D1565137

FLEETING THINGS

Fleeting Things

English Poets and Poems
1616–1660

Gerald Hammond

Harvard University Press
Cambridge, Massachusetts
London, England   1990

Library of Congress Cataloging-in-Publication Data

Hammond, Gerald.
  Fleeting things: English poets and poems, 1616–1660 / Gerald Hammond.
    p.   cm.
Bibliography: p.
Includes index.
ISBN 0-674-30625-2 (alk. paper)
1. English poetry—Early modern, 1500–1700—History and criticism.
2. Literature and society—Great Britain—History—17th century.
I. Title.
PR541.H36 1990   89-15434
821'.309–dc20   CIP

Acknowledgments

Part of Chapter 3 is based on my Chatterton lecture, "Richard Lovelace and the Uses of Obscurity," delivered to the British Academy in May 1985 and published in the Academy's *Proceedings*, 71 (1985), 203–234. Part of Chapter 6 is based on my article "Milton's 'On Shakespeare,'" *Southern Humanities Review*, 20 (1986), 115–124. Part of Chapter 10 was originally published as "Poetry and the Common Sense" in *Poetry Nation Review*, 14 (1987), 11–16. I extend my thanks to all three journals and to the British Academy for permission to use the material here.

I would also like to acknowledge some more personal debts: to Elizabeth Palmer and Kenneth Palmer, my first and best teachers; to Ward Allen, my idea of a true scholar and critic; to Michael Schmidt for his great help in getting this book ready; and to Patsy, my best friend.

Contents

Illustrations

"Half a crown," said Wegg meditating. "Yes. (It ain't much, sir.) Half a crown."

"Per week, you know."

"Per week. Yes. As to the amount of strain upon the intellect now. Was you thinking at all of poetry?" Mr Wegg inquired, musing.

"Would it come dearer?" Mr Boffin asked.

"It would come dearer," Mr Wegg returned. "For when a person comes to grind off poetry night after night, it is but right he should expect to be paid for its weakening effect on his mind."

Charles Dickens, Our Mutual Friend

In this book I discuss about 250 poems by more than fifty poets, taken from many sources. The only rationalization I have imposed is to modernize spellings. I have left other incidentals, such as punctuation, capitalization, and italicization, as they occur in the edition I have used (cited at the first quotation of each poet's work). This leads to some inconsistency, but nothing likely to cause misunderstandings. Biblical quotations are from the Authorized Version, except where otherwise stated. Proverbs are from W. G. Smith and F. P. Wilson, eds., *The Oxford Dictionary of English Proverbs,* 3d ed. (Oxford, 1970).

Introduction: Thresholds

I learned to enjoy poetry at University College, London, so Jeremy Bentham, whose stuffed remains preside at its portals, seems a good place for me to start. That keen poetry hater saw the only possible moral utility in any of the arts lying in their use as "excellent substitutes for drunkenness, slander and the love of gaming," adding that "prejudice apart, the game of push-pin is of equal value with arts and sciences of music and poetry." [1] I value games a little more highly than Bentham did, and do not disapprove at all of gaming; but, faced with the new utilitarianism of the academies which justifies the study of poetry as a source of meaning or meaninglessness, whereby we can better understand the human condition, I prefer his push-pin analogy. In the poetry written between the death of Shakespeare and the Restoration, the period covered by this book, poetry was sometimes a substitute for, sometimes a reinforcement of, drunkenness, slander, gaming, and the many other activities which make life enjoyable. It gestured toward abstract meaning as often as any art form does, but its enduring value lay in the materials which it used to convey these meanings.

The compasses in Donne's "A Valediction: forbidding Mourning" may set us on our way. Signifying constancy, fidelity, and mutual influence over vast distances, the great pleasure they offer, by way of "leans, and hearkens after," is a new perception of compasses. Rather than argue that the poem affects our attitudes toward love in absence, I would settle for the claim that it alters the way we regard this piece of geometrical equipment. The poem makes us less likely to look again at a pair of compasses as if they were inanimate measuring instruments, but persuades us to see them as potentially alive, slender pieces of steel packed with emotion. The kind of critical discussion I want to pursue is related more to the shape, nature, and the use made of compasses in the late sixteenth century than to tracing the history of the emblematizing of constancy.

Too often critical discussion ignores the thing and explores only the idea. Another famous Donne image offers a fair example, at the opening of "The Good Morrow":

> I wonder by my troth, what thou, and I
>   Did, till we loved? were we not weaned till then,
> But sucked on country pleasures, childishly?
>   Or snorted we in the seven sleepers' den?

A. J. Smith's editorial glosses on these lines are representative enough. He begins by explaining that "the central metaphor of the poem is an awakening to a new life," explicates the child-rearing images of "weaned" and "sucked on country pleasures"—"in the seventeenth century the infants of well-to-do families were sent to be wet-nursed in the country"—and then explains that the "seven sleepers' den" was "the cave in which seven Christian youths, walled up alive in the persecution of Decius (A.D. 249), slept miraculously for 187 years."[2] So much for childish things, which are firmly put away by that last note. The modern reader now knows that the poem has begun to detach itself from the common experiences of life and should be understood as the recounting of a mystical experience. But a seventeenth-century reader would have kept in contact with the childishness at least a little longer, for *sevensleeper* was a dialect word for a dormouse (as in the German *Siebenschläfer*), and it gives more life to the opening lines to see in "sucked," "snorted," and "den" the image of the lovers as a couple of mice, awake after hibernation, for whom one little room really would be an everywhere.

Like mice and men, poetry and push-pin are paired partly through the attractions of alliteration and partly for their yoking of the most valued and the most trivial. That men should illogically value poetry so highly was Bentham's point, one which most seventeenth-century poets would happily have accepted. Edmund Waller's last poem, titled "Of the Last Verses in the Book," shows a reluctance to separate life from art which is typical of the century, for the poem is as much concerned with his own imminent death as with bringing the collection to a fitting conclusion. It recognizes the triviality and childishness of the poems he has written, and yet it offers a powerful defense of their existence:[3]

> When we for age could neither read nor write,
> The subject made us able to indite;
> The soul, with nobler resolutions decked,
> The body stooping, does herself erect.
> No mortal parts are requisite to raise

Her that, unbodied, can her Maker praise.
   The seas are quiet when the winds give o'er;
So, calm are we when passions are no more!
For then we know how vain it was to boast
Of fleeting things, so certain to be lost.
Clouds of affection from our younger eyes
Conceal that emptiness which age descries.
   The soul's dark cottage, battered and decayed,
Lets in new light through chinks that time has made;
Stronger by weakness, wiser men become,
As they draw near to their eternal home.
Leaving the old, both worlds at once they view,
That stand upon the threshold of the new.

"Stronger by weakness" works two ways, justifying the wisdom of age which can look backward at life and forward to death so clearly, and explaining that such a vision could have been achieved only by continuous pursuit of the fleeting things which made up his life and were the material for his poems. "Fleeting things, so certain to be lost" epitomizes seventeenth-century poetry's vain efforts to restore what is no longer there or to hold on to something which is already sliding out of the grasp. When all is gone, then "that emptiness" appears. This book's concern is with the things which temporarily hid the emptiness from the century's eyes—fans and muffs, kings and queens, wine and roses.

Ships and thresholds figure in it also, to take two images from Waller's poem. "The soul's dark cottage" links them, the building emerging from the hulk which has been battered by passionate seas, then nudging us toward the threshold which stands at the very end of Waller's poetry. Though much praised in the next century as a genuine precursor of Augustan rationality in verse, Waller's poetry is actually full of the glorious imprecisions which make the seventeenth-century lyric so distinctive, as this image shows. It works by impression rather than by logic, and one can imagine Dr. Johnson finding fault with a soul which at one moment is a building, at the next a figure standing on a threshold. He might also have felt uneasy with the strength of the image, which, like Donne's compasses, overpowers meaning. What we remember from Waller's poem is not the moral that through weakness we find spiritual purpose, but the picture of a deserted, delapidated building. If we know Waller's earlier poetry, then we are moved by the contrast between this humblest of habitations and his more youthful celebrations of great public buildings such as St. Paul's and Somerset House.

Because of the cottage's dominance over the last part of the poem, the threshold is more literal than figurative. Once words lose their immediate connection with real things they begin to slip first into abstraction then into cliché. *Threshold* is a word which in our time stands on the threshold of such a decay, by way of Freudian psychology and the measurement of medication dosages. Good poetry revives and restores words by relating them to solid experience: Waller's threshold reminds us of real doorways rather than abstractions such as tolerance or limits of consciousness. His "fleeting things," too, is less of the cliché it had become in the seventeenth century because of its link, by way of the sea passage, with the original sense of the word *fleet,* to float on the water. These things float into and across our consciousness before sinking into oblivion.

Push-pin deteriorated too, so that by the time Bentham used it it had become merely a synonym for a "trivial or insignificant occupation, child's play, triviality" (*OED*). To give it back its original strength we need to see its employment by a fine seventeenth-century poet, Robert Herrick:[4]

> *Love's play at Push-pin.*
> Love and my self (believe me) on a day
> At childish Push-pin (for our sport) did play:
> I put, he pushed, and heedless of my skin,
> Love pricked my finger with a golden pin:
> Since which, it festers so, that I can prove
> 'Twas but a trick to poison me with love:
> Little the wound was; greater was the smart;
> The finger bled, but burnt was all my heart.

The game was played by two children and required little skill other than a capacity to get excited over trivialities. Joseph Strutt, writing at the beginning of the nineteenth century, in his *Sports and Pastimes of the People of England,* gave it less space than any other game, describing it as "a very silly sport, being nothing more than simply pushing one pin across another."[5] Herrick knows it well and the tiny dangers it presents to small, eager fingers. The game he describes is a real enough one, ending in blood and tears, although the opponent is not, as usual in his poems, a person, but only an abstraction. Great disturbances are signaled here, with a whole existence poisoned by what had seemed to be only a piece of trivial flirtation. Under the adult gaze nothing could be more childish than a game of push-pin, yet the memories of such experiences haunt our later lives, fleeting things which, once lost, we long vainly to restore. Herrick is thinking back to a threshold experience in which a game governed by rules which made triumph and loss inconsequential suddenly opened up prospects of cruelty, humiliation, and pain.

This is the experience of love, and any account of seventeenth-century poetry which did not open with a love lyric is not likely to represent its subject fairly. But, if we are to believe theorists like Lauro Martines, we ought to learn how to read such poems for their political subtexts too.[6] His list of rules whereby we may find the real purposes of apparently innocuous poems is an admirable piece of critical theory, vitiated only by his unwillingness to attempt any readings of specific poems. Still, there are enough explicitly political poems to make the parallels between the game of love and the game of power. Richard Lovelace, looking back in the 1650s at a public life which had seen the Royalist cause shot to pieces, offered this trivial poem as an introduction to *The Royall Game of Chess-Play*, a book claiming to describe a game which was "sometimes the recreation of the late king, with many of the nobility":[7]

To Dr. F. B. On his Book of Chess

Sir, now unravelled is the Golden Fleece:
Men that could only fool at Fox and Geese,
Are new made politicians by thy book,
And both can judge and conquer with a look.
The hidden fate of princes you unfold;
Court, clergy, Commons, by your law controlled;
   Strange, serious wantoning, all that they
      Blustered, and cluttered for, *you play.*

Fox and geese is a child's board game, petty in comparison with chess; but chess itself, though the grandest of games, is still closer to push-pin than to the arts of statesmanship. But not necessarily in retrospect: Lovelace, looking back, sees all that the court, clergy, and commons blustered about as simply one more childish way of passing the time, not too far removed from Marvell's image of Charles being trapped by Cromwell's wiser art in "An Horatian Ode."

Lovelace's poem is a threshold piece, designed to carry the reader into F. B.'s book. George Herbert preferred to write his own introductions, following his dedication with a section called "The Church-Porch," as literal a representation of the threshold as it is possible to find. Under that porch Herbert offers precepts for the living of a good Christian life. Like "An Horatian Ode" these too are aimed at the forward youth who would appear:[8]

> Thou, whose sweet youth and early hopes enhance
> Thy rate and price, and mark thee for a treasure;
> Hearken unto a Verser, who may chance
> Rhyme thee to good, and make a bait of pleasure.
>   A verse may find him, who a sermon flies,
>   And turn delight into a sacrifice.

Part of Herbert's purpose in *The Temple* is to instruct his youthful reader to put away childish things, as he himself has done. Included among these are the games which Englishmen were so fond of. The first section of the volume has frequent images of dicing, gambling, and card playing:

> Play not away the virtue of that name,
> Which is thy best stake, when griefs make thee tame
>
> .   .   .   .   .
>
> Never exceed thy income. Youth may make
> Ev'n with the year: but age, if it will hit,
> Shoots a bow short, and lessens still his stake
>
> .   .   .   .   .
>
> If yet thou love game at so dear a rate,
> Learn this, that hath old gamesters dearly cost:
> Dost lose? rise up: dost win? rise in that state.
> Who strive to sit out losing hands, are lost
>
> .   .   .   .   .
>
> Get a good stock of these, then draw the card;
> That suits him best, of whom thy speech is heard
> . . . a proud ignorance will lose his rest,
> Rather than show his cards . . .
>
> .   .   .   .   .
>
> We are all but cold suitors; let us move
> Where it is warmest. Leave thy six and seven;
> Pray with the most: for where most pray, is heaven.[9]

Amy Charles, writing about the Herbert family, seems puzzled by one of her findings: "Rather surprisingly, Gorse mentions card-playing as another diversion of the household: on one occasion Mrs Herbert had been playing cards and losing money and had to send to Gorse for funds to pay off her debt."[10] Really she ought not to be surprised, for *The Temple* repeatedly sets the eternal Christian truths within the context of the most ephemeral pursuits, card games in particular: as in the primero image from "Jordan," "Riddle who list, for me, and pull for prime."

The shortest poem in the volume is this one:

$$Ana\text{-}\begin{cases}MARY\\ARMY\end{cases}gram$$

> How well her name an *Army* doth present,
> In whom the *Lord of Hosts* did pitch his tent!

I suspect that this is the one poem for which the prospect of publication meant loss rather than gain. In Herbert's italic hand the *g* and *y* were similar enough for the *gram* to be read backward as *mary*—one meaning of *anagram* is "written backward"—the parenthesis being her and her mother, Anne, standing for the womb in which she and the whole Christian host were conceived. That effect is now lost, and there are further signs that Herbert had concerns about the poem, for it is the only alteration in the order of the poems as set out in the Bodleian manuscript ("the original of Mr George Herbert's Temple; as it was first licensed for the presse") and its 1633 publication. It originally sat between "Church-music" and "Church-lock and key," rather spoiling the sequence of four "church" poems; so the decision to move it is understandable. But why put it where it now stands, between "Avarice" and "To all Angels and Saints"?

In "Avarice" man's hunt for gold is presented as a parody of God's creation, as man stamps his image upon the gold he digs out of the ground. There is an echo of this in the title of "To all Angels and Saints," for the angel pun on the coin of this name was a virtual cliché. But while the anagram gets slightly in the way of the echo, it does prepare for the real theme of the following poem, what C. A. Patrides describes as "a tactful censure of Mariolatry, especially the Roman Catholic tendency to regard the Virgin as co-redemptrix with Christ":[11]

> ### To all Angels and Saints
> Oh Glorious spirits, who after all your bands
> See the smooth face of God, without a frown
>   Or strict commands;
> Where ev'ry one is king, and hath his crown,
> If not upon his head, yet in his hands:
>
> Not out of envy or maliciousness
> Do I forbear to crave your special aid:
>   I would address

My vows to thee most gladly, blessed Maid,
And Mother of my God, in my distress.

Thou art the holy mine, whence came the gold,
The great restorative for all decay
              In young and old;
Thou art the cabinet where the jewel lay:
Chiefly to thee would I my soul unfold:

But now (alas!) I dare not; for our King,
Whom we do all jointly adore and praise,
              Bids no such thing:
And where his pleasure no injunction lays,
('Tis your own case) ye never move a wing.

All worship is prerogative, and a flower
Of his rich crown, from whom lies no appeal
              At the last hour:
Therefore we dare not from his garland steal,
To make a posie for inferior power.

Although then others court you, if ye know
What's done on earth, we shall not fare the worse,
              Who do not so;
Since we are ever ready to disburse,
If any one our Master's hand can show.

If we pick up the resonances of "hands" (5), "unfold" (15), "bids" (18), "court" (26), and the showing of hands at the end, then we reinforce the theological point with a card-playing image. The English church has played the king to the Catholic queen and scooped the pot.

Later in *The Temple* the poem called "The Jews" ends with the hope of this race's eventual conversion, that moment at the end of time which Marvell's "To His Coy Mistress" uses as an image of the apocalypse:

        Oh that my prayers! mine, alas!
Oh that some Angel might a trumpet sound;
At which the Church falling upon her face
Should cry so loud, until the trump were drowned,
And by that cry of her dear Lord obtain,
        That your sweep sap might come again!

When God does choose to play the last trump, then all games come to an end. One response is to lose gracefully, but a child may well do what Herbert does in the poem which follows, "The Collar," banging the table and shouting "no more"—"sweeping the board" meant taking all the cards. Unwilling to be still in suit—the suit is hearts—he is restored to himself only by the reminder that such behavior is childish.

Love, politics, and religion take up much of what follows, but poetry figures too. Here is another threshold poem, the first verses in the Shakespeare first Folio, written by Ben Jonson:[12]

To the Reader

> This figure, that thou here seest put,
> It was for gentle Shakespeare cut;
> Wherein the graver had a strife
> With nature, to outdo the life:
> O, could he but have drawn his wit
> As well in brass, as he hath hit
> His face; the print would then surpass
> All, that was ever writ in brass.
> But, since he cannot, reader, look
> Not on his picture, but his book.

S. Schoenbaum describes these as "a few perfunctory lines of commendation," a remark aimed not so much at Jonson as at the wretched Droeshout portrait to which the poem refers.[13] Jonson may well have regarded the portrait wryly, and his lines reflect this; but the poem itself is not a negligible thing, no more than is the doodle of any great artist. Its theme of art battling with nature is the very one which is carried through the next poem in the Folio, Jonson's great eulogy praising Shakespeare for the effort he took in writing—an effort which needs to be given as much recognition as his facile naturalness. In Droeshout's vain effort to capture the fleeting image of Shakespeare lies an emblem of all art's failure, and the need for its spectator, or reader, to turn the dead into the living line. The wit lies in Jonson's establishing a parallel between the art of engraving—in technical terms such as "cut," "graver," "brass," "print," and perhaps even the "put" of the opening line—and the imagery of funerary poetry being written in brass. In trying to catch the living image the engraver has confirmed Shakespeare's death: only the words which follow have power to restore life. Submerged in the imagery, too, is the sport of fencing, in "drawn," "hit," and "point," as if Jonson

Martin Droeshout's portrait for the 1633 Shakespeare Folio edition, with Jonson's poem so placed that it is nearly impossible for the reader to obey the injunction of the final couplet.

were judging Droeshout's efforts in the way he might have judged the many fencing contests which were held in the theaters in that time.

The poem may be only a doodle, but it is packed with Jonson's responses to the world around him, which his dead friend no longer shares, and which survives only in poetry. This passage from his *Discoveries* provides some sense of how Jonson's mind worked around the same images (my italics):

> Indeed, the multitude commend writers, as they do *fencers,* or wrestlers; who if they come in robustiously, and *put* for it, with a deal of violence, are received for the braver fellows: when many times their own rudeness is a cause of their disgrace; and a slight touch of their adversary, gives all that boisterous force the *foil.* But in these things, the unskilful are *naturally* deceived, and judging wholly by the bulk, think rude things greater than polished; and scattered more numerous, than composed: nor think this only to be true in the sordid multitude, but the neater sort of our gallants: for all are the multitude; only they differ in clothes, not in judgement or understanding.
>
> I remember, the players have often mentioned it as an honour to Shakespeare, that in his writing (whatsoever he penned) he never blotted out line. My answer hath been, would he had blotted a thousand . . . [14]

"Truth, exactitude of every kind, is fatal to poetry," wrote Bentham, adding that "the poet must see everything through coloured media, and strive to make every one else do the same." [15] So, for Jonson, no philosophy links memories of Shakespeare, the art of engraving, and the practice of fencing, only his own memory, experience, and observation of things. Out of them he fashions his memorial poem, rather like the engraver who restores Shakespeare out of the memories of those who knew him, or the reader of Shakespeare who needs to balance the portrait against the poet's words to understand the man. Ideas are little help in such critical acts; only obstacles, in fact, for they impose order upon an art whose purpose is nothing if not to register the chaos of living in the present. The readers of Jonson's poem experience just such a confusion. Instructed by his closing couplet to look forward to the words and ignore the portrait, their eyes inevitably move back to the image of the poet as a thing which promises more knowledge of the man than all the pages which follow. Jonson's poem occupies a fleeting, chaotic present moment, between the image of the past and the future experience of reading his words.

"Not ideas about things, but the thing itself," is how one poet describes his art; more succinctly, another claims "No ideas but in things"; and more simply another describes himself as a man who "used to notice such things." [16] Some of the things noticed by seventeenth-century poets were very important: the king, Parliament, and the king's counselors, for instance, and this book begins with them. Others were plainly trivial, such as the hair, roses, and games with which it ends. In time, however, the important and the trivial change places. Handy-dandy, three and a half centuries later, the Duke of Buckingham turns out to be more of a fleeting thing than a game of push-pin, if only because Robert Herrick wrote a better poem about the game than about the duke; and it is, after all, only the poetry which endures.

PART ONE

Counselors and Kings

1   Obduracy: Praising and Blaming

The fact of life which affected most seventeenth-century poets was the need to write in praise of powerful people. Such poetry is easy enough to write in an age of shared beliefs but becomes problematic when factionalism takes over the state. The 1620s throw up some good examples of this, particularly in the poems of Richard Corbett. Corbett, eventually to become the Bishop of Oxford, pinned his colors firmly to the Duke of Buckingham's mast, using what gift for poetry he had to cultivate Buckingham's support for his constant place hunting. Having been made Dean of Christ Church, he wrote "A New Year's Gift, to my Lord Duke of Buckingham" to express his gratitude for a gift which could compare only, so he said, with the debts he owed to his parents and his king. Corbett's problem seems to have been that he felt he could not match the sums which others were prepared to offer Buckingham in return for preferment, so he praises the duke for his discernment of the true value of men and his realization that he should promote only those who genuinely cared for his interests. The poem ends like this:[1]

> O you that should in choosing of your own,
> Know a true *Diamond* from a *Bristow stone;*
> You know those men always are not the best
> In their intent, that loudest can protest;
> But that a *Prayer* from the Convocation
> Is better than the Commons' *Protestation.*
> Trust those that at your feet their lives will lay,
> And know no Arts, but to *Deserve,* and *Pray;*
> Whilst they, that buy preferment without praying,
> Begin with bribes, and finish with *betraying.*

This is not very inspired stuff—sub-Jonsonian assertions within a tightly bound set of couplets—but it does its job efficiently enough. Corbett, you will notice, is not attacking the offering of bribes, merely the offering of them without accompanying prayers for Buckingham's welfare. The diamond–Bristol stone image is designed to appeal to the duke's values. He certainly would appreciate the difference between the two. Corbett also takes care to remind his patron that factionalism has set in—in a couplet only loosely related to his main theme—by contrasting the Church of England's support for his policies with Parliament's assertion of its rights (the Protestation of December 1621 had asserted Parliament's right of freedom of discussion). The coded message of these lines is that Buckingham will need genuine supporters like Corbett in high places.

Within a couple of years Corbett wrote "A Letter to the Duke of Buckingham, being with the Prince of Spain." The tone now is witty bantering, but the praise is as fulsome as ever. Buckingham's departure with the prince means that England has been transported across the seas. The conceit is that since Buckingham and Charles embody virtually everything of value in the country, their departure means that the country itself has gone with them:

> Sir:
> I've read of islands floating, and removed,
> In *Ovid's* time, but never heard it proved
> Till now: that Fable, by the *Prince* and *you,*
> By your transporting *England,* is made true.
> We are not where we were; the *Dog-star* reigns
> No cooler in our climate, than in *Spain's;*
> The self same breath, same air, same heat, same burning
> Is here, as there; will be, till your returning:
> Come, ere the Card be altered, lest perhaps
> Your stay may make an Error in our maps;
> Lest England should be found, when you shall pass,
> A thousand miles more Southward than it was . . .

Knowing how often the wit of seventeenth-century poets is firmly rooted in experience, we may guess that the summer of 1623 was a hot one. Had it been miserable Corbett would no doubt have spun out an image around the absence of England's sun and its consequences for the climate. The poem's banter increases as Corbett comes round to relating the spate of rumors which the journey has encouraged in London. Meant to be a secret, the mission to make a marriage between Charles and the Spanish princess had soon become public knowledge, and all kind of gossip was generated, from the most trivial—how much the pair had lost at cards (although this would not be so trivial to the English taxpayers)—to the real opposition of the powerful Count of Olivares. "Poets of Pauls" are cited for their descriptions of how (55–62)

> in one cross week
> My Lord hath lost a thousand pound at gleek.
> And though they do allow but *Little* meat,
> They are content your losses should be *great*.
> False, on my *Deanery!* falser than your fare is;
> Or then your difference with *Cond' de Olivares;*
> Which was reported strongly for one tide,
> But, after six hours' floating, ebbed, and died.

Corbett's purposes are threefold. He is warning Buckingham that such things are being said. He is mocking the rumors as the products of envy aimed at greatness ("Poets of Pauls" is a euphemism for starving hacks whose only way of earning a crust is to provide something sensational). Most of all, Corbett is place hunting. This becomes embarrassingly clear toward the poem's end, where, after a vision of King James flanked by the duke and his son, as obvious equals, the poet claims his reward:

> In this I have a part, In this I see
> Some new addition smiling upon me:
> Who, in an humble distance, claim a share
> In all your greatness, what so e'er you are.

The last phrase is a little puzzling since Buckingham had been made a duke earlier in the year, and it is difficult to imagine how he might be more highly favored. But more puzzling is how Corbett could have let his mask slip so obviously. Gone are all the little turns of wit which normally dress up the flattery, and there is no attempt at all to disguise the self-interest. Contemporaries, well used to having their supplications presented in a coded form, among professions of modesty and altruism, must have been struck by Corbett's clumsiness here. Indeed, they were. Corbett's editors note examples of the popular disdain to which this poem gave rise, and counterpoems were written, attacking Corbett "for his flattering verses sent into Spaine."[2]

The point is that Corbett had obviously taken care not only to send the

verses into Spain but also to have them well known in England: the number of manuscript versions shows its wide circulation long before Corbett's poems were published in 1648. The place of poetry in the patronage
system had obviously moved on since the 1590s, when, as Shakespeare's
sonnets demonstrate, the poet's purpose was merely to compete with others in singing his patron's praises. Now the poems present praise in action, mocking the patron's political opponents and rehearsing with wit
the arguments in favor of his political maneuverings.

Some of Corbett's later poems show how combative panegyric poetry
had become by the 1630s. As well as directing his efforts toward his principal patron, he followed the course of most of his contemporaries and
wrote poems to the royal family. Poems to Elizabeth I had been apolitical,
except insofar that any celebration of a royal icon must be part of an
ideological enterprise. But by the accession of Charles I even poems of
royal praise dipped into the seas of practical politics. When Corbett
wrote his poem celebrating the birth of a male heir, instead of merely
praising the worth and potency of the father and the fecundity of the
mother, he took the opportunity, by way of the happy reign which he
prophesied for the child, to offer what is virtually an anatomy of the
causes of factionalism in the country:

On the Birth of Prince Charles
What Joy that Shunamite did once inherit
After her dead Son had received his Spirit,
Such did the dead World take at the new birth
Of Charles his Son, the Wish of the whole earth:
And if the Priest do yet remain a Seer,
As he was wont, then hear the Prophet, hear.
  This Child shall have attending his sweet reign
Reverence and Love; his Common vulgar Train
Laborious and not wise; his Citizen
A better Judge of wares than news or men;
A Gentry more Obedient than Learn'd;
And his Nobility shall be discerned
By b'ing as Kings (for Love, not Power) desiring
The Crown may flourish, to it not aspiring;
No strife for Offices, when any fall.
Virtue shall marry Honour: and this shall
The sole Contention be, to deserve best:
Wealth without Vice; and Law for who gives Least:

That Peace, rich warlike Peace, I mean Consent
Between the Closet and the Parliament;
No Trumpet sounding Wars, and when it must
It shall be foreign, fortunate, and just;
His Victories not grievous unto those
Whom he shall conquer, no, not to his Foes;
Religion Pure and Practised, argued less:
A preaching Pulpit and a silent Press.
Doubts put to Synods, to Divines that know;—
What should the Law do with the Gospel, tro'?
In his best Strength three Children shall he have:
A late old age, and Heav'n after his Grave.

Between the real state of the nation and Corbett's prescription for a return to order lie rifts filled with opportunities for irony. The wish that
Charles's subjects should be "laborious and not wise" and should stick to
judging wares rather than "news or men" and be "more obedient than
learned" could just as easily have come from a Puritan satirist aping the
prejudices of opponents who look back nostalgically to a feudal society.
It is surprisingly easy to read the poem as an exercise in irony all the way
to the closing question, which argues for a separation between law and
gospel.

As well as this extended vision of a future happy state, Corbett wrote a
shorter poem on the royal birth; but even in this squib he could not resist
marrying the conceit of Charles's birth as a source of new wealth to a dig
at the rebellious Parliament which the king had dissolved the year before:

> *On the Birth of the Young*
> *Prince Charles*
>
> When private men get sons they get a spoon,
> Without eclipse, or any Star at noon;
> When kings get sons, they get withal supplies
> And succours, far beyond five Subsidies.
> Welcome, God's Loan, great tribute of the state,
> Thou Money new come in, rich fleet of plate:
> Welcome, blest babe, whom God thy father sent
> To make him rich without a Parliament.

This did receive an ironic reading. It appears in the diary of John Rous,
under the entry for 27 June 1630, together with Rous's conjecture that it

had been written by a Puritan.³ It is easy to see why. Take the view of the private man rather than that of the king, and his objection to greater and greater taxes to support more and more ostentation, and then the poem becomes a wry comment on ways in which other sources of revenue might be tapped—perhaps a future Spanish marriage is on the cards—as well as a contrast between private values of thrift and royal profligacy. Parliament had unprecedentedly offered five subsidies to the king in 1626, and five more in 1628, as the poem disdainfully notes.

Marvell's "Horatian Ode," the most celebrated political poem of the century, makes conscious use of such ironies, but in these public poems written two decades earlier it is even more of a problem to guess how critical the poet is being. Thomas Carew, though from a more elevated rank of the gentry than Corbett, nonetheless came from a family down on its luck; and while his poetry generally reinforced the image he presented to the world of an elegant lounger at court, some of it was obviously aimed at making the right noises in the right places. He wrote two poems on Buckingham's death—of which more later—and one of the purest celebrations of Stuart rule, the masque *Coelum Britannicum*. Carew's other, less obviously propagandist poems threaten to be torn apart from within by his efforts to contain the country's dissensions within the ideal vision of kingship which the masque proclaimed. In "A New Year's Gift to the King" the conventional movement of the poem, which begins by looking back at the old year and all the years which have gone before, and then looks forward to the next, presents an apparently untroubled view of Charles's heritage and his prospects—all adds up to "one great continued festival." This would have been enough for an Elizabethan poet, but Carew feels constrained to end his poem with visions of peace dissolving into revolt and rebellion:⁴

> Circle with peaceful olive boughs,
> And conquering bays, his Royal brows.
> Let his strong virtues overcome,
> And bring his bloodless Trophies home:
> Strew all the pavements where he treads
> With loyal hearts, or Rebels' heads . . .

Even more revealing are the tensions within the poem on Charles's sickness.⁵ Carew's conceit here is of the body politic feeling the infection which is tormenting the king (19–20):

Ent'ring his royal limbs that is our head,
Through us, his mystic limbs, the pain is spread.

Carew does not go on to say that troubles in the kingdom are symptoms
of the illness. Instead he focuses on a less positive, more troubling idea,
that there are actually subjects indifferent to the king's suffering—or,
what is worse, subjects who positively welcome it (21–24):

That man that doth not feel his part, hath none
In any part of his dominion;
If he hold land, that earth is forfeited,
And he unfit on any ground to tread.

Carew's vision for the rest of the poem stays with the court, but there are
powerful negatives implicit within it:

This grief is felt at Court, where it doth move
Through every joint, like the true soul of love.
All those fair stars that do attend on Him,
Whence they derived their light, wax pale and dim.
That ruddy morning beam of Majesty,
Which should the Sun's eclipsed light supply,
Is overcast with mists, and in the lieu
Of cheerful rays, sends us down drops of dew:
That curious form made of an earth refined,
At whose blest birth, the gentle Planets shined
With fair aspects, and sent a glorious flame
To animate so beautiful a frame:
That Darling of the Gods and men, doth wear
A cloud on's brow, and in his eye a tear:
And all the rest, (save when his dread command
Doth bid them move,) like lifeless statues stand;
So full a grief, so generally worn
Shows a good King is sick, and good men mourn.

This is good poetry, celebrating the centrality of the court vision to the
country's mystic existence, and at its center the suffering body of the king,
which has frozen courtiers and ladies-in-waiting into statues. But the
closing couplet implicitly contrasts this paralysis with the sense that some
men are not still with suspense or grief, but are on the move. They are not

good men, but they indubitably exist; and the acknowledgement that they do contaminates the ideal vision which the poem attempts to celebrate.

The most puzzling of Carew's public poems is his "Answer" to Aurelian Townshend, written upon the death of Gustavus Adolphus. Its full title is "In Answer of an Elegiacal Letter upon the death of the King of *Sweden* from *Aurelian Townshend,* inviting me to write on that subject." In part this panegyric is dedicated to the dead Swedish king, but it turns into a celebration of the peaceful state of England under Charles's rule— a haven of tranquillity in contrast to war-torn Europe. Perhaps the only one of Carew's public poems which is widely known today is his elegy on the death of John Donne, from which many of the critical opinions of Metaphysical poetry have been derived. This may be a consequence of the insularity of literary criticism, especially of seventeenth-century literature, because the poem of Townshend is at least as well-written and has much broader interests than the Donne elegy. Its subject is insularity. The year is 1633, the same as that of the elegy, and Carew is revolving some of the same ideas through his mind, such as the contrast between prose and poetry and, developing from this, the question of the future of English poetry. It opens:

> Why dost thou sound, my dear *Aurelian,*
> In so shrill accents, from thy *Barbican,*
> A loud alarum to my drowsy eyes,
> Bidding them wake in tears and Elegies
> For mighty *Sweden's* fall? Alas! how may
> My Lyric feet, that of the smooth soft way
> Of Love, and Beauty, only know the tread,
> In dancing paces celebrate the dead
> Victorious King, or his Majestic Hearse
> Profane with th'humble touch of their low verse?
> *Virgil,* nor *Lucan,* no, nor *Tasso* more
> Than both, not *Donne,* worth all that went before,
> With the united labour of their wit
> Could a just Poem to this subject fit . . .

Townshend's hint that Carew should write a heroic Protestant poem is met by coy reluctance.[6] Partly this is a modesty topos, well-worn even this early in the century, but one which was practiced by poets of all hues—think of Milton's disclaimers at the opening of *Lycidas.* But whereas Milton's unreadiness stems from a lack of inward ripeness, Carew's is a product of the masque and tourney-ridden culture which dominates the court life he inhabits. The reference to Donne is revealing. Even his line of masculine expression, now lost to English poetry, could not have matched the king's achievements—so leave the task to prose historians (15–16):

> His actions were too mighty to be raised
> Higher by Verse, let him in prose be praised.

Poetry's purpose, it transpires, is neither elegiac nor heroic, but lyric. The old pun on metrical and real feet is given a further witty turn in the "dancing paces" which would be out of place in funeral rites. And Carew's purpose as a national poet rather than a European one is to sing of revels and gently inspire the pastoral pipe "till all our swains admire / Thy song and subject." Europe may be full of soldiers, but England is a country of shepherds.

The second half of the poem offers a celebration of English peace. Donne is recollected in the way the court masques act out a mysterious version of "The Canonisation," bringing "from above / A pattern of their own celestial love." But, as Carew says at the end, on the way to this vision he has achieved what he had disclaimed at the beginning: the first half of his poem, in its sweep over Gustavus Adolphus' victories, elevates English rhyme to a form of heroic poetry. The syntax in the first fifty or so lines is expansive, the diction and imagery austere, as in this representation of the whole of Europe as the Swedish king's churchyard (25–34):

> Leave we him then to the grave Chronicler,
> Who though to Annals he cannot refer
> His too-brief story, yet his Journals may
> Stand by the Caesar's years, and every day
> Cut into minutes, each, shall more contain
> Of great designment than an Emperor's reign;
> And (since 'twas but his Church-yard) let him have
> For his own ashes now no narrower Grave
> Than the whole *German* Continent's vast womb,
> Whilst all her Cities do but make his Tomb.

In the second half of the poem all of this strength melts away. The diction is softer, the images repeal the exiled train of gods and goddesses, and the syntax sits itself down comfortably within the couplet form. The move from heroic to lyric begins around the point where Carew contrasts warring Europe with tranquil England (43–53):

> Then let the Germans fear if *Caesar* shall,
> Or the United Princes, rise, and fall,
> But let us that in myrtle bowers sit
> Under secure shades, use the benefit
> Of peace and plenty, which the blessed hand
> Of our good King gives this obdurate Land,
> Let us of Revels sing, and let thy breath
> (Which fill'd Fame's trumpet with *Gustavus'* death,
> Blowing his name to heaven) gently inspire
> The past'ral pipe, till all our swains admire
> Thy song and subject . . .

This land owes its peace and plenty to the "blessed hand / Of our good king," but in the same line it is described as "obdurate"—the oddest and most revealing word in the poem. How easily might Carew have described it as "excellent" or even "obedient"; but "obdurate" sinks shafts of discontent into the poem. And with the discontent come ironies.

Carew's focus on England's present peaceful state develops from a vision of the court masques which he and Townshend had written (55–104):

> For who like thee (whose loose discourse is far
> More neat and polished than our Poems are,
> Whose very gait's more graceful than our dance)
> In sweetly-flowing numbers may advance
> The glorious night? When, not to act foul rapes,
> Like birds, or beasts, but in their Angel-shapes
> A troop of Deities came down to guide
> Our steerless barks in passion's swelling tide
> By virtue's Card, and brought us from above
> A pattern of their own celestial love.
> Nor lay it in dark sullen precepts drowned
> But with rich fancy, and clear Action crowned
> Through a mysterious fable (that was drawn
> Like a transparent veil of purest Lawn
> Before their dazzlng beauties) the divine
> *Venus,* did with her heavenly *Cupid* shine.

The story's curious web, the Masculine style,
The subtle sense, did Time and sleep beguile,
Pinioned and charmed they stood to gaze upon
Th'angelic forms, gestures, and motion,
To hear those ravishing sounds that did dispense
Knowledge and pleasure, to the soul, and sense.
It filled us with amazement to behold
Love made all spirit, his corporeal mould
Dissected into Atoms melt away
To empty air, and from the gross allay
Of mixtures, and compounding Accidents
Refined to immaterial Elements.
But when the Queen of Beauty did inspire
The air with perfumes, and our hearts with fire,
Breathing from her celestial Organ sweet
Harmonious notes, our souls fell at her feet,
And did with humble reverend duty, more
Her rare perfections, than high state adore.
    These harmless pastimes let my *Townshend* sing
To rural tunes; not that thy Muse wants wing
To soar a loftier pitch, for she hath made
A noble flight, and placed th'Heroic shade
Above the reach of our faint flagging rhyme;
But these are subjects proper to our clime.
Tourneys, Masques, Theatres, better become
Our *Halcyon* days; what though the German Drum
Bellow for freedom and revenge, the noise
Concerns not us, nor should divert our joys;
Nor ought the thunder of their Carabins
Drown the sweet Airs of our tuned Violins;
Believe me friend, if their prevailing powers
Gain them a calm security like ours,
They'll hang their Arms up on the Olive bough,
And dance, and revel then, as we do now.

I shall not often quote at such length; but there is no other way of showing the hypnotic state which this second half of the poem creates. To ex-
plicate it fully would require establishing detailed parallels with Townshend's and Carew's masques, for this is a purely verbal equivalent to
their spectacle and sound. In those masques, as here, action is frozen into
postures of wonder and admiration. At the center, of course, are the king

and queen, the ultimate objects of the arts' worship. It is possible, even probable, that Carew meant this vision of paralyzed insularity to be read without irony, but certainly from our hindsight, and to any contemporary who was not part of the court milieu, such an untainted reading is not sustainable.

In Marvell's "An Horatian Ode" the clinching contrast is between Cromwell as actor and Charles as actor, in the two very different senses of the word. Cromwell is the man who "doth both act and know," Charles the "royal actor." Charles's death is a final performance, achieved so splendidly because of his long experience of spectacular theater. Cromwell's action is in the line of Gustavus Adolphus—and Marvell ends his poem by setting out Cromwell as the Swedish king's successor, prepared to conquer Catholic Europe. His admiration for Cromwell is only slightly tempered by respect for Charles's performance. In Carew's poem, written twenty years earlier than Marvell's, the emphasis is, apparently, the opposite—apparently, because it is genuinely puzzling to try to estimate Carew's awareness of what is building up in the country. Parliament has already been dissolved for four years. Popular discontent with Charles's foreign policy—more Catholic than Protestant in its favoring of Spanish interests—is part at least of the burden of "obdurate," and its existence readily undermines the notion of an island blessedly cut off from the Continental turbulence. Even Aurelian Townshend, a fellow purveyor of illusions to royalty, has been affected by the Protestant hero's death and calls for commitment. Carew's answer is a brave attempt to hold the line, although such a military metaphor simplifies the situation. Unlike the Swedish king's adventures, England's situation is more sinister: there are enemies within. It may be going too far to claim that somewhere in Carew's poem is a vision of civil war, but the material for such a vision is not lacking—not only in the poem's closing images of the court reveling to the sound of violins and distant gunfire, but also in its opening citation of Townshend's alarum delivered from his house in the Barbican, a reminder of fortress London, the center of the present obduracy and soon to be the site of armed resistance.

It is not lacking, either, in a poem very like Carew's, written three years earlier. Sir Richard Fanshawe's "Ode Upon Occasion of His Majesty's Proclamation in the year 1630. Commanding the Gentry to reside upon their Estates in the Country" likewise contrasts the Thirty Years' War with England's peace. England is presented idyllically:[7]

> Only the Island which we sow,
> (A world without the world) so far

From present wounds, it cannot show
                An ancient scar.
White Peace (the beautiful'st of things)
Seems here her everlasting rest
To fix, and spreads her downy wings
                Over the nest.

But 1630 is a revealing time to write such a poem, just one year after Charles, in Fanshawe's words "the Augustus of our world," has suspended Parliament. The poem develops for more than 130 lines its vision of a contented gentry who follow their king's example and retire from the city to their country estates, with scarcely a hint of the domestic turbulence which is building up. Only at the end does Fanshawe admit some possibility of bloodshed, in this highly stylized scene of the estates' gardens and their "commonwealth of flowers":

The Lily (Queen), the (Royal) Rose,
The Gillyflower (Prince of the blood),
The (Courtier) Tulip (gay in clothes),
                The (Regal) Bud,
The Violet (purple Senator),
How they do mock the pomp of State,
And all that at the surly door
                Of great ones wait.
Plant Trees you may, and see them shoot
Up with your Children, to be served
To your clean boards, and the fair'st Fruit
                To be preserved:
And learn to use their several gums,
" 'Tis innocence in the sweet blood
Of Cherries, Apricocks and Plums
                To be imbrued."

The material for analysis of the state is present here, in the gardens' parody of the social structure—those who retire to them carry with them their experiences at the surly doors of the men of power—but Fanshawe absolutely refuses to concede anything to the realities of the political situation. His is still an ideal state of a king presiding over a benevolent aristocracy. Cities exist only as places from which to escape. The country's values are enduring and dominant.

    The city versus the country was already an old theme of English poetry, going back at least as far as Spenser's Colin Clout, who loses his inspiration by forsaking his rural muse for the city's Rosalind. But whereas in Elizabeth's time the court lay at the center of the city, Carew's poem to Townshend shows how alienated the two were becoming from each other. Just as in Fanshawe's poem, the court now stands for some sort of country ideal. Poets like Townshend and himself should, Carew says, celebrate harmless pastimes in rural tunes. These pastimes include the taming of the erotic to the purposes of a virtuous court. In his younger days Carew had written "A Rapture," a poem so full of sexual acrobatics that it is hard to resist retitling it as a rupture. Aimed at a young city audience such as might be found at the Inns of Court, it lovingly describes the buildup toward and achievement of copulation. Here the woman guides his penis into its harbor:

> My rudder with thy bold hand, like a tried
> And skilful pilot, thou shalt steer, and guide
> My bark into love's channel, where it shall
> Dance, as the bounding waves do rise and fall.

In the answer to Townshend this is redefined in Platonic terms:

> in their Angel-shapes
> A troop of Deities came down to guide
> Our steerless barks in Passion's swelling tide
> By virtue's Card, and brought us from above
> A pattern of their own celestial love.

In *Paradise Lost* Milton presents his angels as beings who copulate—it is part of Raphael's reassurance to Adam that if mankind does evolve into something spiritual he will not lose what he most enjoys, making love to Eve—but Carew's masque-derived angels mean no such thing. They are products of the new court philosophy championed by the queen. When she presses for a love "made all spirit" her aim is, to quote from Carew's "To the Queen," to choke the impure flames of love and replace them with "chaste desires." Playing at sex instead of doing it is the pattern for all the court's actions. Carew was in the exquisitely impotent position of having to purvey anemic visions to such a court while appreciating how bloodless they are, and his poem to Townshend says as much. It is not clear how far, in 1633, he was aware of the hollowness of the "calm security" he praises at the end of the poem, but safety was a concept about which, as we shall see, he had already, at Buckingham's death, found good cause to be skeptical.

Another poet in a similar position to Carew's was William Davenant, Jonson's unofficial successor as poet laureate. He too celebrated the Stuart ideal for the court while the ingredients of rebellion bubbled up all around. But of a different temperament from Carew, and twelve years younger, Davenant has little of the melancholia which runs through all the elder poet's work. When war did break out both men took up arms— but it is markedly harder to engage in warfare at the age of forty-five than it is at thirty-three. There are few sadder poems in the century than Carew's "To my friend G. N. from Wrest." Written soon after the disastrous expedition into Scotland in the so-called Bishops' War, where all visions of chivalric warfare were annihilated by a northern winter, the poem is a masterpiece of nostalgic control. Carew is dying from the rigors of the campaign for which he, together with the rest of the army, had been unprepared. He starts by contrasting what he has just experienced with the peace of his present retirement:

> I breathe (sweet *Ghib:*) the temperate air of *Wrest*
> Where I no more with raging storms oppressed,
> Wear the cold nights out by the banks of Tweed,
> On the bleak Mountains, where fierce tempests breed,
> And everlasting Winter dwells; where mild
> *Favonius,* and the Vernal winds exiled,
> Did never spread their wings: but the wild North
> Brings sterile Fern, Thistles, and Brambles forth.
> Here steeped in balmy dew, the pregnant Earth
> Sends from her teeming womb a flowery birth,
> And cherished with the warm Sun's quick'ning heat,
> Her porous bosom doth rich odours sweat;
> Whose perfumes through the Ambient air diffuse
> Such native Aromatics, as we use
> No foreign Gums, nor essence fetched from far,
> No volatile spirits, nor compounds that are
> Adulterate, but at Nature's cheap expence
> With far more genuine sweets refresh the sense.

The poem then expands into one more celebration, in the line of Jonson's "To Penshurst," of the country house ideal. The catalogue of praise runs for nearly 100 lines, as if Carew were trying to reconstruct the social ideal as an exorcism of the dissensions which were splitting the country apart—as in this account of a society perfectly structured, in which every class not only knows its place but is happy with it too (35–46):

> at large Tables filled with wholesome meats
> The servant, Tenant, and kind neighbour eats.
> Some of that rank, spun of a finer threat
> Are with the Women, Steward, and Chaplain fed
> With daintier cates; Others of better note
> Whom wealth, parts, office, of the Herald's coat
> Have severed from the common, freely sit
> At the Lord's table, whose spread sides admit
> A large access of friends to fill those seats
> Of his capacious circle, filled with meats
> Of choicest relish, till his Oaken back
> Under the load of piled-up dishes crack.

Perhaps Carew really believes in this peace which has been temporarily patched up, but the poem's final four lines hint at other futures, omens personal and national. Saying goodby to his friend, and celebrating his pleasure in the harmless pursuit of stag hunting, he sees the rural ideal dissolve into memories of other hills and slaughter:

> Thus I enjoy my self, and taste the fruit
> Of this blest Peace, whilst toiled in the pursuit
> Of Bucks, and Stags, th'emblem of war, you strive
> To keep the memory of our Arms alive.

Davenant, in contrast, prided himself on his soldiering experience, and when war came embraced it readily enough. Earlier, in the 1630s, he had tried to shore up the pseudo-philosophical vanities of the masques with some more heroic matter in his poems, most notably in "Madagascar," written in praise of Prince Rupert's impracticable idea of conquering the island and setting up a colony there, with himself as viceroy. Davenant writes as if the enterprise, still in its planning stage, had been successfully completed, with battles fought and won, and reputations gained—a wished-for reversal of English foreign policy in the 1630s, from shameful passivity to the reawakening of Elizabethan heroics. Except, of course, that none of it was allowed to happen. Charles flirted with the idea for a time, but wiser counsels prevailed and the plug was pulled on the whole enterprise. This did not stop Davenant giving the poem pride of place in his volume; hence Carew's beautifully tongue-in-cheek poem to Davenant on "Madagascar":

> When I behold, by warrant from thy pen
> A prince rigging our fleets, arming our men,
> Conducting to remotest shores our force
> (Without a Dido to retard his course),
> And thence repelling in successful fight
> Th'usurping foe, whose strength was all his right,
> By two brave heroes (whom we justly may
> By Homer's Ajax or Achilles lay):
> I doubt the author of the Tale of Troy,
> With him that makes his fugitive enjoy
> The Carthage Queen, and think thy poem may
> Impose upon posterity, as they
> Have done on us. What though romances lie
> Thus blended with more faithful history;
> We of th'adulterate mixture not complain,
> But thence more characters of virtue gain;
> More pregnant patterns of transcendent worth
> Than barren and insipid Truth brings forth:
> So oft the bastard nobler fortune meets
> Than the dull issue of the lawful sheets.

Flippant this may be, but it touches on sensitive matters. The prospect of a prince who would lead Englishmen in a true fight strikes chords with much of the popular discontent of the decade. Ballads of the 1630s often fasten upon English neutrality in the Thirty Years' War as a source of national shame, as in "Gallants, to Bohemia" (ca. 1632):[8]

> Some seek in foreign Lands to thrive,
>   we like Bees do keep our hive:
> Some get riches, Pearl and Gold,
>   we sitting still grow faint and cold:
> Once again let it be said,
>   we foreign actions never feared,
> The true Religion to maintain,
>   *Come let us to the wars again.*
>
> In fair *Bohemia* now is sprung,
>   a Service which we looked for long:

Where Soldiers may their valour try,
    when cowards from the field will fly:
It never shall of us be said,
    that English Captains stood afraid:
Or such adventures would refrain,
    Then let us to the wars again.

Of late we had within our Land,
    a noble number of command:
Of gallant Leaders brace and bold,
    that almost all the world controlled:
As *Essex, Cumberland* and *Drake,*
    which made both Sea and Land to shake,
The *Indian* silver to obtain,
    Then let us to the wars again.

Davenant's piece of wish fulfillment shares with the ballad, as Carew shrewdly notes, a resistance to the "Barren and insipid" truth of the necessary circumspection of England's foreign policy.

A few years earlier, in 1630, Davenant had written a New Year's poem to the king in which he called for peace obtained through victory, not one "compassed by / Expensive Treaties." The poem as a whole is a celebration of Charles as "th'example and the Law, / By whom the good are taught, not kept in awe"; but in the context of the conventional excesses of panegyric poetry, Davenant's allusion to the dearly bought treaties of Susa and Madrid is emphatic, if coded, criticism of the way the country is being run. Davenant had supported Buckingham's Continental adventures, so the new spirit of neutralism held few attractions for him. The blame, of course, is not Charles's—that would be going too far for any court poet—and the poem pins it firmly on those members of Parliament who argue for the sake of personal aggrandizement and who fail to raise the taxes which would enable England's king to match Sweden's:[9]

A Session too, of such who can obey,
As they were gathered to consult, not sway:
    Who not rebel, in hope to get
    Some office to reclaim their wit:
        Let this year bring
        To *Charles* our King:
To *Charles;* who is th'example and the Law,
By whom the good are taught, not kept in awe.

Praetors, who will the public cause defend,
With timely gifts, not Speeches finely penned;
   To make the Northern Victor's Fame
   No more our envy, nor our shame;
     Let this year bring
     To *Charles* our King:
To *Charles;* who is th'example and the Law,
By whom the good are taught, not kept in awe.

As Davenant's editor notes, the odd feature of all of this is that Parliament had been dissolved for nearly a year: "presumably . . . Davenant was expecting, or expressing the hope, that a more pliant parliament would be recalled in 1630."[10] Perhaps, but it is not difficult to see Davenant's problem. In a country splitting into factions, in which the king had assumed total authority, any allusion to popular discontent needed a scapegoat to deflect blame from the king. And so obvious was the discontent becoming that it was hard to write in praise of Charles without mentioning it, given the ironic readings to which poems of undiluted praise, such as Corbett's, could be subjected.

Admittedly some poets could keep writing as if nothing were happening—not least Edmund Waller, whose capacity to fool himself into believing that all was going well became legendary. But even Waller's poetry betrays some doubt and concern within its fixed purpose of offering Charles nothing but praise.

In 1631, under Bishop Laud's prompting, Charles appointed commissioners to raise money for the repair of St. Paul's cathedral. The enterprise never got very far because the people of England remained spectacularly unmoved by the whole idea. Only £5,400 was subscribed in two years. But like Davenant's "Madagascar," Waller's poem on the matter, "Upon his Majesty's Repairing of St Paul's," treats the enterprise as if it had been successfully concluded, the intent standing for the deed. The poem's wit lies in its praise of Charles for his lack of personal ambition: other kings would have built new edifices to carry their names into history, but Charles's greatness is secure enough for him merely to rebuild and renew. The whole enterprise is then portrayed as the pursuit of peace through beauty (39–42):

For doubtful reason few can apprehend,
And war brings ruin where it should amend;
But beauty, with a bloodless conquest, finds
A welcome sovereignty in rudest minds.

Here all those who doubt the wisdom or morality of English neutrality are taken issue with, and the poem ends by praising Charles for his resolute peacefulness. Had he chosen war he would naturally have triumphed; but the achievements of peace are harder and greater:

> Glad, though amazed, are our neighbour kings,
> To see such power employed in peaceful things;
> They list not urge it to the dreadful field;
> The task is easier to destroy than build.

The pursuit of beauty made up much of the material and purpose of the court masques of the 1630s. In the case of Davenant, who wrote a fair number of them while at the same time hankering after military adventures, the contradictions make his public poetry more interesting in this decade than Waller's unquestioning support for whatever the king wanted. But Waller has at least one poem which encourages a skeptical reading. This is "The Apology of Sleep, for not approaching the lady who can do anything but sleep when she pleaseth." It is not, as its title implies, a companion piece to his poem "Of the Lady Who Can Sleep When She Pleases," for that lady was Waller's flame, Sacharissa, and that poem is merely one in the long catalogue of seventeenth-century addresses to sleeping ladies. This is quite different, for the lady is wide awake; and, what is more, this lady is the queen.

As in his St. Paul's poem Waller's purpose is to use wit to transform a more or less shabby reality into a transcendent illusion. There the king's lack of means to repair his capital's cathedral becomes an emblem of magnanimity; here the queen's restlessness comes not, as one might reasonably conjecture, from worry about present turmoils and future threats, but rather from her freedom from cares. Sleep is nature's tool for easing a troubled mind; no troubled mind, so no need for sleep, is how the logic runs:

> My charge it is those breaches to repair
> Which Nature takes from sorrow, toil, and care;
> Rest to the limbs, and quiet I confer
> On troubled minds; but nought can add to her
> Whom Heaven and her transcendent thoughts have placed
> Above those ills which wretched mortals taste.
> Bright as the deathless gods, and happy, she
> From all that may infringe delight is free . . .

There are shades of "Let them eat cake" here, but Waller's panegyric does not alter its course in the slightest. It is this inflexibility which makes the poem so interesting, for it is hard to imagine any contemporary reader not perplexed by a queen whose mind is untroubled, who is free from cares, and who presides over a court which has all the joys and glories which three kingdoms can offer, with none of its responsibilities. These joys and glories are, as one might expect, the court entertainments, particularly the masques. Waller wittily claims that what they embody far outshines anything which the dreams of sleep could provide (11–20):

> Such real pleasures, such true joys suspense,
> What dream can I present to recompense?
>   Should I with lightning fill her awful hand,
> And make the clouds seem all at her command;
> Or place her in Olympus' top, a guest
> Among the immortals, who with nectar feast;
> That power would seem, that entertainment, short
> Of the true splendour of her present court,
> Where all the joys, and all the glories, are
> Of three great kingdoms, severed from the care.

Given the massive expenditure lavished on the masques, and the elaborate machinery and costumes which they contained, Waller's conceit may well not be as hyperbolic as it first seems; and this emphasis upon such ostentation makes it the more uncomfortable in its absolute refusal to consider how fragile the court's position has become. Nonetheless, the very fact of the queen's restlessness undermines Waller' vision, although by the poem's end he has wish-fulfilled himself into the position of being able to promise her sleep at last.

Of course, one might argue that the queen could, by virtue of her position as consort, be held free from the responsibilities, and therefore the cares, of state. But Waller's readers would know this to be a fiction. Charles was no single-minded man of strength; he was impressionable and dependent upon those closest to him, especially his queen, whose flirtation with the prospect of a restored Catholicism was responsible for much of the popular resentment. Moreover, in the masques which reinforced Charles's view of himself as an absolute ruler—what he would have liked to be rather than what he was—the queen was given important roles to play, sometimes as worshiper-in-chief, as in Davenant's masque *Luminalia,* presented by the queen and her ladies in 1638, and always as

Charles's intimate partner, the two of them making a complete, Platonic ideal. The best example of this is Davenant's *Salmacida Spolia* (1640), the last of the Stuart court masques, presented so close to the civil wars that Carew's vision of violins drowning out cannon fire is very nearly realized.

In this masque Davenant tries to create out of the nation's chaos one more picture of Charles's benevolence curing all. He is characterized as Philogenes, "lover of the people." Concord bewails his predicament thus (19–22):

> much I grieve, that though the best
> Of Kingly science harbours in his breast,
> Yet 'tis his fate to rule in adverse times,
> When wisdom must awhile give place to crimes.

The third song of the masque is addressed to the king, "when he appears with his lords in the Throne of Honour." Davenant's editor says of the New Year's poem to the king that although he was poet laureate it appears to be the only one which he directly addressed to Charles. Part of the reason for this may well have been the difficulty of writing such panegyric verse in the 1630s, but the comment tends to ignore the fact that in his masques Davenant was addressing the king very directly, as here (song III):

> Those quar'ling winds (that deafened unto death
>   The living, and did wake men dead before)
> Seem now to pant small gusts, as out of breath,
>   And fly, to reconcile themselves on shore.
>
> If it be Kingly patience to out last
>   Those storms the people's giddy fury raise,
> Till like fantastic winds themselves they waste,
>   The wisdom of that patience is thy praise.
>
> *Murmur's* a sickness epidemical;
>   'Tis catching, and infects weak common ears;
> For through those crooked, narrow Alleys, all
>   Invaded are, and killed by Whisperers.
>
> This you discerned and by your mercy taught,
>   Would not (like Monarchs that severe have been)
> Invent Imperial Arts to question thought,
>   Nor punish vulgar sickness as a sin.

Nor would your valour (when it might subdue)
   Be hindered of the pleasure to forgive;
Th'are worse than overcome (your wisdom knew)
   That needed mercy to have leave to live.

Since strength of virtues gained you Honour's throne,
   Accept our wonder, and enjoy your praise!
He's fit to govern there, and rule alone,
   Whom inward helps, not outward force, doth raise.

The poem praises Charles's discretion at this dangerous stage, a theme which concerned Davenant greatly. But it transforms the political realities of the situation into praise of Charles's prescience, the one quality which he certainly lacked. Most striking is the way in which the realism of the first three stanzas gives way to illusion in the next three. In the first two stanzas the praise of kingly patience scarcely outweighs the description of England in 1640 as a land battered by storms. Then comes the marvelous double image of murmur burrowing its way through the channels of the ear. Those "crooked, narrow alleys" are also the streets of London, warrens of conspiracy and sedition. But all of this dissolves into wish fulfillment in the rest of the poem, which, although it never quite loses sight of Charles's helplessness, contrives to support his view of himself as one fitted to rule alone. Then the queen and her ladies descend and the masque resolves itself first into a celebration of the queen's virtuous power—glancing at her ridiculous notions of Platonic love (song IV, 25–28):

   All that are good she did inspire!
Lovers are chaste, because they know
It is her will they should be so;
   The valiant take from her their Fire!

and finally addressing the king and queen together (song VI, 1–8):

   So musical as to all Ears
Doth seem the music of the Spheres,
Are you unto each other still,
Tuning your thoughts to either's will.

All that are harsh, all that are rude,
Are by your harmony subdued;
Yet so into obedience wrought,
As if not forced to it, but taught.

Nothing could be further from the real situation than this vision of the royal couple as one mind and one spirit, governing all and by their harmony teaching the nation to act obediently, as if the alleys of London were on a different planet rather than a mile or so away.

The most daring poem which Davenant wrote was addressed directly to the queen, either in 1640 or early 1641. Intended or not, the writing of it was an act of *Realpolitik* for Davenant, for later in 1641 when in danger of prosecution by Parliament he defended himself by claiming that "it is not long since I wrote to the Queen's majesty in praise of her inclination to become this way the People's advocate." [11] Presumably this is the poem to which he refers:

To the Queen

Madam; so much peculiar and alone
Are Kings, so uncompanioned in a Throne,
That through the want of some equality
(Familiar Guides, who lead them to comply)
They may offend by being so sublime,
As if to be a King might be a crime;
All less than Kings no more with Kings prevail
Than lesser Weights with greater in a Scale:
They are not moved (when weighed within a Throne)
But by a greatness equal to their own.
To cure this high obnoxious singleness
(Yet not to make their power but danger less)
Were Queens ordained; who were in Monarchs' breasts
Tenants for life, not accidental Guests;
So they prevail by Nature, not by chance;
But you (with yours) your virtue does advance,
When you persuade him (in the People's cause)
Not to esteem his Judges more than Laws.
In Kings (perhaps) extreme obdurateness
Is as in Jewels hardness in excess:
Which makes their price: for we as well call stones
For hardness as for brightness, Paragons:
And 'tis perhaps so with obdurate Kings
As with the best impenetrable things.
No way to pierce or alter them is found,
Till we to Diamonds use a Diamond.

This argument that the queen is the only one who can soften the king's obduracy—a diamond to cut a diamond—is continued through the poem until it closes in scorn for those who might consider any form of yielding a weakness (41–44):

> Accursed are those *Court-Sophisters* who say
> When Princes yield, Subjects no more obey.
> Madam, you that studied Heaven and Times
> Know there is Punishment, and there are Crimes . . .

This is an extraordinarily troubled, and for that reason highly political, poem, testimony to Davenant's strengths. It is difficult to think of any other court poet who was prepared to wrestle so openly with the problem of how to persuade Charles to act with discretion. Most fascinatingly, it shows a poet immersed in the techniques of panegyric and patronage poetry having to bend them to breaking point—perhaps beyond this point, for it is difficult now, and must have been equally so then, to read the poem as anything but a powerful criticism of Charles's behavior.

The loaded word is "obdurate," the one which only seven or eight years earlier Carew had used to describe the people. Now it describes Charles and applied to a king, recalls the pharaoh of Exodus whose heart was hardened to the degree that he destroyed many of his own people. Davenant's opening lines are revealingly clumsy as the panegyric strains to explain why obduracy is the consequence of regal isolation. "As if to be a King might be a crime" is a line packed with doubt about the future of kingly power: the king's mere existence as king makes him a cause of offense. This is an attempt to understand and convey Charles's predicament, but the poem does not shrink from finding fault with him: telling the queen to advise him not to favor his judges above his laws is as direct a piece of blame as any of Charles's opponents could have wished, and in its contrast of judges and laws it sets up the conflict which the rest of the poem explores between the king's wish to help his supporters and his need to respect the laws of the country. The queen's mission is to persuade him to make proper constitutional use of his prerogative, and not protect those who have broken the law: "there is Punishment, and there are Crimes."

Whether Davenant actually saw the queen as willing to use her influence in such a way is doubtful, but much significance lies in his impulse to write the poem. No doubt part of his motive was to take out some kind of insurance against catastrophe, but it is possible to be more charitable and to see some consistency in his endeavors. Rather than being a "strong contrast" to the 1630 poem, as has been claimed, this poem should be read, within the coded conventions of the panegyric and the masque, as a continuation: there he criticized Charles's expensive treaties, now he criticizes his obduracy; just as in the masques, behind the froth and illusion, he had conveyed some sense of the discord to which poets such as Waller would give no explicit recognition.

2 "All Time's Story": Strafford and Buckingham

Davenant's poem to the queen, asking her to become the people's advocate, ends with a carefully measured balancing of mercy and bloodshed:

> Madam, you that studied Heaven and Times
> Know there is Punishment, and there are Crimes.
> You are become (which doth augment your state)
> The Judge's Judge, and People's Advocate:
> These are your Triumphs which (perhaps) may be
> (Yet Triumphs have been taxed for Cruelty)
> Esteemed both just and mercifully good:
> Though what you gain with Tears, cost others Blood.

It is possible to understand Davenant's meaning in the final line to be something like the idea that by her effective pleading the queen will save others from having to achieve the same end by shedding blood. But it is more likely, given the account of cruel triumphs which precedes it, that Davenant is pointing to a double sacrifice which must now be made. The queen must weep and men must bleed. If so, the most obvious victim for sacrifice is the Earl of Strafford.

Strafford had, in the 1620s, opposed the government's arbitrary taxations and equally arbitrary imprisonment of opponents: he was imprisoned himself for a short period. But after the Duke of Buckingham's death his distaste for the increasingly militant Puritanism of the Parliamentary party led him to move closer to the king's side. He ruled Ireland through the 1630s, returning to England in September 1639, soon after the debacle of the first Bishops' War. Now Charles's chief adviser, he supported the idea of a second Scottish campaign against Parliament's wishes. He commanded the English army, and its defeat at Newburn during his illness led to threats of his impeachment. He tried to forestall this by charging Parliament's leaders with treachery, but was outmaneuvered, ending up a prisoner in the Tower. Charles, characteristically, pursued contrary courses of action: one, peaceable, to win over Parliament's leaders; the other, aggressive, to liberate Strafford by force. When this "army plot" was discovered the House of Lords passed the Commons' bill of attainder, which it had hitherto blocked. Charles had promised Strafford that he would not suffer "in life, honour or fortune," but the earl now wrote releasing him from the promise. On 10 May 1641 Charles signed the bill, and Strafford was executed two days later.

Many poets ruminated on Strafford's trial and execution with an air of puzzlement. For one thing, it was difficult to judge the degree to which his downfall had been engineered or was self-induced. For another, scarcely anyone writing at the time could guess its consequences, whether it was a sacrifice which would help to heal the country's divisions or one which showed up the king's weaknesses so emphatically that it made the prospect of rebellion stronger. It was possible to take a fairly simple view and see the earl's fate as entirely self-induced. *The Rump* includes a poem whose title, "Upon Ambition. Occasioned by the Accusation of the Earl of Strafford, in the year 1640," fits it neatly into the genre of poems warning against attempts to climb up to the slippery top:[1]

How uncertain is the State
    Of that greatness we adore,
When Ambitiously we soar,
    And have ta'en the glorious height,
'Tis but Ruin gilded o'er,
    To enslave us to our fate,
Whose false Delight is easier got, than kept,
Content ne'er on its gaudy Pillow slept.

Then how fondly do we try,
    With such superstitious care,
To build Fabrics in the Air?
    Or seek safety in that sky,
Where no Stars but Meteors are,
    That portend a ruin nigh?
And having reached the object of our aim,
We find it but a *Pyramid* of flame.

The poem is not very good, not merely because its images are hackneyed and the development of its ideas confused, but because it evades, rather than faces, Strafford's situation. It was probably written before the trial, but there is nothing in it to encourage speculation about what has happened or what will. *The Rump* collected poems which reflected well on "our late Sovereign of Glorious Memory," and this one example of a Strafford-connected poems fits its bill nicely. There is no hint of Charles's involvement here, nor of the politicking which led to Strafford's arraignment, only a condemnation of his ambition which sets him into a long line of statesmen who aspired too high.

A poem which works the opposite way is "The Fall," Richard Fanshawe's translation of a Spanish original by Gongora. A poem about the fallen statesman Don Rodrigo Calderon, written in 1621, its closeness to the details of Strafford's case is fascinating, and obviously struck Fanshawe forcibly.[2] He had served under Strafford in Ireland and was a good friend of the earl's son. His translation of what might have seemed to be an archetypal account of fallen ambition becomes a hauntingly specific rendering of Strafford's fate:

> The bloody trunk of him who did possess
>   Above the rest a hapless happy state,
>   *This little Stone* doth Seal, but not depress,
>   And scarce can stop the rolling of his fate.
>
> Brass Tombs which justice hath denied t'his fault,
>   The common pity to his virtues pays,
>   Adorning an Imaginary vault,
>   Which from our minds time strives in vain to raze.
>
> Ten years the world upon him falsely smiled,
>   Sheathing in fawning looks the deadly knife
>   Long aimed at his head; That so beguiled
>   It more securely might bereave his Life;
>
> Then threw him to a Scaffold from a Throne,
> *Much Doctrine lies under this little Stone.*

Fanshawe's poem is so good because within the sonnet's pretty room it gives space to all the circumstances of Strafford's life and death—the fault of his ambition, his restlessness, the sense of destiny which marked his rise, the respect and hatred which he engendered, and also Charles's part

"None stood so, or so fell": Thomas Wentworth, first Earl of Strafford. After Anthony Vandyke, ca. 1633.

THE TRUE MANER OF THE EXECUTION OF THOMAS EARLE OF STRAFFORD, LORD
Lieutenant of Ireland vpon Tower-hill the 12ᵗʰ of May. 1641.

A. Doctor Vsher, Lord Primate of Ireland.
B. the Sherifes of London.
C. the Earle of Strafford.
D. his kindred and Friends.

Execution des Grafen Thoma von Stafford Statthalters in Irland auf dē Tawers platz in London 12 Maj 1641.

A. Doct. Usher Primat in Irland.
B. Rahts Herren von Londen.
C. Der Graf von Stafford.
D. Seine anverwanten vnd freunde.

Strafford's execution. Great falls bring about many smaller ones: note the collapsing grandstand opposite the scaffold. Wenceslaus Hollar, ca. 1643.

in his downfall. Kept out of the poem until the couplet, the throne exists only as an impassive object from which Strafford is hurled to his fate. How far Charles can be identified with, or removed from, the world which fawns on Strafford in the third quatrain is as impossible for us to judge as it was for Strafford's contemporaries to estimate his behavior toward the earl. Implicit too is some sense of the consequences of the statesman's fall. This comes from an appreciation of the poem's lapidary status: Strafford was denied a fitting burial and a suitable monument with engraved brass, so the sonnet acts as the stone which seals the grave.[3] But so powerful is Strafford's spirit that it is barely containable: "rolling" is a word full of threat, of revolution, as well as of resurrection when the stone is rolled away from the grave. A lesson is promised in the final line, but not so much the generalized "beware of ambition" of the *Rump* poem as a specific warning of what will follow Strafford's death.

Fanshawe wrote a longer poem, "On the Earl of Strafford's Trial," but it has nothing of the compressed power of the sonnet. It faintly anticipates Marvell's "An Horatian Ode," seeing the trial as a theatrical performance (11–18):

> Then if 'twill prove no *Comedy,* at least
> To make it of all *Tragedies* the best.
> And that he'll do; I know not what past fact
> May speak him less, but for his life's *last act,*
> *Times* shall admiring read it, and *this age,*
> Though now it *hiss, claps* when he leaves the Stage;
> So *stand* or *fall,* none *stood* so, or so *fell;*
> This far-famed *Trial* hath no parallel.

But the poem as a whole does not go far beyond this focus upon the drama of the trial. It praises Strafford for his bearing there and for his resolution in determining to die rather than fight for his life at the cost of civil war, presenting his self-sacrifice as an act of nobility, necessary to keep national peace and restore Charles's power. In the margin of the following lines Fanshawe notes "The Earles pathetical Letter to the King, which is to be seene in print, wherein hee begges of his Majesty, to passe the Bill for his death, to quiet the Kingdomes"(33–40):

> Nor shall he die, unless these broils t'assuage
> A yet *more Civil War* himself shall wage,
> Turn (what he used so well for his defence)
> Against *himself,* his conquering *Eloquence,*

Spend his whole stock of favour too, to bring
To the *Three Kingdoms* a *fourth* Power, *the King:*
A *Fourth Estate* add to the *Parliament:*
And to the *Royal* give his own assent.

Despite the poem's length (forty-two lines), too many questions are left unasked. In contrast to the sonnet, it is a public poem whose purpose is to continue Strafford's policy after his death. The fewer questions asked, the better are Charles's chances; but the sonnet offers a more skeptical view of the whole process.

A similar wish for secrecy, not so much from fear for personal safety as for general political reasons, may attach to a highly popular poem, an epitaph, which appeared soon after Strafford's death. It was probably written by John Cleveland, though in only two of its fifteen manuscript versions is it attributed to him, and the chief manuscript source of Cleveland's writings does not include it.[4] A fair number of modern readers have found it so unlike his other poems that they have doubted the ascription to him, and Cleveland's editors keep it in their "Poems Probably by Cleveland" section, with the justification that although it is unlike any of his other poems, "considering the extreme tact enjoined by the event upon a Fellow of St John's not yet irretrievably committed to the King's cause, it is what one might expect: a trail of consciously clever antitheses, half-shielding and sophisticating the pathos of bloody 'riddles.'"[5] "Extreme tact" may be putting it too strongly, for the most tactful action would have been to write nothing at all. No one required or ordered such a poem, so either it is the result of a poet's irresistible need to respond to the event or it has a public purpose. Or both, of course—but its public purpose is worth emphasizing, for if it had been written only as an individual response, then there is no reason for it to have left the poet's desk drawer (just as most of Marvell's stayed shut away until Mary Palmer collected them):

> *Epitaph of the Earl of Strafford*
> Here lies Wise and Valiant Dust,
> Huddled up 'twixt Fit and Just:
> STRAFFORD, who was hurried hence
> 'Twixt treason and Convenience.
> He spent his Time here in a Mist;
> A *Papist,* yet a *Calvinist.*
> His Prince's nearest Joy, and Grief.
> He had, yet wanted all Relief.

> The Prop and Ruin of the State;
> The People's violent Love, and Hate:
> One in extremes loved and abhorred.
> Riddles lie here; or in a word,
> Here lies Blood; and let it lie
> Speechless still, and never cry.

Poems on Strafford kept appearing for the next ten years, but no one knew how to make sense of the man or his fate. The writer of *Eikon Basilike* had to deal very early with the earl's death. He has Charles defending himself against the apparent injustice of his sacrifice of Strafford, and revealing his bad conscience over the matter; but he also takes care to sow enough seeds of doubt about the earl's "great abilities," which were "like enough to betray him to great errors and many enemies."[6] Cleveland's poem is a more honest piece. "Huddled up" gets just the tone of shoddiness and shabbiness which brought about Strafford's fall. He is already a corpse before the verdict has been declared. In the *Eikon* Charles appears as the victim of competing forces: his conscience, the clamor of the people, and his best advisers. In the "Epitaph" Strafford is, more properly, seen as the real victim of impersonal forces. All the abstractions which are pulling the country apart come to a point under this stone: fit, just, treason, convenience, prince, people. All add up to "riddles," whose counterpart is "blood." Blood is thicker than the dust which opens the poem, and is the most terrible answer to the riddles, for blood will not lie speechless: "the voice of thy brother's blood crieth unto me from the ground." "Wise and valiant dust" is, in the opinion of Cleveland's editors, a sophistication of the pathos of Strafford's death, but "blood" certainly is not. For all the expressed hope that the dead man's influence will end there and then, that one word is enough to predict the horrors to come: "Blood will have blood." Cleveland may not understand Strafford, but he grasps the consequences of his execution. In this sense the poem, in all its brevity, is a marvelous clarification of what has happened. Strafford's death is not, as Fanshawe's public poem would have it, a sacrifice which will help secure peace and stability. It resolves the muddle in another way. Men who claim to be arguing political theory and principle have become, more simply, men of blood.

In finding exactly the right word the poem becomes part of the event. Riddles to which there is no answer leave us speechless. The aim of Strafford's opponents was not just to defeat him but also to silence him. The trial showed what formidable powers of oratory he could deploy. And the king, too, had no need to give any explanation of his acquiescence in the event. But the flood of poems and writings purporting to be Strafford's own became increasingly embarrassing, so much so that Parliament had to threaten prosecution to halt it.[7] Not only does Cleveland's "Epitaph" give the most striking account of Strafford's fall, fixing it firmly and precisely in the public consciousness, but it does so by giving him the power of speech which Pym's Bill of Attainder and Charles's pious vacillations had taken away from him. He has only the one word, but it is the most evocative word imaginable. Blood lies speechless only when it is being revenged; until then it cries out.

The other well-known poem on Strafford's fall is John Denham's "On the Earl of Strafford's Trial and Death." Admirable enough on its own, it fades when set next to Cleveland's because it too easily makes Strafford a victim of "they" who, in their "legislative frenzy," desired his death. The repeated "'twixt" of Cleveland's "Epitaph" may appear clumsy, but it emphasizes how all sides wished for Strafford's death, grinding him between them. In Denham's poem the king and his supporters are passed over. A couplet like this one might have signified the contests between Charles and the Commons (17–18):[8]

> Now private pity strove with public hate,
> Reason with rage and eloquence with fate.

Instead it merely represents Strafford's fight for his life. Such a view of the affair is too simple, and Cleveland's "Epitaph" explains why. Rather than there being only two sides, one marked by pity and reason, the other by hate and rage, the more complex truth is that all of these forces operate within all the protagonists. Strafford's mixed nature—a man who had everything and wanted everything—is symptomatic of the nation as it slipped into civil war, and for the rest of the century it governed poets' perceptions of the men who struggled for power (such as Marvell's Cromwell and Dryden's Zimri).

Englishmen's interpretations may have varied as to just when sensibilities became dissociated, so that heart and mind pulled against each other, but it seems fair to assume that many would have looked back to the assassination of George Villiers the first Duke of Buckingham as a key incident in the country's fragmentation. Buckingham's star had risen through James I's reign, due partly to his good looks and graces, but mainly because of his ruthless political intelligence. By James's death he had become the most powerful and hated man in the country, responsible for a series of foreign adventures which had wasted much taxpayers' money, with thousands of English soldiers left dead on the Continent.

"This child of honour": George Villiers soon after he had been created Earl of Buckingham. Attributed to William Larkin, 1616.

Naturally, Charles came increasingly under his control, until, in 1628, Buckingham was stabbed to death by John Felton, variously described as a disaffected servant or a new Brutus. The poems written about that event provide both parallels and contrasts with Strafford's fall. Most significantly, there begins the perception that things can never be so simple again. The one word which Carew found to portray this realization is *safe*. A word which had appeared to be full of value and meaning has, after Felton's stabbing of the duke, ceased to mean anything at all:

> Reader, when these dumb stones have told
> In borrowed speech, what Guest they hold,
> Thou shalt confess, the vain pursuit
> Of human Glory yields no fruit,
> But an untimely Grave. If Fate
> Could constant happiness create,
> Her Ministers, Fortune and Worth
> Had here that miracle brought forth;
> They fixed this child of Honour, where
> No room was left for Hope, or Fear,
> Of more, or less: so high, so great
> His growth was, yet so safe his seat.
> Safe in the circle of his Friends:
> Safe in his Loyal heart, and ends:
> Safe in his native valiant spirit:
> By favour safe, and safe by merit;
> Safe by the stamp of Nature, which
> Did strength, with shape and Grace enrich:
> Safe in the cheerful Courtesies
> Of flowing gestures, speech, and eyes:
> Safe in his Bounties, which were more
> Proportioned to his mind than store;
> Yet, though for virtue he becomes
> Involved Himself in borrowed sums,
> Safe in his care, he leaves betrayed
> No friend engaged, no debt unpaid.
>   But though the stars conspire to shower
> Upon one Head th'united power
> Of all their Graces, if their dire
> Aspects, must other breasts inspire
> With vicious thoughts, a Murderer's knife
> May cut (as here) their Darling's life.

> Who can be happy then, if Nature must
> To make one Happy man, make all men just?

The difficult thing in assessing such a poem is to guess how much of this Carew believed. Detestation of Buckingham was so deep and so widely voiced that for the poet to proclaim his virtue, worth, dignity, and honesty in this way is to assert that only the court's perceptions have any validity at all. So, too, the notion of Buckingham as in any way safe is bizarrely at odds with all that had happened. As was well known, Buckingham had not only been threatened with death many times, but had confided his expectations of a violent end to many friends. And the hacking to death of his protégé Dr. Lamb on the streets of London a few weeks earlier had been a potent enough warning of what was in store for the duke if he were careless enough to let his guard slip.

Epitaph poetry encourages the glossing over of such uncomfortable facts, but the poems which responded to Buckingham's death were less epitaphs than elements in a continuing political struggle. On the streets were being widely circulated poems which applauded Felton's act and which celebrated it as a great release for the country. Carew's poem is an act of counterpropaganda, not only affirming Buckingham's greatness but also doing its best, against all the evidence, to show that the murder was entirely unexpected and explicable only through the natural antipathy of bad to good. Another poem which he wrote on the event, "On the Duke of *Buckingham*," comes only a little closer to the popular perception of it, by casting Felton not just as a figure of the stars' opposition, but as a deluded victim of factionalist politicians (1–15):

> When in the brazen leaves of Fame,
> The life, the death, of *Buckingham*
> Shall be recorded, if Truth's hand
> Incise the story of our Land,
> Posterity shall see a fair
> Structure, by the studious care
> Of two Kings raised, that did no less
> Their wisdom, than their Power express;
> By blinded zeal (whose doubtful light
> Made murder's scarlet robe seem white,
> Whose vain-deluding phantasms charmed
> A clouded sullen soul, and armed
> A desperate hand, thirsty of blood)
> Torn from the fair earth where it stood;
> So the majestic fabric fell.

"Zeal" is the key word which sets up Felton as an enthusiastic fool manipulated by Puritan preachers skilled in making murder acceptable. But what is most striking here is the element of uncertainty in the conditional "if" of the third line, for this lets in a doubt about whose version of Buckingham's death will prevail. The other poem, for all its professed concern with the annihilation of safety, betrays no such perception that the duke's death is part of a struggle for power which involves the whole country, rather than being the rash act of a desperate zealot. Because he is so firm a supporter of the established order, with everything to lose if it collapses, the doubt which Carew admits is only a faint one. But it is worth noting the curious choice of image with which he presents Truth's writing of history. To *incise* the story of our land is to engrave it in enduring brass, but it also mimics Felton's act of stabbing Buckingham. Again, there is just the glimmer of recognition that truth is variable, to be defined by the victors, who might even represent Felton as the instrument of righteousness.

Some other court poets present a slightly less simplified view of Buckingham's death. Davenant wrote two poems about it. The more public one is addressed to the duchess. It ignores all the facts of the assassination and simply treats the death as if it were the passing on of any great man, ending like this:

> For gone is now the Pilot of the State,
> The Court's bright Star, the Clergy's Advocate,
> The Poet's highest Theme, the Lover's flame,
> And Soldier's Glory, mighty *Buckingham*.

The other poem, kept in manuscript, bears all the signs of being a genuinely personal piece of writing. As Corbett's poems show, Buckingham attracted a crowd of sycophantic hangers-on, but here and there in the poems addressed to him it is possible to detect real emotion. Herrick, for example, pays a short tribute in *Hesperides* which he claims adds the final luster to his book. Its title, "To the High and Noble Prince, GEORGE, Duke, Marquess, and Earl of *Buckingham*", betrays the hero worship involved here:

> Never my Book's perfection did appear,
> Till I had got the name of VILLIERS here.
> Now 'tis so full, that when therein I look,
> I see a Cloud of Glory fills my Book.
> Here stand it still to dignify our Muse,
> Your sober Hand-maid; who doth wisely choose,

Your Name to be a *Laureate Wreath* to Her,
Who doth both love and fear you *Honoured Sir.*

Herrick, with no aspirations to a bishopric, seems simply pleased to have the name Villiers included in his poems; but some sense of the awe which Buckingham's power inspired is apparent in the somberness of the poem. The poem makes no attempt at wit, but bows down in reverence—the fear equal to, if not outweighing, the love which Herrick bears. But Davenant, in his unpublished poem on the duke's death, tries hard to bend the conventions of panegyric elegy to include his own real sorrow. It was customary for the poet to begin by depreciating his competitors as mercenaries who are motivated by greed rather than real feeling, but Davenant uses this convention to convey both his own horror at what has happened and his sense of the duke's restlessness, now the condition of his wandering soul. The poem, titled "An Elegy on the Duke of Buckingham's Death" in one manuscript, opens like this:

No Poet's trivial rage, that must aspire
And heighten all his hymns by enforced fire,
Shall his loud dirges mix with my sad choir;
And he that husbands grief, that his dull sight
And moisture spends not on thy funeral Night
T'augment the Balmy store (when only good
And glorious eyes shall melt into a flood)
Doth want the noble Touch; he mourns by Art,
His breast contains a pebble, not a heart.
Buckingham, oh my Lord; so may I find
With strict endeavour of my sight, the wind
That viewless posts about the world, as thy
Great soul, now wandering through the purple sky.

And the poem seems unfinished. At the point where Davenant returns to the idea of Buckingham's military genius, he portrays himself as an old soldier, moved to action by the news of the murder:

Let a dull soldier greet thee with a groan;
I heard thy death, and clapped my Corslet on,
For a distracted rage did so enflame
My powerful Blood, wonder so shake my frame,
That, but the Iron sheet did fast combine
My flesh, my Ribs had started from my Chine.

These are the last lines, unusual in such poetry for their personal intensity. They do not provide an expected rounding off, but close it abruptly,
at the point where Marvell begins his ode, by strapping armor on. But
this is the 1620s, not the 1650s, and the question is: whom to fight?

In one sense the answer is that Davenant is making a coded wish that
Buckingham's adventurous foreign policy be continued. As the poem explains earlier, his influence had been to replace decadence with valor (35–
40):[9]

> Luxurious Sleep, and surfeits that have made
> This Nation tame, and spoiled our glorious Trade,
> Loud Iron war, he did dismiss the Court,
> And taught our Churlish youth the noble sport.
> The soft and whispering Lute he straight struck dumb
> With noise, and made them dance unto the drum.

Teaching the young noblemen of England to fight foreign wars to expand
the nation's trading opportunities is one thing, but the poem also makes
room for a more disturbing kind of war, to be waged against the enemy
within. In a passage at the center of the poem Davenant fixes the blame
for the murder on "the precise," that is, the Puritans. Revealingly, his view
of their mischief concentrates on the way their poets will celebrate Buckingham's death—a further gloss on Carew's doubt about who will write
the story of these days (53–64):

> Their Poets drink Town Breath, t'infuse some Qualm
> That may Convert the story to a Psalm.
> Now rare Divinity, If the precise
> Do relish murder as a Sacrifice,
> Dull easy faith and Ignorance no more
> Shall flatter crooked Bondage as before,
> Predominance shall cease, the sons of men
> Shall now enjoy Equality again;
> For ruminate, oh trivial fools, If high
> Heroic Princes are constrained to die
> By oblique force, while your Religion too
> Applauds their fate, what will become of you?

If Davenant wrote the whole of this poem at the time, then such lines as
these offer a remarkably clear prophecy of the issues over which the civil
wars will be fought.

The young Edmund Waller also wrote a poem on Buckingham's death. Unlike Carew and Davenant, he is not concerned with rival views of the event, only with its immediate aftereffects. The title, "Of His Majesty's Receiving the News of the Duke of Buckingham's Death," shows it to be a poem concerned more with Charles than with Buckingham. True to form, Waller knows there is always more to be gained from praising the living. The duke is reduced through the course of the poem to a mere emblem, to a lopped-off limb which Charles has already replaced. Waller's purpose is to praise a majesty which can hear the news of Buckingham's death, as Charles famously did, and continue to the end of his prayers before betraying emotion (1–8):

> So earnest with thy God! can no new care,
> No sense of danger, interrupt thy prayer?
> The sacred wrestler, till a blessing given,
> Quits not his hold, but halting conquers Heaven;
> Nor was the stream of thy devotion stopped,
> When from the body such a limb was lopped,
> As to thy present state was no less maim,
> Though thy wise choice has since repaired the same.

There is some self-interest behind these lines. Though one of the richest poets in England, Waller was still ambitious and knew that Buckingham's death had left a great hole into which plenty of smaller figures could, with luck, insert themselves; hence the focus, in the rest of the poem, upon Charles's wisdom in arranging for Buckingham's "best friends" to be looked after in spite of their great patron's sudden death. But like many of Waller's panegyric poems, this one flirts dangerously with embarrassment. After all, the story of Charles's reception of the report of Buckingham's death is not as simple as Waller is determined to make it seem. When the news was brought to him, according to Clarendon, Charles "continued unmoved, and without the least change in his countenance, till prayers were ended." Waller presents this as the reaction of a lonely, resolute, and ideal monarch. Others sensed in it something close to relief, as Clarendon observed:

> Yet the manner of his receiving the news in public, when it was first brought to him in the presence of so many, (who knew or saw nothing of the passion he expressed upon his retreat,) made many men to believe that the accident was not very ungrateful; at least, that it was very indifferent to him; as being rid of a servant very ungracious to

the people, and the prejudice to whose person exceedingly ob-
structed all overtures made in Parliament for his service.[10]

Less uncharitably, others might have been tempted to see Charles's silence
as a form of irresolution, the simple indecisiveness which marked his betrayal of Strafford a few years later. Only a hint of this intrudes into Waller's poem, in the phrase "no sense of danger," which points to Charles's
imperviousness to the possibility of there being wider conspiracies in
train than the official view of Felton as a deranged zealot might present.

That there were dangers afoot, if not actual conspiracies, is borne out
by the anti-Buckingham poetry of the 1620s, in which virulent hatred of
the duke is accompanied by varying degrees of abuse for Charles. At one
extreme is the accusation that the king and Buckingham were partners in
all kinds of loose and immoral behavior, as in the anonymous "Upon the
Duke's Going into France":[11]

> And wilt thou go, great duke, and leave us here
> Lamenting thee, and eke thy pupil dear,
> Great Charles: O who shall then the sceptre sway
> And kingdoms rule, when thou art gone away?
> Is there no whore at court to stay thee? must
> Thy hate to Spain and France excite thy lust?
> Hast thou no niece to wed, is there no inn?
> Nor bawdy house t'afford thee any kin
> To cuckold lords withal? hast thou no foe
> Unpoisoned left at home? then mayest thou go,
> And think poor England plagued sufficiently.
> Most graceless duke we thank thy charity,
> Wishing the fleet such speed, as thou but lost,
> Though we be conquered we have quitted cost.

Wishing for national defeat in war so long as Buckingham gets killed in
the process is by no means the most extreme example of popular hatred
for the duke. And with regard to Charles's pupilage to Buckingham's lessons in lewdness, Milton trotted out the same well-remembered charge
some twenty years later: "Can you praise the purity and continence of
one who is known to have joined with the Duke of Buckingham in every
act of infamy? There is no need to investigate his more private habits and
hidden retreats when even in the theatre he kisses women wantonly, en-
folds their waists and, to mention no more openly, plays with the breasts
of maids and mothers."[12]

At the least, Charles was accused of negligence, of letting Buckingham steer the ship of state onto the rocks, as in this squib:[13]

On the Duke, 1628

When only one doth rule and guide the ship,
    Who neither card nor compass knew before,
The master pilot and the rest asleep,
    The stately ship is split upon the shore,
But they awaking, start up, stare, and cry,
    "Who did this fault?"—"Not I"—"Nor I"—"Nor I!"
So fares it with a great and wealthy state,
    Not governed by the master, but his mate.

"Mate" completes the ship of state analogy nicely, but its potential sexual overtones would not have been lost upon a public which knew how close the two men were. One of the most telling poems written before the duke's death builds a beautiful conceit on the idea that when he does eventually arrive in hell he will take control of Lucifer's throne, just as he has done to Charles's here on earth. The poem ends by addressing Lucifer and drawing obvious parallels between the king and the devil:[14]

But why should I persuade you to bestow
The place and honour on him that you owe?
His highness shall command it, and his port
O'er-sway the greatest noble in your court.
He shall be king there, sit in the king's throne,
Or else command the king, and that's all one.

Such poems played a part in Buckingham's murder. When Carew and Davenant glance at the opposition writers they are not engaged in a mere rival-poet game, but in a battle for hearts and minds. Their view of things would obviously triumph at court, but on the streets the anti-Buckingham balladeers were carrying the day. They provided, at the least, a reflection of popular distaste. Moreover, in the eyes of the establishment they were not simply reflecting, but were leading public opinion. When Felton finally struck he felt that he was acting in tune with the expressed wish of the people. Their hatred of the duke had not only been registered in Parliament but was daily reinforced in the rhymes which were on everyone's lips. Significantly, a number of these were written by men who could hardly be described as members of a zealot faction. Martin Parker, for instance, a balladeer who remained doggedly loyal to

Charles in the 1640s, rejoiced at the murder of Dr. Lamb, Buckingham's protégé, in the streets of London. His ballad on that event begins:[15]

> Neighbours cease to moan,
> And leave your lamentation:
> For Doctor *Lamb* is gone,
> The Devil of our Nation,
>   as 'tis known.
>
> A long time hath he lived,
> By cursed conjuration:
> And by enchantments thrived,
> While men of worthy fashion,
>   have connived.

How far up the scale "men of worthy fashion" should go is questionable—certainly to Buckingham, probably not as far as Charles; but it would not be a great leap for many of Parker's readers to make. The ballad, in good penny-dreadful style, goes into the way Lamb was carved up, and ends:

> Thus Doctor *Lamb* is dead,
> That long hath wronged our Nation.
> His times accomplished,
> And all his conjuration,
>   with him is fled.
>
> As his life was lewd,
> Damnable and vicious:
> So he did conclude
> His life, and none propitious,
>   pity showed.

Extending these phrases to Buckingham would not be difficult, and the ballad might easily by taken as an incentive to further action. Lamb died on 14 June 1628. Buckingham, beside himself with fury, instigated Charles to threaten to withdraw the charter of the city of London and to fine it £6,000. But only ten weeks later he was assassinated by Felton.

The striking thing about Felton's action, according to all witnesses, was his failure to take the opportunity of escape which the general panic of the moment offered him. He seems to have been resolute and desperate, paralyzed by the sense that although he had served his country and king he had destroyed himself in the act. His self-sacrifice was seized upon by the anti-Buckingham poets. Some presented him as a national hero simply and unquestionably. A poem called "Felton's Tombstone" begins: "Is Felton dead? it's that he did desire"; praises his "art", which made "all Buckinghamians quake"; and describes his action succinctly:[16]

> He did endeavour by one stroke to make
>   The king and commons (by him put asunder)
> Join all in one, and resolution take
>   To mend all things unto the world's great wonder.

Another, by Zouch Townley, has Felton exulting at his torture:[17]

> Serve in your sharpest mischiefs: use your rack;
> Enlarge each joint, and make each sinew crack:
> Thy soul before was straitened, thank thy doom,
> To show her virtue she hath larger room.

Townley goes on to claim that Felton's act has saved England—and Charles—from the corruptions of Buckingham's politicking:

> Farewell: for thy brave sake we shall not send
> Henceforth commanders enemies to defend:
> Nor will it ever our just monarch please
> To keep an admiral to lose our seas.

It takes some mental gymnastics to accept the phrase "just monarch" here. How Charles could be held aloof from the huge loss of life and the humiliations which Buckingham's policies brought upon the state is difficult to comprehend, but it fits the pattern of much seventeenth-century poetry, which tries hard to separate princes from responsibility for their actions; Dryden's Absalom is only the most obvious example. This poem by Townley, as we shall see later, circulated among the citizens of London, to the embarrassment and danger, of Ben Jonson.

Because Charles's position was impregnable it was important for all but the most politically extremist poets either to ignore his complicity with Buckingham's actions, as Townley does, or, at the least, to present Felton's act as reasonable and justifiable in law. An anonymous poem "Upon the Duke's Death" begins with a bald statement of national relief:[18]

The duke is dead, and we are rid of strife,
By Felton's hand, that took away his life.

Then comes a reasoned defense of Felton's action. First, the case against
is presented:

> Whether that fact were lawful or unjust,
> In two short arguments may be discussed.
> One: though the duke were one whom all did hate,
> Being supposed a grievance to the state,
> Yet he a subject was; and thence we draw
> This argument; he ought to die by law.
> Another: were he traitor most apparent,
> Yet he that killed him had no lawful warrant,
> But as a murderer he did it act,
> And ought himself to die for such a fact.

This is not the stuff of great poetry, but it is persuasive in its exhibition of
control: here is no rabid zealot speaking, but one who has weighed the
arguments carefully. Not surprisingly, the rest of the poem argues the case
for Felton.[19] Buckingham had put himself above the law, so assassination
was the only answer. The image used is the same as Waller's, but with the
opposite emphasis:

> A rotten member, that can have no cure,
> Must be cut off to save the body sure.

Still, the poet has to deal with the fact that Felton was a murderer, so he
balances Charles's culpability in supporting Buckingham against Felton's
sin:

> So was the duke: for when he did withstand
> The ancient course of justice of this land,
> Thinking all means too weak to cast him down,
> Being held up by him that wears a crown;
> Even then, when least he did expect or know,
> By Felton's hand God wrought his overthrow.
> What shall we say? was it God's will or no,
> That one sinner should kill another so?
> I dare not judge . . .

But a judgment is eventually offered, that a precedent has been created which is a true mirror for magistrates:

> But when his sin was ripe it then must down:
> God's sickle spares not either king or crown.

Better poets than this one responded positively to Felton's act. Their verses on the event show how extensively cultured and intelligent men had begun to question the nature of authority in the country. A poem "On the Murder of the Duke of Buckingham," tentatively attributed to Owen Feltham, begins by approaching Buckingham's death in a manner similar to Carew:[20]

> Sooner I may some fixed statue be,
> Than prove forgetful of thy fall and thee;
> Canst thou be gone so quickly, can a knife,
> Let out so many titles and a life?

But already the idea of the knife letting out not blood but "so many titles" points to a sardonic view of Buckingham's aggrandizement. Like anyone else, all he really had to lose was "a life." Soon Charles's judgement is brought into the balance. The granter of many of those titles is still called "wise," but the poet makes it clear that, like his father, he had been manipulated by Buckingham, to the nation's cost (11–12):

> The eclipse of two wise princes' judgments sure
> Thou wast, whereby our land was still kept poor.

Reasoned doubts about Felton's justification are entertained, but set against the extreme guilt of his victim (17–22):

> And when the time to come shall want a name
> To startle greatness, here is Buckingham;
> Fallen like a meteor; and 'tis hard to say
> Whether it was, that went the straighter way,
> Thou, or the hand that slew thee; thy state
> Was high, and he, resolute above that.

The poem closes with a fine sense of its writer's being caught between his appreciation of the justified popular hatred of Buckingham and his concern that Felton's action is a horrifying precedent, an offense against the religious principles which should govern the use of power:

> Yet should I speak the vulgar, I should boast
> Thy bold assassinate, and wish almost
> He were no christian; that I up might stand
> To praise the intent of his misguided hand;
> And sure when all the patriots in the shade
> Shall rank, and their full musters there be made,
> He shall sit next to Brutus, and receive
> Such bays as heathenish ignorance can give;
> But then the christian, checking that, shall say,
> Though he did good, he did it the wrong way;
> And oft they fall into the worst of ills,
> That act the people's wish without their wills.

Doing things the wrong way becomes a favorite refrain of the century, along the lines of Marvell's cool comment that the cause was too good a one to have fought for. This poet finally decides a similar thing about killing Buckingham—that it was too necessary to be done—but not before he has given space to the popular resentment which spurred Felton on.

Traditionally, literary critics have taken such events as the deaths of Prince Henry or Edward King as central to any discussion of seventeenth-century elegiac poetry, for in their poems on these representative deaths the poets could make expansive use of the traditions which they had inherited from the Elizabethans. They celebrate a cultural continuity even while they lament the disorder which death throws into worldly affairs. The deaths of Buckingham and Strafford, in contrast, put the culture under pressure, and their elegies reveal discontinuities. Cleveland's epitaph on Strafford is so celebrated because its terse, austere analysis of the enigma which its subject's life and death represented seems nearly unprecedented in accounts of recently buried great men. Bitterness, in conventional elegiac poetry, is voiced in a stately, dignified manner, and political concerns are expressed only in the most oblique ways, if at all; for one of elegy's chief concerns is to convey contempt for the world, and in such a context politics is a virtual irrelevance. Cleveland's Strafford, though dead, is still a living symbol of the tensions which are tearing the country to pieces, not a soul looking down upon the things of this earth in contempt.

Strafford's treatment was not quite unprecedented. One John Hepe wrote an equally terse epitaph on Buckingham. Though lacking Cleveland's paradoxes, it rivals his poem in its revelation of the bitterness which now must mark political struggles in the country:[21]

> I that my country did betray,
> Undid the king that let me sway
> His sceptre as I pleased; brought down
> The glory of the English crown;
> The courtiers' bane, the country's hate,
> An agent for the Spanish state;
> The Romists' friend, the gospel's foe,
> The Church and kingdom's overthrow;
> Here a damned carcase dwell,
> Till my soul return from hell.
> With Judas then I shall inherit,
> Such portions as all traitors merit.
> If heaven admit of treason, pride, and lust,
> Expect my spotted soul among the just.

This is an extreme example of the hatred which Buckingham engendered: the poem's brevity is an expression of the hatred. He deserves, and will be allowed, no ornamentation, his absolute corruption being comprehensible only if offered in the plainest possible language. But such language is, paradoxically, the vehicle for riddles too, and it requires only a little twist of the register to turn Buckingham into a model for the more complex statesman who died a few years later. James Shirley did just this in his "Epitaph on the Duke of Buckingham," a poem which stands in a direct line between Hepe's bit of hatred and Cleveland's enigma:[22]

> Here lies the best and worst of Fate,
> Two kings' delight, the people's hate,
> The courtiers' star, the kingdom's eye,
> A man to draw an Angel by.
>   Fear's despiser, *Villiers'* glory,
>   The Great man's volume, all time's story.

Shirley's little poem is probably the best thing written about Buckingham. For all the efforts of the professional court praisers, it was either the haters of Buckingham or, even more significantly, the praisers of Felton whose poems had and have most effect. One poem in particular stands out as a tour de force—a celebration of Felton's achievement which takes full account of the long and deep tradition of epitaph poetry. In this sense it is all the more a political statement because it counters the establishment's efforts to degrade Felton in ways reminiscent of the indignities later visited upon Cromwell's corpse. After having been hanged at Tyburn, Felton's body was sent to Portsmouth, the scene of the crime, and left hanging in chains. The writer of this poem transforms humiliation into triumph:[23]

Felton's Epitaph

Here uninterred suspends (though not to save
Surviving friends th'expences of a grave,)
Felton's dead earth; which to the world must be
Its own sad monument, his elegy;
As large as fame, but whether bad or good
I say not: by himself 'twas writ in blood;
For which his body is entombed in air,
Arched o'er with heaven, set with a thousand fair
And glorious diamond stars. A sepulchre
That time can never ruinate, and where
Th'impartial worm (which is not bribed to spare
Princes corrupt in marble) cannot share
His flesh; which if the charitable skies
Embalm with tears; doing those obsequies
Belong to men: shall last, till pitying fowl
Contend to bear his body to his soul.

"Felton's dead earth" is not simply the commonplace that flesh is dust, but, because of the burial he has been denied, a conceit that he is his own burial ground. Equally, he has to become his own monument and epitaph. The great political victory of the poem comes when it points out that because he has not been interred Felton can never be eaten by worms. Here Buckingham enters the poem, both as a form of worm himself who, unlike the more mundane variety, is bribed to flatter princes that they are not like other men, and as a corpse already being eaten by a host of politic worms while Felton hangs free. The phrase "princes corrupt in marble" is a brilliantly compacted piece of contempt for the whole image of royalty which dresses rank flesh in imposing exteriors. And just when the reader thinks that the poet has missed the obvious point that Felton's corpse, though free of the depredations of worms, must be subject to the possibly more hideous fate (because more public) of being pecked to bits by the birds, the poem ends with the image of these very birds carrying his body piece by piece to heaven.

This is a formidable piece of writing: a warning to the official poets that they had to contend not merely with muckraking balladeers, but with rivals who could manipulate the conventions of wit with some subtlety. But the situation itself was still relatively simple compared with that of the early 1640s. The two sides were fairly easily drawn. On the one were court poets, on the other the anti-Buckinghamites, ranging from fractious zealots to people like this poet, capable of writing for a sophisticated audience. And although there were doubts about how far the king had been tarnished by Buckingham's policies, he still escapes relatively uncriticized. His were the orders to leave Felton's body hanging for the birds to devour, so the epitaph is something of a direct challenge to his authority; and the parenthesis about bribing princes and their corruption makes its point forcefully enough. But it was, after all, a commonplace that courts were inhabited by flatterers and that princes are subject to time, so even this poem leaves Charles the opportunity to detach himself from Buckingham's notoriety. Twelve years later Charles's complicity is so deep that it is difficult to read even the simplest account of Strafford's death innocently. And after Strafford's death the king himself became the chief riddle for poets of all hues to puzzle over.

3 Doing Nothing Common: The King

In his collection of ballads "illustrating the period of the Great Rebellion" Hyder Rollins includes one by Laurence Price on Strafford's fall, called "The true manner of the life and Death of Sir *Thomas Wentworth* . . ." This ballad gives Rollins reason for pause, for Price, a confirmed dissenter, was one of the relatively few Puritan balladeers in the 1640s; most of the popular songs were Royalist. But this account of Strafford's rise and fall shows "great devotion to the king and the royal family, and . . . hearty approval of the execution of Thomas Wentworth, Earl of Strafford."[1] One explanation may be that Price, like all balladeers, had an eye for the best audience and gave it what it wanted. Another may be that the praises of Charles, though expressed in the most simply loyal way imaginable, are not what they seem. This is the ballad, to be sung to the tune "Welladay, welladay":

> Country men list to me
> Patiently patiently,
> And you shall hear and see,
> As time gives leisure,
> The object of mishap,
> Caught fast in his own trap,
> Cast out of fortune's lap,
> Through his own folly.
>
> Sir *Thomas Wentworth* he,
> At the first at the first
> Rose to great dignity,
> And was beloved,
> *Charles* our most gracious King
> Graced him in many a thing,

And did much honour bring,
On his proceedings.

Fame's Trumpet blazoned forth
His great name, his great name
Lord president of the North,
So was he called,
And as I understand,
He had in Ireland,
A place of great command,
To raise his fortunes.

More honour did befall,
Unto him unto him
He was Lord general
Of the King's army,
These titles given had he
By the King's Majesty,
And made assuredly
Knight of the Garter.

But here's the spoil of all,
Woe is me, woe is me,
Ambition caused his fall,
Against all reason,
He did our laws abuse,
And many men misuse,
For which they him accuse,
Quite through the kingdom.

New laws he sought to make,
In Ireland in Ireland
If he the word did speak,
None durst withstand him,
He ruled with tyranny,
And dealt most cruelly,
To men in misery,
The like was ne'er heard of.

The Second part, To the same tune

He hath done thousands wrong
As 'tis known as 'tis known

And cast in prison strong,
Our King's liege people,
Such cruelty possessed
His black polluted breast,
He thought himself well blessed,
In acting mischief.

But those that climb highest of all
Oftentimes oftentimes,
Do catch the greatest fall,
As here appeareth,
By this unhappy wight,
Who wronged his Country's right,
And overcame by might,
Our good king's subjects.

To London Tower at last,
He was brought, he was brought,
For his Offences past,
And just deservings,
And after certainly,
He was condemned to die,
For his false treachery,
'Gainst King and Country.

It being the twelfth day
In this month of May,
As true reports do say,
He came to his trial,
The Nobles of our land,
By Justice Just command,
Pass sentence out of hand,
That he should suffer.

When the appointed time,
Was come that he should die,
For his committed crime,
The axe being Ready,
Up to the scaffold he,
Was brought immediately,
Where thousands came to see,
Him take his death.

After some Prayers said,
And certain speeches made,
O' th' block his head he laid,
Taking his farewell.
The headsman bloodily,
Divided presently,
His head from his body,
With his keen weapon.

Heaven grant, by his downfall
That others may take heed,
Lord send amongst us all,
True peace of conscience,
And may our King and Queen,
Amongst us long be seen,
With all their branches green,
To all our comfort.

It is hard now to be certain about the way to read pieces such as this, unless we assume that they should be treated as simply as possible. Certainly the balladeer affects complete simplicity in his recording of Strafford's rise to power. The "as I understand" which introduces the account of his rule in Ireland puts him on the level of his popular audience, dependent upon whisper and rumor and reporting things in black-and-white terms of which he has no direct knowledge. Such ballad formulas were used by much more sophisticated poets—Marvell's notorious account of Irish satisfaction at Cromwell's behavior in "An Horatian Ode" fits this register exactly—but there is no reason to think that the balladeers themselves were not aware of their more complex uses too. In this case the simplicities allow Price to make easy generalizations about Strafford's responsibility for his own fall, presenting him as an ambitious and tyrannical man. But they also provide a too-unquestioning view of the king's part in his rise and fall. Charles is first the bestower of titles and power upon the earl and then the figurehead betrayed by him. Strafford imprisons "our King's liege people," overcomes "our good king's subjects," and generally acts against "King and Country." The unspoken thing in all of this is the king's responsibility for letting him go so far; and leaving it so obviously unspoken casts an ironic light upon the pious platitudes which end the ballad, especially as they follow Price's call for "true peace of conscience." And even if we decide not to read any ironies into the ballad's transparencies, so complex is the situation around the trial and execution that treating Charles in such a way—as if he were detached from the whole matter—is either a damning refusal to believe his well-known torments of conscience at allowing Strafford to be tried, or an equally damning ignoring of them.

History soon enough added its own ironies to Price's last verse, Strafford's trial and execution acting as a model for the king who did not take sufficient heed. Between these two executions, poets who tried to write in praise of Charles, whatever their audience, found themselves pulled in two contrary directions. One was to see their subject as a man, the other to present him as an icon. In this they were repeating and paralleling the representations of the artists: Charles on horseback and in armor is a symbol of militant Protestant kingship, but we remember too his sorrowful eyes and the many domestic images of a man and his family.

How hard it was to sustain the two images together is borne out in an early poem by John Cleveland, "Upon the King's Return from Scotland," a piece he contributed to a Cambridge collection of poems celebrating Charles's return, in November 1641, from trying to come to some kind of accommodation with the Presbyterians. What Cleveland did was to recast a poem he had already written, "Parting With a Friend Upon the Road." Both poems make use of Donne's "Good Friday 1613, Riding Westward," but whereas "Parting With a Friend" employs its conceits playfully, and reflects in its clumsiness Cleveland's disorientation at leaving his friend, the poem on the king's return merely retreats into more and more fanciful expressions of Charles's greatness.[2] Nothing of the king's actual effort in making the journey or the frustrations he met with in Scotland is allowed to come through. Instead he is presented as a godlike conciliator whose every action leads to harmony and resolution.

The royal progress had figured strongly in poetry about royalty since the days of Elizabeth I. It is an important element in country-house poetry too, as in Carew's "To the King at his Entrance into *Saxham*." But in the 1640s the image of a traveling king took on a poignancy as it gradually shifted from a king in a state of peace—as when he drops in at a house such as Saxham—to a king in pursuit of peace—as in Charles's journey to Scotland—to a king leading his troops into battle, and finally to a king on the run, as in "An Horatian Ode." A brief lyric written by Thomas May for his *Tragedy of Cleopatra* (ca. 1626) gives the clue to the fate of a king doomed to wander:[3]

> Not he that knows how to acquire,
>   But to enjoy, is blessed.

> Nor does our happiness consist
>   In motion, but in rest.
>
> The gods pass man in bliss, because
>   They toil not for more height,
> But can enjoy, and in their own
>   Eternal rest delight.
>
> Then, princes, do not toil, nor care;
>   Enjoy what you possess;
> Which whilst you do, you equalise
>   The gods in happiness.

The point which May expresses epigrammatically, that happiness consists in rest, not in motion, becomes a commonplace in poems of retirement in the 1640s and 1650s; but it was difficult for the poets to consider Charles in this light because of his iconic standing. That final admonition to princes is all very well, but it assumes that princes are masters of themselves, and by the 1640s this was patently untrue—as Richard Lovelace implicitly observes at the end of "The Grasshopper," when he contrasts his and Charles Cotton's peace with the fate of kings who "want themselves."

In earlier, happier times the icon of the king on the move could be used to contrast with the peace of the family to which he returned. Henry King's poem about one of Charles's earlier journeys to Scotland celebrates his return in a triumphant image of a man returning to the blisses of his wife's embraces:[4]

> Here may You henceforth stay! There need no Charms
> To hold You, but the Circle of Her arms,
> Whose fruitful Love yields You a rich increase,
> Seals of your Joy, and of the Kingdom's Peace.
> O may those Precious Pledges fix You here,
> And You grow old within that Crystal Sphere!

These are the pieties of a poet intent on praising the monarch's domestic virtues, but by the beginning of the 1640s the various celebratory poems on royal births and royal journeys betray an increasing concern with images of disturbance. Waller, writing in 1640 to welcome the birth of the queen's fourth son, in July, gives out signals that at this time the king is absent, leading an army against the Scots:

Puerperium

You gods that have the power
To trouble, and compose,
All that's beneath your bower,
Calm silence on the seas, on earth impose.

Fair Venus! in thy soft arms
The God of Rage confine;
For thy whispers are the charms
Which only can divert his fierce design.

What though he frown, and to tumult do incline?
Thou the flame
Kindled in his breast canst tame
With that snow which unmelted lies on thine.

Great goddess! give this thy sacred island rest;
Make heaven smile,
That no storm disturb us while
Thy chief care, our halcyon builds her nest.

Great Gloriana! fair Gloriana!
Bright as high heaven is, and fertile as earth,
Whose beauty relieves us,
Whose royal bed gives us
Both glory and peace,
Our present joy, and all our hopes' increase.

Read in the light of the kind of thing which earlier poets such as King had written, the poem reveals dissonances which Waller possibly intended his readers to pick up. There are two casts of characters in the poem: Venus and Mars, and Charles and Henrietta Maria; but the image of Venus confining Mars in her arms so closely overlaps the various representations of Henrietta embracing Charles that we are persuaded to very close parallels between the two sets of lovers. *Puerperium* is the act of giving birth—"confinement." Waller's call to the god and goddess to confine themselves to an issue of peace has its national purposes too, as the final verse makes clear. Behind the hope that the royal birth will signify a national peace there seems to be some kind of warning to Charles to resist Strafford's persuasion to make war on the Scots with his newly arrived Irish army. At the heart of the poem is a real sense of the politics of the royal bedchamber, the queen embracing and whispering persuasions to Charles to moderate his policies.

Less of a politician than Waller was the devotedly loyal Sidney Godolphin. His "To the King and Queen" has no such undertone, but it betrays its own kind of nervousness in some of its wishes to the royal pair:[5]

> Be all your senses blessed with harmony,
> Proportioned objects meet each faculty,
> All appetites find such a just supply,
> That you may still desire, still satisfy.
>
> May present things with present pleasure pay,
> Every contentment be entire, and way
> To the next joy, may every new success
> Recall the past, and make one happiness.
>
> May you then all your joys reflected see
> In other's breasts, may that reflection be
> Powerful on you, and though none can project
> Beams to reach you, yet what you cause, reflect.
>
> May you not need the art to multiply
> Joys, in the fancy's unsafe flattery;
> But may your pleasures be still present, pure,
> Diffusive, great, and in their truth, secure.

The wishes of the first two stanzas are common enough in seventeenth-century poetry. Self-sufficiency and absolute contentment in the present moment, with no bad memories and no future fears, are the stock elements of most retirement poems of the midcentury. The king and queen are the one couple who cannot achieve such a state, for where they go the court goes too, a fact which gradually intrudes into the poem. In the third stanza their effulgence influences the crowd which surrounds them, but they will remain free of it themselves—a pointer toward the "flattery" of the final stanza. And the poem closes firmly on "secure," a word which is to figure greatly in royal poetry of the next two decades, itself an echo of Carew's "safe" in his reflections on Buckingham's death.

That monarchs are no less safe than any other man has always been a commonplace, but some fine poems appeared around 1640 which honed this lesson to a fine point. William Habington included in his 1640 edition of *Castara* a poem, "Nox Nocti Indicat Scientiam," which had not been in earlier editions. The first half of the poem takes an overview of human life and behavior similar to Henry Vaughan's "The World"; then, from his lofty detachment Habington sees the futility of human endeavor typified in the self-satisfaction of kings who cannot see what is awaiting them (21–44):[6]

> It tells the conqueror
>   That far-stretched power,
> Which his proud dangers traffic for,
> Is but the triumph of an hour;
>
> That from the farthest north,
>   Some nation may
> Yet undiscovered, issue forth,
> And o'er his new-got conquest sway:
>
> Some nation yet shut in
>   With hills of ice
> May be let out to scourge his sin
> Till they shall equal him in vice.
>
> And then they likewise shall
>   Their ruin have;
> For as yourselves your empires fall,
> And every kingdom hath a grave.
>
> Thus those celestial fires,
>   Though seeming mute,
> The fallacy of our desires
> And all the pride of life confute:
>
> For they have watched since first
>   The world had birth;
> And found sin in itself accursed,
> And nothing permanent on earth.

The north, of course, is the biblical source for any unexpected and dangerous threat. Habington may be looking to a nation much farther north than Scotland and warning a monarch quite different in nature from Charles, on whom the title "conqueror" would sit bizarrely, but the fatalism of the poem fits in with the spirit of the time exactly. Because nothing is permanent nothing can be secure.

In Samuel Harding's meditation on death from the same time, the details of majesty are reduced to images of humiliating impotence:[7]

Of Death

Noblest bodies are but gilded clay:
>> Put away
> But the precious shining rind,
The inmost rottenness remains behind.
Kings, on earth though gods they be,
Yet in death are vile as we;
He, a thousands' king before,
Now is vassal unto more.
> Vermin now insulting lie,
> And dig for diamonds in each eye:
> Whilst the sceptre-bearing hand
> Cannot their inroads withstand.
> Here doth one in odours wade
> By the regal unction made,
> While another dares to gnaw
> On that tongue, his people's law.
Fools! ah, fools are we, who so contrive,
>> And do strive,
> In each gaudy ornament,
Who shall his corpse in the best dish present.

Here again the king is representative of all of us, but he also is specially chosen by death for the greatest degradations. Such poems are, because of the time when they were written, more than simple *memento mori* pieces. They enact the processes, just beginning, whereby kings are stripped of power. The worms which dig for diamonds in the eye and gnaw away the tongue which gave so many commands are only thinly disguised members of Pym's party. The word which Harding chooses, "vermin," is just the one which Charles's supporters would have used in reference to them; Dryden uses it a generation or so later in "The Medal," to describe another threat to Stuart rule, with Shaftesbury the "vermin wriggling in the usurper's ear" (31). And most telling is the "regal unction" through which one of the worms wades. The oil is both symbol of royal office and the embalming fluid which, even in death, strives to keep kings separate from fellow mortals by repelling the agents of corruption. But all it actually does is present a more tasty dish.

While it was possible in such oblique ways to touch upon the king's predicament as a real man in real trouble, poets who wrote directly to or about Charles in the early 1640s were still bound to treat him as an icon.

Here is the most ceremonial of seventeenth-century poets, Robert Herrick, addressing the king's most godlike function, the ritual curing by the laying on of the royal hand:

T O   T H E   K I N G
To cure the Evil

To find that Tree of Life, whose Fruits did feed,
And Leaves did heal, all sick of human seed:
To find *Bethesda,* and an Angel there,
Stirring the waters, I am come; and here,
At last, I find, (after my much to do)
The Tree, Bethesda, and the Angel too:
And all in Your Blest Hand, which has the powers
Of all those supple-healing herbs and flowers.
To that soft *Charm,* that *Spell,* that *Magic Bough,*
That high Enchantment I betake me now:
And to that Hand, (the Branch of Heaven's fair Tree)
I kneel for help; O! lay that hand on me,
Adored *Caesar!* and my Faith is such,
I shall be healed, if that my KING but touch.
The Evil is not Yours: my sorrow sings,
Mine is the Evil, but the Cure, the KING'S.

The idea that the kings of England and France could cure scrofula by their touch has been connected with the notion that these two monarchs were the only ones to be anointed with the pure chrism rather than with "ordinary" sacred oil, so in some ways Herrick's poem is a nice counterpoint to Harding's. Touching for the evil became an important piece of symbolism for the Stuarts: Charles II, and later the Old Pretender and his two sons, continued the practice avidly while in exile. In Herrick's poem Charles is the static figure, the tree of life and the angel troubling the waters, to which the poet, as one of the sick, travels. But it is fairly clear that in spite of the large number of sufferers from the disease—Charles II is said to have touched over 100,000—the poem is concerned with something even more widespread. Herrick's wish-fulfillment narrative sees Charles as the healer of the whole country's woes. The crucial observation is made in the closing couplet. While a phrase like *the king's evil* could be taken to mean that the evil belongs to—or is even caused by—the king, Herrick's purpose is to argue otherwise. The king's possession of it carries no implication that Charles is responsible for the state's illness, nor that he is a fellow sufferer, but that only he can heal it because only he is aloof from it.

Alongside its idealization of Charles, there is a strong personal content in Herrick's poem, as if the poet were the certain man in the biblical story, who, troubled for thirty-eight years, had not been able to enter the pool of Bethesda by himself. This motif recurs a number of times in poems of this decade. In "To Lucasta from Prison" Richard Lovelace, from the obscurity of prison, hopes for a light from his king which will enable him, as well as others, to see more clearly. It is very close to Herrick's appeal in its uncertainty that the help will come. Herrick's poem is pitched at the point where he kneels in entreaty and begins to plead; Lovelace's is placed in his lowest point of isolation. Both poems are born more out of sorrow than out of hope, and perhaps out of some sense of guilt too. Lovelace's self-analysis goes through all the ideas which he could have believed in and fought for: Peace, War, Religion, Parliament, Liberty, Property, Reformation, the Public Faith. All are found wanting and have deserted him, leaving only the king (41–56):[8]

> Since then none of these can be
>   Fit objects for my love and me;
> What then remains, but th'only spring
>   Of all our loves and joys? The KING.
>
> He who being the whole ball
>   Of day on Earth, lends it to all;
> When Seeking to eclipse his right,
>   Blinded, we stand in our own light.
>
> And now an universal mist
>   Of error is spread o'er each breast,
> With such a fury edged, as is
>   Not found in th' inwards of th'abyss.
>
> Oh from thy glorious starry wain
>   Dispense on me one sacred beam
> To light me where I soon may see
>   How to serve you, and you trust me.

The sense of bafflement here is the result of Lovelace's attempt to understand what it is that he should fight for. Kings seen far off are too remote; seen close, they are a source of confusion. Herrick made just this point in an epigram whose purpose is, presumably, to praise Charles, but which could just as well be taken as a warning to fly the courts of princes—or, at the least, not to get too heavily involved with them:

To the King

Give way, give way, now my *Charles* shines here,
A Public Light (in this immensive Sphere.)
Some stars were fixed before; but these are dim,
Compared (in this my ample Orb) to Him,
Draw in your feeble fires, while that He
Appears but in his Meaner Majesty.
Where, if such glory flashes from his Name,
Which is His Shade, who can abide His Flame!
Princes, and such like Public Lights as these,
Must not be looked on, but at distances:
For, if we gaze on These brave Lamps too near,
Our eyes they'll blind, or if not blind, they'll blear.

In line with several of the other poems in *Hesperides* attached to particular persons, part of Herrick's conceit here refers to his book. With Charles as a subject, others must give way, and Charles shines brightest among his constellation of poems. Herrick's pride of possession at having so majestic a subject is signaled in the phrase "my *Charles*," but this becomes a little ironic when the poem develops its vision of a royal progress, with Herrick as a kind of herald announcing his imminent arrival. In the book of poems merely the name Charles flashes enough glory to outshine all the other poems and their subjects: how much more striking would be the real vision of Charles himself. On the other hand, the actual sight of a Stuart monarch was apt to disappoint—increasingly so in the 1640s, when observers frequently commented on Charles's worn-out appearance. "My *Charles*" expresses Herrick's total allegiance, but the intimacy implied in the phrase is belied by the poem's final insistence that Charles is a public light, not a private man. Looking too closely at him—gazing—leaves one like Lovelace's prisoner, so enlightened in darkness that one is blinded by it. Herrick steers carefully between "blind" and "blear," so that his close-up vision of Charles stands somewhere between not being able to see anything at all and not being able to see anything other than the king. In both Lovelace's and Herrick's poems are only slightly muted doubts about the usefulness of such an iconic view of the monarch.

During the war it was natural for poets to respond to victories, or

hoped-for victories, with further idealizations of royalty. Herrick welcomed the victory at Leicester in 1645 with an image of Charles as a kind
of Tamburlaine, turning Fortune's wheel himself:

TO THE KING

Upon his taking of *Leicester*

This Day is Yours *Great* CHARLES! and in this War
Your Fate, and Ours, alike Victorious are.
In her white Stole; now Victory does rest
Ensphered with Palm on Your Triumphant Crest.
Fortune is now Your Captive; other Kings
Hold but her hands; You hold both hands and wings.

To some extent Herrick is justified in associating Charles's fate with his
own: eventually defeat meant displacement for both, although Herrick
could retire while Charles was bound to go the whole distance. Victory's
"white stole" which Charles now wears, ties in with the recurring motif
of the white king, which came to dominate poems about Charles in the
latter half of the 1640s. A year earlier Herrick had welcomed Charles's
incursion into the west as a white-omened harbinger of summer. Again,
the iconic figure transforms all ugliness into beauty (7–10):[9]

> War, which before was horrid, now appears
> Lovely in you, brave Prince of Cavaliers!
> A deal of courage in each bosom springs
> By your access; (O *you best of Kings!*)

But this poem is very soon followed in *Hesperides* by one which draws
attention to the real unhappiness which the king and queen experienced
through their frequent and protracted absences from each other:

> ### To the King and Queen, upon
> ### their unhappy distances
> Woe, woe to them, who (by a ball of strife)
> Do, and have parted here a Man and Wife:
> CHARLES the best Husband, while MARIA strives
> To be, and is, the very best of Wives:
> Like Streams, you are divorced; but 'twill come, when
> These eyes of mine shall see you mix again.
> Thus speaks the *Oak*, here; C. and M. shall meet,

Treading on *Amber,* with their silver-feet:
Nor wil't be long, ere this accomplished be;
The words found true, *C.M.* remember me.

It was a necessary part of the propaganda of both sides in the war to present Charles as both a man and a king. These were not diminishments, however. The view of Charles as a man of blood is a way of fixing a more comprehensive responsibility upon him, as if his personal, willful predilection for punishment and revenge had intensified the awful powers which a head of state necessarily wielded. Lucy Hutchinson makes this clear when she describes Charles at his trial:

> One thing was remarked in him by many of the court, that when the blood spilt in many of the battles where he was in his own person, and had caused it to be shed by his own command, was laid to his charge, he heard it with disdainful smiles, and looks and gestures which rather expressed sorrow that all the opposite party to him were not cut off, than that any were: and he stuck not to declare in words, that no man's blood spilt in this quarrel troubled him except one, meaning the Earl of Strafford.[10]

On the other side, royalist poets needed to stress that Charles was a man who felt and suffered, an emphasis which culminated in the *Eikon Basilike*'s representation of Charles as, virtually, the biblical man of sorrows. Herrick's poem on the king and queen, presumably written some time in the early 1640s, shows the poet slightly uneasy with the enterprise of presenting the royal pair as simply man and woman. Indeed, in one place it is a very uneasy poem. The description of Henrietta Maria as striving to be the very best of wives is potentially sardonic, not the less so because of the interpolated "and is." So loyal was Herrick that he can easily be freed from any such impertinence, but he is rarely so clumsy, and the poem utters a nearly audible sigh of relief as it moves from the mundane to the superterrestrial, transfusing Charles and Maria into a god and goddess and prophesying the return of sunlight to the land with their coming together again.[11]

As well as the man and his wife there was also the man and his sons. Richard Fanshawe addressed two poems to the future Charles II. The first of these draws attention in its title to the image of his father as Caesar, a parallel which continued through the decade until in Marvell's "An Horatian Ode" it is transferred from Charles to Cromwell. Fanshawe's strategy here is deliberately to merge Charles and Caesar with each other in the son's mind:[12]

Presented to his Highness the Prince of Wales
at his going into the West, 1645.
Together with Caesar's Commentaries.

Sir,
Now that your Father, with the World's applause,
Employs your early Valour in his Cause,
Set *Caesar's* glorious Acts before your sight,
And know the man that could so *do* and *write*.
View him in all his postures, see him mix
Terror with *love, Morals* with *Politics*.
That courage, which when fortune ebbed did flow,
Which never trampled on a prostrate Foe,
Admire and emulate. Before he fought,
Observe how *Peace* by him was ever sought:
How bloodless Victories best pleased him still,
Grieving as oft as he was forced to kill.
How most religiously he kept his word,
And conquered more that way than by the sword.
In whom was all we in a King could crave,
Except that *Right* which you shall one day have.
Yet think (Sir) it imports you to make good
With all his worth the title of your blood.

Fanshawe's injunction to "know the man" is specially pertinent. For a son to know the man who is his father is difficult, doubly so when father and son are king and heir; but the son, as he reads Caesar and sees how close the parallels are with his father's actions, will learn to appreciate the burden of kingship which he will inherit. This was a matter which seems greatly to have concerned Fanshawe. The next year he presented another poem to the young Charles. Its title points to its having been written during the prince's stay in the Scilly Isles, after what turned out to be his final parting from his father at Oxford: "Presented to his Highness in the West, Ann. Dom. 1646." The prince is hailed as the "*Royal Plant*, born for your Country's good, / The hoped cure of our great flux of blood." This greeting picks up from the end of the earlier poem, as if Fanshawe had already conceded the impossibility of his father's being able to achieve either victory or conciliation. If we could keep Caesar and Charles I separate, then the close of that poem would present no difficulty; but because of their fusion we understand that while Charles, like Caesar, had all we could crave in a king, he nonetheless lacked the right which the son would have.

It is hard to know how far to press this. A loyal subject such as Fanshawe could never have denied Charles I his right to be king, but there are many signs in the poetry of the mid-1640s that even resolutely Cavalier poets had come to realize that the prospect of his continued sovereignty was impossible to maintain. Something of this comes into Fanshawe's second poem to the son, which takes the form of a translation of a Latin poem written two generations earlier to his grandfather, the future James I, by George Buchanan. For both poets the theme is that good kings get good subjects—and from those subjects comes the right to rule. Such a philosophy, for a member of the Royalist party, takes some arguing by 1646. Indeed, taken in its context, Fanshawe's poem makes disturbing reading, for it first asserts that the cure of England's woes and the promise of

> that peaceful *golden Age,*
> Which to your Grandsire ancient *Bards* presage,
> And we supposed fulfilled in Him, appears
> By Fate reserved for your riper years.

And then it strongly implies that at least part of the responsibility for the troubles lies with the father. Obviously this could not be openly said, but Fanshawe refuses to subscribe to the idea of an obdurate people who have malevolently blocked their monarch's purposes. Much the opposite, they are seen to take their lead from him (23–30):

> No Ship the Rudder so much turns and winds
> As *Princes'* manners do their *People's* minds.
> Not *Prisons, penal Laws,* sharp *Whips,* severe
> *Axes,* with all the instruments of fear,
> Can so constrain, as the dumb eloquence
> Of *Virtue;* and the love and reverence
> Of a well-governed Sceptre shall persuade
> Their wills, by *great Examples* eas'ly swayed.

By repeating Buchanan's lesson Fanshawe can instruct the prince under his care in how to respond to the present troubles.[13] The lesson is very wise, for it ignores the prospect of revenge and continued war, and promises instead that a peaceful reaction, marked by love for the people, will gain their passionate loyalty (45–56):

> So do the *People* fix their eyes upon
> *The King;* admire, love, honour *Him* alone.
> In *Him,* as in a glass, their manners view

And frame, and copy what they see *Him* do.
That which the murdering *Cannon* cannot force,
Nor plumed Squadrons of steel-glittering *Horse,*
Love can. In this *the People* strive t' out-do
The King; and when they find they're loved, love too.
They serve, because they need not serve: and if
A good *Prince* slack the reins, they make them stiff;
And of their own accords invite that yoke,
Which, if enforced on them, they would have broke.

The unasked question behind this is how far the father loved his people—
and "not enough" is the unavoidable answer. Just before this passage
comes the most curious part of the poem, in which Fanshawe seems to be
counseling patience of another kind. The good king is compared to the
phoenix, who returns, as the prince one day will return to England "from
his perfumed cradle (his Sire's Urn)." The phoenix returns to popular ac-
clamation, not because of his regal splendor or because he is rarely seen,

                    but 'cause he brings
His Father's honoured ashes on his wings,
And funeral odours, that it may be known
He climbed not till his death the spicy throne.   (37–40)

The son is being advised not to attempt to accelerate the processes of
history either by pursuing further war or by refusing to wait for his father's death. As one biographer laconically put it, "though in his later
years little piety was observable in Charles towards the memory of his
father, no effort was spared by him to avert the catastrophe of January
1649."[14] This seems to be in tune with Fanshawe's poem; the image of
Charles I which emerges from the poems of the mid-1640s is of a man cut
off from wife and family, whose cause has been abandoned except by the
most sentimental.

    Two poems refer directly to the period when Charles, having lost all
hope of maintaining resistance in England, fled north in disguise with the
desperate aim of trying to come to terms with the Scots. One is John
Cleveland's "The King's Disguise," the other Henry Vaughan's "The King
Disguised," which has the explanatory subtitle "Written about the same
time that Mr John Cleveland wrote his."[15] It is likely that Vaughan wrote
with full knowledge of Cleveland's poem: both make reference to the
myth of the white king who, according to a famous pamphlet of 1643,
after his departure "would wander lost to the view of his people."[16] Both

poems, too, see Charles as already suffering a kind of death. Cleveland's opens:

> And why so coffined in this vile disguise,
> Which who but sees blasphemes thee with his eyes?

and Vaughan's like this:

> A King and no King! Is he gone from us,
> And stol'n alive into his coffin thus?

Both poets work hard and ingeniously to transform Charles's humiliation into forms of triumph. In Cleveland's poem the conceits are largely spun around the notion of darkness and obscurity, as in this passage where the poet's depression about Charles's disguise turns to elation in his realization that out of all this darkness will come a purer light (91–98):

> But pardon Sir, since I presume to be
> Clerk of this Closet to Your Majesty;
> Me thinks in this your dark mysterious dress
> I see the Gospel couched in Parables.
> The second view my purblind fancy wipes,
> And shows Religion in its dusky types.
> Such a Text Royal, so obscure a shade
> Was *Solomon* in Proverbs all arrayed.

Vaughan, to whom the contrast of dark and light was becoming increasingly important—he must already have been writing some of the poems which appear in *Silex Scintillans*—harps on the same theme (9–12, 23–26):

> Poor, obscure shelter! if that shelter be
> Obscure, which harbours so much Majesty.
> Hence profane eyes! the mystery's so deep,
> Like *Esdras'* books, the vulgar must not see't.
> . . . . . .
> But all these clouds cannot thy light confine,
> The sun in storms and after them, will shine.
> Thy day of life cannot be yet complete,
> 'Tis early sure; thy shadow is so great.

These are virtually the last gasps of iconic poetry about Charles, efforts at transforming an increasingly grubby reality into a vision of transcendental splendor. In spite of the king's desperate state, they admit very little appreciation of what he was undergoing. Vaughan writes of his wandering in sheepskin, pursued by wolves. This gives some sense of the danger and the near aimlessness of the flight, but the poem as a whole concentrates on Charles's superhuman ability to rule heroically, even from so obscure a situation (33–38):

> But full as well may we blame night, and chide
> His wisdom, who doth light with darkness hide:
> Or deny curtains to thy Royal bed,
> As take this sacred covering from thy head.
> Secrets of State are points we must not know;
> This vizard is thy privy council now.

Cleveland's poem, much the more consciously witty of the two, is charged more with contempt for the king's enemies than with pity for him, and only at its close does it convey any sense of his straitened situation. But this strategy is most effective: after appearing to move further and further away from the actual situation, the poem unexpectedly turns back with a powerful biblical image to register both Charles's humiliation and his hopeless position (115–124):

> Mount then thou shadow royal, and with haste
> Advance thy morning star, *Charles's* overcast.
> May thy strange journey contradictions twist,
> And force fair weather from a Scottish mist.
> Heaven's Confessors are posed, those star-eyed Sages,
> To interpret an Eclipse thus riding stages.
> Thus *Israel*-like he travels with a cloud,
> Both as a Conduct to him, and a shroud.
> But oh! he goes to *Gibeon,* and renews
> A league with moldy bread, and clouted shoes.

Because of the ambiguity of "with" it is difficult to be sure just who is being compared to whom in the biblical story. In Joshua 9 the inhabitants of Gibeon put on old shoes and take moldy bread with them, to trick the Israelites into believing that they have come from far away. By making a treaty before their real proximity is discovered they ensure their survival, if only as hewers of wood and drawers of water for the Israelites. If

Charles is the traveler, as a strict one-for-one parallel would indicate, then his poverty and inevitable servitude are predicted. If he is the king of Israel, as decorum would insist in such an analogy, then the Bible story is given a mordant twist, making him travel in pursuit of security from men who should be his servants. Either reading offers a bleak conclusion to the pretensions of the rest of the poem.

One element of Charles's obscurity which Vaughan touches upon and which Cleveland develops is the speculation about scandalous state secrets and treacherous privy messages which attended the disintegration of royal power. Rumors about them continued after his death. The *Eikon Basilike* purports to be Charles's own defense, a claim which came to be endorsed by both sides for different reasons. But earlier, with Charles on the move so much, and with his various headquarters being overrun, there were opportunities for revelations of captured secrets—hence Vaughan's protest that "Secrets of State are points we must not know." In Cleveland's poem Charles's cabinet, a matter for counterpropaganda claims after it was supposed to have been taken and opened after Naseby, is related directly to the king's own body (105–114):

> Hence Cabinet-Intruders, Pick-locks hence,
> You that dim Jewels with your Bristol-sense:
> And characters, like Witches, so torment,
> Till they confess a guilt, though innocent.
> Keys for this Cipher you can never get,
> None but St *Peter's* opes this Cabinet.
> This Cabinet, whose aspect would benight
> Critic spectators with redundant light.
> A prince most seen, is least: what Scriptures call
> The Revelation, is most mystical.

Here are boxes within boxes to baffle the most ingenious interpreter. Cleveland's poem is an attempt not so much to explain as to describe the riddle which Charles's behavior and policy had turned into. It is packed with images of encoding and enfolding. The writer of the *Eikon*, too, looking back at this period, has Charles present it in riddling terms:

> I must now resolve the riddle of their loyalty, and give them opportunity to let the world see they mean not what they do, but what they say . . .
> So various are all human affairs, and so necessitous may the state

of princes be, that their greatest danger may be in their supposed safety, and their safety in their supposed danger.

I must now leave those that have adhered to me, and apply to those that have opposed me.

However, Charles goes on to emphasize that in his own mind there are no riddles, only the certainty that what he does is right:

I thank God, no success darkens or disguises truth to me; and I shall no less conform my words to my inward dictates now, than if they had been, as the words of a king ought to be, among loyal subjects, *full of power.*[17]

But Charles was, as the poets now knew, powerless. After the Scots had given him over to his enemies, the only real question was how far the powers of Parliament could stretch. Much would depend upon what might be proved against him, and much ink was used up in speculating about his motives and intentions. At the lowest level is a titleless ballad which Thomason dated 1 April 1645. This tells the story of Stuart malad-ministration, from James I's homosexual relations with Buckingham, and the favors granted in payment, to Charles's carrying on of the same policies after Buckingham had supposedly murdered James (stanzas 2 and 5):[18]

He was both cunning and fearful, we find,
  And loose in his Pockets before and behind;
He kept on with Patents to make the State Poor,
  And still Kept a Minion instead of a whore;
    yet his Wife all his life
      Made him not Vary,
    Though his Nan was a Span
      Longer than Mary.

  . . . . .

When George had rewarded King James with a Fig,
  His Son, being crowned, began to look big,
And Jostled down Parliaments, casting the Men
  Into th' Starchamber; his Counsellors then,
    Who all did Err, some concur,
      But in the Conclusion
    So they wrought as they brought
      All to Confusion.

More than anything else, it is Charles's word which shows him to be a man not worthy of trust. The ballad refers, in turn, to words which he has purportedly committed to paper in different places: a "commission" to the Irish allowing them to cut English throats whenever necessary, his "word" to the Scots which they could not trust and accordingly burned, and an indulgence from Rome "to Pardon his Sins both past and to come."

This is an expression of pure hatred from a writer as extreme in his opposition to Charles as poets such as Cleveland and Vaughan were extreme in their loyalty. Both sides knew that there was a large middle ground which needed to be won over and persuaded of either the king's malevolence or his benevolence toward his subjects. His words, looks, and bearing took on greater significance as he worked to maintain the iconic image while opponents and supporters, for different reasons, looked for the man beneath; as in the interpretations of Lucy Hutchinson's friends at his trial or, at the end, Marvell's carefully ambiguous commentary upon his behavior at his execution. His supporters took care to emphasize his nobility during his various imprisonments, and, with it, his freedom from the taint which his opponents fixed on him of plotting and politicking with England's enemies. In a poem on Charles's execution Henry King continues Cleveland's idea of a king coffined alive and buried in obscurity during his time at Carisbrooke Castle (146–152):

> But Thou hast Lived an Execution,
> Close coffined up in a deceased Life;
> Hadst Orphan Children, and a Widow-Wife,
> Friends, not t'approach, or comfort, but to mourn
> And weep their unheard plaints, as at Thy Urn?
> Such black Attendants Colonied Thy Cell,
> But for thy Presence, Car'sbrooke had been Hell.

And while he was at Carisbrooke there emerged again the idea of Charles's cabinet being rifled, this time by Colonel Hammond, his custodian on the island. King in an epigram transforms this potential propaganda victory for Parliament into Charles's triumph, as the opened cabinet reveals only a riddle whose answer may prophesy not his but Hammond's fate:

> Hammond his Master's Cabinet broke ope,
> Yet nothing found included but a Rope:
> A fatal Emblem, which in Justice might

A treach'rous Heart, and guilty conscience fright;
And shows what mortal dangers 'gainst him lie
Who into Prince's secrets dares to pry.
    That Casket think thy Lottery, false man!
Where thou thy End may'st calculated scan:
To which Two Titles thy corrupted faith
Both as a Picklock and a Traitor hath.
And were thy wages measured by that Line
Haman's tall Gallows scarce could equal thine.

That Charles's cabinet should contain only a rope is one more riddle. To hang himself with? To use to help his escape, as he apparently tried to do "with a cord"?[19] Or is it there simply in anticipation of Hammond's treachery, a mute but eloquent remonstrance, as King would have it? Or perhaps it merely shows how impoverished Charles has become, owning nothing of importance in spite of his enemies' suspicions. For Hammond the answers are only self-revelations; the closer one pries into a king's affairs the more bleared one's eyes become, as Herrick had already proclaimed.

Herrick himself wrote one last poem to Charles. *Hesperides* was published in 1648, and this may be the latest datable poem in the volume.[20] When Charles arrived at Hampton Court in mid-1647 he was greeted by this poem—or, more probably, it was Herrick's wish that he should be greeted by it: there is no evidence that it was "set and sung" as its subtitle claims, and very little likelihood that Herrick would have been able to get near him at this time:

TO THE KING,

Upon his welcome to Hampton-Court.
Set and Sung.

Welcome, *Great Caesar,* welcome now you are,
As dearest Peace, after destructive War:
Welcome as slumbers; or as beds of ease
After our long, and peevish sicknesses.
O Pomp of Glory! Welcome now, and come
To repossess once more your longed-for home.
A thousand Altars smoke; a thousand thighs
Of Beeves here ready stand for Sacrifice.
Enter and prosper; while our eyes do wait
For an *Ascendant* throughly *Auspicate:*
Under which sign we may the former stone

Lay of our safety's new foundation:
That done; O *Caesar,* live, and be to us,
Our *Fate,* our *Fortune,* and our *Genius;*
To whose free knees we may our temples tie
As to a still protecting Deity.
That should you stir, we and our Altars too
May (*Great Augustus*) *go along with You.*
Chor. Long live the King; and to accomplish this,
We'll from our own, add far more years to his.

It is difficult to conceive of anything more heroically naive than this effort. Charles is welcomed as if he were a returning conqueror rather than a humiliated captive of the army. The same image of the auspicious stone which will lay the foundation for better times will soon be used by Marvell in "An Horatian Ode," only there it is the king's bleeding head in which "the State / Foresaw its happy Fate." The oddest phrase in Herrick's poem is the exclamation "*Pomp of Glory!*" *Pomp* had already, by this time, begun to acquire its negative, sardonic connotations, and, given the context of the poem, we might well have expected it to introduce some kind of meditation upon the turns in fortune's wheel which had led Charles, once seen in all his splendor at Hampton Court, now to be reduced to a prisoner under house arrest in the same place. Instead it means what it says, with no apparent undertone, as if the king were still at the center of adoring throngs of supplicants.

While Herrick works against all the odds to preserve the fading image of royalty, Richard Lovelace, in a poem also written during the king's stay at Hampton Court, casts a far colder eye upon this image. Lovelace's appreciation of the making and breaking of such images makes it one of the most profound poems about royalty written in the century. Its title is "To my Worthy Friend Mr *Peter Lilly:* on that excellent Picture of his Majesty, and the Duke of York, drawn by him at *Hampton Court.*" The Lely portrait referred to depicts one of the occasional visits which Charles's son was allowed to pay him during his time at Hampton Court. The first half of the poem seems uncannily prophetic of the *Eikon Basilike,* as it develops a series of rapturous paradoxes very much in the manner of a Counter-Reformation poet praising a martyr. Its opening image of a clouded majesty recalls the closing image of "To Lucasta from Prison," that is, the vision of the king threatened by obscurity:

See! what a *clouded Majesty!* and eyes
Whose glory through their mist doth brighter rise!
See! what an humble bravery doth shine,

"Clouded Majesty": Sir Peter Lely's portrait of Charles under house arrest at Hampton Court in 1648, being visited by the Duke of York.

And grief triumphant breaking through each line;
How it commands the face! so sweet a scorn
Never did *happy misery* adorn!
So sacred a contempt! that others show
To this, (o'th'height of all the wheel) below;
That mightiest Monarchs by this shaded book
May copy out their proudest, richest look.
    Whilst the true *Eaglet* this quick lustre spies,
And by his *Sun's* enlightens his own eyes;
He cares his cares, his burden feels, then straight
Joys that so lightly he can bear such weight;
Whilst either either's passion doth borrow,
And both do grieve the same victorious sorrow.

The picture has come to be known as "Clouded Majesty," after the poem, and its title fits its apparent propaganda purpose well. Majesty emerges from obscurity all the greater, whether the clouds and mists which obscure it are the confinements to which it is subjected or the tears through which it must look (tears, of course, for its suffering people). Eyes are the key to the poem, and Lovelace looks carefully at the eyes of both sitters, seeing the younger take luster from his father's eyes. At this point we see the triumphant image of a pair of royal eagles, so that the clouds and mists which began the poem now turn out only to have been those which hide the mountaintop from our eyes, but through which the eagle himself can see clearly. The obscurity is ours, not his. All this is reinforced by a Crashaw-like series of baroque paradoxes, of which "*clouded Majesty*" is the first, followed by "humble bravery," "grief triumphant," "*happy misery*," and "sacred . . . contempt."

Structurally this poem is very like Lovelace's best-known poem, "The Grasshopper." Both, in the first half, describe an image of the king. Then, exactly halfway through, they turn in direct address to a friend, a maneuver which asks us to revise our allegiances. These are the next four lines of the Lely poem (17–20):

> These my best *Lilly* with so bold a spirit
> And soft a grace, as if thou didst inherit
> For that time all their greatness, and didst draw
> With those brave eyes your *Royal Sitters* saw.

Here the syntax is doubly elliptical: as the Royalist vision comes under pressure, our scrutiny turns from the *basileus* to the *eikon*. For a start, the sentence turns out to be no sentence at all, "These my best *Lilly*" being neither the subject nor object of a verb. Then there is the compression of "those brave eyes your *Royal Sitters* saw." The principal sense requires us to insert something like "through which" between "brave eyes" and "your *Royal Sitters*," reinforcing the idea that Lely, during the time he painted this picture, put on much of his subjects' greatness. But this is, itself, a shrewd appreciation of the whole curious phenomenon of having such a picture painted at such a time. The one thing we know about Charles's strategy in these last years of his life is that his overriding concern was to preserve the image of majesty which he embodied: he carried it through his trial, right down to the two shirts he wore at his execution. He became, as this poem puts it, a pattern for princes to "copy out their proudest, richest look."

This is how Lely's sitters intended to be seen and, were they artists, how they would have portrayed themselves. That Lely should see through their eyes is Lovelace's recognition of the total work of art which Charles's life had become. But Lovelace, it turns out, is more interested in Lely's art than in Charles's suffering, and a more straightforward interpretation of that piece of syntax makes the eyes Lely's, not Charles's, requiring only "which" to be inserted between "brave eyes" and "your *Royal Sitters.*" As those sitters came under Lely's scrutiny they saw how bravely he saw them. Artists are eagles as much as monarchs are, because of the keenness of their sight, and also because they can so fearlessly look on suffering monarchs.

Through all the apparent excesses of the first half of the poem Lovelace's eyes are actually fixed on the artistic process through which the suffering king has been portrayed. "*Clouded Majesty*" is literally true, for the whole right half of the double portrait is dominated by its backcloth of thick, dark clouds, behind the Duke of York's head, mirroring his taller father's expression on the left half. The ecstasy of suffering in "grief triumphant" is tempered by the phrase "breaking through each line," for "line," like other words in the first half of the poem—"show," "shaded," "copy out," "lustre," "borrow"—carries a technical, artistic sense too. The lines on Charles's face are the lines of art, no less than Cromwell's warts would prove to be. "How it commands the face!"—grief, of course, but the grief the artist has, to take a word from later in the poem, "designed." This is, after all, a very technically absorbed poem, and it should not surprise us that its use of the word *sitter,* in the sense of one who sits for a portrait, is the first recorded in English. The remainder of the poem concentrates on the details of the craft:

> Not as of old, when a rough hand did speak
> A strong Aspect, and a fair face, a weak;
> When only a black beard cried Villain, and
> By *Hieroglyphics* we could understand;
> When Crystal typified in a white spot,
> And the bright Ruby was but one red blot;
> Thou dost the things *Orientally* the same,
> Not only paint'st its colour, but its *Flame:*
> Thou sorrow canst design without a tear,
> And with the Man his very *Hope* or *Fear;*
> So that th'amazed world shall henceforth find
> None but my *Lilly* every drew a *Mind.*

There are implications here that the days of icons such as Charles and his son are numbered; but, in any case, the striking thing is how, by the end of the poem, the intensity of their suffering has given way to a panegyric on the power of the new realism in art, in which Charles is diminished to the shadows of a "Man" and a "*Mind.*" The artist himself is not affected by what he is supposed to see: "Thou sorrow canst design without a tear" refers principally to Lely's ability to penetrate the stoical appearance of his royal sitters, but it also describes the artist's necessary detachment, that he paints their sorrow without himself feeling it.

PART TWO

Poets

4 "Light and Airy Man": Ben Jonson at Court

"The king said Sir P. Sidney was no poet. Neither did he see ever any verses in England to the sculler's."[1] "The sculler" was John Taylor, the water poet. James I was probably joking, knowing that Ben Jonson, who reported these judgments to William Drummond of Hawthornden, was inclined to be nettled by the mere existence of Taylor. In *Discoveries*, just before the passage in which he laments how mean a mistress poetry has been "in this latter age," Jonson uses Taylor to illustrate the perversity of public taste:

> The puppets are seen now in despite of the players: Heath's epigrams and the sculler's poems have their applause. There are never wanting, that dare prefer the worst preachers, the worst pleaders, the worst poets: not that the better have left to write, or speak better, but that they that hear them judge worse; *Non illi pejus dicunt, sed hi corruptius judicant.* Nay, if it were put to the question of the water-rhymer's works, against Spenser's; I doubt not, but they would find more suffrages; because the most favour common vices, out of a prerogative the vulgar have, to lose their judgments, and like that which is naught.[2]

But James's stated preference stuck in Jonson's mind, adding him to the crowd, who prefer the worthless to the well-wrought.

Indeed, Jonson seems to have wondered whether Taylor was not some kind of *Doppleganger* appointed by a malign fate: "Taylor was sent along here to scorn him."[3] There are uncanny similarities in the two men's backgrounds, and Taylor clearly guyed Jonson a little, not to the extent that he tortured Thomas Coryat, but by such things as walking to Scotland (meeting Jonson on the way back) and issuing his banalities under the title *Works*. More perplexingly, perhaps, Taylor's writing sometimes has the authentic Jonson touch in its characteristic autodidact's readiness to throw in as many learned allusions as possible. Accordingly, it would be easier for the ignorant or envious to compare Taylor with Jonson than to compare him with Spenser or Sidney. Jonson's yoking of Taylor with another poetaster, John Heath, reveals his unease here, for Heath's *Two Centuries of Epigrams* parallels nothing in Spenser or Sidney, but contemporaries certainly did compare it with Jonson's own volume of epigrams.

Having complained about the scant reward offered to good poets, Jonson draws the lesson which his recollection of James's preference for Taylor's works bore out—that lack of judgment was to be found not only in "the sordid multitude" but also in "the neater sort of our gallants: for all are the multitude; only they differ in clothes, not in judgment or understanding." [4] This is the context in which to approach Jonson's famous, and now notorious, conservatism. Much has been made of it recently, and in any left-of-center reading of seventeenth-century poetry his influence is likely to be regarded as, at best, a support for authoritarianism, at worst a buttress to tyranny. It hardly needs to be said that most of the court poets were to a greater or lesser extent of the tribe of Ben. His are the forms and terms of praise which they so lovingly polish. To take just the one example, Carew's "safe" and the other poets' "secure" rely on a key Jonsonian formula. In his "Epode" for *Love's Martyr* he uses both words in the opening lines, which make the moral life closely parallel to the responsible rule of a state:

> Not to know vice at all, and keep true state,
>   Is virtue, and not Fate:
> Next, to that virtue, is to know vice well,
>   And her black spite expel.
> Which to effect (since no breast is so sure,
>   Or safe, but she'll procure
> Some way of entrance) we must plant a guard
>   Of thoughts to watch and ward
> At the eye and ear (the ports unto the mind)
>   That no strange, or unkind
> Object arrive there, but the heart (our spy)
>   Give knowledge instantly,
> To wakeful reason, our affection's king:
>   Who (in the examining)
> Will quickly taste the treason, and commit

Close, the close cause of it.
'Tis the securest policy we have,
To make our senses our slave.

Set against "The Phoenix and the Turtle" or, for that matter, Donne's celebrations of platonic love, this opening demonstrates just how politically engaged Jonson's poetry is. These may be traceable commonplaces, but the context they provide for the description of a love built on love of virtue points to a crucial difference between his praise of the couple and Shakespeare's. Whereas "The Phoenix and the Turtle" insists upon their differentiation and, accordingly, their separation, from the world, Jonson's poem thrusts them back into it. Their relationship has, in the widest sense, political implications (51–54):

this bears no brands, nor darts,
To murder different hearts,
But, in a calm, and god-like unity,
Preserves community.

If the couple really were Elizabeth and Essex, then such an emphasis would be doubly important. The poem's final line pits the two vital terms against each other: "*Man may securely sin, but safely never.*" Again, the contrast is a commonplace, but Jonson's purpose is to bring it to new life by showing how intimately public and private behavior are bound together.

The key text for understanding Jonson's belief in the central position of poetry in the life of the state is *The Poetaster*. There he exploits Rome's class structure rather as Shakespeare did in his Roman plays. Crispinus, the poetaster, is used by tribunes whose purpose is to disgrace Horace, and with him the values he stands for. Envy is the presiding genius over their actions. His prologue opens the play, egging the audience on to do that most threatening of things for an author—misapply his words so that they are given specific, damning reference to the actions of great men. As the armed prologue soon says:[5]

know 'tis a dangerous age,
Wherein who writes had need present his scenes
Forty-fold proof against the conjuring means
Of base detractors and illiterate apes
That fill up rooms in fair and formal shapes.

The play's action demonstrates how many are the pretenders to poetry, and how many more its misappliers; but the Rome which Jonson creates is a wish-fulfillment state over which presides the ideal ruler. Augustus Caesar not only can tell the difference between poets and poetasters; he also knows what use to make of them. At one point in the play Jonson has Augustus virtually forcing Virgil to take his place on the throne (V.ii):

> Let us now behold
> A human soul made visible in life,
> And more refulgent in a senseless paper
> Than in the sensual complement of kings.
> Read, read thyself, dear Virgil, let not me
> Profane one accent with an untuned tongue:
> *Best matter, badly shown, shows worse than bad.*
> See then this chair, of purpose set for thee
> To read thy poem in: refuse it not.
> *Virtue, without presumption, place may take*
> *Above best kings, whom only she should make.*

Caesar's wisdom brings about the prophecy which Ovid utters at the beginning of the play, that "heavenly poesy no death can fear. / Kings shall give place to it, and kingly shows."

When Jonson came to call James the best of kings and the best of poets early in his *Epigrams* he had much evidence to show that this was no Augustus Caesar. Indeed, the placing of the epigram fourth in the book, after epigrams addressed "To the Reader," "To my Book," and "To my Bookseller," demonstrates well enough that the expected hyperbole of the address to James is part of a hardheaded commercial venture. Not that commercial interest should be taken to be distinct from moral purpose. As often as Jonson claims a moral design behind his plays and poems, so he complains about the lack of rewards which poets suffer. The two ideas run side by side through *The Poetaster*, focused principally on the character of Horace.[6]

Jonson's poverty is an ambivalent thing. It marks him out as one who neither bows to popular taste nor panders to the whims of great men, but it is also a badge of the viciousness of the times. In his ideal state his ideal king would ensure that he was sufficiently rewarded, at least as well as the rich lawyers and merchants to whom he often compares the neglect of poets. Jonson's epigrams, then, show a continuous movement between self-interest and contempt for those whom it is in his interest to flatter. Shortly after pouring the oil of ideal kingship and great poet upon James's

head, he includes an epigram which tersely expresses the corruption of
the court over which that king presides:[7]

On a Robbery

Ridway robbed Duncote of three hundred pound,
Ridway was ta'en, arraigned, condemned to die;
But, for this money was a courtier found,
Begged Ridway's pardon: Duncote, now, doth cry,
Robbed both of money, and the law's relief,
The courtier is become the greater thief.

Probably the best-known examples of this initial movement toward
praise and then retreat from it are the two epigrams addressed to Robert,
Earl of Salisbury, followed by Jonson's address to his muse (nos. 63–65).
The first tribute to the earl ends with the couplet:

Cursed be his muse, that could lie dumb, or hid
To so true worth, though thou thyself forbid.

The second, addressed to Salisbury "Upon the Accession of the Treasure-
ship to Him," begins with Jonson's disclaimer that he writes in hope of
reward or to get a suit granted, nor is he glad out of fashion or the desire
to flatter, "nor of wit"—by which I assume he means that he is not just
taking an opportunity to spin out a nice poetic conceit. Instead,

I am glad to see that time survive,
Where merit is not sepulchred alive.
Where good men's virtues them to honours bring,
And not to dangers. When so wise a king
Contends to have worth enjoy, from his regard,
As her own conscience, still, the same reward.
These (noblest Cecil) laboured in my thought,
Wherein what wonder see thy name hath wrought!
That whilst I meant but thine to gratulate,
I have sung the greater fortunes of our state.

In the next epigram Jonson turns on his muse as the cause of his troubles.
The theme is the familiar one, that poetry leads to poverty, but the matter
is more carefully explained here as poverty deriving from his failure to
achieve the patronage which he has angled for:

To My Muse

Away, and leave me, thou thing most abhorred
That hast betrayed me to a worthless lord;
Made me to commit most fierce idolatry
To a great image through thy luxury.
Be thy next master's more unlucky muse,
And, as thou hast mine, his hours, and youth abuse.
Get him the time's long grudge, the court's ill will;
And, reconciled, keep him suspected still.
Make him lose all his friends; and, which is worse,
Almost all ways, to any better course.
With me thou leav'st an happier muse than thee,
And which thou brought'st me, welcome poverty.
She shall instruct my after-thoughts to write
Things manly, and not smelling parasite.
But I repent me: stay. Who'er is raised,
For worth he has not, he is taxed, not praised.

It is difficult to conceive of a reader who could miss the point here, that the worthless lord is Robert Cecil. Mere juxtaposition achieves this, emphasized by the play on worth in the three poems. True worth inspires the muse in 63; worth enjoys its proper reward in 64; then 65 is framed by "worthless" and "worth he has not." Embedded in all this is not only detestation of the Earl of Salisbury and of having had to flatter him, but contempt for the king's judgment too; for in praising Cecil's worth Jonson's poverty has at least given him an excuse denied to James.

In his three volumes of poetry Jonson offers enough counterflattery and contempt for abuse of power to satisfy the most radical readers. His conservatism is deeply grounded in complete respect for institutions, and he sees the poet's purpose as one which makes men fit to wear the titles they inherit or gain. As he wrote in "An Epistle to Master John Selden" (21–23):

I have too oft preferred
Men past their terms, and praised some names too much,
But 'twas with purpose to have made them such.

This is not to say that Jonson ceased to write in praise of vicious men. He had to live, and poems to such as Lord Weston, a later lord treasurer, are virtually indefensible except on the mere grounds of survival. His "Epistle Mendicant" to Weston in 1631 makes this clear, but the poem he addresses to Weston "Upon the Day he was Made Earl of Portland," praising him as the eye of state who seldom sleeps, and whom only bad men hate, is about as far removed from reality as it is possible to get. Hence, perhaps, the venom of his response "To my Detractor." That detractor, probably John Eliot, had mocked a third poem which Jonson wrote to Weston—"To the Right Honourable, the Lord High Treasurer of England. An Epigram"—by claiming that Jonson had earned £40 through it: "These verses then being rightly understood, / His lordship, not Ben Jonson, made them good." [8] Jonson's reply is that the purpose of a man like Eliot is "to make cheap the lord, the lines, the price"; and he closes on an image of beating the man to death, dashing out "thy dirty brains," so that men may "smell thy want of worth." Clearly Eliot's gibes had stung, and although the word is too common to build much upon it, Jonson's closing his reply with "worth" may signal the distress generated by too close an identification of his poetry with simple parasitism.

There are some signs of Jonson's independence to set against this kind of thing. For one, there are no poems to Buckingham, an omission obvious enough to any of his contemporaries—although Buckingham was one of Jonson's patrons. [9] And when Buckingham was assassinated Jonson was interrogated as the possible author of one of the many pro-Felton verses—testimony enough to their efficacy and learned composition, one would have thought, and perhaps the only occasion when Jonson and Puritan zealotry come into association with each other. [10] Jonson disclaimed the poem but admitted to having seen a copy of it at Sir Robert Cotton's house, "the paper of thes verses liing ther uppon the table after dinner." [11] This takes us back to the finest poem in his *Epigrams*, "Inviting a Friend to Supper," in which Jonon is the host, and poems lie upon the table:

> Tonight, grave sir, both my poor house, and I
> Do equally desire your company:
> Not that we think us worthy such a guest,
> But that your worth will dignify our feast,
> With those that come; whose grace may make that seem
> Something, which, else, could hope for no esteem.
> It is the fair acceptance, sir, creates
> The entertainment perfect, not the cates.
> Yet you shall have, to rectify your palate,

An olive, capers, or some better salad
Ush'ring the mutton; with a short-legged hen,
If we can get her, full of eggs, and then,
Lemons and wine for sauce: to these, a cony
Is not to be despaired of, for our money;
And, though fowl, now, be scarce, yet there are clerks,
The sky not falling, think we may have larks.
I'll tell you of more, and lie, so you will come:
Of partridge, pheasant, woodcock, of which some
May yet be there; and godwit, if we can:
Knat, rail, and ruff too. Howso'er, my man
Shall read a piece of Virgil, Tacitus,
Livy, or of some better book to us,
Of which we'll speak our minds, amidst our meat;
And I'll profess no verses to repeat:
To this, if aught appear, which I know not of,
That will the pastry, not my paper, show of.
Digestive cheese, and fruit there sure will be;
But that, which most doth take my muse, and me,
Is a pure cup of rich canary wine,
Which is the Mermaid's, now, but shall be mine:
Of which had Horace, or Anacreon tasted,
Their lives, as do their lines, till now had lasted.
Tobacco, nectar, or the Thespian spring,
Are all but Luther's beer, to this I sing.
Of this we will sup free, but moderately,
And we will have no Pooly, or Parrot by;
Nor shall our cups make any guilty men:
But at our parting, we will be, as when
We innocently met. No simple word,
That shall be uttered at our mirthful board,
Shall make us sad next morning: or affright
The liberty, that we'll enjoy tonight.

By seventeenth-century standards it may not be a great feast which Jonson promises, but it is more than merely decent—the kind of offering which one might sit down to at a prosperous lawyer's or merchant's. Perhaps Jonson was in unusually good financial circumstances at the time, or perhaps he expected his guest to read it as the vision of an ideal meal, just as the real James is shaped into the ideal monarch in the earlier epigram. Anyhow, the important thing is to see how the liberality of the entertainment matches the vision of freedom which the poem proclaims. At least three of Martial's epigrams feed into Jonson's poem, but none of them quite prepares us for the concern with freedom of speech which comes to dominate Jonson's poem. Introduced halfway through as the innocent speaking of minds about Virgil, Tacitus, or Livy, the insistence upon the right to speak freely leads Jonson to promise his friend that there will be no government spies present, nor anything in their conversation which might lead them to self-incrimination or the incrimination of others. The interview with the attorney general after Buckingham's death reinforces Jonson's point here, that going to dinner in Jacobean London could be a dangerous experience. Either Cotton or one of his company set Jonson up, testing whether or not he was the writer of the pro-Felton poem; or an informer had been present and had reported all. Jonson's deposition makes uncomfortable reading because he too is forced to inform, if only to clear himself, without knowing how much his inquisitor knew:

> this examinant was asked concerning thos verses, as if himself had been the auther thereof; theruppon this examinant redd them, & condemned them & with deep protestations affirmed that they were not made by him, nor did he knowe who made them, or had ever seen or herd them before, & the like protestations he nowe maketh uppon his christianity & hope of salvation / he saith he took noe coppy of them, nor ever had coppy of them; he saith he hath herd of them since, but ever with detestation / he being further asked wheather he doth knowe who made or hath herd who made them, he answereth he doth not knowe, but he hath herd by common fame that one mr Townleye should make them, but he professeth truly that he cann not name any one singuler person who hath soe reported it / Being asked of what quality that mr Townly is, he saith his name is *zouch Townlye,* he is a scholler and a divine by profession & a preacher / but wher he liveth or abideth he knoweth not, but he is a student of Christs church in oxford / Being further asked wheather he gave a dagger to the said Mr Townlye? and uppon what occasion? and when / he answereth, that on a Sunday after this examinant had herd the said mr Townly preach at St Margarets church in westminster, mr Townly taking a liking to a dagger with a white haft which this examinant ordinaryly wore at his girdle & was given to this examinant this examinant gave it to him two nights after, being invited by mr Townly to supp but without any circumstaunce & without

any Relation to thos or any other verses, for this examinant is well assured this was soe done before he sawe thes verses, or had herd of them . . . [12]

Here Jonson is trapped between two suppers: one with Sir Robert Cotton, when he first saw the poem; and an earlier one with Zouch Townley, when he gave him a dagger and when, so he unconvincingly protests, no poems were discussed. The police-state conditions of early seventeenth-century England make any social contact, no matter how apparently innocent, a potential trap when put under the scrutiny of so excellent an interrogator as this one. Jonson's lies and evasions become more embarrassing as the interview proceeds—ignorance of Townley's domicile is contradicted by that invitation to supper, and the claim that he cannot remember who told him about Townley's supposed authorship is patently unconvincing. In such a context virtually any topic, even discussion of Virgil, Tacitus, or Livy, could be interpreted as evidence of subversive tendencies.

Envy begins *The Poetaster* by encouraging the audience to read into Jonson's Horace, Crispinus, and Virgil matter which he can "force . . . to the present state." The armed prologue pins his hopes upon an audience of "free souls," and Jonson continues his protest against misinterpretation in his "Apologetical Dialogue," where he describes his position as one surrounded by a nest of hornets which

> fly buzzing mad about my nostrils,
> And like so many screaming grasshoppers
> Held by the wings fill every ear with noise.[13]

"Inviting a Friend to Supper" takes place in a room with close friends and trusted servants (especially if the "man" was Alexander Brome). The night which frames the poem is both threat and guarantor of safety. Men such as Pooly and Parrot work in darkness—Pooly had Marlowe stabbed after dinner in the Deptford pub—but Jonson's control over his household, with the cultural tradition which governs his actions, promises the visitor that this will be one occasion when he can feel free to talk. The poem closes on freedom, guilt, innocence, simplicity, and liberty, rejecting daylight sadness and the fears of the night.

The inheritors of this epigram were the Royalists of the late 1640s and the 1650s, Jonson's night anticipating the Cavalier winter during which solace could be found only with a trusted friend in a warm room with good food and drink. Lovelace's "Grasshopper" is the best-known example. But the Jonsonian example was not influential so much because of the shared royalism as because Jonson's poetry is, in large part, a poetry of resistance. This is one reason for his attractiveness to Yeats—that his poetry fuses an immense respect for tradition to a language studded with expressions of resistance and revolt. The great Jonsonian moral imperatives—conveyed in words such as "stand," "turn," and "go"—are frequently given aggressive or even warlike connotations. Jonson's man stands against opposition, turns and goes to meet it. The fact that he never openly counsels seditious action makes the implicit resistance of such words and ideas all the more compelling. A good example is the ode which he wrote to James, Earl of Desmond. (The *Underwood* 25). It opens with an apparently innocent invocation:

> Where art thou, genius? I should use
>   Thy present aid: arise invention,
> Wake, and put on the wings of Pindar's muse,
>   To tower with my intention
>   High, as his mind, that doth advance
> Her upright head, above the reach of chance,
>   Or the time's envy.

The inclusion of "envy" marks the piece as Jonson's, and "advance" already begins to strike the familiar military note. But the adversity toward which Desmond had to advance was singularly nasty. He had been imprisoned since the age of nine and by 1600, the probable date of Jonson's poem, had spent sixteen years in the Tower of London. He was well known as the "Tower earl", hence Jonson's use of "tower" in his opening lines. Desmond becomes a type of individual persecuted because of his family connections, a victim of reasons of state. Jonson calls upon him to tower above his persecutions rather than be tainted by them. The poem ends ominously with the prophecy that a light will shine in Desmond's darkness:

> O then (my best-best loved) let me importune,
>   That you will stand,
> As far from all revolt, as you are now from fortune.

This counsel to Desmond not to join in or encourage Tyrone's rebellion is a testimony to Jonson's love of civil order, for he makes clear in the course of the poem his understanding of the sordid political maneuverings which had caused the earl so much suffering (27–39):

Nor think yourself unfortunate,
If subject to the jealous errors
Of politic pretext, that wries a state,
    Sink not beneath these terrors:
    But whisper; O glad innocence
Where only a man's birth is his offence;
    Or the disfavour,
    Of such as savour
Nothing, but practise upon honour's thrall.
    O virtue's fall,
When her dead essence (like the anatomy
    In Surgeon's hall)
Is but a statist's theme, to read phlebotomy.

A critic calls this poem "confusing and pretentious." [14] Perhaps this is a reaction to Jonson's efforts to harness the Pindaric ode to the compression of epigrammatic lines such as "Palm grows straight, though handled ne'er so rude" or "Gold, that is perfect, will outlive the fire." On the other hand, there is a lot about Jonson's publication of the poem which is the opposite of pretentious. When it appeared in *The Underwood* it was given the subtitle "Writ in Queen Elizabeth's Time, Since Lost and Recovered." It could hardly have been otherwise, for Desmond, having shown the patient trust which Jonson counseled, had resisted the temptation to rebel. For his loyalty he arrived back in England expecting a pension, the return of some of his lands, or both. Cecil saw to it that the earl was kept in poverty, and within a few months he was dead, little more than thirty years old. So, for Jonson to promise light in the darkness after the earl's death would have been simple idiocy; but the bravery of publishing the poem is involved with the recognition that his advice had been wrong, an admission that he was a failed prophet. In this sense "finding" the poem is both a retrospective praise of Desmond as a victim of state oppression and a marker for men such as Zouch Townley when they came to write in praise of later political prisoners.

The ode has parallels with plays which Jonson was writing around the turn of the century, in particular *The Poetaster*. The stoical advice given to the earl, that "fury wasteth / As patience lasteth," is followed by lines whose martial imagery connects with the armed prologue of the play (48–52):

No armour to the mind! He is shot-free
    From injury,

That is not hurt; not he, that is not hit;
    So fools we see,
Oft scape an imputation, more through luck, than wit.

This idea is taken up in the "Apologetical Dialogue" to *The Poetaster,* in
which Jonson claims that his enemies

Have nothing left but the unsavoury smoke
Of their black vomit to upbraid themselves,
Whilst I, at whom they shot, sit here shot-free
And as unhurt of envy as unhit.[15]

But in both cases the sentiment is heavily qualified by its context. Desmond's sordid treatment and quick death show how palpably hurt he had
been, and in Jonson's dialogue begins the long, sustained resentment
which he felt at his treatment by both the people and the authorities.
According to the preamble "to the reader" he had the dialogue delivered
on the stage only once, as "all the answer I ever gave to sundry impotent
libels then cast out (and some yet remaining) against me and this play."[16]
The preamble was written in 1616, so the idea that the libels yet remain
shows how deeply Jonson felt about them; and that this anger is directed
not simply against the popular response but also against official conniv-
ance is borne out by the statement issued to readers of the 1602 Quarto,
that "in place of the Epilogue, was meant to thee an Apology from the
Author . . . but (since he is no lesse restrain'd, then thou depriv'd of it, by
Authoritie) hee praies thee to thinke charitably of what thou hast read."[17]
The dialogue closes with Jonson's ill-fated design to turn from comedy to
tragedy,

Where, if I prove the pleasure but of one,
So he judicious be, he shall b'alone
A theatre unto me.

This anticipation of Milton's fit audience is striking enough, the more so
for its having been written just at the point where Jonson could begin to
look forward to an appreciative and influential audience of one, the best
of kings and best of poets who would shortly succeed Elizabeth.

Among the other professions which Jonson frequently pretended to
consider as alternatives to his ill-rewarded life as a dramatist-poet, at
least once, probably playfully, he scouted the idea of going into the
church. He told Drummond: "He hath a mind to be a churchman, and so

he might have favour to make one sermon to the king, he careth not what thereafter should befall him: for he would not flatter though he saw death." [18] Drummond could have replied that Jonson had had more opportunity than most churchmen to address the king by way of his contributions to court masques; but so morally vacuous were these entertainments that Jonson might well have countered to the effect that with someone like Inigo Jones in control of the spectacle it was virtually impossible not to consider them as extended pieces of flattery.[19] In contrast, however, there was certainly one occasion when Jonson could preach a dramatic sermon to the king. This was the second performance of *Bartholomew Fair*, given at court in November 1614.

It may initially seem to be a dry academic exercise to label a play so funny and so lively as *Bartholomew Fair* a sermon; but seventeenth-century sermons were often entertaining, even rumbustious performances. Certainly it is important to counter the general perception of the play as little more than a romp spiced with anti-Puritan satire. Whereas the masques removed the king from reality into the stratosphere of gods, goddesses, and Jones's machines, *Bartholomew Fair* shoved him back into the country he ruled. Like Claudius watching the dumb show in *Hamlet*, it is a matter for speculation as to how far James could appreciate what was going on in front of him. Only the year before Jonson and Jones had presented at court the masque *Love Freed from Ignorance and Folly*.[20] There Love's search to solve the Sphinx's riddle seems doomed to failure until, lost in ignorance and folly, he is instructed by the muses' priests to look to the chief spectator for the answer:

> Gentle Love, be not dismayed.
>   See the muses, pure and holy,
>   By their priests have sent thee aid
>   Against this brood of folly.
> It is true that Sphinx, their dame,
>   Had the sense first from the muses,
>   Which in uttering she doth lame,
>   Perplexeth, and abuses.
> But they bid that thou should'st look
>   In the brightest face here shining,
>   And the same, as would a book,
>   Shall help thee in divining.

The brightest face to which Love should look is of course James. He and his court knew exactly how to respond to such a compliment, as do modern commentators, who carefully track down and elucidate the formidable scholarship which Jonson brought to such affairs—something which Taylor playfully imitated by constantly referring to his own scholarship, meaning, really, scullership. Still, it is arguable that for all its use of such sources as Alciati or Ripa, *Love Freed from Ignorance and Folly* is at best morally empty, at worst an example of art employed for the purpose of encouraging tyranny. James's court would have been well aware of this. If his face was shining when the above compliment was delivered, it was probably the result of his ogling the latest young man-about-town. Jonson preserves some dignity by turning James into a text to be read by Love and, one assumes, by the other spectators too. His purpose is to unperplex poetry from the riddle into which the child of the muses, the Sphinx, had turned it. As Love piously goes on to proclaim (286–291):[21]

> The King's the eye, as we do call,
> The sun the eye of this great all;
> And is the light and treasure too.
> For 'tis his wisdom all doth do,
> Which still is fixed in his breast,
> Yet still doth move to guide the rest.

There is a whole world between this mumbo jumbo and the Induction to *Bartholomew Fair,* where the stage-keeper slangs off the dramatist for his failure to hit the humors of the fair. Among the list of things which the audience at the Hope Theatre will not see, but which they would see at Smithfield, is the well-educated ape who goes "over the chain for the king of England, and back again for the Prince, and sit[s] still on his arse for the Pope and the king of Spain." [22] Any suggestion that spectators can remove themselves from the world of the fair is quashed by Quarlous' reprimand to Winwife, who wants merely to watch and not be approached, that "our very being here makes us fit to be demanded, as well as others" (II.v). They are fit victims of poetry too. Jonson exposes as an academic fiction the notion that fine words can have a moral purpose: Nightingale's ballad warning all to beware of cutpurses, with its refrain "Youth, youth, thou hadst better be starved by thy nurse, / Than live to be hanged for cutting a purse" is praised by Adam Overdo as, at last, a piece of valuable, purposeful poetry, while the audience sees it as the decoy to attract an audience whose purses can be cut by Edgworth. In this fashion all claims to authority and power over others, from the poet's to the magistrate's, are shown up for the shams they really are. James might have laughed at his magistrate's downfall, but he might just have picked up the meaning behind Overdo's most heartfelt line, that "as we are public persons, what do we know?" (II.i).

Jonson uses the fair as a controlling metaphor for the state in a time of social change. All classes have to come to it—even the king—and while there they must obey Quarlous' injunction or end up the worse, like Overdo's wife, who is revealed drunk and on the point of being turned into a whore in the final scene. Overdo himself does everything the ideal magistrate should do, not standing aloof from the people he governs, but mixing with them and seeing for himself rather than relying on spies and informers. There are parallels: Henry V on the night before Agincourt, who learns, with Shakespeare's typical lack of sentimentality, how lacking in ideals are the men he is sending into battle. A closer parallel is the duke in *Measure for Measure,* whose disguised, godlike benevolence puts on the stage some of James's most cherished theories about how the best of kings should rule—practices, too, for James famously went in disguise to see how his merchants conducted themselves.[23] Adam Overdo may well be a mockery of Shakespeare's duke: if so, he is a mockery of James's idealism also, as Jonson shows how difficult it is either to govern people or to judge them. Again, Quarlous is Jonson's spokesman, reminding Overdo that he is "but Adam, flesh and blood"—followed shortly by Jonson's epilogue telling James that "this is your power to judge."[24]

The one royal function which still proclaimed the ideal of a king who could go among his people doing active good was the custom of touching to cure the king's evil—as we saw in the way Herrick's poem reinforced this practice so favored by Stuart monarchs. Herrick balked at calling it the king's evil, when it belonged to the king only insofar as he was the only one who could cure it. In this quibble he was probably recollecting Jonson's "Epigram to King Charles, for a £100 he sent me in my sickness. 1629" (*Underwood* 62):

> Great Charles, among the holy gifts of grace
> Annexed to thy person, and thy place,
> 'Tis not enough (thy piety is such)
> To cure the called King's evil with thy touch;
> But thou wilt yet a kinglier mastery try,
> To cure the poet's evil, poverty:
> And, in these cures, dost so thyself enlarge,
> As thou dost cure our evil, at thy charge.
> Nay, and in this, thou show'st to value more
> One poet, than of other folk ten score.

O piety! So to weigh the poor's estates!
O bounty! So to difference the rates!
What can the poet wish his king may do,
But, that he cure the people's evil too?

This is a squib, but nonetheless interesting. "Called King's evil" makes
the same point as Herrick's poem, absolving the king of any responsibility. Charles is no more to be blamed for scrofula than he is for Jonson's
poverty. The poem then praises him for his capacity to weigh men and
judge who deserves most help, and ends with a form of repayment, the
poet's using his gift to wish for peace between the monarch and his
people. How should we understand "the people's evil": as a parallel to
"the King's evil," and therefore miscalled, or as a contrast to it, because
the people are responsible for the country's troubles? Probably the second
is the answer, if Jonson's other poems to Charles are any guide. An epigram written in the same year, on Charles's anniversary, seems to pin the
whole blame for the collision with Parliament upon the people's ingratitude: (*Underwood 64*):

> An Epigram. To our Great and Good King
> Charles on His Anniversary Day. 1629
> Most happy were the subject if he knew,
> Most pious king, but his own good in you!
> How many times, live long, Charles, would he say,
> If he but weighed the blessings of this day?
> And as it turns our joyful year about,
> For safety of such majesty, cry out?
> Indeed, when had great Britain greater cause
> Than now, to love the sovereign, and the laws?
> When you that reign, are her example grown,
> And what are bounds to her, you make your own?
> When your assiduous practice doth secure
> That faith, which she professeth to be pure?
> When all your life's a precedent of days,
> And murmur cannot quarrel at your ways?
> How is she barren grown of love! Or broke!
> That nothing can her gratitude provoke!
> O times! O manners! Surfeit born of ease,
> The truly epidemical disease!
> 'Tis not alone the merchant, but the clown,
> Is bankrupt turned! The cassock, cloak, and gown

Are lost upon account! And none will know
How much to heaven for thee, great Charles, they owe!

Although the reasons for the conflicts between Charles and Parliament were many and various, the point of collision was usually money. Parliament's opposition to Buckingham's demands for increased expenditure forms the subtext of Jonson's poem—and also of the epigram thanking Charles for his £100 gift, for in its strongest complaints at Charles's excesses, the expense of the royal household and of royal entertainments also came under Parliament's scrutiny. A hundred pounds for a poet could hardly ever be thought of as a last straw, but it could be taken as symptomatic of the king's wrong priorities. For Jonson, of course, the gift showed that his priorities were, at last, sorting themselves out properly; hence his praise for Charles's estimation of a poet as worth a hundred other people—the relative values of the £100 given to him and the £1 given to sufferers from scrofula.

But Jonson is in danger of running into ironies in his praise of Charles. Some readers might have found reason to quibble with the idea that Charles cured the poet's evil at his own charge. If they did, then Jonson's response would be the one framed in the anniversary poem, a position which assumed, at bottom, that the crown should not have its executive authority controlled by Parliament. But the reality of the political situation was, now, that Parliament could and did withhold the necessary funds for the crown to do what it wished (which principally meant the funding of Buckingham's adventures). Jonson's poem argues that although Parliament clearly holds this power, its reluctance to finance Charles is based on ingratitude, one of the more insidious forms of Jonson's cardinal sin, envy. Again the idea of weighing is employed. This time the people are asked to balance what they owe to Charles with how little they give him. They owe safety and security, guaranteed by his virtuous example. Their failure to pay is a consequence of bankruptcy spread across all classes. The operative word is "broke"—"How is she barren grown of love! Or broke!"—used to signify lack of funds and the proroguing of Parliament.[25] By this time Parliament's strategy to force Charles into bankruptcy was clear to all, and Jonson's poem traces its origins to a national moral bankruptcy, from which only Charles is exempt.[26] Peeping out of the poem, too, in the rhyme word which Jonson finds for "secure," is the zealous faction which has control of Parliament, those whose faith is professedly "pure."

In his poems to Charles, then, the king becomes another type of Jonson himself, rejected by the people who should love him and in dire financial straits. All of the embedded rebellion in Jonson's poetry finds its purpose in defending the king against the envy of an ungrateful nation. An ode "In Celebration of Her Majesty's Birthday, 1630" has the muses insisting upon celebration in the teeth of obvious popular hostility. It opens with these revealing verses, delivered by Clio and Melpomene (*Underwood* 67):

1 CLIO.
Up public joy, remember
This sixteenth of November,
    Some brave uncommon way:
And though the parish steeple
Be silent, to the people
    Ring thou it holiday.

2 MEL.
What, though the thrifty tower
And guns there, spare to pour
    Their noises forth in thunder:
As fearful to awake
This city, or to shake
    Their guarded gates asunder?

"Uncommon" seems to have been uncommon enough for it to have stuck out even more to its contemporary readers that it does to us.[27] Certainly the contrast which Jonson sets up between the uncommonness of the celebration and its appeal to the people becomes the paradox which develops through the poem—that Charles is and is not popular. Popular refusal to celebrate monarchy, to the extent that church bells stay unrung and public funds are not wasted on firing salutes, is set against popular joy at their king and queen's happiness. The poem closes with images of Charles and his queen at the center of public rejoicing:

7 CALLI.
See, see our active king
Hath taken twice the ring
    Upon his pointed lance:
Whilst all the ravished rout
Do mingle in a shout,
    Hey! for the flower of France!

8 URA.
This day the court doth measure
Her joy in state, and pleasure;
    And with a reverend fear,
The revels, and the play
Sum up this crowned day,
    Her two and twentieth year!

9 POLY.
Sweet happy Mary! All
The people do her call!
    And this the womb divine!
So fruitful and so fair,
Hath brought the land an heir!
    And Charles a Caroline!

One way to resolve the paradox is to take up the Parliamentary implications of "uncommon" and to assume that Jonson is arguing that Parliament is not representative of popular feeling, but only of the resentments of the zealous faction. Nonetheless, the ironies are still heavy in the contrast between the city's parsimony and the court's revels. Jonson may welcome the second, but, like the other royal poems of the 1630s, Jonson's carry as part of their freight the growing tensions in the country. Indeed, because he is the ruler of the tribe, his poems set the pattern for the rest.

Most striking are Jonson's repeated reminders to the king of his troubles, as in "To the King. On His Birthday. An Epigram Anniversary. November 19, 1632" (*Underwood* 72). The poem opens by declaring that this is King Charles's day, and the king might well have hoped that for once its celebrants would play only cheerful tunes. Most did, but the old poet insisted upon warts and all. The marvelous image of Charles's island ringed with a continuous salute from his fleet, reinforcing the peal of church bells throughout the land, gives way to doubt and resentment:

This is King Charles his day. Speak it, thou tower,
Unto the ships, and they from tier, to tier,
Discharge it 'bout the island, in an hour,
As loud as thunder, and as swift as fire.
Let Ireland meet it out at sea, half way,
Repeating all Great Britain's joy, and more,
Adding her own glad accents, to this day,
Like Echo playing from the other shore.

What drums or trumpets, or great ordinance can,
The poetry of steeples, with the bells,
Three kingdoms' mirth, in light and airy man,
Made lighter with the wine. All noises else,
At bonfires, rockets, fireworks, with the shouts
That cry that gladness, which their hearts would pray,
Had they but grace, of thinking, at these routes,
On the often coming of this holiday:
   And ever close the burden of the song,
     Still to have such a Charles, but this Charles long.
The wish is great; but where the prince is such,
What prayers (people) can you think too much?

It is possible that one authentic version of this poem lacked the closing couplet.[28] The couplet makes obvious the latent contradiction of "Had they" in line 15 and, by doing so, reveals the whole poem to be the poet's wish, not a description of popular celebration. As a piece of wish fulfillment it might be thought to fit neatly into the line of Royalist poems of the 1630s and early 1640s, but it has a much greater value than such worthless pieces of puffery as Waller's because it reflects back on to the heroic enterprise of Jonson's final years, that of rebuilding the whole state within his head. A suspected textual problem in this poem is "light and airy man" in line 11, made lighter with the wine in the next line, or, as some manuscripts have it, "made loftier by the winds." Changing "man" to *Man*—that is, the Isle of Man—has been suggested, or emendation to *moan*.[29] But perhaps "man" is right, with "light and airy" being a tribute to the imagination which interprets in the haze of wine or in the roaring wind the noises of celebration which should ring through this November day. Jonson, of course, had always been the opposite of light and airy. He weighed 280 pounds when he walked to Scotland. But by this time he had lain paralyzed for many months, unable to see for himself, and forced to interpret what he could hear. From 1628 until his death in 1637 "he appears . . . to have been confined to his chamber, and finally to his bed."[30] As early as 1632 he seems to have slipped out of the public consciousness: one correspondent is on record as having noted with surprise the announcement of *The Magnetic Lady's* forthcoming performance, by "Ben Jonson, who I thought had been dead."[31]

But Jonson knew that a true poet could be compared to only one other man in terms of eternal fame. In the final line of the epilogue to *The New Inn*, the first play he completed after his two strokes, he proclaimed that although "mayors and sheriffs may yearly fill the stage: / A king's or poet's birth do ask an age." [32] This was a sentiment which caught the attention of the water poet, who rephrased it to make the better point—one that Jonson would surely have agreed with—the poets outlive even kings: "When heaven intends to do some mighty thing, / He makes a poet, or at least a king." [33]

5 "The Utmost Bound of a Fable": Ben Jonson in Bed

For the last nine years of his life Ben Jonson was probably grossly fat, certainly paralyzed, and confined to one room. He ought to have been better prepared than most for such a fate, having invested imaginatively in it during the previous twenty years. Volpone's bed dominates the stage and becomes the character's fate as he is directed to "lie in prison, cramped with irons, / Till thou be'st sick and lame indeed."[1] And if Bartholomew Fair sits at the center of English life, at the fair's own center is the pig-woman's tent. She had been active enough in her earlier life—Overdo has had Ursula before him as "punk, pinnace and bawd, any time these two and twenty years" (II.ii). Now her huge bulk anchors her to her tent, and her one effort at vigorous movement leads to a scalding and virtual immobility for the rest of the play, as she sits in a chair giving directions and shining like Ursa Major.

For a long time Jonson himself was a great bear directing all around him. In his "Epistle to Mr Arthur Squib" (*The Underwood* 54) he boasts of being only two pounds short of twenty stones in weight, and in a poem to the painter William Burlase (*Underwood* 52) he directs the artist to describe him by "a monogram / With one great blot." A sense of his own bulk seems to underlie his famous dismissal of himself as lying "careless . . . / Buried in ease and sloth," (*Underwood* 23) and it certainly hinders him in potential amorous encounters, as the final lines of "My Picture Left in Scotland" (*Underwood* 9) make humorously clear. But the bulk is seen positively too, notably in Jonson's identification of himself with Horace. "An Elegy" in *The Underwood* (42) begins:

> Let me be what I am, as Virgil cold;
> As Horace fat; or as Anacreon old

recollecting the little fat Horace of *The Poetaster* who shares that other Jonsonian affliction, poverty.

The elegy then brings out the great paradox, as Jonson perceived it, of his fatness (3–18):

> No poet's verses yet did ever move,
> Whose readers did not think he was in love.
> Who shall forbid me then in rhythm to be
> As light, and active as the youngest he
> That from the muses' fountains doth endorse
> His lines, and hourly sits the poet's horse?
> Put on my ivy garland, let me see
> Who frowns, who jealous is, who taxeth me.
> Fathers and husbands, I do claim a right
> In all that is called lovely: take my sight
> Sooner than my affection from the fair.
> No face, no hand, proportion, line, or air
> Of beauty; but the muse hath interest in:
> There is not worn that lace, purl, knot or pin,
> But is the poet's matter; and he must
> When he is furious, love, although not lust.

There is some self-mockery here. One of the poem's antecedents is Epicure Mammon, whose grossness includes bizarre fantasies of love and lust, with parents acting the part of bawds. But Jonson's purpose in the poem is to show how fine and delicate is the sensibility trapped inside the bulk. Those eyes apparently libidinously ogling some wife or daughter are really supersubtle threaders through each filament of clothing, capable of the finest shades of perception and feeling. The poet's identity, vastly at odds with his appearance, is Puckish, even fairylike. Jonson repeatedly registers in his songs the most exquisite sensations, not only to eye and ear, but also to touch. The images are of fat flesh rubbing against swansdown and beaver wool, and fingering the bag of the bee or a skein of silk without a knot.

Jonson was obviously aware of, and himself exploited, the images of Falstaffian fatness which his appearance encouraged—as in his song to the bouncing belly in *Pleasure Reconciled to Virtue* which piles up pictures of a vaster and vaster stomach, all finally bursting out with a fart. But it does not take much reading into Jonson's later poems to see how his physical plight tormented him. Like Ursula in her chair, Jonson in his bed seems to live in a state of perpetual anger, railing and fulminating against individuals such as Inigo Jones and against people in general who could no longer understand him. In this sense it is not stretching things too far to say that his poetry in his last few years is a species of prison poetry.

Jonson had experienced prison at least a couple of times earlier in his life, but apart from the threat of close questioning it is hard to think that he could have found it much of a punishment: it must have provided him with plenty of material for low-life scenes. But this final prison was paralysis and pain, the more tormenting because the mind within the helpless bulk was as lively as ever. This is the burden of his epilogue to *The New Inn:*

> Plays in themselves have neither hopes nor fears,
>> Their fate is only in their hearers' ears:
> If you expect more than you had tonight,
>> The maker is sick and sad. But do him right,
> He meant to please you: for he sent things fit
>> In all the numbers both of sense and wit,
> If they ha' not miscarried! If they have,
>> All that his faint and faltering tongue doth crave
> Is that you not impute it to his brain.
>> That's yet unhurt, although, set round with pain,
> It cannot long hold out. All strength must yield.
>> Yet judgment would the last be i' the field
> With a true poet. He could have haled in
>> The drunkards and the noises of the inn
> In his last act; if he had thought it fit
>> To vent you vapours in the place of wit:
> But better 'twas that they should sleep or spew
>> Than in the scene to offend or him or you.
> This he did think; and this do you forgive:
>> Whene'er the carcass dies, this art will live.
> And had he lived the care of King and Queen,
>> His art in something more yet had been seen;
> But mayors and sheriffs may yearly fill the stage:
>> A king's or poet's birth do ask an age.

"Faint and faltering tongue" seems literal rather than figurative, as if Jonson's paralysis extended to slurring of his speech, probably a form of aphasia. In such circumstances his earlier advice to such prisoners as the Earl of Desmond to bear all stoically and not rebel could hardly have been sustained: now Jonson was the philosopher with the toothache. When *The New Inn* failed—inevitably, one supposes, not because of weaknesses in the play, but because Jonson could not be present to direct it—his response was a howl of rage, his infamous and much-answered ode "Come Leave the Loathed Stage," otherwise known as his "Ode to Himself." But in the epilogue he seems already to have anticipated the play's fate, and in it he takes pains to tell posterity what he shrewdly guesses his contemporaries cannot perceive, that the failure comes not from senility but from his refusal to pander to the audience's preference for clowning over real wit. Between the two comments on his own physical state, "all strength must yield" and "the carcass dies," comes the careful analysis of what he could have done in the last scene and what he chose to do instead because of the continued reliability of his judgment.

This concern for structure and decorum conditions much of Jonson's writing during his last years. *Discoveries,* which presumably comprised the jottings of a lifetime, was probably put into shape then. For all of its use of authority and precedent it is a very personal work, opening with a disquisition on ill fortune, which "never crushed that man, whom good fortune deceived not." These discoveries "made upon men and matter" begin at home with the pain and poverty which he now endures: "He knows not his own strength, that hath not met adversity. Heaven prepares good men with crosses; but no ill can happen to a good man. Contraries are not mixed. Yet, that which happens to any man, may to every man. But it is in his reason what he accounts it, and will make it." [2]

There are many such observations in the work, alternating with pieces of what we would call literary criticism and literary theory, as well as comment on princes, politics, and education. There is a problem in all of Jonson's last things in seeing them as a whole. *The New Inn,* for instance, alternates between so many different styles that critics are tempted to treat the elements which they find discordant as forms of parody, as with the Romance ending, whereby the play closes very much in the style of moldy *Pericles.* It may be, however, that the problems are ours, not his, failures resulting from our compartmentalizing, whereas he was finding ways of breaking down distinctions. Certainly, strange things happen in *Discoveries,* as if Jonson could no longer distinguish between art and life—or would not. At one place he more or less says as much, explicitly:

I have considered, our whole life is like a play: wherein every man, forgetful of himself, is in travail with expression of another. Nay, we so insist in imitating others, as we cannot (when it is necessary) return to ourselves: like children, that imitate the vices of stammerers so long, till at last they become such; and make the habit to another nature, as it is never forgotten.[3]

The faltering tongue again; but these sentences parallel in a much broader way what is said and done in *The New Inn,* particularly by the host, the disguised, errant Lord Frampul. Having opted out of the life he had been born to, his practice is to sit at ease in his inn and

> Imagine all the world's a play;
> The state and men's affairs all passages
> Of life, to spring new scenes, come in, go out,
> And shift and vanish . . .   (I.iv)

Jonson himself may not have been at ease, but, imprisoned in his palsied flesh and the one room in which there was "nothing . . . to be seen but the bare walls, and not anything to be heard but the noise of a saw", he inhabited a world built almost entirely on memory and imagination.[4] Who knows what legions of angels or devils he saw circling about his big toe when he had no choice but to lie and look at it. There are hints enough in *Discoveries* that imagination and reason are fighting each other; as when he turns to giving his judgment on Horace, always the poet with whom he most closely compared himself, and the rationality of the language barely covers what is a piece of complete self-dramatization:

> My conceit of his person was never increased toward him, by his place, or honours. But I have, and do reverence him for the greatness, that was only proper to himself, in that he seemed to me ever, by his work, one of the greatest men, and most worthy of admiration, that had been in many ages. In his adversity I ever prayed that God would give him strength: for greatness he could not want. Neither could I condole in a word, or syllable for him; as knowing no accident could do harm to virtue; but rather help make it manifest.[5]

Most striking is the sentence about God's giving Horace strength in his adversity. It can scarcely apply to Horace, who is long dead and gone and, presumably, saved as one of the righteous heathen. Jonson, of course, still needs strength.

Most of all, he needs it to manage the end gracefully. In this sense his considerations in *Discoveries* on the style and structure of a work of art should be related to Jonson's life too. There are elements of self-parody; thus, when he is discussing one species of bad writing he describes it as "a fleshy style, when there is much periphrasis, and circuit of words; and when with more than enough, it grows fat and corpulent; *arvina orationis,* full of suet and tallow."[6] More often the analogy is between the body politic and the body in pain. In counseling discretion rather than puritanical zeal in the hunting out of false pastors, Jonson writes: "The body hath certain diseases, that are with less evil tolerated, than removed. As if to cure a leprosy, a man should bathe himself with the warm blood of a murdered child: so in the church, some errors may be dissimuled with less inconvenience, than can be discovered."[7] In either case the implied resolution of disease is suicide, national or personal. But although Jonson's classical authorities might recommend such an ending, his Christianity forbade it, so the question was how to give shape and purpose to a life which seemed to be decaying into stammering senility.

Another poet who considered this matter at this time was George Herbert. "The Forerunners" welcomes senility as a full and proper ending to a life of service to God. But for Herbert this is a relatively easy conclusion, completely in line with his continued emphasis on the necessity of affliction and the insignificance of human achievement when set against the imitation of Christ's suffering. In *The Temple* the poet's creativity and control of language are presented as much inferior to a simple groan, so that being left only with the capacity to mumble "Thou art still my God" is an apotheosis, not a degradation. Nothing could be further from Jonson's position, where the emphasis is always on human achievement, resistance, and rebellion against whatever dehumanizes. When the human is restricted by paralysis and confinement, the need is not to accept this as a welcome annihilation of self, but to transform it into something active. Lying careless, apparently buried in sloth, is to present an image of merely growing "like a tree / In bulk," that is, "standing long an oak, three hundred year, / To fall a log at last, dry, bald, and sere." These lines come, of course, from the Cary-Morison Ode, whose proper title is "To the Immortal Memory and Friendship of that Noble Pair, Sir Lucius Cary and Sir H. Morison" (*Underwood* 69). This great poem, written soon after Jonson's stroke, moves between a celebration of Morison's short, happy life, and the counsel to Cary on how to live a long life. It is not merely a matter of endurance, but of shaping. Like the infant of Saguntum at the beginning of the poem, who turned back at his birth in contempt for the horrors of the world he was entering, all men must learn to make their circle perfect.[8]

Jonson introduces Cary to this responsibility in the most complex stanza of the poem (53–64):

> Go now, and tell out days summed up with fears,
> And make them years;
> Produce thy mass of miseries on the stage,
> To swell thine age:
> Repeat of things a throng,
> To show thou hast been long,
> Not lived; for life doth her great actions spell,
> By what was done and wrought
> In season, and so brought
> To light: her measures are, how well
> Each syllabe answered, and was formed, how fair;
> These make the lines of life, and that's her air.

The "stage" / "age" rhyme, repeated at the beginning of his "Ode to Himself," points toward Jonson's inclusion of himself in this stanza, as an older counterpart to Morison who will help guide Cary through his remaining life; but aside from the advice to set his suffering into some kind of artistic form, it is not easy to follow the train of Jonson's thought here. My guess is that the "days summed up with fears" and the period in which Cary has been "long not lived" is specifically the time that has elapsed between Morison's death and Jonson's poem. A subgenre of mourning poems in the seventeenth century consisted of poems counseling surviving relatives or friends against immoderate mourning; Buckingham's widow seems to have been offered a hatful of them. Such mourning makes days seem years and, as in Donne's "A Nocturnal Upon St Lucy's Day," turns living into a purely negative experience. Jonson's poem, like others of the genre, is aimed at leading the mourner back to a sense of purpose. In this case there is much self-preoccupation too, for the idea of producing "thy . . . miseries" on the stage, with words like "mass" and "swell," is largely self-referential—and this stanza is followed by the images of growing like a tree in bulk and standing long an oak.

Jonson moves himself explicitly into the poem soon after this, straddling stanzas. The initial reference is to Morison (79–89):

> He leapt the present age,
> Possessed with holy rage,

To see that bright eternal day:
Of which we priests, and poets say
Such truths, as we expect for happy men,
And there he lives with memory: and Ben.

THE STAND
Jonson! Who sung this of him, ere he went
Himself to rest,
Or taste a part of that full joy he meant
To have expressed,
In this bright asterism . . .

There is more imaginative use of form and syntax here than in a myriad of Metaphysical shaped poems, especially if we do as Richard Petersen advises and ignore the common emendation which removes the period after "Ben."[9] Jonson, in this movement across stanzas, anticipates the development of the poem, which moves from the great personal friendship of the two young men, signaled in their Christian names Lucius and Henry, to their standing as monuments of virtue for surviving ages as "great surnames / And titles." It also represents Jonson's inclusion and then exclusion. As "Ben" he presides over their lives as he did over all the other sons of Ben, but as "Jonson" he becomes the public poet who transforms the individual into a law for mankind. Something of this movement occurs earlier in the poem, when he corrects himself in recounting Morison's early death (43–47):

Alas, but Morison fell young:
He never fell, thou fall'st my tongue.
He stood, a soldier to the last right end,
A perfect patriot, and a noble friend,
But most a virtuous son.

The correction fits the decorum of the Pindaric ode, with its stress on emotional currents sweeping the poet in different directions. Added to this is some sense of Jonson's own stammering, if his stroke has impaired his speech, so that his mind outruns his tongue. His is a small example of the greater theme, that personal loss must give way to recognition of enduring values. The poem's emphasis on standing, in form as well as in subject, makes Jonson's bedridden state the more pathetic. Morison dead is more alive than the paralyzed Jonson or the immoderately mourning Cary.

By moving from "Ben" to "Jonson" the poem acts out a personal valediction as intimacy retreats into the formality of surnames. "Jonson," who "sung this of him, ere he went / Himself to rest," seems almost to be wishing that this were the last poem he could write. A peaceful glide into death would unite him with this dead son. Instead he is left to straddle life and death, trapped between words and silence as his name lies across the void between stanzas. Morison dead and Cary alive make a comparable couple—fate's alternating design—who act as an example for everyone in the final stanza:

THE STAND
And such a force the fair example had,
As they that saw
The good, and durst not practise it, were glad
That such a law
Was left yet to mankind;
Where they might read, and find
Friendship, in deed, was written, not in words:
And with the heart, not pen,
Of two so early men,
Whose lines her rolls were, and records,
Who, ere the first down bloomed on the chin,
Had sowed these fruits, and got the harvest in.

There are three great oppositions here. Youth and age, with which the poem ends, is the most obvious. Yeats remembered this poem when he mourned Major Robert Gregory and, by implication, started to recount his own sense of aging, recognizing Jonson as his great precursor as the poet of old age. In contrast with Jonson, these young men had lived hardly any longer than the infant of Saguntum, but their circle was already drawn. The second opposition is between the active and the passive, in the curious image of good men who dare not practice goodness being gladdened by the example of these two who dared to do so. The third, between words and silence, is in effect an extension of the second, for activity means deeds over words, inactivity means the pen rather than the heart.

A paragraph in *Discoveries* explores these last two oppositions further:

Good men are the stars, the planets of the ages wherein they live, and illustrate the times. God did never let them be wanting to the world: as Abel, for an example, of innocency; Enoch of purity, Noah of trust in God's mercies, Abraham of faith, and so of the rest. These, sensual men thought mad, because they would not be partakers, or practisers of their madness. But they, placed high on the top of all virtue, looked down on the stage of the world, and contemned the play of fortune. For though the most be players, some must be spectators.[10]

Acting rather than action is the behavior of the majority, the real actors standing aloof, appearing only to be spectators. But the great irony of the stage image here becomes apparent when related to the contemning spectators in Jonson's "Ode to Himself," who sat aloof and mocked *The New Inn.* The parallel points up Jonson's predicament in his last years. Forced into stasis and increasing detachment from the world, and intellectually appreciative of the opportunity it provides for him finally to leave the world to its follies and crimes, his temperament pushes him into greater and greater involvement with it—more words rather than silence. Like an actor who will not get off, but ad-libs to pad out his part, Jonson hears the audience calling for his removal, telling him to leave the stage. Despite all his protestations to the contrary he wants to be a player, not a spectator.

The dramatic figure who comes closest to self-representation in Jonson's last plays is the host of the New Inn, who turns out finally to be the cockbrained Lord Frampul. Before ending up as mine host he had abandoned wife and family and

> measured all the shires of England over:
> Wales and her mountains, seen those wilder nations
> Of people in the Peak and Lancashire;
> Their pipers, fiddlers, rushers, puppet-masters,
> Jugglers, and gipsies, all the sorts of canters,
> And colonies of beggars, tumblers, ape-carriers,
> For to these savages I was addicted,
> To search their natures and make odd discoveries!   (V.v)

Jonson does not explore his motives for doing this—the addiction is a given, in the fashion of the Romance elements of the play—except that some sense of his discontent emerges when he joins with his future son-in-law, Lord Lovel, in mutual dissatisfaction at the degeneration of the times. It is impossible to resist the comparison with Michael Oldisworth's account of a visit to Jonson in 1632:[11]

> His whole Discourse
> Was how Mankind grew daily worse and worse,
> How God was disregarded, how Men went
> Down even to Hell, and never did repent,
> With many such sad Tales . . .

But one suspects that Jonson was having fun acting the part of a tetchy old moralist, and that, like Lord Frampul, his spirit was really out with the jugglers and gypsies.

The most Romantic element of *The New Inn* is the inn itself, its symbolic essence demonstrated in the signs which are explicated at the play's opening and realized in its providing, like Bartholomew Fair, a locus where representatives of the whole of society gather. All who come to the inn are necessarily players and serve the scene—the games played with clothes reinforce this point explicitly—and Jonson's equivalent to the layers of illusion in *A Midsummer Night's Dream* reaches its climax when Lovel rises from his bed to find that all he has dreamed has come about (V.v):

> *Lovel* Is this a dream now, after my first sleep?
> Or are these fantasies made i' the Light Heart?
> And sold i' the new inn?
> *Host*   Best go to bed,
> And dream it all over. Let's all go sleep,
> Each with his turtle.

There is a huge wish fulfillment in this happy ending, but no sentimentality, for Jonson's dream includes a hardheaded appraisal of his own position. When asked a little earlier in the play to define true valor, Lovel states (IV.iii):

> The things true valour is exercised about
> Are poverty, restraint, captivity,
> Banishment, loss of children, long disease:
> The least is death.

As an active man Lovel means that his purpose should be to defend the old, sick, and grieving; but his words are just as applicable to Jonson's passive situation, a counseling of heroic endurance in the face of the tribulations which he lists.

The least may be death, but the problem still lies in the ending. Dreams can be awakened from, and stage plots may be untied in a few lines, as when the host reveals his true identity; but life corresponds to the neatness of art only in the rare case of a Morison. Some sense of life's refusal to end in a fitting way comes through in the host's despair in the opening scene of the last act. He feels as if the action is slipping away from him:

> I had thought to ha' sacrificed
> To merriment tonight, i' my Light Heart, Fly,
> And like a noble poet to have had
> My last act best: but all fails i' the plot.
> Lovel is gone to bed; the Lady Frampul
> And sovereign Pru fallen out: Tipto and his regiment
> Of mine-men all drunk dumb from his whoop, Barnaby,
> To his hoop, Trundle: they are his two tropics.
> No project to rear laughter on but this,
> The marriage of Lord Beaufort with Laetitia.
> Stay! What's here! The satin gown redeemed!
> And Pru restored in't to her lady's grace.

As in all good comedies, the point of greatest despair suddenly turns to lightness and jollity: in the last two lines of his speech the host welcomes the unexpected entrance of Lady Frampul and Pru. Now all moves toward reconciliation. And, as we have seen, the host's dismay that all the lower orders are in a drunken stupor gives way to the dramatist's celebration of their absence, in his epilogue, as a final preservation of decorum, preferring wit to vapors.

Fittingly enough, *Discoveries* closes on a discussion of how to end things properly. Jonson's point is that a well-wrought poem or play begins to end from its opening line. The end of something is not merely its last scene, but an integral part of the whole:

> Now, in every action it behoves the poet to know which is his utmost bound, how far with fitness, and a necessary proportion, he may produce, and determine it. That is, till either good fortune change into the worse, or the worse into the better. For, as a body without proportion cannot be goodly, no more can the action, either the comedy, or tragedy, without his fit bounds. And every bound, for the nature of the subject, is esteemed the best that is largest, till it can increase no more: so it behoves the action in tragedy, or comedy, to be let grow, till the necessity ask a conclusion.[12]

So, by keeping the drunkards offstage throughout the final act of his play Jonson is true to his fable, not sacrificing it to the indecorous demands of an audience whose judgment is warped. The ending of a play is as much a part of that play as any other element of it—no more, no less—and not something which can be tacked on or altered to suit the demands of different audiences. Indeed, one sign of the drama's decline was the growing habit through the 1620s and 1630s of altering the endings of plays, often at royal demand. As the closing paragraph of *Discoveries* has it: "For the whole, as it consisteth of parts; so without all the parts it is not the whole; and to make it absolute, is required, not only the parts, but such parts as are true. For a part of the whole was true; which if you take away, you either change the whole, or it is not the whole." [13]

All of this has a direct relation to Jonson's final years. The very imagery of this discussion in *Discoveries* is as self-referential as anything he wrote elsewhere. Many of its words and phrases might relate equally to Jonson's body or character, such as "a body without proportion," "till it can increase no more," "to be let grow," or the emphasis on *true* in the final paragraph; and this discussion of the "utmost bound of a fable," as Jonson's marginal note describes it, opens with an account of plots in which "either good fortune change into the worse, or the worse into the better." This is a recollection of the very opening of *Discoveries,* where Jonson asserts that "ill fortune never crushed that man, whom good fortune deceived not." For the man, even more than for the dramatist, the difficulty lies in knowing where "necessity ask[s] a conclusion." Given that the old Roman way of finishing an exhausted life was denied to a Christian, Jonson's concern with the rounding off of his life is not simply a matter of knowing when to die—that, after all, can be left confidently to providence—but in knowing when to stop writing, so that the Works exist in their entirety as a complete summation of Ben Jonson, from which nothing can be taken, to which nothing need be added, and whose ending makes the circle whole.

Jonson kept writing up to the last two years of his life, expanding and amplifying the circle, certain that while he kept the center just its proper shape would hold. Poems to Charles I and other members of the royal family alternated with masques, further plays, attacks on Inigo Jones, celebrations of Venetia Digby, and even an epithalamium. This was a tremendous feat of imagination in circumstances which ought to have impelled him toward silence. These poems ring with life, giving the lie to such descriptions of him as "an old poet, struggling with disease and want, wringing plays and entertainments from a jaded and reluctant brain." [14] The definitive poem by which to measure the man is the "Epistle

Mendicant" which he wrote in 1631, "To the Right Honourable, the Lord High Treasurer of England"—Jonson's equivalent to Donne's "Hymn to God My God in my Sickness" (*Underwood* 71):[15]

> MY LORD,
> Poor wretched states, pressed by extremities,
> Are fain to seek for succours and supplies
> Or princes' aids, or good men's charities.
>
> Disease, the enemy, and his engineers,
> Want, with the rest of his concealed compeers,
> Have cast a trench about me, now, five years;
>
> And made those strong approaches, by faussbraies,
> Redoubts, half-moons, horn-works, and such close ways,
> The muse not peeps out one of hundred days;
>
> But lies blocked up and straitened, narrowed in,
> Fixed to the bed and boards, unlike to win
> Health, or scarce breath, as she had never been.
>
> Unless some saving honour of the crown
> Dare think it, to relieve, no less renown
> A bed-rid wit than a besieged town.

Donne's poem is justly celebrated, Jonson's largely ignored. Still, they bear comparison. Both develop their conceit in some detail. Donne's comparison of himself to a map extends through a pun on *straits* into a parallel between oceans flowing into oceans and the poet's journey into the next life. Jonson's poem is an extended metaphor, based on the image of his bedridden self as a city-state under siege by Disease and Want. Donne's poem is a hymn, a form devoted to praise of God, whereas Jonson describes his as an "Epistle Mendicant," that is, a begging letter. In that contrast lies the strength of the Jonson poem. Where Donne's straits are pains and doorways into other worlds, Jonson's are pains and wants, still bound tightly into this world. *Straitened* has its figurative siege-warfare sense—the *OED* lists frequent siege uses—but even this sense lays more and more emphasis on Jonson's literal recumbency. Donne's soul is on the way toward escaping from its body, and notwithstanding its images of pain, sweat, and blood, the hymn is an essentially intellectual and spiritual piece, as if the mind, as the torture intensifies, schools itself into detachment and aloofness, to the point where it can stare down at the body lying flat on its bed. Jonson's body remains stubbornly present and felt in all the pain of the confinement, blockages, and breathless-

ness which he is experiencing. Escape here is not the soul's release from
the body's torment, but release of inspiration into poetic creation. The
sheer pressure of pain prevents the composition of poetry—except that
the poem has got itself written, with its inspiration coming from the pain
and indigence.

The most glorious thing about Jonson's poem is that in spite of its concern with disease and want it nonetheless contrives to be vigorous, vital,
even funny. The extreme formality of its title sets the right context. Here
is an address from the lowest to the highest, but the lowest has an equal
dignity which allows him to cast even this most conventionally unctuous
and self-abasing communication between one man and another, the begging letter, into a subgenre which can be set in the Works alongside examples of the Ode Enthusiastic, the Ode Allegoric, or the Epigram Anniversary. This is very close to self-parody, and the poem never loses hold of
its parodic elements for all its account of the desperation of the poet's
state, right down to the near-dismissive piece of self-description in the
final line, "a bed-rid wit." The effect would have been subtly different if
Jonson had written "poet" instead of "wit," but a wit who is confined to
bed is a rather more comical image, a wit being commonly defined as a
social being, not a private one.

That Jonson should mock himself in the act of begging, and mock, too,
his apparent helplessness, is a valuable balance for the anger which informs many of his later poems. The anger is understandable when one
considers the vulnerability to attack which he seems always to have felt.
Envy was always the greatest vice in his book, worse than greed, pride,
or impiety, because it always leads to one person's—or many's—attack
upon another. Compared with envious people, mere confidence tricksters
or cutpurses are innocuous. Confined as he now was, fixed to the bed and
boards, Jonson was more than ever vulnerable to the envious, a sitting
duck rather than a moving target. This is why the siege image works so
well, because although the besiegers are abstractions, Disease and Want,
"the rest of his . . . compeers" lets in the picture of the poet in his room
being actively undermined, bombarded, and assaulted by the many human enemies whom, in his more vigorous times, he had been able to fend
off. Their aim is annihilation, reducing him to a state as if he had never
been.

The best-known example of such an attack was the assault upon *The
New Inn,* at which, according to Jonson's retaliatory ode, the hostile
Bankside audience had jeered to the point where it could not be acted
properly.[16] There is also a second epilogue, "but the play lived not in
opinion, to have it spoken." [17] From it we may deduce that the audience
jeered most at Jonson's effort to give the lady's maid, then called Cicely—

later changed to the potentially symbolic, and therefore more defensible, Prudence—the governing role of the play:

> A jovial host and lord of the new inn
>> Cleped the Light Heart, with all that passed therein,
> Hath been the subject of our play tonight,
>> To give the King and Queen and Court delight:
> But then we mean the Court above the stairs,
>> And past the guard; men that have more of ears
> Than eyes to judge us: such as will not hiss
>> Because the chambermaid was named Cis.

The painful imagining of an audience's derisive hissing goes right back to the induction to *The Poetaster,* where Envy, the spokesman for Jonson's antagonists, opens the play by thrusting snakes at his audience as a kind of mirror image of their contempt for the dramatist and his works (44–55):

> Here, take my snakes among you, come and eat,
> And, while the squeezed juice flows in your black jaws,
> Help me to damn the author. Spit it forth
> Upon his lines and show your rusty teeth
> At every word or accent; or else choose
> Out my longest vipers, to stick down
> In your deep throats, and let the heads come forth
> At your rank mouths, that he may see you armed
> With triple malice, to hiss, sting and tear
> His work and him; to forge, and then declaim,
> Traduce, corrupt, apply, inform, suggest:
> O, these are gifts wherein your souls are blessed.

This is a preemptive strike, Jonson hissing at his audience before they can do so at him. As Envy somewhat disappointedly says (56–58):

> What, do you hide yourselves? Will none appear,
> None answer? What, doth this calm troop affright you?
> Nay, then I do despair . . .

To be sure that his audience had been silenced Jonson's actor may have used real snakes here in as threatening a manner as possible, so that "this calm troop" is heavily ironic.

When the prophet Jeremiah comes to the city of Jerusalem, he connects the sound of hissing to the want and suffering brought about by the Babylonian siege it must undergo (19:8–9):

> And I will make this city desolate, and an hissing, so that every one that passeth thereby, shall be astonished and hiss because of all the plagues thereof.
> And I will feed them with the flesh of their sons, and with the flesh of their daughters, and every one shall eat the flesh of his friend in the siege and straitness, wherewith their enemies, that seek their lives shall hold them strait.   (Geneva Version)

If these verses were in Jonson's mind when he wrote his "Epistle Mendicant" and the second epilogue to *The New Inn*, then they point to a political parallel for his personal predicament. Jeremiah is the prophet of siege, factionalism, and civil war—and, eventually, imprisonment. Poetic versions of his lamentations were popular in the first half of the century. They were related most directly to the torments endured on the Continent in the Thirty Years' War, but they provided an increasingly relevant imagery for events closer to home, as in Donne's version (chapter 2, stanzas 15–16):

> The passengers do clap their hands, and hiss,
>   And wag their head at thee, and say, Is this
> That city, which so many men did call
>   Joy of the earth, and perfectest of all?
>
> Thy foes do gape upon thee, and they hiss,
>   And gnash their teeth, and say, "Devour we this,
> For this is certainly the day which we
>   Expected, and which now we find and see."

The derisive hiss emanating from England's chief city was aimed, ultimately, after the removal of men such as Buckingham and Strafford, at the king. Hissing is a peculiarly powerful image for Jonson because he had always preferred the ear above the eye. Other animal noises fit the bill too. There are the buzzing hornets and screaming grasshoppers described in the "Apologetical Dialogue" to *The Poetaster*; Inigo Jones, the ultimate traducer of the spoken word, is portrayed as a braying ass, and there is probably a play on *false brays* in the "faussebraies" of the "Epistle Mendicant"; and Alexander Gill's attack on *The Magnetic Lady* is described as a dog's barking.[18] But the snake's unique malevolence comes from its mixture of derisive noise, venomous bite, and ability to creep into the holiest places of all. Jonson's "Ode to Himself" ends with a triumphant prophecy that he will leave the stage and turn to singing the glories of his king, to the discomfiture of his—and the king's—enemies:

> Leave things so prostitute,
> And take the Alcaic lute;
> Or thine own Horace, or Anacreon's lyre;
> Warm thee by Pindar's fire:
> And though thy nerves be shrunk, and blood be cold,
> Ere years have made thee old,
> Strike that disdainful heat
> Throughout, to their defeat:
> As curious fools, and envious of thy strain,
> May blushing swear, no palsy's in thy brain.
>
> But when they hear thee sing
> The glories of thy king;
> His zeal to God, and his just awe of men,
> They may be blood-shaken, then
> Feel such a flesh-quake to possess their powers,
> That no tuned harp like ours,
> In sound of peace or wars,
> Shall truly hit the stars
> When they shall read the acts of Charles his reign,
> And see his chariot triumph 'bove his wain.

In the second epilogue to *The New Inn* this movement is more tentatively described, almost in the terms of a military retreat rather than in terms of a move to higher things. The height is not, as here, among the stars, but up into a *sanctum sanctorum,* "the Court above the stairs, / And past the guard," where there are still "men that have more of ears / Than eyes to judge us."

But even there, in the privy chamber, the snake can penetrate. "The Humble Petition of Poor Ben to the Best of Monarchs, Masters, Men, King Charles" (*Underwood* 76) starts as a jolly, almost Skeltonic, reminder to Charles that it is the duty of kings to reward good poets (1–22):

> . . . Doth most humbly show it,
> To your majesty your poet:
>
> That whereas your royal father,
> James the blessed, pleased the rather,

Of his special grace to letters,
To make all the muses debtors
To his bounty; by extension
Of a free poetic pension,
A large hundred marks annuity,
To be given me in gratuity
For done service, and to come:
    And that this so accepted sum,
Or dispensed in books, or bread,
(For with both the muse was fed)
Hath drawn on me, from the times,
All the envy of the rhymes,
And the rattling pit-pat noise,
Of the less-poetic boys;
When their pot-guns aim to hit,
With their pellets of small wit,
Parts of me (they judged) decayed,
But we last out, still unlaid.

For all the poem's apparent lightness, some of Jonson's most heartfelt themes crowd in here—want, and its relief; the king's need for a poet being as great as a poet's need for the king's support; opposition of the envious, with their derisive noise; and the triumphant assertion of his own vigor and life in spite of all contrary appearances. *Still unlaid* is usually glossed according to the *OED*'s tentative definition: "?laid out (as a corpse); laid in the grave." But this is the only example given, and I prefer the hint of grim self-mockery which would come from the more common meaning, "unexorcised"—as in Shakespeare's "ghost unlaid forbear thee."

    This is not a poem which has enjoyed much critical esteem, but it is worth recognising that Jonson thought it merited inclusion in *The Underwood,* a poem "of lesser growth" admittedly, but still an estimable part of the corpus which he wished to preserve. So, perhaps the apparently trivial verse form—octosyllabic couplets declining into septisyllabics—is meant to signify the poet's impoverishment and, hence, his straitened inspiration. But Charles should be reminded that he still needs his poet's services. The poem ends not so much Skeltonically as satanically, with the hissing of the envious (23–30):

    Please your majesty to make
Of your grace, for goodness sake,

Those your father's marks, your pounds;
Let their spite (which now abounds)
Then go on, and do its worst;
This would all their envy burst:
And so warm the poet's tongue
Youl'd read a snake, in his next song.

These lines are commonly taken to refer to Aesop's fable of the farmer who warmed a frozen snake back to life by putting it into his bosom, only to have it bite him. There are problems with this, as Ian Donaldson's note explains: "Charles is evidently being warned that it is dangerous to tolerate one of Jonson's rivals, though the point is clumsily made: Jonson forgets that he has already rendered Martial's *invidus* (= jealous man) by a plural."[19]

Tying the poem to the Martial epigram on which it is based would introduce the idea of a rival poet, but Jonson did not often make the kind of mistake he is accused of here, even in his dotage. It might be that the poet is the same one as in the rest of the poem, namely Jonson himself. Charles will need a snake to hiss back at his detractors, and keeping Jonson warm and alive will offer him such protection.

Commentators usually describe these begging poems in a way flattering to the petitionees, with a note to the effect that the poet's request was granted. Still, there is one hint that it was as much a politic as a humane gesture on their part: adding Jonson to the mounting list of articulate opponents would not have been wise. John Aubrey's notes on Jonson include the cryptic comment "v. None-such-Charles. when B.J. was dyeing. K.Ch: sent him but xii."[20] *The None-Such Charles his Character* was an anonymous work published in 1651, which included this anecdote: "Now men may see, how much reason *Ben. Jonson* had, when as, lying sicke in his bed, very poore, and that after much importunity of courtiers, ten pounds were sent to him by the King, after the receit of which, *Ben.* threw them through the glasse windowes, saying, *this mans soule was not fit to live in an alley.*"[21]

6 A Justly Suspected Easiness: Reading Shakespeare

Who says this?

> The things true valour is exercised about
> Are poverty, restraint, captivity,
> Banishment, loss of children, long disease:
> The least is death. Here valour is beheld,
> Properly seen; about these it is present:
> Not trivial things which but require our confidence.

The speaker is Lord Lovel in *The New Inn* (IV.iii), so it is tempting to interpret the lines as Jonson's own definition of true valor. They come close to home, for perhaps only banishment in the list of afflictions is not directly relevant to his own experience at the time he wrote them. But even if we ignore the biographical relevance the lines are still worth requoting for the sense they offer of an alternative Jonson to the model presented in the *Epigrams, The Forest,* or *The Underwood.* This is blank verse, whereas every poem which Jonson wrote is in rhyme, even the one which attacks rhyme. As its title "A Fit of Rhyme Against Rhyme" confesses, the more angry rhyme makes him, the more confined by it he becomes—note the play on *fit* in the title and line 2 (*Underwood* 29):

> Rhyme, the rack of finest wits,
> That expresseth but by fits,
> > True conceit,
> Spoiling senses of their treasure,
> Cozening judgment with a measure,
> > But false weight.
> Wresting words, from their true calling;

> Propping verse, for fear of falling
>   To the ground.
> Jointing syllabes, drowning letters,
> Fastening vowels, as with fetters
>   They were bound . . .

Here, of course, Jonson was playfully engaging in the debate begun by Campion and Daniel in their respective attack on and defense of rhyme. Jonson told Drummond that he disagreed with both of them. Apart from couplets "he detesteth all other rhymes." [1] The debate continued through the century, with Dryden finally settling it all in favor of the heroic couplet; but the best-known document on the way was Milton's attack on rhyme as a barbarism in his foreword on "the Verse" for the second edition of *Paradise Lost*.

Milton could well have written the lines from *The New Inn* with which this chapter opened. We are so used to tracing the influence of Spenser and Shakespeare upon him that we have tended to ignore the Jonsonian elements. And yet if we were to look for a model for the strenuous blank verse of his mature epic writing those lines would not be a bad place to start: not only the language—particularly words such as "exercised," "restraint," "least," and "confidence"—but also the compression of the list running from "poverty" to "disease," and, most of all, the sentiment itself. All are potentially Miltonic: actually so, if we change "valour" to *virtue* or *fortitude*.

It is not unreasonable to guess that Milton might have seen *The New Inn*. If the play was performed at the Blackfriars Theatre soon after it was licensed in March 1629, then Milton, home from Cambridge after having graduated in the same month, could well have attended this fashionable theater, not far from his Cheapside home, with his old school friend Alexander Gill. Gill, the son of his headmaster at St. Paul's, was not strictly a peer of Milton's, being twelve years older. He had been one of the wild men about town, most notoriously in the scrape which got him hauled before the Star Chamber and nearly led to the loss of his ears. It began with Gill's drinking a toast to Buckingham's assassin in Oxford in 1628 and reached its most dangerous point when the authorities discovered anti-Charles and anti-Buckingham verses in his lodgings. For this he was fined £2,000 and sentenced to have one ear amputated in Oxford, the other in London. After intercession by influential friends of his father, his ears were left attached to his head and the fine mitigated. The signs are that after this shock Gill turned to softer targets for his satirical wit, notably the paralyzed Ben Jonson.

Gibing at Jonson would have put Gill in good, fashionable company and been relatively safe—hence his attack on *The Magnetic Lady,* performed at Blackfriars in 1632. Jonson's play he describes as "the child of your bed-ridden wit": it should have been performed to hoi polloi at the Fortune rather than to the discerning audience of Blackfriars, and Jonson ought to go back to work as a bricklayer because he has not the capacity to satisfy "this strict age." Gill ends his poem with a contemptuous reference to Jonson's resolution in his "Ode to Himself" to "leave the loathed stage":[2]

> Fall then to work in thy old age again,
> Take up thy trudge and trowel, gentle Ben,
> Let plays alone: or if thou needs will write,
> And thrust thy feeble muse into the light;
> Let Lowen cease, and Taylor scorn to touch
> The loathed stage, for thou hast made it such.

Jonson did not treat this with the silent contempt it deserved. Instead he took the opportunity to remind Gill of his luck in keeping his ears, made a couple of swipes at Gill's father on the way, and showed in the compression of his final couplet that it was still dangerous to bait this old bear:[3]

An Answer to Alexander Gill

> Shall the prosperity of a pardon still
> Secure thy railing rhymes, infamous Gill,
> At libelling? Shall no Star Chamber peers,
> Pillory, nor whip, nor want of ears,
> All which thou hast incurred deservedly;
> Nor degradation from the ministry,
> To be the Denis of thy father's school,
> Keep in thy barking wit, thou bawling fool?
> Thinking to stir me, thou hast lost thy end;
> I'll laugh at thee, poor wretched tyke; go send
> Thy blatant muse abroad, and teach it rather
> A tune to drown the ballads of thy father:
> For thou has naught in thee to cure his fame,
> But tune and noise, the echo of his shame.
> A rogue by statute, censured to be whipped,
> Cropped, branded, slit, neck-stocked; go, you are stripped.

All of this is relatively trivial, except to show how vicious the infighting of literary London could be, and to give one example of the hostile forces which laid siege to Jonson. But it also gives a context for Milton's one specific reference to Jonson, in "L'Allegro." There is no way of dating this poem with any precision; best guesses put it somewhere around 1631, and it may well be that Milton would not have favored Jonson with such a mention after the insults aimed at Gill junior and senior, although it is worth remembering that Jonson's enmity toward the father went back to the 1620s. Still, Milton's perfect summer's day ends with a trip to the theater, with an enviable choice between a Jonsonian or Shakespearean comedy (129–134):[4]

> . . . Such sights as youthful poets dream
> On summer eves by haunted stream.
> Then to the well-trod stage anon,
> If Jonson's learned sock be on,
> Or sweetest Shakespeare fancy's child,
> Warble his native wood-notes wild . . .

This well-known and often-repeated tribute to Shakespeare's naturalness should not entirely obscure the compliment paid to Jonson with the epithet "learned." It was more than Milton was prepared to offer his Cambridge tutors, and Jonson would certainly have been pleased with it. In many ways these lines set the agenda for posterity's view of our two greatest dramatists, one the poet of nature, the other the spokesman for classical values.

But we should emphasize Milton's pairing of Jonson and Shakespeare, rather than the contrast, and praise the young man for having made so exactly right a choice, in spite of fashion and possible personal prejudices. Jonson, as we have seen, was being hooted off the stage, regarded by such intellectuals as Gill as being too rude for the new, polished age. Shakespeare was, apparently, a fading name. Bentley's *Jacobean and Caroline Stage* lists only sixteen productions of his plays between 1616 and the closure of the theaters, compared with fifty by Beaumont and Fletcher. The poet of "L'Allegro," though only in his early twenties, is either a nostalgia buff, taking delight in swimming against the tide, or a truly perceptive student of dramatic poetry who recognizes what has enduring value—or both.

That Milton had, or had access to, a Shakespeare Folio is probable, given the intimate knowledge of his plays and poems which his own poems, from *Comus* onward, demonstrates. That he also had a copy of

Jonson's works, if not the *Works* itself, is likely, for while Milton's editor lists thirty-two "indisputable echoes" of Shakespeare in the masque, Jonson comes third on the list, after Sylvester, with seven. It was never a possibility that Milton would have become one of the sons of Ben, any more than he could have become a Metaphysical poet, but the signs are that he was more attracted by the Jonsonian mode than by Donne's example. As well as *Comus* and "Arcades" there is the "Epitaph on the Marchioness of Winchester" to show that the young Milton was preparing to move into Jonson's territory—indeed, Milton's poem is better than Jonson's lame piece on the death of the same lady. Milton's control over his couplets, varying between octosyllabics and septisyllabics, matches the best of Jonson's octosyllabic epitaphs in *The Underwood*. It surpasses them, in fact, in the daring way it switches from the third person funerary register—"This rich marble doth inter / The honoured wife of Winchester"—to the intimacy of direct address—"Gentle lady may thy grave / Peace and quiet ever have."

Milton's epitaph was probably written soon after the marchioness's death in April 1631 and may have been intended for a proposed volume of Cambridge elegies, in the fashion of *Lycidas* six years later. No such volume appeared, and Milton's first published poem had to wait another year. This was his tribute to Shakespeare, which was printed anonymously among the preliminary matter of the Shakespeare Second Folio. There it was titled "An Epitaph on the admirable Dramatic Poet, W. Shakespeare." In the 1640 Folio it was again printed, this time over Milton's initials; and then it appeared in his own 1645 volume, where he gave it a new title and added the date of composition:

On Shakespeare. 1630

What needs my Shakespeare for his honoured bones,
The labour of an age in piled stones,
Or that his hallowed relics should be hid
Under a star-ypointing pyramid?
Dear son of memory, great heir of fame,
What need'st thou such weak witness of thy name?
Thou in our wonder and astonishment
Hast built thyself a live-long monument.
For whilst to the shame of slow-endeavouring art,
Thy easy numbers flow, and that each heart
Hath from the leaves of thy unvalued book,
Those Delphic lines with deep impression took,

> Then thou our fancy of itself bereaving,
> Dost make us marble with too much conceiving;
> And so sepulchred in such pomp dost lie,
> That kings for such a tomb would wish to die.

Though an epitaph, the mode of this poem is a little closer to Donne than to Jonson, its couplet structure being overridden in the second half by the living monument conceit. The syntax runs across the lines and makes the gradually weakening rhymes seem even fainter. There was good cause to avoid the Jonsonian example in such a poem: at the head of the Second Folio, as it had been at the head of the First, was Jonson's magisterial epitaph on Shakespeare, "To the Memory of My Beloved, the Author, Mr William Shakespeare, and What he hath Left Us."

Since Dryden there has been a tendency to depreciate Jonson's poem, either as a mistaken effort to remold Shakespeare in Jonson's own image or, less charitably, to see it as a piece of sustained irony. Both responses go back eventually to the palpable contrast between Jonson's frequent comments on Shakespeare's unhealthy facility and the poem's emphasis upon the hard work which Shakespeare must have put in to achieve the effects he did. The charge of irony is hard to refute once it has been posited; I can only say that those who believe that Jonson's poem is meant ironically must have tin ears (excluding Dryden: he had other reasons for attacking the poem). I cannot imagine the lines on the muses' anvil being read in anything other than a strenuous and wholly committed way, as Jonson bends and shapes the syntax in imitation of the effort involved in writing a living line (55–70):

> Yet must I not give nature all: thy art,
> My gentle Shakespeare, must enjoy a part.
> For though the poet's matter, nature be,
> His art doth give a fashion. And, that he,
> Who casts to write a living line, must sweat,
> (Such as thine are) and strike the second heat
> Upon the muses' anvil: turn the same,
> (And himself with it) that he thinks to frame;
> Or for the laurel, he may gain a scorn,
> For a good poet's made, as well as born.
> And such wert thou. Look how the father's face
> Lives in his issue, even so, the race
> Of Shakespeare's mind, and manners brightly shines
> In his well-turned, and true-filed lines:

> In each of which, he seems to shake a lance,
> As brandished at the eyes of ignorance.

There is nothing degrading in the *shake spear / shake lance* pun, any more than Donne's punning on his own name degrades what God has done with him; and the image is wholly consistent with what leads up to it. All of the hammering on the anvil and twisting, turning, and shaping the steel results finally in the making of something as clean and straight as a spear. Jonson's editors quote the lance brandished in the face of ignorance as an example of Jonson's painting Shakespeare in his own image.[5] I would suggest that this reaction amounts to a curious disregard for the large amount of learning which Shakespeare put into his plays, enough to keep the academic factories working for years. Jonson's point, borne out by the reams of commentary upon him, to which no end is ever in sight, is that the right epithet for Shakespeare is "learned." That we still prefer to see him as fancy's child says more about the partiality of our view of Shakespeare than about Jonson's judgment in this poem. Our partial view, to be fair, is partly Jonson's doing. It goes back to his earlier comments about Shakespeare's fluency; to Heming and Condell's statement in their preface to the First Folio that he wrote as he thought, "with that easinesse, that wee have scarce received from him a blot in his papers"; and to Milton's reference to him in "L'Allegro" and, most of all, to Milton's poem describing how his "easy numbers" flow.

In praising Shakespeare's easy numbers Milton was setting him against the whole Jonsonian ethos. In *Discoveries* Jonson advised aspiring writers not to trust their first thoughts, but to choose carefully the words they use: "no matter how slow the style be at first, so it be laboured and accurate." Ease in writing should always be distrusted: "the safest is to return to our judgment, and handle over again those things, the easiness of which might make them justly suspected."[6] These are purely literary directions, but words such as "safest" and "justly suspected" might alert us to the political implications which underlie any discussion of style in the 1620s and 1630s.

If you think this is going too far, then a useful corrective would be a reading of *The English Grammar*, which Jonson wrote during his bed-ridden period. As an example of a pioneering attempt to describe and classify the elements of English it is an admirably scientific piece. But read in another way, with concentration on the illustrations which Jonson offers, it is halfway to becoming a political document. In the first book the examples of letters, words, and conjugations seem haphazard enough, but in the second most of the illustrations of syntactic paradigms are taken from sources with contemporary relevance. They begin with quotations of personal significance, rather as *Discoveries* begins with the plunge from good to evil fortune. Showing how a "vowel may be cast away, when the word next following beginneth with another," Jonson cites:[7]

> Th'outward man decayeth:
> So th'inward man getteth strength.
>
> If ye'utter such words of pure love, and friendship,
> What then may we look for, if ye'once begin to hate?

And in showing how vowels "suffer also this *Apostrophus* before the consonant *h*," he quotes from Chaucer's *Troilus and Criseyde*:

> For of Fortune's sharp adversity,
> The worst kind of infortune is this:
> A man to'have been in prosperity,
> And it remember when it passed is.

It then becomes increasingly difficult not to perceive a political purpose in the chosen quotations. For example, illustrating how "two singulars are put for one plural": "All *Authority*, and *Custom* of men, exalted against the word of God, must yield *themselves* prisoners."[8] Or, showing how *that* is used "for a Relative": "Sedition is an Aposteme, which, when it breaketh inwardly, putteth the State in great danger of Recovery; and corrupteth the whole Commonwealth, with the rotten fury, *that* it hath putrefied with."[9] Or, as an example of how the verb governing another verb may be understood: "For if the head, which is the life, and stay of the body, betray the members, must not the members also needs betray one another; and so the whole body, and head go altogether to utter wreck, and destruction?"[10] It is not surprising, then, to find the *Grammar* closing with an extended quotation from Sir John Cheke, calling for wise magistrates to impose martial law when the populace gets out of order.

If even such a thing as an elided vowel can be given a political context, then how much more can the opposition of ease and labor. While Shakespeare was alive Jonson had been content to see himself as the laborer, wrestling with words to achieve hard-won results, while Shakespeare, dashing off whatever came into his head, picked up easy rewards. The consolation was that it would be Jonson's works which would last forever. But after Shakespeare's death Jonson's view changed, and although his ode still praises Shakespeare's naturalness, it sets this praise within the realization that such apparent ease could only have been the result of great effort.

There is a genuine revaluation involved here, Jonson now accepting Shakespeare as his equal. His prologue to the poem (lines 1–16) carefully makes this clear. He begins by asserting that he is right for the task which Heming and Condell have set him. His poem is to have pride of place in the volume, put there for its instructional value for potential readers of the plays. The editors write in their preface "To the Great Variety of Readers" that Shakespeare should be read "again and again," and if the reader does not like what he reads, then he must be "in some manifest danger, not to understand him." Their preface closes with this advice: "And so we leave you to other of his Friends, whom if you need, can bee your guides: if you neede them not, you can leade your selves, and others." Jonson's poem follows straight after, as the first and foremost of the guides.

Its opening lines make a characteristic Jonsonian movement, the sweeping away of envy:

> To draw no envy (Shakespeare) on thy name,
> Am I thus ample to thy book, and fame . . .

Here is his first qualification for interpreting Shakespeare for us. He is fat enough not to be considered an envious person who will maliciously distort a rival's words—Jonson returned to this theme in one of his attacks on Inigo Jones: "I am too fat to envy him. He too lean / To be worth envy." [11] Other qualifications follow. He is neither ignorant nor blindly affectionate nor malicious (5–12):

> But these ways
> Were not the paths I meant unto thy praise:
> For seeliest ignorance on these may light,
> Which, when it sounds at best, but echoes right;
> Or blind affection, which doth ne'er advance
> The truth, but gropes, and urgeth all by chance;
> Or crafty malice, might pretend this praise,
> And think to ruin where it seemed to raise.

These are the credentials which clear him of any ill intention or failure to understand, and the ode proper begins by praising Shakespeare the dramatist, using the same "age" / "stage" rhyme which opens his "Ode on Himself" (17–18):

> I therefore will begin. Soul of the age!
> The applause, delight, the wonder of our stage!

And it ends with another rhyme for "stage" as Jonson closes his celebration of Shakespeare's achievement with his familiar theme of the stage's decline (77–80):

> Shine forth, thou star of poets, and with rage,
> Or influence, chide, or cheer the drooping stage;
> Which, since thy flight from hence, hath mourned like night.
> And despairs day, but for thy volume's light.

"Rage," the new rhyme for "stage," is the classic term for the frenzy of poetic creation, completing Jonson's careful balance through the poem between inspiration and effort. It was an ideal glanced at in the little poem which he wrote to describe the engraver's success, or lack of it, in drawing Shakespeare's portrait for the Folio.

Milton's redating of his poem to 1630 may be significant: perhaps a denial that it was meant to be read in any other context than an uncommissioned piece of inspired praise for the dead poet. But even though it was not written specially for the Second Folio, Milton surely composed it in full knowledge of Jonson's ode. How he contrived to get it included in the preliminary material of the Folio is a matter for speculation, but in doing so Milton ensured, as one of the "other friends" of Shakespeare, that his appreciation would be set against Jonson's. As with the epitaphs on the Marchioness of Winchester, there was some element of rivalry, in spite of the great difference in their ages. There did not have to be. Had Milton been a keen son of Ben, a Robert Herrick, for instance, he might merely have repeated what Jonson had already said. And to begin with it seems as if he is going to do so. That Shakespeare does not need "the labour of an age in piled stones" and that his "live-long monument" is "our wonder and astonishment" seem only elaborations of these lines from Jonson's ode (22–24):

> Thou art a monument, without a tomb,
> And art alive still, while thy book doth live,
> And we have wits to read, and praise to give.

But from the point where Milton praises Shakespeare's "easy numbers," opposing them to "the shame of slow-endeavouring art," the challenge is offered to Jonson's vision of Shakespeare as an artist who labored hard for what he achieved.

At bottom there are cultural, even political, implications in the opposition between easy and labored writing. When the argument to the October eclogue of Spenser's *Shepheardes Calender* described Cuddie's poetic rage, it introduced into the English cultural vocabulary the word *enthusiasm,* albeit still in its Greek form. The word soon burst its literary-critical banks and became one of the key terms for describing Puritan claims to be channels for the divine word. Not the least of the lessons which Milton learned from his sage and serious master was a belief in the primacy of inspiration over any other claim to poetic authority. It begins in this celebration of Shakespeare's easiness, and culminates in the last of the invocations in *Paradise Lost,* in the plea for an answerable style from the muse who "inspires / Easy my unpremeditated verse" (9:23–24). The connection between the two becomes all the tighter when we take into consideration, too, the idea that in calling him a "son of memory" Milton makes Shakespeare a brother of the muses, in effect a source of his own inspiration. At the least, Milton appropriates Shakespeare to a Puritan view of inspired expression, the flat contrary to Jonson's balanced praise.

The irony is that at the time he wrote the poem nothing could have been further from Milton's own experience. If by 1667 he could describe his own verse as easy and unpremeditated, this was only after more than thirty years of effort. "Slow-endeavouring art" is only one of many such formulations in his early writings, but nearly all are self-referential. In the seventh Prolusion he speaks of his desire "to strive earnestly after a true reputation by long and severe toil, rather than to snatch a false reputation by a hurried and premature mode of expression";[12] in the "Elegia Sexta," written in 1629, he opposes to the lightness of elegiac poetry the long preparation needed by the heroic poet which he intends to be, just as "Il Penseroso" presents a truer self-image in the student reading far into the night than the summer-inspired poet of "L'Allegro"; and *Lycidas,* famously, opens with yet one more confession that he is too little prepared to undertake the task in hand, the words being forced from him before they are ripe to emerge. The great attraction of his Shakespeare poem comes, in this context, from the self-excoriation of the living monument conceit.

Another way in which Milton's praise differs from Jonson's—and from most of the other commendatory poems in the Folio—is that it ignores Shakespeare's role as a dramatist and treats him only as a poet, very much in the spirit of Heming and Condell's advice to read him again and again. Reading other poets is an important part of Jonson's education of the aspiring poet: "to read the best authors" is the first of his "three necessaries" for a man to write well.[13] While it is possible to argue for this as one way of finding inspiration, it is not the recommended route to enthusiasm, where the only text to rely on would be the divinely inspired one. Some Puritan sects went further and rejected all reading as an obstacle to speaking in tongues.[14] Milton, who lived for and in books, could never have accepted such a philosophy, but the Shakespeare poem more than hints at a suspicion that there may be something to it. The "live-long monument" is, it turns out, the reader of Shakespeare:

> Thou in our wonder and astonishment
> Hast built thyself a live-long monument.
> For whilst to the shame of slow-endeavouring art,
> Thy easy numbers flow, and that each heart
> Hath from the leaves of thy unvalued book,
> Those Delphic lines with deep impression took,
> Then thou our fancy of itself bereaving,
> Dost make us marble with too much conceiving . . .

Not just any reader of Shakespeare is described here but, more particularly, the poet who reads him. "Live-long monument" is an interesting phrase, deriving ultimately from Horace's "Exegi monumentum aere perennius" (3:30) by way of dozens, if not hundreds, of Latin and English poems. "Live-long" gives it a new twist. *Livelong* before Milton used it was simply, as the *OED* defines it, "an emotional intensive of *long,* used of periods of time." By applying it to a monument rather than a period of time Milton gives new life to the cliché. The *OED* defines its appearance here as a nonce use, meaning "that lives long or endures; lasting"; but if we allow it its adjectival rather than substantival pronunciation, then it also means "life-long."

That the paralysis induced by reading Shakespeare might last one's whole life is the fear behind Milton's poem. In "L'Allegro" Shakespeare is the child of fancy. Here he bereaves the reader of his own fancy and turns him into marble with too much conceiving. So many ideas come into the poet's mind as he reads Shakespeare that his imagination stifles itself in the throng of conceits generated by the great original. There is a procreation image here too, the reader taking the feminine role as he is made to conceive by Shakespeare; but the conception ends in stillbirth, like the Marchioness of Winchester, in the next poem Milton wrote, who died in childbirth, made marble by too much conceiving. The fear is of complete possession, for to become Shakespeare's monument is to become not a pile of stones or a pyramid, but an image of Shakespeare himself, sitting on top of his tomb, with all of one's own identity lost.

Jonson and Milton both write of "my Shakespeare." Jonson can do so because he loved him this side of idolatry. Ample enough to praise without adoration, he had overcome the fears of envious rivalry. Like Cary, forced to live on after the death of Morison, he knows that the two of them together will shine on future ages as a bright asterism. Milton's Shakespeare is, in contrast, a god, the poem not one by an equal, but from the next generation, by a son of Will not ready yet to challenge the father's influence but haunted by his example. In any history of bardolatry "On Shakespeare" must be a prime document, and although it opens with a claim to possession of Shakespeare, it closes the opposite way, in the fear that Shakespeare has possessed him, and will possess generations of poets.

Perhaps this accounts for the grudging attitude with which Milton later regarded his Shakespeare, for although his poetry kept on echoing him—it is impossible to think of the Satan of *Paradise Lost* without remembering Macbeth and Richard III—after "On Shakespeare" and "L'Allegro" he allowed him no further acknowledgment, only implied disdain, as in the account of tragedy which he fixed to the beginning of *Samson Agonistes,* where he traced the deterioration of the form's standing down to the infamy it had incurred through modern poets' "error of intermixing comic stuff with tragic sadness and gravity." [15]

He did use Shakespeare's name once more, with reference to another reader who, confined to his closet, perhaps had his paralysis of will intensified by thinking too much about the conceits which Shakespeare's plays fed into his imagination. This reader was Charles I. The context is Milton's refutation of *Eikon Basilike's* efforts to make him seem a pious victim of persecution:

> the Poets also, and som English, have bin in this point so mindfull of *Decorum,* as to put never more pious words in the mouth of any person, then of a Tyrant. I shall not instance an abstruse Author . . . but one whom wee well know was the Closet Companion of these his solitudes, *William Shakespeare;* who introduces the Person of *Richard* the third, speaking in as high a strain of pietie, and mortification, as is uttered in any passage of this Book. [16]

PART THREE

Life and Death

7 "You Never Saw Thing Made of Wood So Fine": Ships and the Sea

In many accounts of the rise of Cromwell and militant Puritanism we hear much about the New Model Army, little of the navy; and yet it, too, was remodeled. When the Civil War broke out Charles had only 42 ships under his command. At the Restoration the navy consisted of 154 ships. In spite of this fourfold increase, total tonnage had risen only from 22,400 to 57,400.[1] The new model, then, was more, lighter, and faster.

Underpinning the religious differences which led to war were powerful economic strains, not least the general and sustained resistance to the paying of ship money, culminating in the trial of John Hampden in 1637. Later in the same year, in October, the most extreme example of Charles's desire for naval aggrandizement was launched, the great flagship the *Sovereign of the Seas*. At 1,637 tons it was more than double the size of the English flagship when the Armada was defeated. As another measure of comparison, the *Mayflower* was 180 tons.

That England's navy was inadequate to protect its growing, ever-outward-spreading merchant fleet was obvious to all. Charles's pretext for ship money was to protect English merchantmen against pirates' depredations. His greater interest, guessed by many, was to keep his side of secret treaties with Spain, made against the Dutch. In neither case, however, was something as large as the *Sovereign* likely to be of much practical help. To the hardheaded merchant class it represented yet another example of Stuart ostentation.

Naturally enough, the poets weighed in, trying at this late stage to argue that excessive royal expenditure was no bad thing if the grudging populace would only appreciate its symbolic value. Richard Fanshawe wrote his poem on the *Sovereign* while it was still under construction. He could hardly have chosen a more tactless opening than his apostrophizing the vessel as "Escurial of the Sea," given the suspicions of collusion with

The *Sovereign of the Seas* soon after launching. Ornately carved all over and with cannon of brass, she cost six times as much as a normal great ship. After a cruise of twenty-four days she was laid up for fifteen years as "a great charge

Spain. Then, in scouting possible names for the ship, after suggesting Charlemagne, he offers the possibility of calling it Edgar, in memory of "that warlike king" during whose reign Britain stood "bright 'mongst neighb'ring crowns." Edgar's custom was to circumnavigate his land once a year, and he once steered a galley rowed by tributary kings toward Chester church (49–56):[2]

> It did both seal his claim, and represent
> The image of a perfect Government,
> *Where, sitting at the helm the Monarch steers,*
> *The Oars are laboured by the active Peers,*
> *And all the People distributed are*
> *In other offices of Peace and War.*
> Whilst he that in the Common-wealth doth bear
> No calling, is the Sea-sick passenger.

Puritan propaganda laid special claim to pre-Conquest England, so Fanshawe's suggestion of making Charles a second Edgar represents a kind of restoration of the continuity of English history; but his symbolic image of a perfect government recognizes that there is a subclass that does not fit into the commonwealth—those with no calling, who are as useful as seasick passengers. More pedantic readers might point out also that Fanshawe's image works for a galley but not for a ship such as the *Sovereign*, which did not use oars.

This moment of unease is soon overcome, and Fanshawe's vision moves beyond the nearly finished hulk in front of him to its launching on the Thames, its use in peace or war, and then its final voyage (95–110):

> When running in the *Ocean* thy last stage,
> Being then to end thy watery pilgrimage,
> Let it not be by wrack; nor, feeble grown
> With years, by any foe be overthrown;
> (Too proud a victory!) Nor pine away
> Of slow consumption in inglorious Bay;
> Nor like patched *Theseus'* Ship (whereof the name
> Of what it was only remained the same)
> By mending still, and by that fallacy
> Affect a perishing eternity;
> But, lodged b'a happy storm upon some sphere,
> Be launched a *sailing Constellation* there.
> And thence (as *Adm'ral of the World*) hang forth

> A brighter Star than that which from the North
> Lights the benighted Seaman through the Main:
> So *Charles* his Ship shall quite Eclipse his *Wain*.

The sea and ships often have this effect upon poets, pushing them toward symbolic narratives; think forward to Cowper and Tennyson. The temptation here is to see behind the great ship the great king whose inspiration it is. By late 1637 Charles's narrative is well on its way, heading almost inevitably toward one of the destinies which lie in wait for the *Sovereign:* worst of all would be a constant patching up as bit by bit the monarchy was dismantled, until it could affect only "a perishing eternity." The wish-fulfillment alternative to all such indignities is to be asterized into the immortality of the North Star. It is a stubborn evocation of the ideal of monarchy in the face of political realities, the most obvious of which was the growing inadequacy of the man who wore the crown.

Waller's poem "To the King, On his Navy" realizes the apocalyptic implications. It might have been written at any time in the 1620s or 1630s, and a date as late as 1636 has been proposed.[3] In it Waller plays with the idea of a second Flood, after which Charles would ride triumphant over the whole drowned globe because of the glory of his fleet (19–24):

> Should nature's self invade the world again,
> And o'er the centre spread the liquid main,
> Thy power were safe, and her destructive hand
> Would but enlarge the bounds of thy command;
> Thy dreadful fleet would style thee lord of all,
> And ride in triumph o'er the drowned ball . . .

Again, pedants might have pointed out that such an apotheosis would involve the drowning of England as well as the rest of the globe, but perhaps Waller might regrettably have accepted the need for such a catastrophe. How else to deal with the enemy within?

Awe-inspiring as it was, the *Sovereign of the Seas* was a symbol, not, as Fanshawe would have it, of the unity of the state, but of the increasing helplessness of the king. Seasick passengers might, after all, be not so much incapacitated by nausea, as mutinous against the whole enterprise to which the ship had been committed. Henry King's "Salutation to his Majesty's Ship the Sovereign" gradually reveals this unease:

> Move on thou Floating Trophy built to Fame!
> And bid Her Trump spread Thy Majestic Name;

That the blue Tritons, and those petty Gods
Which sport themselves upon the dancing Floods,
May bow as to their Neptune, when they feel
The awful pressure of thy potent Keel.
 Great Wonder of the Time! whose Form unites
In one aspect Two warring Opposites,
Delight and Horror; and in them portends
Diff'ring events both to thy Foes and Friends.
To These thy Radiant brow, Peace's bright Shrine,
Doth like that Golden Constellation shine
Which guides the Seaman with auspicious Beams
Safe and unship-wracked through the troubled Streams.
But, as a Blazing Meteor, to Those
It doth ostents of blood and death disclose.
For thy Rich Decks Lighten, like Heaven's fires
To usher forth the Thunder of thy Tires.
 O never may cross Wind or swelling Wave
Conspire to make the treach'rous Sands thy Grave:
Nor envious Rocks in their white foamy laugh
Rejoice to wear thy Loss's Epitaph.
But may the smoothest, most successful Gales
Distend thy Sheet, and wing thy flying Sails:
That all Designs which must on Thee embark
May be securely placed, as in the Ark.
May'st Thou, where'er thy Streamers shall display,
Enforce the bold Disputers to obey:
That They, whose Pens are sharper than their Swords,
May yield in Fact, what they Denied in Words.
Thus when th'amazed World Our Seas shall see
Shut from Usurpers, to Their Own Lord Free,
Thou may'st, returning from the conquered Main,
With thine own Triumphs be crowned Sovereign.

Charles his ship is King's theme, with the language of royal praise being extended to the majesty of the vessel. The power lies in the title "sovereign," awe-inspiring to foes and friends. Such is the ideal of the first half of the poem, as the people of England are rendered secure from fear of rough seas by the mightiness of the ship in which they sail, while their enemies are blasted into submission. When the poem turns to predicting the future its certainty begins to fade. As in Jonson's poetry, "secure" is added to "safe" to complete the picture of national harmony, but it occurs in a passage of increasing political implication—treacherous sands, envious rocks which laugh in triumph, designs, disputes, and the wielders of pens who deny what only military force can make them yield. Ostensibly directed at enemies abroad, it is increasingly difficult to read the second half of the poem without bringing into it Hampden, Fiennes, and all others who would usurp the king's right to levy ship money. In another sense too King's unease was well merited. A frequent and bitter refrain of popular Royalist poetry in the early 1640s was anger at the way the navy so readily went over to Parliament's side. Those very ships which had so grandly symbolized Stuart pretensions to rule far and wide now blockaded his forces and kept him in close confinement on bigger or smaller islands.

The ships themselves were readily anthropomorphized, or, rather, gynomorphized, as in Mildmay Fane's "In Praise of Fidelia":[4]

> Get thee a Ship well-rigged and tight,
> With Ordnance store, and Manned for fight,
> Snug in Her Timbers' Mold for th' Seas,
> Yet large in Hold for Merchandise;
> Spread forth her Cloth, and Anchors weigh,
> And let her on the Curled-waves play,
> Till, Fortune-towed, she chance to meet
> Th'Hesperian home-bound Western Fleet;
> Then let her board 'um, and for Price
> Take Gold-ore, Sugar-canes, and Spice;—
>   Yet when all these Sh'hath brought ashore,
>   In my Fidelia I'll find more.

That ships are female is a long-established idea, but seldom so craftily presented as here. The title alerts us to the woman behind the well-rigged ship; the feminine pronouns help it along; and it is largely built upon the double-entendres, not only "well-rigged" and "tight," but also "manned," "snug," "large in hold," "curled waves," and "board 'um." Love and war are exotically amalgamated in the image of a privateer raiding the western fleet and a lady in gorgeous silks and perfumes.

The process could work the opposite way just as evocatively. Here is Fanshawe looking at the newly completed *Sovereign* and anticipating its launching in the Thames (67–70):

> Behold she comes, decked like a Royal Maid!
> Her Anchors are tucked up, her Flags displayed,

Which fan the Air, and offer in a scorn
Waves to the River, Purple to the Morn.

Milton's Dalila belongs to this tradition, the ship as stately queen or the queen as stately ship. In Fanshawe's poem this is an important part of the symbolic association of the great ship with the royal family. Charles's mastery over it is analogous with his mastery over his queen. The whole passage has the aura of one of the court masques in which the queen and her ladies danced for her husband's enjoyment, the whole spectacle being an image of power and beauty. Fane's poem has something of this quality too, as if he were painting a moving picture of the ship under sail, the imperatives "Get thee a ship," "Spread forth her Cloth," "let her board 'um" being directions to the imagination.

To these images of luxury we should add, inevitably, others of danger and shipwreck. This is a poem by a Jesuit, Henry Hawkins, published in 1633:[5]

The Star

The glorious Sun withdrew his beams of light;
My Sin was cause. So I, in dismal night,
Am sailing in a stormy dangerous Main;
And ere the Sun, I fear, return again,
Shall suffer shipwrack, where the freight's my Soul.
My only Hope's a Star, fixed near the Pole;
But that my Needle now hath lost its force,
Once touched with grace, and sails out of course.
Star of the Sea, thy Sun hath given thee light:
Till he brings day guide me in sin's dark night.
    I seek what Sages heretofore have done,
    Guided by thee, a Star, to find the Sun.

Despite the emphatic difference in motive and message, this does not stand far removed from Fane's poem. The details are of navigation rather than of rigging, and the freight is infinitely more precious, but both poems work so well upon our imagination because of our readiness to see the man on the ship on the sea as the essential metaphor for human achievement in the face of overwhelming dangers. In Fane's poem the achievement is beauty—its appreciation and value, gained from fortune's auspicious winds. For Hawkins, loss of direction, night and stormy seas, and a decaying compass are all pitted against the one star by which his wandering bark can still sail a course. Most of all, both poems share a sense of present time, of the thing happening at this moment. They describe, in the old meaning of the word, fleeting things. As in Donne's calm and storm, the voyage itself is the enduring thing. Fane's ship gets home at the end of the poem, but the final line looks forward to future voyages.

The seagoing metaphor spread through all classes. Martin Parker, probably the most prolific of the balladeers, set one of his most successful songs in the mouths of the sailors of England. "Sailors for my Money" was written sometime around 1635. It combines protestations of piety with most impious actions at the end, but gets away with this by presenting everything in the context of the dangers which sailors undergo and which gentlemen in England now at ease rarely think about:[6]

Countrymen of England, who live at home with ease,
And little think what dangers are incident o' the seas:
Give ear unto the sailor who unto you will show
     His case, his case: Howe'er the wind doth blow.

He that is a sailor must have a valiant heart,
For when he is upon the sea, he is not like to start;
But must with noble courage all dangers undergo:
     Resolve, resolve: Howe'er the wind doth blow.

Our calling is laborious and subject to much care,
But we must still contented be, with what falls to our share.
We must not be faint-hearted, come tempest, rain or snow,
     Nor shrink, nor shrink: Howe'er the wind doth blow.

Sometimes on Neptune's bosom our ship is tossed with waves,
And every minute we expect the sea must be our graves.
Sometimes on high she mounteth, then falls again as low,
     With waves, with waves: When stormy winds do blow.

Then with unfeigned prayers, as Christian duty binds,
We turn unto the Lord of hosts with all our hearts and minds;
To him we flee for succour, for he, we surely know,
     Can save, can save: Howe'er the wind doth blow.

Then he who breaks the rage, the rough and blusterous seas,
When his disciples were afraid, will straight the storms appease,
And give us cause to thank, on bended knees full low,
     Who saves, who saves: Howe'er the wind doth blow.

Our enemies approaching, when we on sea espy,
We must resolve incontinent to fight, although we die;
With noble resolution we must oppose our foe,
   In fight, in fight: Howe'er the wind doth blow.

And when by God's assistance, our foes are put to the foil,
To animate our courages, we all have share o' the spoil.
Our foes into the ocean we back to back do throw,
   To sink, or swim: Howe'er the wind doth blow.

The attraction here is the clarity of the sailor's position. Despite the dangers, they work in a realm where the issues are of simple survival, either against angry waves or against foes who would, if victorious, treat them the way they are treated at the poem's end. Much seventeenth-century poetry devoted a lot of effort to the hunt for certainty; hence the many images of pilgrims or soldiers going to the wars; but the sailors of Parker's poem have it the most clearly of all. Their simple language emphasizes their privileged position. Here is nothing subtle, complex, or sophisticated—man against nature, Englishmen against foreigners, with God on the side of the righteous. Sailors are hardworking and careful. They have to be to survive, and they have all to pull together because of the ferocity of the opposition. But such is the flexibility of the ship image that even such certainties can fragment with only a slight touch of the rudder, as in Davenant's "The Winter Storms." Davenant, an experienced soldier, must have known well the attitudes—and the songs—of the sailors who carried him to and from the continental wars. His poem is only a little more sophisticated than Parker's, and might just as easily have been called "Sailors for my Money":

Blow! blow! The Winds are so hoarse they cannot blow.
Cold! cold! our Tears freeze to Hail, our Spittle to Snow!
   The Waves are all up, they swell as they run!
     Let them rise and rise,
     As high as the skies,
And higher to wash the face of the Sun.

Port, Port! the Pilot is blind! Port at the Helm!
Yare, yare! For one foot of shore take a whole Realm,
   Alee, or we sink! Does no man know to wind her,
     Less noise and more room!
     We sail in a Drum!
Our Sails are but Rags, which Lightning turns to Tinder.

> Aloof, aloof! Hey, how those Carracks and Ships,
> Fall foul and are tumbled and driven like Chips!
> Our Boatswain, alas, a silly weak Gristle,
>   For fear to catch cold,
>   Lies down in the Hold,
> We all hear his Sighs, but few hear his Whistle.

From at least as early as Skelton's *Bouge of Court* the image of the ship of state had figured large in drama and poetry. *The Tempest* begins its exploration of uses and abuses of authority with a foundering ship on which passengers and crew are at odds. Davenant's poem is a clear recollection of that scene—as might be expected from a true son of Will—although the call "Aloof, aloof!" nods in the direction of Jonson's great enemies of state, the wolf and the dull ass. It is not possible to date the poem precisely, but best guesses put it sometime in the late 1630s.[7] Apparently it was not written as part of any dramatic performance, but simply for its own sake, perhaps as an attempt to fit the popular manner of such as Parker's poem. But its allegorical undertones are unmistakable. In a shipwreck every man shifts for himself, and if the poem is dated from around the late 1630s then its relevance would be obvious. A blind pilot and a bosun's whistle which few can hear are the framing elements of two stanzas which describe a ship out of control in perilous seas. Desperate calls for it to steer alee or aloof signal the paralysis of those on board. The prevailing image is of their simple inadequacy to cope with huge forces which they do not understand. The political allegory is underpinned by the very naturalness of the way nautical language fits the discourse of government: the *OED* gives an example of *pilot* used in such a sense from 1653—"the pilots of the Commonwealth had an eye to the dangers that lay in the way"—and has such a usage traceable back to the ninth century. Then the recollection of Richard III on Bosworth field in the offer of a whole realm for one foot of shore makes the ship of state image unavoidable. Again, though, the most effective thing is the poem's present tense. This is all happening now, and the poem itself becomes the whistle which few can or will hear; not that the warning can be of much use at this late stage.

The vision of Parker's "Sailors for my Money" is separated from Davenant's "Winter Storms" by only a paper-thin margin. All the organization and unity which make the crew so successful in keeping their ship afloat in rough seas and in defeating the enemy can crumble to pieces in the face of one fierce blast. The refrain "Howe'er the wind doth blow" is hopeful rather than definitive. Indeed, the refrain in the second stanza is virtually that of the Royalist party in the next two decades: "Resolve, resolve: Howe'er the wind doth blow." Herrick had said a similar thing to his friend John Wickes:[8]

> Well then, on what Seas we are tossed,
> Our comfort is, we can't be lost.
> > Let the winds drive
> Our Bark; yet she will keep alive
> > Amidst the deeps;
> 'Tis constancy (my *Wickes*) which keeps
> The Pinnace up; which though she errs
> I'th'Seas, she saves her passengers.

And in a poem set in the same tradition, Lovelace tells his brother how easily fortunes can collapse:[9]

> Frank, wilt live handsomely? trust not too far
> Thyself to waving seas, for what thy star
> Calculated by sure event must be,
> Look in thy glassy-epithet and see.
>
> > Yet settle here your rest, and take your state,
> And in calm halcyon's nest ev'n build your fate;
> Prithee lie down securely, Frank, and keep
> With as much no noise the inconstant deep
> As its inhabitants; nay steadfast stand
> As if discovered were a New-found-land
> Fit for plantation here; dream, dream still,
> Lulled in Dione's cradle, dream, until
> Horror awake your sense, and now you find
> Yourself a bubbled pastime for the wind,
> And in loose Thetis' blankets torn and tossed;
> Frank to undo thyself why art at cost?

This is a striking opening because of the way it pulls the reader into the dream of security which Lovelace feels his brother has fallen into, rather like the calm seas which seem to promise unending peace. The awakening for both is as rude as for the sailors who wake to find themselves in a hideous storm.

Sleep and storm at sea are frequently paired in mid-seventeenth-century poetry—perhaps *billow* and *pillow* made too tempting a rhyme, but the ultimate antecedents are Jonah, who "was gone down into the sides of the ship; and he lay and was fast asleep," in spite of the mighty tempest which threatens to overwhelm the ship (1:4–5); and, of course, Jonah's antitype in Mark 4:37–38:

> And there arose a great storm of wind, and the waves beat into the ship, so that it was now full.
> And he was in the hinder part of the ship, asleep on a pillow: and they awake him, and say unto him, Master, carest thou not that we perish?

In a Shakespearean adaptation, *The Law against Lovers,* which was performed early after the Restoration, and which might have been written at any time in the 1650s, Davenant has Viola contrasting the troubled state of lovers in this world with the peace of the dead, by way of a sea image in which the passengers sleep while the crew faces the storm (III.i):

> Wake all the dead! what ho! what ho!
> How soundly they sleep whose Pillows lie low!
> They mind not poor lovers who walk above
> On the decks of the World in storms of love.

Later in the play Lucio turns from the crew to the captain to give an image of the government out of control (V.i):

> Our ruler has got the vertigo of State;
> The World turns round in his politic pate.
> He steers in a Sea where his course cannot last,
> And bears too much Sail for the strength of his Mast.

In such circumstances the ship is doomed. Either the sail will soon be torn to shreds and it will be left to drift or it will capsize because it is top-heavy. In contrast, the sailors of Parker's "Sailors for my Money" have a more reliable captain, the Lord of Hosts, whose very métier is the howling wind; hence the explicit reference to those verses of Mark:

> Then he who breaks the rage, the rough and blusterous seas,
> When his disciples were afraid, will straight the storm appease,
> And give us cause to thank, on bended knees full low,
>   Who saves, who saves: Howe'er the wind doth blow.

Parker was no Puritan. Much the opposite, he appears to have been an alehouse keeper, and during the 1640s he was frequently attacked as a notorious and scurrilous Royalist balladeer. Hyder Rollins quotes one enraged Puritan naming him as a "Poeticall, Papisticall, Atheisticall" ballad maker who printed rhymes "against the truest Protestants." [10] Yet Parker was inevitably writing for an audience with strong Puritan sympathies, particularly in the streets of London, and "Sailors for my Money," while it may be poetical, has nothing papistic or atheistic about it. Indeed, it comes very close to an ideal Puritan vision: a state in which there are no officers or captains apparent, only a body of men pulling together under the direction of God, in a world whose dangers are apparent and omnipresent. More than anything else, they have a vocation for what they do, stated at the very point where the ballad turns from the third to the first person:

> Our calling is laborious and subject to much care,
> But we must still contented be, with what falls to our share.
> We must not be faint-hearted, come tempest, rain or snow,
>   Nor shrink, nor shrink: Howe'er the wind doth blow.

The sailors are no longer a race apart to whom countrymen in England give little or no thought, but all of us, involved in a laborious enterprise. Again the present tense pulls us into the experience of the poem. Note, too, that although the register is quite different, we are not very far removed from the labor/ease opposition of Milton's poem on Shakespeare. The idea of a laborious calling very neatly sums it up, as does the image of the sailors' hard work being relieved by the inspired word which calms the storm.

Perhaps the one non-Puritan element in Parker's ballad, given the time it was written, is the complete national harmony which it suggests, for such a condition could only prevail during the rule of the Saints. Under the Stuarts and Laud there could be only factions, dissent, and persecution. As it happens, there is a version of the ballad called "Neptune's Raging Fury; or, the Gallant Seaman's Sufferings," in the *Roxburghe Ballads* (6:432) which was possibly written in the middle or late 1630s, and which injects into Parker's relatively innocent celebration of the seaman's vocation no small degree of resentment. Its opening gives the clue. Instead of "countrymen of England," it begins "You gentlemen of England"; and although it follows Parker's ballad fairly closely, at the point where the sailors fall to prayer this version gives vent to the class antagonisms implicit in its opening:[11]

Then down again we fall to prayer with all our might and
   thought;
When refuge all doth fail us 'tis that must bear us out;
To God we call for succour, for He it is, we know,
That must aid us and save us *when the stormy winds do blow.*

The lawyer and the usurer that sits in gown of fur,
In closets warm, can take no harm, abroad they need not stir;
When winter fierce with cold doth pierce, and beats with hail
   and snow,
We are sure to endure *when the stormy winds do blow.*

We bring home costly merchandise, and jewels of great price
To serve our English gallantry with many a rare device;
To please the English gallantry our pains we freely show,
For we toil and we moil *when the stormy winds do blow.*

We sometimes sail to the Indies to fetch home spices rare,
Sometimes again to France and Spain for wines beyond compare
Whilst gallants are carousing in taverns on a row
Then we sweep o'er the deep *when the stormy winds do blow.*

The ballad closes with its heroic mariners drinking themselves senseless
in a pub, but its images of enemies within make its heroes appear only
dupes who substitute drunkenness for rebellion against their exploiters.

The sailors did rebel. The revolt of the navy was the key event in the
early stages of the Civil War. Soon after the flight of the five members two
thousand sailors marched on Guildhall to offer their services to the Com-
mittee of the House of Commons. Their spokesman put it like this: "We,
who are used to tempests, never stood in fear of a greater than this on
land. That great vessel, the Parliament-house, which is so richly fraught
with no less value than the price of a kingdom, is fearfully shaken, and in
great danger. Rome has rocks, and Spain quicksands to swallow her
up." [12] Charles is reported to have asked, "how is it I have lost the hearts
of these water-rats?" The answer was quite simple. Sailors in rags, not
paid for years, discontented to the point that out of one crew of 250 in
1636 no fewer than 230 deserted, had nothing to hope for from further
Stuart mismanagement and everything to gain from Parliament's promises. The palpable luxury of the *Sovereign of the Seas* must have been as
galling to the sea rats as the tales of court masques were to the London
citizenry. To quote from a ballad celebrating its launching, "Upon the
great Ship": [13]

I mean the ship so lately built,
Without, within so richly gilt;
O never man saw rapier hilt
         So shine.
I think there's none since Noah's flood
Was ever like to prove so good;
You never saw thing made of wood
         So fine.

This balladeer recognizes that some on land "were discontent / And thought their money had been lent / In vain," but he believes the sight of the splendid ship will cheer them so much that they would now "double it if need shall be." This was one poet, very much a king's man, whose claims to prophetic powers were very poor.

During the Commonwealth the navy was restructured on the pattern of the New Model Army, run by committees with a new draft of officers qualified by talent more than by birth. As Blake's victories showed, this Puritan navy came closest to realizing the ideal vision of Parker's ballad. Blake's laureate was Andrew Marvell, but in a better poem than the one he wrote in praise of the admiral, he spoke for an earlier group of Puritan sailors, the refugees from Laud's persecution who found their haven in Bermuda:[14]

Bermudas
Where the remote Bermudas ride
In the ocean's bosom unespied,
From a small boat, that rowed along,
The listening winds received this song.
    What should we do but sing his praise
That led us through the watery maze,
Unto an isle so long unknown,
And yet far kinder than our own?
Where he the huge sea-monsters wracks,
That lift the deep upon their backs,
He lands us on a grassy stage,
Safe from the storms, and prelate's rage.
He gave us this eternal spring,
Which here enamels everything,
And sends the fowls to us in care,
On daily visits through the air.
He hangs in shades the orange bright,

Like golden lamps in a green night,
And does in the pom'granates close
Jewels more rich than Ormus shows.
He makes the figs our mouths to meet,
And throws the melons at our feet,
But apples plants of such a price,
No tree could ever bear them twice.
With cedars, chosen by his hand,
From Lebanon, he stores the land,
And makes the hollow seas, that roar,
Proclaim the ambergris on shore.
He cast (of which we rather boast)
The gospel's pearl upon our coast,
And in these rocks for us did frame
A temple, where to sound his name.
Oh let our voice his praise exalt,
Till it arrive at heaven's vault:
Which thence (perhaps) rebounding, may
Echo beyond the Mexique Bay.
   Thus sung they, in the English boat,
An holy and a cheerful note,
And all the way, to guide their chime,
With falling oars they kept the time.

Here the luxury and ostentation are all nature's. In a sense the island is like a great ship, its trees the masts, the oranges the lamps in its rigging. The real boat of the poem is the small one which the Englishmen are rowing. It is not possible to be absolutely clear about the narrative. Either they are settlers, already familiar with the island, rowing around it; or they have just arrived and are rowing toward it for their first landing. I prefer the second if only because it is more consistent with Marvell's general interest in first encounters. But whichever narrative we choose the poem remains, as one editor has described it, a "psalmic and descriptive lyric." [15] In the first-encounter narrative it is just that—the description is one of anticipation and gradual revelation, the oranges and pineapples gradually being perceived for what they are, the shape of the rocks being slowly discerned, as the boat approaches the island.

The psalmic element is worth stressing too, for the register is not so much the Prayer Book's Great Bible version of the Psalms, but Sternhold and Hopkins's doggerel versification of them. It is amusing nowadays to come across such comments as this, written in 1908, evaluating poetic treatments of naval battles in the seventeenth century: "a greater poet, and more renowned than Marvell, Edmund Waller, celebrated Stayner's capture of the Spanish galleons off Cadiz." [16] Such low estimates of Marvell could only have been reinforced by the reading of a poem such as "Bermudas," which, for all the attractiveness of its imagery, is a wretched metrical performance. So regular in its rhythm is it, and so lamely does it bend syntax to fit the demands of meter and rhyme, that it is impossible to read it in anything other than a monotone. We differ from earlier critics in our appreciation that this is deliberately done, although the kind of editorial comment I have just quoted—"psalmic and descriptive lyric"—makes me wonder if we all do. I suspect that some commentators believe that Marvell is wholly at one with the Puritans in the boat as they chant their metrical psalm.[17]

The story behind "Bermudas" seems to belong to John Oxenbridge, a fellow of Eton College. When Marvell went there as William Dutton's tutor in July 1653, Dutton was Oliver Cromwell's ward. Oxenbridge had been a refugee from Laud's persecutions in the 1630s and had made two trips to the Bermudas. Marvell's poem seems to be an imaginative effort to recapture the feelings of the refugees of twenty years before, probably based on the tales Oxenbridge had to tell. His motives for doing this need not be pressed too closely; after all, a lyric poem can be generated by the most casual of stimuli. Still, in the case of a poet so much thought about as Marvell now is, even passing moments of fancy deserve research. I am not sure, anyway, that this is so casual a piece. We have genuine difficulties in knowing how to respond to the many innocences and naïvetés of his lyric poetry—not just the nymph complaining over her dead fawn, or the mower over the artificiality of gardens, but of Marvell himself when, for instance, he assures us that the Irish appreciate Cromwell's goodness and justice.

Perhaps Cromwell is not entirely absent from "Bermudas." A famous story which once held strong currency had Cromwell and Pym as potential colonists of the Americas in the 1630s. It is as if, in going back twenty years, Marvell is researching the purest originals of the now prevailing Puritan temperament. Their art is crude, but necessarily so, for the psalm's metrical regularity is doubly functional: praise of God, which is the whole defense of poetry which hardline Puritans would think worth offering; and music to work by, a rowing song, in which the rhythm matches the singers' movements. In exploiting this second element Marvell is getting back even beyond the ballad to the most basic form of the popular lyric, the one which survived into this century in sea-shanties and in soldiers' songs of the world wars. With the emphasis entirely on function, there is as little place for ornament or style as there is in a Puritan church for stained-glass windows.

One of the first things which the Puritan settlers did was to build a church. Like rowing, it was hard, practical work done to the singing of metrical psalms. In the case of "Bermudas," however, the church is already present, part of the beneficence of providence which has already brought them through rough seas and the danger of shipwreck to a paradise where everything they could wish for is there for the taking. There may well be little exaggeration in this vision. The Bermudan pamphlets which Shakespeare drew on for *The Tempest* described how the earliest visitors to the islands had only to put out their hands, wait for game birds to settle on each, and then keep hold of the heavier one for the pot.[18] Hence the "daily visits" of the fowls to Marvell's settlers, together with the figs which fall into their mouths and the melons lying at their feet. He who stills the winds and calms the storms has led them through the watery maze to a bay smooth enough for them to row to shore. The rough seas and rocks beyond the bay make their paradise complete, giving it the fence which all gardens need to keep intruders out.

Their delight is total, but they exist in the psalm's present tense. The poem itself is more reflective, framing the psalm within Marvell's retrospective narrative. The psalm is praise and ease, the frame is effort. God's providential aid promises the settlers a life of ease. Even the most instinctive of Puritan acts, the erection of a building in which to praise God, is rendered unnecessary by the natural church framed by the rocks. The clue to Marvell's view of the whole enterprise lies in the echo. It is difficult for modern readers to close their minds to the notion of satellites bouncing sound from one part of the world to another when they come to the Puritans' wish to conquer and proselytize Catholic America:

> Oh let our voice his praise exalt,
> Till it arrive at heaven's vault:
> Which thence (perhaps) rebounding, may
> Echo beyond the Mexique Bay.

Possibly it is not wrong to do so. Marvell's poetry shows much interest in the latest scientific findings in optics. He is likely to have been interested in research into sound too, and the production of echo by sound bouncing off surfaces gives a hard edge to the central section of his "Ode to his Coy Mistress," where "echo" and "vault" also occur close together. Zeal will transform paradise into what the modern Bermudas have become. Fences which keep intruders out will be broken down by the settlers themselves as they spread their message to the whole New World. They may have arrived where they are through inspiration, but they will transform their paradise into a place where they can labor, even if it means sailing back into the hollow seas.

Even Bermuda, it seems, will offer only a very temporary safety. The prevailing image is of a smooth sea which can suddenly turn rough again. In "The Garden" Marvell compares the world to an ocean as he sinks into a reverie. Lovelace reminded his brother that the most solid land, even apparent paradise, is as unstable as the roughest sea:[19]

> Nor be too confident, fixed on the shore,
> For even that too borrows from the store
> Of her rich neighbour, since now wisest know,
> (And this to Galileo's judgment owe)
> The palsy Earth itself is every jot
> As frail, inconstant, waving as that blot
> We lay upon the deep, that sometime lies
> Changed, you would think, with's bottom's properties;
> But this eternal strange Ixion's wheel
> Of giddy earth, ne'er whirling leaves to reel
> Till all things are inverted, till they are
> Turned to that antic confused state they were.

In *Paradise Lost* the garden of Eden finally floats away in the great Flood (11:829–835):

> then shall this mount
> Of Paradise by might of waves be moved
> Out of his place, pushed by the horned flood,
> With all his verdure spoiled, and trees adrift
> Down the great river to the opening gulf,
> And there take root an island salt and bare,
> The haunt of seals and orcs, and sea-mews' clang.

Of Oxenbridge, the probable inspirer of "Bermudas," a biographer later wrote, charting his troubles in the 1660s after he was ejected from his living, that he "tumbled about the world in unsettled times . . . in the general shipwreck that befell nonconformists we find him swimming away to Surinam."[20] Fortunately he ended up in New England, but not before he had thoroughly learned the lesson that, if you consider things properly, shipwreck is everywhere.

8   A Just Recompense: *Lycidas*

Si recte calculum ponas, ubique naufragium est was the motto for the collection of poems in memory of the recently drowned Edward King, for which Milton wrote *Lycidas* in 1637. Ben Jonson died in the same year, but Milton obviously thought that King was the one who deserved to be mourned in verse. A smaller irony is that while the *Sovereign of the Seas* was nearing completion, with its figurehead of King Edgar who was rowed in triumph into Chester, the sinking of a much lesser craft just outside that city generated the finest poem which had so far been written in English.

The boat is important in any consideration of Milton's poem, for of all the elegists who contributed to the Cambridge volume, only he and one other blamed it for the death of King. The majority thought the sea was to blame.[1] Perhaps Milton was keener to blame the ship because one of his purposes in *Lycidas* was to show that shipwreck could happen anywhere—in other words, that there is no real difference between the sea and the land. The resurrected figure who stands on the shore at the end of the poem and is "good / To all that wander in that perilous flood" is not simply to be regarded as a guardian of mariners and others who go down to the sea in ships, but as a guide to all men. "Wander," as always, is Milton's word for living in this fallen world. The flood is everywhere, sea or land. We are all afloat in the Irish Sea.

Nineteen years earlier John Donne, preparing to sail to the Continent, pursued the same idea. "A Hymn to Christ, at the Author's Last Going into Germany" opens like this:

> In what torn ship soever I embark,
> That ship shall be my emblem of thy ark;
> What sea soever swallow me, that flood

Shall be to me an emblem of thy blood;
Though you with clouds of anger do disguise
Thy face; yet through that mask I know those eyes,
   Which, though they turn away sometimes,
      They never will despise.

There is a beautiful blurring of the literal and figurative here. The ship itself is real enough. So, probably, is its torn state, its rotten boards and fraying sails; but "torn" points to an allegorical reading of the ship as the frail human body which is sailing toward its ultimate and inevitable shipwreck. *Lycidas* has been read in the same way, with the fatal bark "built in the eclipse man has endured since Adam's fall."[2] The sea as an emblem of death is too general to need illustration, but Donne's twist is to make its horror merely a mask for Christ's benevolence. His second stanza wishes a flood upon the whole of Britain (9–12):

   I sacrifice this Island unto thee,
   And all whom I loved there, and who loved me;
   When I have put our seas 'twixt them and me,
   Put thou thy sea betwixt my sins and thee . . .

And he ends the poem with a yearning for the drowning which he will sooner or later have to experience (30–32):

   To see God only, I go out of sight:
      And to 'scape stormy days, I choose
         An everlasting night.

This is a precise image. Going out of sight means sinking into the depths of the sea. It is all darkness there, but calm in spite of the storm which lashes up the waves on the surface.

Lycidas presents a slightly different kind of shipwreck. There was no storm (98–99):

   The air was calm, and on the level brine,
   Sleep Panope with all her sisters played.

Instead, the storm comes after the sinking. The corpse does not lie sunken in the peaceful depths, but is swept across the seas of the world, falling and rising as it meets various crosscurrents (154–158):

Ay me! Whilst thee the shores, and sounding seas
Wash far away, where'er thy bones are hurled,
Whether beyond the stormy Hebrides
Where thou perhaps under the whelming tide
Visit'st the bottom of the monstrous world . . .

But this is only Edward King's body. His soul has found peace; hence the injunction to the sorrowing shepherds to weep no more.

That a good man's sufferings are ended by death is a given of seventeenth-century elegiac poetry—naturally so, since any other opinion would be a monstrous denial of Christian values. This was the more necessary because of the frequency with which young people died. This meant not only that their present sufferings were cut short, but also that they had been released from the otherwise inevitable suffering into which extended life would have led them. This is part of Donne's purpose when he chooses to "'scape stormy days." William Hammond wrote a sequence of poems on the death of his brother-in-law, who was drowned in his youth around the same time that Edward King died. One of them develops the conceit of the boat as the body of man from which the soul is released upward as it sinks beneath the waves:[3]

The Boat

How well the brittle boat doth personate
     Man's frail estate!
Whose concave, filled with lightsome air, did scorn
     The proudest storm.
Man's fleshy boat bears up; whilst breath dost last,
     He fears no blast.
Poor floating bark, whilst on yon mount you stood,
     Rain was your food:
Now the same moisture, which once made thee grow,
     Doth thee o'erflow.
Rash youth hath too much sail; his giddy path
     No ballast hath;
He thinks his keel of wit can cut all waves,
     And pass those graves;
Can shoot all cataracts, and safely steer
     The fourscorth year.
But stoop thine ear, ill-counselled youth, and hark
     Look on this bark.
His emblem, whom it carried, both defied

> Storms, yet soon died;
> Only this difference, that sunk downward, this
> Weighed up to bliss.

A later poem in the sequence explains to the mourning wife that by dying
so young her husband has escaped all the dangers which longer life would
have held for him—hinted at already in the presumptuous course charted
by the youth who confidently thinks he will live past the age of eighty.
This poem, called "The Reasons," closes like this:[4]

> Ask but the sacred oracle, you there
> Shall find, untimely deaths no windfall are.
> The grand example, miracle of good,
> (In virtue only old) slain in the bud,
> Newly disclosing man. It were a shame
> To wish, than that of his, a longer flame.
> Who would not die before subdued by age?
> That conquest oft Fortune pursues with rage;
> Or sin in that advantage wounds him worse:
> To wish him long life, then, had been a curse!

The lesson is that shipwreck of the body, while young, will save you from
the greater danger of a shipwrecked soul. It becomes, then, almost axio-
matic that the good die young, or, even more providentially, that the
young die good. Survivors, because of the greater number of temptations
they must face and their growing decrepitude, are likely to be at best
weak, at worst vicious. John Ashmore mourns the death of Elizabeth
Briggs, "daughter to the discreet matron and widow, Beatrice Briggs," by
consoling himself and her mother with the thought that the fairest flowers
fade soonest:[5]

> Come, Virgins, come! why do you linger so,
>   With streams of tears that from your swol'n eyes show'r?
> Her Grave with Roses and with Lilies strow
>   That of your Garland was the fairest flower.
>   Lilies and Roses soon decay and perish,
>   While bitter Worm-wood and sharp Nettles flourish.
>
> Your Garlands break! henceforth no garlands bear;
>   Their fading doth your fading state express
> For Garlands, deadly Yew and Elder wear,

And branches of the saddest Cyparess.
   Lilies and Roses soon decay and perish,
   While bitter Worm-wood and sharp Nettles flourish.

Ye Holly-hocks, why hold you down your heads?
   And violets, why pine you so away?
Because (alas!) that she from you is fled,
   That dressed you and hath ta'en her leave for aye?
   Lilies and Roses soon decay and perish,
   While bitter Worm-wood and sharp Nettles flourish.

The contrast between lilies and roses, which die young, beautiful, and virtuous, and wormwood and nettles, which live on, is generally a comfort, not least because it sets the bitterness of mourning within the dispensation of providence: it is the price they pay for having survived the death of their children. The seminal poem in all of this is Jonson's Cary-Morison ode, which is as much concerned with consoling the surviving friend as it is with mourning the dead. The sentiment spans the whole century. Dryden's mourning for Oldham is equally a lament for his own fate, having to live on when the youth and vigor which made him write so well are only a memory. Oldham's early death means that he will always be a poet of energy and strength. Dryden's survival means that he may write much more, and that his best verse will be swallowed up by the poetry of his decrepitude.

Another late seventeenth-century poem which finds a powerful image for such a fate is "The Meditation," by John Norris. Norris was no more than thirty when he wrote it, but his last stanza gives a graphic representation of what it feels like to survive while all around you die:[6]

So when the spacious globe was deluged o'er,
   And lower holds could save no more,
On th'utmost bough th'astonished sinners stood,
And viewed th'advances of th'encroaching flood.
O'er topped at length by th'element's increase,
With horror they resigned to the untried abyss.

This is 1687, when Christian certainties are beginning to fade, and fear of death has begun to be a fear of oblivion rather than of what will happen to one's soul. Two or three generations earlier, the good man could face death with more of the equanimity of Donne about to sail to Germany, or of Robert Herrick writing, significantly, to a friend:

No Shipwreck of Virtue. To a friend

Thou sail'st with others, in this *Argus* here;
Nor wrack, or *Bulging* thou hast cause to fear:
But trust to this, my noble passenger;
Who swims with Virtue, he shall still be sure
(*Ulysses*-like) all tempests to endure;
And midst a thousand gulfs to be secure.

"Sure"/"endure"/"secure" are Jonsonian rhymes, and, following Jonson, Herrick is not proposing that virtue offers safety, but that it guarantees security. It may be literally shipwrecked and forced to swim through rough seas, but it can never be figuratively shipwrecked, in the sense of St. Paul's use of the image in 1 Timothy 1:18–19:

This charge I commit unto thee, son Timothy, according to the prophecies which went before on thee, that thou by them mightest war a good warfare;

Holding faith, and a good conscience; which some having put away concerning faith have made shipwreck.

"*Bulging*" is the staving in of the bottom or sides of a ship. It was precisely this which happened to Edward King's ship when it struck a rock.

This is Masson's translation of the Latin paragraph which opens *Justa Edovardo King naufrago . . .* , the collection of Latin and Greek poems mourning Edward King, followed by *Obsequies to the memory of Mr Edward King,* to which *Lycidas* was a contribution:[7]

P. M. S. Edward King, son of John (Knight and Privy Councillor for the Kingdom of Ireland to their majesties, Elizabeth, James, and Charles), Fellow of Christ's College in the University of Cambridge, happy in the consciousness and in the fame of piety and erudition, and one in whom there was nothing immature except his age, was on his voyage to Ireland, drawn by natural affection to visit his country, his relatives and his friends,—chiefly, his brother Sir Robert King, Knight, a most distinguished man; his sisters, most excellent women, Anne, wife of Lord G. Caulfield, Baron Charlemont, and Margaret, wife of Lord G. Loder, Chief Justice of Ireland; the venerable prelate Edward King, Bishop of Elphin, his godfather; and the most reverend and learned William Chappell, Dean of Cashel and Provost of Trinity College, Dublin, whose hearer and pupil he had been in the University,—when, the ship in which he was having struck on a rock not far from the British shore, and being stove in by the shock, he, while the other passengers were fruitlessly busy about their mortal lives, having fallen forward upon his knees, and breathing a life which was immortal, in the act of prayer going down with the vessel, rendered up his soul to God, Aug. 10, 1637, aged 25.[7]

Masson comments on the clumsiness of the original, which, I suppose, is prima facie evidence for Milton's not having seen it; otherwise he might well have persuaded the editors to write something more elegant. On the other hand, it has been argued that Milton saw everything and that *Lycidas* is a summary of the whole volume.[8] Whether or not this was the case, the one really Miltonic element of the preliminary paragraph—one which must have struck him forcibly whenever he read it—was the description of King as "one in whom there was nothing immature except his age."[9]

Youth and maturity were great Miltonic concerns. Nearly all of his early poetry turns at some point to consider his own unreadiness, often in contrast to more timely-happy spirits, and *Lycidas* itself begins with a succession of images of immaturity. King, though two years younger, was certainly more settled, and had qualified himself for the Christian ministry which he would soon enter—but then, as the list of his family connections in that paragraph shows, he had all the advantages. Milton was forced to rely on his father's support with few or no influential connections, making his apparent decision not to enter the ministry something worth note. After all, it was the one obvious career for a man of his learning who had no inclination for "the wide open road leading toward piles of money."[10] Whereas Edward King was heading somewhere definite, Milton, to all external appearances, was only drifting. He had been in retirement in Horton for five years, his furthest journey being only to London, having given himself up "with the most complete leisure" to a life of study.[11] It is possible to argue that such apparent leisure is actually hard labor, but to any observer it must have seemed a life of ease.

Earlier in the century Samuel Daniel had opposed the attractions of ease and labor in "Ulysses and the Siren." The siren tempts Ulysses with the prospect of a life of ease as an observer of the human struggle:[12]

> Come, worthy Greek! Ulysses, come,
>   Possess these shores with me:
> The winds and seas are troublesome,
>   And here we may be free.
> Here we may sit and view their toil

> That travail in the deep,
> And joy the day in mirth the while,
> And spend the night in sleep.

In the dialogue which follows Ulysses sternly rejects the siren's temptation, partly because a life of ease is as hard as a laborious one (29–32):

> For toil doth give a better touch
> To make us feel our joy,
> And ease finds tediousness as much
> As labour yields annoy.

and partly because of his sense that the world demands involvement, even at the cost of blood and hurt (57–64):

> But yet the state of things require
> These motions of unrest;
> And these great spirits of high desire
> Seem born to turn them best;
> To purge the mischiefs that increase
> And all good order mar;
> For oft we see a wicked peace,
> To be well changed for war.

The debate is a familiar one, and the evidence is that in late 1637 when Milton came to write *Lycidas* he had decided on movement rather than stasis. By May 1638 he had set sail for France, on his way to Italy and, he hoped, Sicily and Greece. Now travel was to fulfill exactly what retirement had previously offered—knowledge. It is as if he had decided that in a world where all was in a state of flux it was better to travel than to drift. The sirens' temptation was, anyway, an illusion. The dry land which they offered to Ulysses was not a shore but a reef upon which his ship would be wrecked. Edward King's boat went down in a similar manner. Coasting in smooth waters just off Chester, it struck a rock and its planks were stove in.

The way King died, as much as the fact of the death, might have affected Milton strongly. Since Tillyard it has become common to think of *Lycidas* as if it were principally a projection of the poet's own fears about the apparent unfairness of providence: here he was, devoting himself to a life of laborious study, but with no guarantee that it would ever come to anything. Such a reading is impoverished, avoiding the more probing question which the poem directs at providence, one which is connected to the way King chose to die. I use this phrase because it is fairly clear that King's death was at least as much a positive act as a passive one. In Martin Parker's "Sailors for my Money" the sailors go down on their knees on the deck in gratitude to the Lord who calms the seas:

> Then he who breaks the rage, the rough and blusterous seas,
> When his disciples were afraid, will straight the storms appease,
> And give us cause to thank, on bended knees full low,
>   Who saves, who saves: Howe'er the wind doth blow

This is an act of passive obedience. Edward King, who also went down on his knees, did something slightly different, for his ship was obviously doomed. While the rest of the passengers were "fruitlessly busy about their mortal lives" he went down on his knees and rendered his soul to God.[13] As it happens, not all his fellow travelers' efforts were fruitless. Even if we had no other account than the preface to the Cambridge collection, this would be a fair deduction, for without a survivor there could have been no account of the manner of his death.

There are all kinds of ways to justify King's act. He may well have been praying for the souls of all the crew and passengers as well as his own. He may have decided that he should sacrifice himself to make room for someone else. He may have felt in such a state of readiness for death that the prospect of continued life in this world could only have been one of an inevitable moral degeneration. It was part of the baggage of every seventeenth-century individual to welcome the moment of death and to be constantly ready for it. John Donne is the most famous example, showing such control in his final illness that he composed his limbs in the proper attitude and whispered to his soul to go. Edward King seems to have died in such certainty, already "breathing a life which was immortal."[14]

There is another way of looking at King's death—that it was very close to being an act of suicide. Only a saint could be so certain of his actions, at the age of twenty-five, to make no effort to save himself, particularly when others did so. There are grave dangers in such certainty:

> Alas! we may fall & drown at the last stroke: for to sayle to heaven it is not enough to cast away the burdenous superfluities which we have long carried about us, but we must also take in a good frayte. It is not lightnesse, but an even-reposed stedfastnesse, which carries us thither.

This is Donne questioning, in *Biathanatos,* the early Christian martyrs' willingness to die.[15] Clearly, the compilers of *Justa Edovardo King* believed that their dead friend had, despite his youth, possessed such an ever-reposed steadfastness; hence their proclamation of his maturity in everything but age. And assuredly the manner of his death proved it. A little later in *Biathanatos* Donne offers a relevant image for a death such as King's, in answer to the objection "that in a tempest, it were the part of an idle and treacherous Pylot, to sinke the Ship":

> But I say, if in a Tempest we must cast out the most precious ware aboard to save the lives of the Passengers, and the Marchant who is damnified thereby cannot impute this to any, nor remedie himselfe, how much more may I, when I am weather-beaten, and in danger of betraying that precious soule which God hath embarqued in me, put off this burdenous flesh, till his pleasure be that I shall resume it? For this is not to sink the ship but to retire it to safe Harbour, and assured Anchor.[16]

It is possible, if unlikely, to be weather-beaten by the age of twenty-five.

Milton seems not to have been entirely convinced of King's maturity. Lycidas is "dead ere his prime." This is where the questioning of providence becomes a more pointed thing than simply a complaint about the unfairness of an early death, for in King's case it is not merely the death of the body which is being lamented, but the death of many souls. At the heart of the poem is the contrast between the surviving bad pastors and the death of this potentially very good one, in St. Peter's complaint (113–129):

> How well could I have spared for thee, young swain,
> Enow of such as for their bellies' sake,
> Creep and intrude, and climb into the fold?
> Of other care they little reckoning make,
> Than how to scramble at the shearers' feast,
> And shove away the worthy bidden guest;
> Blind mouths! that scarce themselves know how to hold
> A sheep-hook, or have learned aught else the least
> That to the faithful herdman's art belongs!
> What recks it them? What need they? They are sped;
> And when they list, their lean and flashy songs
> Grate on their scrannel pipes of wretched straw,

> The hungry sheep look up, and are not fed,
> But swoll'n with wind, and the rank mist they draw,
> Rot inwardly, and foul contagion spread:
> Besides what the grim wolf with privy paw
> Daily devours apace, and nothing said . . .

The recollection here is of 2 Peter 2, in which St. Peter inveighs against the false prophets and false teachers: not only will they "bring upon themselves destruction," but also "many shall follow their pernicious ways." Such preachers will lead those who follow them into eternal damnation (4–5):

> For if God spared not the angels that sinned, but cast them down to hell, and delivered them into chains of darkness, to be reserved unto judgment;
>   And spared not the old world, but saved Noah the eighth person, a preacher of righteousness, bringing in the flood upon the world of the ungodly . . .

To put it in the simplest terms, if King had lived and, say, one bad pastor had drowned, there would have been hundreds of souls saved who will now be cast into the outer darkness. St. Peter may complain that he could well have spared one of the vicious. One may ask him, as an agent of providence, why he did not do so.

One answer is that providence has no control over suicide. Since King chose to die rather than to live, providence cannot be held responsible; otherwise the possibility of free will is unacceptably circumscribed. It may be that if King were of the same persuasion as Milton, the prospect of entering the ministry would have held out only the danger of involvement with corruption. As is well known, when Milton reprinted the poem in his 1645 volume, he added the headnote which claimed prophetic powers:

> In this monody the author bewails a learned friend, unfortunately drowned in his passage from Chester on the Irish Seas, 1637. And by occasion foretells the ruin of our corrupted clergy then in their height.

There is as much pragmatism as idealism here: Milton needed to offer some explanation not just for having written poetry, but also for having kept poetic company with the likes of John Cleveland. To the extremists who were gaining power, and with whom he had to deal if he hoped to gain any position of influence, the simple fact of his being a poet was enough to make him an object of suspicion. So, the demonstration that *Lycidas* had energetically attacked Laudian corruption while all around little or, according to Milton's emendation, nothing was said, was testimony to his ideological reliability.

Nonetheless, such pragmatism does not hide the facts that the lines were written in 1637 and that they sum up what anyone but a high church Anglican was likely to have felt about the church under Laud. Entering that church and subscribing to its increasingly questionable tenets and practices might well have led even a resolute man into corruption. In Milton's case the answer was to retire into private study. In King's case it might have made the engulfing waves a satisfyingly simple solution, apparently offered by providence. Still, there is no evidence that King thought in this way. His extant writings show merely a willing puffery of the Stuarts who had encouraged Laud. And to choose so simple an answer is to ignore the implications of the Noah image which St. Peter uses in the verse quoted above. Noah, the "preacher of righteousness," was required to resist the Flood, not acquiesce in it. As Peter goes on to say, in the next chapter (3–7):

> Knowing this first, that there shall come in the last days scoffers, walking after their own lusts,
>
> And saying, Where is the promise of his coming? for since the fathers fell asleep, all things continue as they were from the beginning of the creation.
>
> For this they willingly are ignorant of, that by the word of God the heavens were of old, and the earth standing out of the water and in the water:
>
> Whereby the world that then was, being overflowed with water, perished:
>
> But the heavens and the earth, which are now, by the same word are kept in store, reserved unto fire against the day of judgment and perdition of ungodly men.

It may be a mixing up of the literal and the figurative to claim that the very last way the good man should now choose to die is by drowning, because death by water belonged to the old dispensation and the next one will be death by fire; but for a pious man the moment when the remorseless deep closes over his head is a moment when there is not any space for the figurative. Biblical verses would become entirely literal. Certainly, by the end of the poem Milton has removed King from the water to the blazing fire of the sun as it "flames in the forehead of the morning sky."

In heaven King can now intercede for all those who are still in the element of water (182–185):

> Now Lycidas the shepherds weep no more;
> Henceforth thou art the genius of the shore,
> In thy large recompense, and shalt be good
> To all that wander in that perilous flood.

I want to explore the implications of "henceforth" and "recompense"; the latter term first. Milton uses the same word in *Paradise Lost*, in a technical explanation of the power of the sun (5:423–426):

> The sun that light imparts to all, receives
> From all his alimental recompense
> In humid exhalations, and at even
> Sups with the ocean . . .

This is not, as we might expect, from one of the astronomical passages of the poem, but illustrates Raphael's account of how every created thing, including angels, exits by feeding: "of elements / The grosser feeds the purer, earth the sea" (415–416). There are two connected ideas here, both relevant to *Lycidas*. One is of a gradual movement upward, the other of natural process. Movement upward links Milton to the mainstream of Puritan thought and such literary expressions of it as *The Pilgrim's Progress*. It is not confined to Puritanism: when the attendant spirit opens *Comus* by praising those that "by due steps aspire" (12) his words can just as easily be given a Neoplatonic gloss, arguing for a gradual refinement toward the ideal state. The idea is Darwinian too. Darwin's main reading on his excursions from the *Beagle* was *Paradise Lost*, and he must have been struck by Milton's close adherence to the maxim *Natura non facit saltum*.[17]

Edward King did and did not jump. Macbeth's wish, standing upon this bank and shoal of time, to "jump" the life to come, is normally glossed by editors as "risk," but it is likely that many an auditor would also take the sense of jumping into the life to come. Insofar as King's death was willed he did exactly that, not so much aspiring by due steps, but leaping over the many years which were left to him, straight into eternity. Literally, however, he did not jump, but knelt in prayer and let the waters close over his head. This acquiescence is much more in tune with the natural process which "recompense" recalls in *Paradise Lost,* whereby earth feeds sea, sea feeds air, and eventually the sun, whose rays repay the earth.

In the Bible *recompense* is a predominantly neutral term, much more so than the list of meanings offered by the *OED* might indicate. Its five headings are: (1) "reparation or restitution . . . for some wrong"; (2) "compensation for some loss or injury"; (3) "return or repayment for something given or received"; (4) "compensation or return for trouble, exertion, service, or merit"; (5) "Retribution for some injury or offence." Only the last of these begins to convey some of the negative possibilities of the word as it was used by the Bible translators, as in St. Paul's warning to the Romans that they should "recompense to no man evil for evil" (12:17), or Jeremiah's invoking of "the Lord God of recompenses" who will requite Babylon (51:57). Technically *recompensation,* like other seventeenth-century *re*–concepts, such as *restoration* or *remonstrance,* is a neutral thing, to be defined only and completely by its context. This is at the heart of Milton's philosophy. Later, in *Paradise Lost,* in the characters of Satan and the rebel angels, he teaches his reader to mistrust such apparently positive concepts as pity, loyalty, courage, even compassion. When felt by devils they are evil feelings, just as pity for Charles I is a "seditious pity." [18] The lady puts it most simply in *Comus:* "none / But such as are good can give good things" (701–702).

King's death, like any other human action, is neutral until properly interpreted and given a context whereby it may be judged or justified. Suicide is defensible. Donne found examples for *Biathanatos.* Sabrina, in *Comus,* throws herself into the river to escape worse tribulations than death, and thereby becomes a presiding genius. But it is equally possible to think of King as deluded, lured to his death by the sirens who promise him immortality, peace, and detachment from human suffering. When listening to the lady's song Comus thinks back to his mother's consorts who lulled men to their doom (251–260):

> I have oft heard
> My mother Circe with the Sirens three,
> Amidst the flowery-kirtled Naiades
> Culling their potent herbs, and baleful drugs,
> Who as they sung, would take the prisoned soul,
> And lap it in Elysium, Scylla wept,
> And chid her barking waves into attention,

> And fell Charybdis murmured soft applause:
> Yet they in pleasing slumber lulled the sense,
> And in sweet madness robbed it of itself . . .

Here smooth seas are the setting for damnation. Another analogue is Samson. Like him King probably went to his voluntary death moved by inner promptings. The doubt is whether they were from heaven or hell.

Lycidas by its end allows no such doubt, and uses the simplest moral terms to make the points that King was a good man and that the afterlife of his action will be good: "henceforth thou . . . shalt be good." "Henceforth" is closely connected with the poem's present tense. The drowning is in the past, together with the life which the poet and Lycidas shared, but the poem eventually comes into the present with speculation on the whereabouts of the corpse. At the end of this, secure in the knowledge that Lycidas is in heaven, "henceforth" pitches the poem into the future with its image of King as a benevolent figure who will be good to us survivors, a saint in a society of saints. But sainthood was an equivocal concept in the seventeenth century. King's claim to the title corresponds to the long-established view in which saints are the blessed dead in heaven, the holiness of their lives qualifying them for an exalted station in the next world. In this respect holiness is synonymous with wholeness. Sainthood is judgment upon the life as a whole, complete thing. Most of all, it is the end which gives it shape, the *finis* crowning the opus; and saints frequently qualify for their exalted position by dying spectacularly for God. Extreme deaths have extreme dangers. In Donne's words, "we may fall and drown at the last stroke." But they offer the opportunity for a climactic rounding off to a holy existence. As Donne explained, such an opportunity was a great temptation, a siren song to the early Christian martyrs.

Puritans were quite prepared to march to violent or sudden deaths. John of Leiden and his Anabaptists had become virtually proverbial examples of their foolhardy readiness to do so. But Puritanism had a tough-minded interest in labor and effort to oppose such manifestations of the inspired call to self-destruction, and it emphasized the biblical sense of sainthood over the Catholic one. Technically, Puritan saints are the elect under the New Covenant. Practically, this means that sainthood belongs at least as much to life as to death, and that the slow accumulation of virtues and development of one's soul are infinitely more important, and much more difficult, than ending one's life spectacularly. Michael promises Adam that a life of temperance may allow one to escape much pain and suffering (11:535–538):

So mayst thou live, till like ripe fruit thou drop
Into thy mother's lap, or be with ease
Gathered, not harshly plucked, for death mature:
This is old age . . .

"Ease" here is not a condition of casual achievement, but the effect of much effort, of living laborious days (538–545):

but then thou must outlive
Thy youth, thy strength, thy beauty, which will change
To withered weak and gray; thy senses then
Obtuse, all taste of pleasure must forego,
To what thou hast, and for the air of youth
Hopeful and cheerful, in thy blood will reign
A melancholy damp of cold and dry
To weigh thy spirits down . . .

By dying young Edward King escapes all of this. The prototype is Cary's Morison in Jonson's ode in memory of the pair (79–84):

He leapt the present age,
Possessed with holy rage,
To see that bright eternal day:
Of which we priests, and poets say
Such truths, as we expect for happy men,
And there he lives with memory . . .

Jonson's "memory" is Milton's "henceforth." The ode is partly an elegy for Morison, but partly a plan for Cary's life. His fate is the harder, for (95–96):

fate doth so alternate the design,
Whilst that in heaven, this light on earth must shine.

Now this poem has twinned them even more securely than they were twinned in life, so that as exemplars of virtue the survivor carries the burden not only of his own existence but also of Morison's memory. Unless he continues to live virtuously, no matter how long his life nor how many the temptations, it will not be possible to proclaim, as Jonson can do at the present moment of the ode, "nothing perfect done / But as a Cary or a Morison." Henceforth, from the moment that *Lycidas* is written and known, Edward King will do good to people, and it is part of Milton's life burden that he should continue to do so.

It is worth pointing out how *Lycidas* and the other poems in the Cambridge collection, differ in their estimation of King's loss. The other elegists, obeying convention and the preface's description of King's maturity, stress his achievements. He "dressed the Muses in the brav'st attire / That e'er they wore"; his was a "rare prodigious life's perfection"; in him "Neptune hath got an University"; he is a drowned Vatican, "his brain a centre . . . / To learning's circularity."[19] The constant refrain is loss. *Lycidas,* too, begins with loss, but its purpose is to transform this into gain, restoration, and recompense. In choosing the death he did King deprived heaven of hundreds, perhaps thousands, of souls. In choosing to mourn King in the way he does, Milton transforms that death into an instrument of providential salvation. Henceforth through reading his poem many more souls will be gained than were lost. The scrivener's son knew that recompense was not a matter of simple repayment, but involved the calculation of interest too. By 1645 he could be even more certain of his rightness in choosing to be a poet rather than a churchman, his prophecy of the ruin of the corrupt clergy having so soon come about. If his poem had played even the tiniest part in the process which was leading to the role of the Saints then it had restored many more souls than King's death had lost.

Something of this purpose is implicit in the way the poem restores King's corpse. Its loss is potentially the greatest injustice of all, for not to have a bier, grave, or tombstone is to have no objective evidence that such a person existed. This is why the sea is always the most powerful image of annihilation: after the Flood Noah and his family had restored to them not a world of wreckage and corpses, but one completely empty, as if those who had drowned had never been. The notion survives in the more sinister uses of the word *liquidate.* It is customary for elegiac poetry to reify itself as the actual gravestone, with the prospect of a longer survival than mere brass or stone. *Lycidas* does this and goes further by reconstituting the corpse (172–181):

> So Lycidas sunk low, but mounted high,
> Through the dear might of him that walked the waves;
> Where other groves, and other streams along,
> With nectar pure his oozy locks he laves,
> And hears the unexpressive nuptial song,
> In the blest kingdoms meek of joy and love.
> There entertain him all the saints above,

In solemn troops, and sweet societies
That sing, and singing in their glory move,
And wipe the tears for ever from his eyes.

The effect is one of a curious superimposition. At the very moment of apotheosis, with the image of Lycidas mounted high among the heavenly host, there is a secondary image of a corpse rescued from the sea, laid out on its bier, its hair being washed clean, the water wiped off its face, and mourners singing the exequies. The only way to solve the paradox of a poem which both brings its subject back to life and lays him to rest is to appreciate that the poem is the subject: Edward King is not just Lycidas; he is also *Lycidas*.

9 Caught in the Web of Dreams: The Dead

Superimposing the living upon the dead and the dead upon the living is one of seventeenth-century poetry's major concerns. Having no body to bury makes Milton restore it at the end of *Lycidas,* the sea giving it back at the moment when the poet celebrates Edward King's entry into heaven. Theologically this is nice. Here are man's two bodies, the corruptible and the incorruptible. While seawater is cleaned off the first, tears are wiped away from the second. The mind's eye has to hold both in view, together if possible—otherwise, alternately, like Jonson's Cary and Morison, the one on earth and the other in heaven. Look at Cary as he ages and you see how Morison would have grown old. Remember Morison forever young and in his prime and you remember how Cary used to be: "each styled by his end, / The copy of his friend" The living shepherd heading eastward to new pastures at the end of *Lycidas* is a reflection of his dead friend, the sun dropped into the western bay. The eye holds both images together.

At its most basic this is a matter of optics. "Upon Appleton House" is the *locus classicus* for altered perspectives and superimpositions, many of them shifting from the dead past to the living present. The merging of Thwaites and Maria, Fairfax and his ancestor, is part of the same process which makes the eye see at one moment cows in a field, at another spots on a face or a constellation in the skies. While much can be described by the new science of optics, more depends upon the knowledge and expectations of the observer. Knowing the history of the Fairfax family encourages Marvell to see the nunnery from whose demolition the stones were taken for the building of the house. The stones themselves are neutral, only their context making them vicious or just. The eye sees both possibilities.

Lovelace's "Aramantha," a pastoral poem which influenced "Upon Appleton House," pins its rambling narrative upon just such a shift in perspective. Two former lovers meet by apparent chance in a wood, mistake each other to the point where violence is imminent, and then suddenly see that they are Alexis and Lucasta, not a shepherd and Aramantha. The moment of recognition is recounted with a significant parallel (298–308):

> Now as in war intestine, where
> I'th' mist of a black battle, each
> Lays at his next, then makes a breach
> Through th'entrails of another whom
> He sees nor knows when he did come
> Guided alone by rage and th' drum,
> But stripping and impatient wild,
> He finds too soon his only child.
>   So our expiring desp'rate lover
> Fared, when amazed he did discover
> Lucasta in this nymph . . .

In a state in which divisions have been driven so deep that civil war has come about, the poet becomes interested in how different eyes see the same thing in different ways, and in how difficult it becomes to hold onto one view of a thing as circumstances alter radically and swiftly.

Lovelace's poetry has many such shifts in appearance and observation. The poem in praise of Lely's portrait of Charles I and his son at Hampton Court alternates between the artist's perception of a subject and a subject's (in the other sense) perception of his king. The focus is carefully blurred. One is looking through tears, sorrowing at the sight of a monarch so reduced; and one is looking at tears, admiring the artist's skill in showing them about to well up, or held back from their subjects' eyes. This is part of Lovelace's vision of the committed Cavalier in prison:[1]

> Stone walls do not a prison make,
>   Nor iron bars a cage;
> Minds innocent and quiet take
>   That for an hermitage;
> If I have freedom in my love,
>   And in my soul am free;

> Angels alone that soar above,
> Enjoy such liberty.

The most liberated man is the one most closely confined. The very tangibility of walls and bars frees the imagination. But this is not the freedom of transcendence or detached meditation, for more than anything else the stanza registers the presence of iron and stone, rather as Jonson's imaginative recreation of the breadth of English society and history in his late plays is fixed firmly to his own immobility and confinement. The focus moves forward and backward, alternating between solid and abstract without losing sight of either. In another poem, "Lucasta's Fan With a Looking Glass in It," Lovelace has Lucasta moving across a ballroom floor in all her finery, with her ostrich-feather fan at her side, to be suddenly perceived as the ostrich itself—the eye alternating between one of creation's most elegant objects and one of its most ungainly.

Herrick's short poems often treat such visual puzzles, when nipples become strawberries or a leg becomes an egg. This is a moment of sudden illusion:

> ### The Silken Snake
> For sport my *Julia* threw a Lace
> Of silk and silver at my face:
> Watchet the silk was; and did make
> A show, as if't'ad been a snake:
> The suddenness did me affright;
> But though it scared, it did not bite.

As usual in Herrick's poetry, the situation is entirely domestic, the ingredients of the poem as commonplace as the "Argument of his Book" promises the readers of *Hesperides,* the behavior of the protagonists entirely harmless—even flirtation would be too strong a word for it. And yet the poem is full of sexuality, violence, and death. Only a fraction of a second is occupied by such possibilities, but it takes only a fraction of a second to die. The suddenness of the whole thing is what frightens him. Within its tiny space the incident reveals her repressed aggression, their potential sexual relationship, his role as victim, and, most of all, how beneath the trained, rational practices of polite behavior there is an instinct always on the alert for the final threat. His eye responds in two ways, simultaneously: civilized man, knowing the games the sexes play, registers the details of color and material as well as motive ("for sport"); savage man sees the predator about to strike.

Milton plays skillfully on just this kind of double sight in *Paradise Lost* when Satan approaches Eve to mount the great temptation. Solitary at last, she stands doing her gardening work, in just such a way as to heighten the fallen reader's responses (9:424–427):

> Eve separate he spies,
> Veiled in a cloud of fragrance, where she stood,
> Half spied, so thick the roses bushing round
> About her glowed . . .

The immediate memory here is of Guyon's temptresses on the way in to the Bower of Bliss in *The Faerie Queene:* their eroticism is magnified by their nakedness being perceived through water. Herrick's poetry is also full of veils and thin tissues of lawn through which the object of beauty is only half or three-quarters perceived. In a brief poem called "The Lawn" this effect is transferred to the skin itself:

> Would I see Lawn, clear as the Heaven, and thin?
> It should be only in my *Julia's* skin:
> Which so betrays her blood, as we discover
> The blush of cherries, when a Lawn's cast over.

While this is a classic piece of seventeenth-century aesthetic appreciation, it is disturbing, too, in its realization of how thin is the membrane which keeps life in. Milton's Eve is veiled and half-spied in a way calculated to delight anyone who shares Herrick's delight in near transparencies: "bushing" is carefully chosen to match the flora to her pubic hair, so that we cannot be quite sure which of the two we are catching glimpses of.[2] Like Satan we are encouraged to approach her in appreciation of her beauty and, as her predator, in appreciation of her defenselessness. Because she is an unfallen creature she lacks any such double vision: Milton describes her as "mindless" (431), conveying all of her vulnerability to the Darwinian world she is soon to enter. In any garden where snakes are common fallen humans stay very mindful of their existence; even Herrick's *homo domesticus* has the instinct. After the Fall Adam soon learns to look at nature with a double eye. In the unfallen garden the human couple make no distinction between the elephant writhing his trunk and the serpent writhing his body; both are elements in the Disney park of entertainment which exists for their amusement. Now, however, the aesthete has to make space for the animal which can be both hunter and hunted (11:184–193):

nigh in her sight
The bird of Jove, stooped from his airy tower,
Two birds of gayest plume before him drove:
Down from a hill the beast that reigns in woods,
First hunter then, pursued a gentle brace,
Goodliest of all the forest, hart and hind;
Direct to the eastern gate was bent their flight.
Adam observed, and with his eye the chase
Pursuing, not unmoved to Eve thus spake.
    O Eve, some further change awaits us nigh . . .

Again, we can see how attractive this poem must have been to a man beginning to formulate a theory of natural adaptation and selection.

Man's most painful adaptation is to the knowledge of his aging and death. This is Herrick's "On Julia's Picture":

How am I ravished! When I do but see,
The Painter's art in thy *Sciography?*
If so, how much more shall I dote thereon,
When once he gives it incarnation?

"*Sciography*" catches the eye: so technical a word in so slight a poem. Herrick is having fun showing how even his fragments can find room for the technicalities of art. But the word which shifts the poem from theory to the real world of life and feeling is "incarnation." The artist incarnates his sciograph by filling it in with a flesh color.[3] In doing this he slides it away from representation toward real existence, which means life, aging, and death. *Incarnation* had, and still has, as its principal sense God's taking on of human flesh. The devil in *Paradise Lost,* who parodies all of Christ's actions, takes on serpent's flesh with the same word (9:163–167):

O foul descent! That I who erst contended
With gods to sit the highest, am now constrained
Into a beast, and mixed with bestial slime,
This essence to incarnate and imbrute,
That to the height of deity aspired . . .

Incarnating an essence is just what happens to Julia in Herrick's poem. *Sciography,* from the Greek *skia,* "shadow," is "that branch of the science of Perspective which deals with the projection of shadows."[4] Julia, sketched in outline, shadows without color, is so essentially recognizable that the image ravishes Herrick: her incarnation will be unbearably exciting. But behind this hope is the frustrating sense that all incarnations are really illusions. The closer her image is brought to a living, breathing human being, the further one is removed from the unchanging essence, for incarnation is a matter of subtle and constant alterations of tone. Satan dismisses it as imbrutement and mixture with bestial slime. We might agree with him about taking on the flesh of a serpent, except that at this stage in the poem the snake is still a creature who goes erect rather than crawling in the dust, and its beauty marks it out among the other beasts in the garden. It comes down to a matter of perspective, to whether we stress the spiritual sense of *incarnation*—that is, its color—or its carnal sense.

John Suckling begins his "Farewell to Love" by describing the ladies whom he abandons as a "well-shadowed landskip." His image of them soon deteriorates into Grand Guignol (21–50):[5]

> Oh! how I glory now! that I
> Have made this new discovery!
>   Each wanton eye
> Inflamed before: no more
> Will I increase that score.
>
> If I gaze now, 'tis but to see
> What manner of death's-head 'twill be,
>   When it is free
> From that fresh upper skin,
> The gazer's Joy and sin.
>
> The Gum and glist'ning which with art
> And studied method in each part
>   Hangs down the heart,
> Looks (just) as if, that day
> *Snails* there had crawled the *Hay*.
>
> The Locks, that curled o'er each ear be,
> Hang like two Master-worms to me,
>   That (as we see)
> Have tasted to the rest
> Two holes, where they like 't best.
>
> A quick corse, methinks, I spy
> In every woman, and mine eye,
>   At passing by,

Checks, and is troubled, just
As if it rose from dust.

They mortify, not heighten me:
These of my sins the Glasses be:
   And here I see
How I have loved before,
And so I love no more.

As the eye, so the object; and when the eye is haunted by images of death, then the more beautiful the sight, the more of a *memento mori* it becomes. Much of Suckling's poetry is concerned with different ways of looking at the same thing, as in the supposed dialogue with Carew on "My Lady Carlisle's Walking in Hampton Court Garden," where Carew's idealism is undercut by Suckling's mental stripping of the lady; or a "Sonnet" which begins:

Dost see how unregarded now
   that piece of beauty passes?
There was a time when I did vow
     to that alone;
   but mark the fate of faces;
That red and white works now no more on me
Than if it could not charm or I not see.

There is more than mere libertinage in these poems. True, they function in part as defenses for inconstancy, but they have an edge of bafflement at the way the eye refuses to hold a stable, unchanging view of a subject whose beauty should command undeviating fidelity. Hence comes the popularity of so much *carpe diem* verse, which pretends to be concerned with seduction, but which is really only using this plea as a stratagem for exploring the processes of aging and death. Like the application of cosmetics it is a means of escaping the tyranny of the present moment. Where the one covers up wrinkles and rouges away the paleness of sickness or age, the other paints in the lines and accelerates youth into experience.

This is part of John Hall's best poem, "The Lure" (49–66):[6]

Come, prithee come, we'll now essay
To piece the scant'ness of the day,
We'll pluck the wheels from th' chariot of the sun,

> That he may give
> Us time to live,
> Till that our scene be done.
>
> W'are in the blossom of our age,
> Let us dance o'er, not tread the stage;
> Though fear and sorrow strive to pull us back,
>   And still present
>   Doubts of content,
> They shall not make us slack.
>
> We'll suffer viperous thoughts and cares
> To follow after silver hairs;
> Let's not anticipate them long before,
>   When they begin
>   To enter in,
> Each minute they'll grow more.

Herrick and Marvell and the host of seventeenth-century singers of mortality crowd in here, but the voice is distinctively Hall's too. This is the greatest and still most unappreciated achievement of the period, its unfailing inventiveness in treating the ways in which death invades life and life death. Often the funeral or *carpe diem* poetry of the century is dismissed as conventional and frigid. Perhaps the unpopularity of death in our own age makes us reluctant to give this poetry its due, for apart from the few excellent surveys of its classical grounding it is hard to think of much good criticism of its variety and range.[7] In these three stanzas even as limited a poet as Hall writes something memorable. Piecing "the scant'ness of the day" is a fine description of the lovers' efforts to repair not just the brevity but also the inadequacy of their experience. Its meagerness comes from their shared sense of death and annihilation. The stanza which precedes the three above end by contrasting the sun's constant renewal with their finite existence:

> He can at will his ancient brightness gain;
>   But thou and I,
>   When we shall die,
> Shall still in dust remain.

These are the fears which threaten to pull them off the stage and the "viperous thoughts" which should wait upon silver hairs. They will not, of course, for the act of trying to exorcise them gives them renewed life. Tiny snakes now begin to grow in the hair. "The Lure" is a poem of Platonic love, and the weaker for it, unless we take the clue that sexuality is rejected not because of some half-baked philosophy but because the fears are mortifying, not heightening, ones. Hall's assertion that fear and sorrow "shall not make us slack" is very nearly an admission of detumescence when faced with his quick corpse.[8]

Waller has a forensic approach to matters of love and death. His "To a Lady in a Garden" opens with just the tone of elegant frigidity designed to flatten away fears or passion. The calculated reserve of "resumes" takes away most of the strength of its object word "glory" in the opening stanza:

> Sees not my love how time resumes
> The glory which he lent these flowers?
> Though none should taste of their perfumes,
> Yet must they live but some few hours;
> Time what we forbear devours!

"Devours," too, is apparently diluted to the level of a mere cliché; but the next stanza brings it back to life:

> Had Helen, or the Egyptian Queen,
> Been ne'er so thrifty of their graces,
> Those beauties must at length have been
> The spoil of age, which finds out faces
> In the most retired places.

"Finds out" is the mischievous phrasal verb which subverts the poem's formality. It may not quite have its modern senses of detecting an offense or penetrating a disguise—which the OED dates from around the beginning of the next century—but its simpler senses of discovery and unriddling are forceful enough in the context. The most retired places are such as the garden of the title—its 1645 title was "To a Lady in Retirement"—but the most retired place of all is the one Andrew Marvell called "fine and private." It may be more reticently delivered, but ultimately the image is the same as in the central passage of "To his Coy Mistress," of worms discovering and unriddling the corpse, devouring the face.

Waller's professed purpose is simple seduction, as in most of the line-and-wrinkle poems. John Cleveland mocks the lady's denial of his advances by asking whether she intends to hold out like Ostend, and "be / Nothing but Rubbish at Delivery" ("To Julia, to Expedite her Promise");

and Thomas Beedome has his disdainful female looking at her mirror and being frightened by what she sees:[9]

> And when thy glass shall it present,
> Without those smiles which once were there,
> Showing like some stale monument,
> A scalp departed from its hair,
>   At thy self frighted wilt not start and swear
>   That I belied thee, when I called thee fair?

These are fairly typical examples of the genre, mocking themselves with their own excesses. Beedome's poem, for instance, despite the striking image of the hairless scalp, is based on the unreal idea that he will stay young while she ages. In contrast, a more reticent poem, Herrick's "Upon Silvia, a Mistress," conveys more powerfully the slide toward death:

> When some shall say, Fair once my *Silvia* was;
> Thou wilt complain, False now's thy Looking-glass:
> Which renders that quite tarnished, which was green;
> And Priceless now, what Peerless once had been:
> Upon thy Form more wrinkles yet will fall,
> And coming down, shall make no noise at all.

This is the stronger because it is not concerned with seduction. There are carefully placed words—"fair" and "false"—to hint at sexual betrayal, aided by the implication that what once was green is now tarnished. What once was green turns white too, for the final image is of wrinkles falling like snow, silent and cold.

Looking at a beautiful woman and being struck by thoughts of age and decay is the most obvious example of death superimposing itself upon life. It took other forms too—most hauntingly in Marvell's vision of the mowers scything their way across the meadows in "Upon Appleton House," which dissolves into an image of the New Model Army cutting through the Royalist ranks. This is the more moving because the same men were involved, Fairfax's workers having not long returned from military service. To the eye partly clouded by tears of memory the new-mown meadow seems like a battlefield (421–424),

> Where, as the meads with hay, the plain
> Lies quilted o'er with bodies slain:

> The women that with forks it fling,
> Do represent the pillaging.

The details of superimposition are very precise—not only the same men, but the same women who followed their men into battle to gather hard-earned profits from the bodies of the slain, and perhaps the same implements, a hay-rake making an ideal tool for dispatching a wounded soldier or forking a body clear of a pile of corpses to be individually searched.

Some of the most powerful images in seventeenth-century poems work in the opposite way, superimposing life upon death. It is, after all, difficult to look at death and see it for what it is. We might imagine that in this period, in particular, the cold reality of the corpse in the grave and its entire loss of identity would be muffled by thoughts of heaven or hell. In fact, speculations on the afterlife of the deceased are not all that common, and it is more usual to see the dead in terms of life in this world, as in this poem by John Fletcher, included in his *The Lover's Progress* (ca. 1623). The context is a welcome offered by the dead host of an inn:[10]

> 'Tis late and cold, stir up the fire;
> Sit close, and draw the table nigher;
> Be merry, and drink wine that's old,
> A hearty medicine 'gainst a cold.
> Your bed's of wanton down the best,
> Where you shall tumble to your rest;
> I could wish you wenches too,
> But I am dead, and cannot do.
> Call for the best, the house may ring,
> Sack, white, and claret, let them bring,
> And drink apace while breath you have;
> You'll find but cold drink in the grave.
> Plover, partridge, for your dinner,
> And a capon for the sinner,
> You shall find ready, when you are up,
> And your horse shall have his sup:
>   Welcome, welcome, shall fly round,
>   And I shall smile, though under ground.

This is the other side of Jonson's "Inviting a Friend to Supper," absorbing into this welcoming genre the topoi of epitaph and *carpe diem* poetry. It is a fine tribute to a late good host and an admonition to drink while we have the opportunity. Its humor comes most of all from its superimposition of the self-interest which lies behind any innkeeper's broad welcome to his patrons and the envy which the dead would feel for us if they could feel anything. The puns ram the contrast home. Catching a cold was a common enough euphemism for dying—as Webster's characters reveal— and tumbling "to your rest" and not being able to "do" focus on the bed as the place where life and death are most obviously jumbled together. The bed is the place where life most often begins and ends, where the short pleasure of doing soon leads to the sadness of realizing how short and fleeting everything is, and where dreams of life merge into nightmares of death. Even "ring" and "sack," two emblems of inn life at its most colorful, have their death sentence of tolling bells and sackcloth. The cold drink in the grave is the water seeping in, and the smile of the host under ground is the grimace of rigor mortis.

William Strode has some of the best mergings of life and death. In "On the Death of Sir Thomas Lea" he mourns the memory of a good host who gave freely to the poor, taking the opportunity to turn Hamlet's image of the feeder fed into one of ultimate benevolence to the lowest creatures of all:[11]

> The man whose table fed
> So many while he lived, since he is dead,
> Himself is turned to food . . .

This is standard epitaph wit, but the poem ends with something more interesting in its contrast of the dead good man with the many living selfish ones:

> Such descants poor men make; who miss him more
> Than six great men, that keeping house before
> After a spurt unconstantly are fled
> Away to London. But the man that's dead
> Is gone unto a place more populous,
> And tarries longer there, and waits for us.

Moving back and forth between their country houses and the city was common among the gentry, and commonly complained about because of the resultant neglect of their estates. This is the satirical surface of the lines, but under it is the sinister image of the vast city, more populous than London, where Sir Thomas Lea patiently waits for his friends to join him for their last supper. During outbreaks of the plague the city of the dead became even less unreal. Thomas Flatman wrote "The Retirement" in the "time of the Great Sickness, 1665." A self-indulgent poem, looking forward to Gray's elegy, it moves from the retired poet musing on his melancholic state in the country, back to the city racked by the plague, which finally appears as a "heap of pyramids," [12]

> Eternal monuments of pride and sin,
> Magnificent and tall without, but dead men's bones within.

This is a last twist to the many recollections of pyramids in Renaissance elegiac poetry. Now every one of the fine buildings of the great city imitates the shape of the piles of bodies which were fetched out onto the carts.

In the 1660s and 1670s poets could still write confidently about heaven, but they seem to have found it increasingly difficult to match this promise of survival for the incorruptible body to the decay of the corruptible one. Notions of identity had begun to shift, and such elements as we now label personality and character were more recognizably located in the body than in the soul: emotions and even ideas were generated by, and realized in, the physical senses. So, Flatman, writing to his dead brother, in one of the very few poems of the century which deliberately recall *Lycidas,* after mourning his death offers a stanza of great contentment at the brother's being now in heaven (67–86):[13]

> There is a state of perfect ease,
> Of never interrupted happiness,
> Thy large illuminated mind
> Shall matter of eternal wonder find;
> There dost thou clearly see how, and from whence
> The stars communicate their influence,
> The methods of th' Almighty Architect,
> How He consulted with Himself alone
> To lay the wondrous corner-stone,
> When He this goodly fabric did erect.
> There, thou dost understand
> The motions of the secret hand,
> That guides th' invisible wheel,
> Which here, we ne'er shall know, but ever feel;
> There Providence, the vain man's laughing-stock,
> The miserable good-man's stumbling-block,
> Unfolds the puzzling riddle to thy eyes,
> And its own wise contrivance justifies.

What timorous man wouldn't be pleased to die,
To make so noble a discovery?

There is no trace of doubt here, only confident celebration of the good
man's enjoyment of eternal bliss, which, in the case of Flatman's brother,
means the answers to the many intellectual problems which perplexed
him while on earth. But such certainty assumes that a reasoning mind can
somehow be abstracted from the brain cells which formerly contained it,
and which are now decaying in the earth. The poem's final stanza turns
back to the corpse (87–105):

> And must I take my solemn leave
>   Till time shall be no more!
> Can neither sighs, nor tears, nor prayers retrieve
>   One cheerful hour!
>   Must one unlucky moment sever
> Us, and our hopes, us and our joys for ever!—
> Is this cold clod of Earth that endeared Thing
>   I lately did my Brother call?
> Are these the artful fingers that might vie
>   With all the sons of harmony
>   And overpower them all!
>   Is this the studious comprehensive head
> With curious arts so richly furnished!
> Alas! thou, and thy glories all are gone,
> Buried in darkness and oblivion.
>   'Tis so—and I must follow thee,
>   Yet but a little while, and I shall see thee,
>   Yet but a little while I shall be with thee,
> Then some kind friend perhaps may drop one tear for me.

We cannot explain the sadness away by pointing to a concept of the resurrection which has all the dead sleeping until Doomsday, for the poet
has already located his brother in heaven, celebrating God's power and
understanding His purposes. What we have, in effect, is a weak poem
torn apart by its inability to reconcile the two identities. *Lycidas* holds
the two together in its superimposition of the corpse upon the angel, but
Flatman's eye is too firmly fixed upon the cold clod of earth, its already
decaying fingers and head which once articulated the personality of this
talented human being. While the soul celebrates in heaven, everything
which went into the making of the brother's identity is buried in darkness

and lost for ever. This seems to be the cause of Flatman's melancholy in "The Retirement"—his difficulty in keeping hold of a sense of his own self while increasing piles of other selves lie heaped anonymously in the buildings of London.[14]

Move back two or three decades, and see how Strode approaches the prospect of a decaying corpse:[15]

> Happy Grave, thou dost enshrine
> That which makes thee a rich mine:
> Remember yet, 'tis but a loan;
> And we must have it back, Her own,
> The very same; Mark me, the same:
> Thou canst not cheat us with a lame
> Deformed Carcase; She was fair,
> Fresh as Morning, sweet as Air:
> Purer than other flesh as far
> As other Souls than Bodies are:
> And that thou mayst the better see
> To find her out: two stars there be
> Eclipsed now; uncloud but those
> And they will point thee to the Rose
> That dyed each cheek, now pale and wan,
> But will be when she wakes again
> Fresher than ever: And howe'er
> Her long sleep may alter Her
> Her Soul will know her Body straight,
> 'Twas made so fit for't. No deceit
> Can suit another to it: none
> Clothe it so neatly as its own.

This is more confident, but not entirely so. The promise that bodies will rise from graves in a new incorruptible state fit for their souls to reenter them is qualified by apprehension that something completely unrestorable has been lost. Restoration haunts the century's poetry, but increasingly with the sense that the second temple could not begin to match the first. So, with Strode's epitaph, the mind may take in notions of survival, but the eye sees decomposition, a lame, deformed corpse, eyes extinguished and the cheek eaten away to the bone. Waller's *find out* recurs here in a similar context, for its subject is the grave, which, when he repays the loan, will supply something quite altered from its original state.

How far one's identity is bound to one's body is always a puzzle, the more so in a period when the very idea of identity was such a novel thing. It was an idea which was tested at all levels. Poems on Charles I's death took the highest view, relating not only body to soul but also king to man, and, naturally, they celebrated the concept of the two identities of the king which the Stuart propagandists had pushed so hard. Charles came to be, in the eyes of friends and enemies, a king and no king. But on lower levels poets speculated on smaller amputations than the decapitation of a monarch. Herrick has a poem on the loss of a finger; Thomas Randolph has two. Herrick's is the shortest of the three and most to the point:

Upon the Loss of his Finger

One of the five straight branches of my hand
Is lopped already; and the rest but stand
Expecting when to fall: which soon will be;
First dies the Leaf, the Bough next, next the Tree.

Trunk is the unspoken word here. Its first three definitions in the *OED* are "the main stem of a tree," "the human body," "a dead body . . . also the body considered apart from the soul or life." Herrick's poem moves through all of these meanings. Whether "expecting" includes a hope of the life to come, the expectation of heaven, or only a patient resignation to the fact of annihilation is left unanswered, but the austerity of the poem allows no room for consolation. Randolph, in contrast, is all wit and extravagance:[16]

On the Loss of his Finger

How much more blest are trees than men,
Their boughs lopped off will grow again;
But if the steel our limbs dissever,
The joint once lost is lost for ever.
But fondly I dull fool complain,
Our members shall revive again;
And thou poor finger that art dust
Before the other members, must
Return as soon at heaven's command,
And reunited be to th' hand
As those that are not ashes yet;
Why dost thou then so envious sit,
And malice Oaks that they to fate
Are tenants of a longer date?

> Their leafs do more years include
> But once expired, are ne'er renewed.
> Therefore dear finger though thou be
> Cut from those muscles governed thee,
> And had thy motion at command,
> Yet still as in a margent stand,
> To point my thoughts to fix upon
> The hope of Resurrection:
> And since thou canst no finger be
> Be a death's head to humble me,
> Till death doth threat her sting in vain,
> And we in heaven shake hands again.

This is the lesser known of the two poems on his lost finger, but the more amusing of the two in the variety of symbols it has the finger playing, right down to the admonitory sign in the margin. And in even so light a piece there is still room for bafflement over the identity which controls the muscles which control the finger. That little piece of flesh and bone has a separate identity, its own body and brain, rendering it capable of a handshake at the end. I suppose there is even the possibility of the finger being saved while the rest of the body, because of its later dissolute life, is damned.

One of Herrick's best death poems, only three lines long, is "On Himself." This title could introduce any kind of epigram, but this is an epitaph. So, with every word counting double in such a tight, little poem, "On" adds to its normal meaning in a title—"About"—a literal location, the inscription on the gravestone:[17]

> Lost to the world; lost to my self; alone
> Here now I rest under this Marble stone:
> In depth of silence, heard, and seen of none.

Few poems say so much in so little space. In spite of its size, Herrick can afford repetition. "Lost," doubly emphasized by its initiating the poem and its repetition, is the other side of *restore*. To lose one's self is a haunting theme of seventeenth-century lyric poetry. How one can say, as Herrick does here, that I have lost my self, is a puzzle, for an I which has no self is difficult to conceive. Riddles lie here, and we have already seen that the grave is the one place where unriddling is guaranteed. That is the job for the worms, creatures not entirely removed from poets and readers of poems who also burrow into echoing vaults and try too-long-preserved virginities. The I who writes Herrick's poem is the I who is alive in the

1630s and 1640s, while the "now" is now, all these hundreds of years after 1674. Hence the title "On Himself" rather than "On Myself," for to the readers of "now" Herrick is a third person whose identity is constructed out of the poems. In "alone" is the terrible alienation of the dead, cut off from everything which gave them their identity; the alienation of the living, also, for the continuum between life and death is virtually unbroken—in Flatman's words, "one unlucky moment" which "sever[s] / Us, and our hopes, us and our joys for ever." Milton writes about Edward King as if his corpse had the power of volition which an identity would allow it, visiting, sleeping, and looking homeward. According to the poem's argument these are no longer the "frail thoughts" of the pathetic fallacy passage, but a new realism in which the poet comes to terms with the absence of King's corpse and its humming around the oceans of the world. But perhaps a concern of *Lycidas* is to show how our frailty prevents us from looking squarely at death. As the Psalmist puts it (39:4): "Lord, make me to know mine end, and the measure of my days, what it is; that I may know how frail I am." The Authorized Version's marginal alternative to "how frail I am" is "what time I have here."

The frailest of all human notions is that the dead are only sleeping or resting. Lycidas sleeps just off Land's End, near St. Michael's Mount. Herrick rests alone under the marble stone. "Rest" is slightly tougher than *sleep* because it allows in a little more of the inanimation which a corpse has—things can rest merely by lying in or on something else, unlike animate creatures, who rest in order to wake refreshed. Herrick rests in "depth of silence." The depth is literal enough, under ground, but slides into the figurative when attached to silence. All seems to find compensation with "heard"—"In depth of silence, heard"—and our frail responses to the duplicity of Herrick's syntax raise the possibilities of some heroic survival of identity in a voice which, through his poems, outbraves the oblivion of death. But "heard" is cruelly extended into "and seen of none," a final reminder that the grave's silence is a double one: we hear nothing and we say nothing.

Herrick was just as austere when mourning others, as in his four-line poem "Upon his Sister-in-Law, Mistress Elizabeth Herrick":

> First, for Effusions due unto the dead,
> My solemn Vows have here accomplished:
> Next, how I love thee, that my grief must tell,
> Wherein thou liv'st for ever. Dear farewell.

Really, the whole statement is contained in the final two words. They fulfill the solemn vows which are introduced in lines 1–2 and declare Her-

rick's love for his dead relative, and explained in lines 3–4. The poem is
about our responsibilities to the dead; hence the careful statement of the
first line, making clear the difference between us and them. They, for all
their individuality, are part of that anonymous crowd labeled "the dead,"
the city more populous than London itself. What we can salvage of their
identity we do with our grief, but the frail illusion of their survival is cut
down by the sudden following of "for ever" with "farewell," a tiny parallel to Milton's shepherd striding off toward the east, his back to the
Irish Sea.

"Dear," Herrick's address to his dead sister-in-law, is a remembered
intimacy. As the corpse decays it becomes ever more difficult to restore
our closeness to it. Strode has a gentle poem, one of the common genre in
which ladies were counseled on how to mourn their dead husbands, in
which he directs "the Right Honourable the Lady Penelope, Dowager of
the Late Viscount Bayning" on how to bear her loss:

> Great Lady,
>   Humble partners of like grief
> In bringing Comfort may deserve belief,
> Because they Feel and Feign not: Thus we say
> Unto Ourselves, Lord Bayning, though away,
> Is still of Christ-Church; somewhat out of sight,
> As when he travelled, or did bid good night,
> And was not seen long after; now he stands
> Removed in Worlds, as heretofore in Lands;
> But is not lost. The spite of Death can never
> Divide the Christian, though the Man it sever.
>   The like we say to You: He's still at home,
> Though out of reach; as in some upper room,
> Or Study: for His Place is very high,
> His Thought is Vision; now most properly
> Returned he's Yours as sure, as e'er hath been
> The jewel in Your Cask, safe though unseen.
>   You know that Friends have Ears as well as Eyes,
> We hear He's well and Living, that well dies.

Here death is entirely domesticated. So strong was the dead lord's personality that his identity is marked upon each room of the house, his absence
felt as temporary. Surely he will soon come through the door or be
glimpsed in the hallway. Strode's poem plays on the frailest of our responses to death, that the dead still haunt us, their identity being so
strongly impressed on our memory that we sense their presence about

and around us. The experience is at once comforting and unnerving. Lady Penelope will welcome the constant reminders of her dead husband's existence as a sign that all is not lost even if all cannot be restored; but there is an alienation built into such experiences, for they will remind her that her own identity is as insubstantial as a dream.

Sleep is where the dead haunt the living most strongly, often refusing to accept that they are different from us. Milton's nineteenth sonnet, written probably in the late 1650s, is the most moving description of such an experience:

> Methought I saw my late espoused saint
>> Brought to me like Alcestis from the grave,
>> Whom Jove's great son to her glad husband gave,
>> Rescued from death by force though pale and faint.
> Mine as whom washed from spot of childbed taint,
>> Purification in the old Law did save,
>> And such, as yet once more I trust to have
>> Full sight of her in heaven without restraint,
> Came vested all in white, pure as her mind:
>> Her face was veiled, yet to my fancied sight,
>> Love, sweetness, goodness in her person shined
> So clear, as in no face with more delight.
>> But O as to embrace me she inclined
>> I waked, she fled, and day brought back my night.

The critical dispute over which of his two dead wives Milton remembers here is unresolved, the preference possibly being for Katharine, who died in February 1658, having borne a daughter in October of the previous year, over Mary, who died three days after their daughter's birth in May 1652. These biographical facts are important to any interpretation of the sonnet's reference to the ceremony of the purification of women after childbirth. Other biographical details which affect our response to the poem are Milton's blindness—he had seen Mary but had never seen Katharine—and the possibilities that Mary is represented in the poem as the virgin Mary in line 5, who "accomplished the days of her purification" (Luke 2:22), or that Katharine, from *katharos*, "pure," is referred to throughout in the repeated insistence upon purification and cleansing. The balance of that evidence points to Katharine, and we might think, too, that "saint" is more appropriate to Katharine Woodcock than to Mary Powell if Milton is using the word in the Puritan sense of a living member of a community of believers.

It is, after all, a very Puritan sonnet in its celebration of married love and its stress on purity of body and mind. It stands as one of the most austere love poems in our literature, the more moving for that, as it harnesses an almost complete incongruity of language and syntax to the most traditional themes of love poetry—the woman coming to the bed, the wished-for embrace, and, eventually, unrequited love. Behind the image which he thinks he sees Milton is remembering Petrarch's Laura, Dante's Beatrice, perhaps Wyatt's newfangled mistress, perhaps even Shakespeare's master-mistress whose appearance in dreams makes "nights bright days," and, certainly, Odysseus' vain attempts to embrace his mother in the underworld in book 11 of the *Odyssey*.[18]

In this book Achilles tells Odysseus that all the visions he sees are not realities, but each is merely an afterimage, an *eidolon;* the only exception being Hercules, who has been genuinely transformed into a higher being.[19] Hercules is in Milton's sonnet too, as "Jove's great son"; but his apotheosis is certain, marked by his power to enter and return from the land of death. In Milton's poem the female vision is an *eidolon* and nothing more—"an image or unsubstantial appearance; a spectre or phantom; a mental image, an idea"[20]—which flees the imaginer's return to full consciousness. The experience is a veiled one, as befits a dream, particularly the dream of a blind man. "Methought I saw" would itself be a powerful piece of wish fulfillment, without the addition of any specific object; so the dream is doubly fantastic, a restoration of sight as well as a restoration of the dead. From this comes the sonnet's harping on "as," the particle best suited to convey similarity while denying identity or certainty. Its use is the more striking because of the poem's apparently confident deployment of absolutes. In spite of the veil, in spite of the approximations, he can be sure he sees purity, love, sweetness, goodness, even clarity.

This mixture of vagueness and certainty is consistent with the nature of deep dreams. Entirely convincing while we are immersed in them, our waking records only a fragment, a movement, gesture, impression. And between the dream and the memory of it is the moment of waking, when the vision flees and the light crowds in. Milton's sonnet, of course, closes with an apparent reversal of this experience, for his waking is a return to our darkness; but the experience is still closely related to ours, for our sight and his blindness are only two slightly different versions of fallen man's fancied sight as opposed to the full sight which our arrival in heaven will grant us. One of the seventeenth-century religious poets' favorite images for our seeing only through a glass darkly is the veil; Henry Vaughan's poems, for instance, are packed with such images. And Milton writes of Eve, in her unfallen state, as needing no veil, being virtue-proof.

Only when Satan moves in for the kill is she described as veiled, "in a cloud of fragrance."

The dream, then, offers a veiled image of a pure state in contrast with which our waking life lacks clarity and intensity. The idea is not just a religious one. A fair number of love poems follow Donne's example in lamenting the lost dream. This is one by William Cartwright, a minor poet who occasionally comes up with unexpected parallels to Milton:[21]

> *A Dream Broke*
> As Nilus' sudden Ebbing, here
> Doth leave a scale, and a scale there,
> And somewhere else perhaps a Fin,
> Which by his stay had Fishes been:
> So Dreams, which overflowing be,
> Departing leave Half things, which we
> For their Imperfectness can call
> But Joys i' th' Fin, or in the Scale.
> If when her Tears I haste to kiss,
> They dry up, and deceive my Bliss,
> May not I say the Waters sink,
> And Cheat my Thirst when I would drink?
> If when her Breasts I go to press,
> Instead of them I grasp her Dress,
> May I not say the Apples then
> Are set down, and snatched up again?
> Sleep was not thus Death's Brother meant;
> 'Twas made an Ease, no Punishment.
> As then that's finished by the Sun,
> Which *Nile* did only leave begun,
> My Fancy shall run o'er Sleep's Themes,
> And so make up the Web of Dreams:
> In vain fleet shades, ye do Contest:
> Awak'd how e'er I'll think the rest.

The "Web of Dreams" is a fine phrase to describe the way most of the poets use their dream experiences. For them responsibility ends in dreams. Cartwright's typical intention is to spend his waking time making up the web, that is, restoring the experience which has trapped his imagination. Here, surely, is the power of Milton's sonnet, that while he gives full expression to the hold the past has upon him, he refuses to be trapped by or in it. It is sometimes revealing to read critics of the poem, for they tend to rewrite it slightly, making the movement toward the embrace as much Milton's as the dead wife's, rather as Cartwright's dream is full of his actions. But Milton in his sonnet is almost entirely passive, the done to rather than the doer. The vision is brought to him, and at the end his night is brought back. His one act is to wake up. In normal circumstances waking is the most passive of actions, the consequence of external stimuli, usually, as in Donne's poem, the sun peeping through the curtains—although in Milton's case the stimulus to awakening would have to be sound, smell, or touch, not sight. We should realize that in the case of this dream Milton's awakening is not passive, but an act of heroic resistance.

Whereas George Herbert chose to begin his *Outlandish Proverbs* with the one about man proposing and God disposing, whoever reprinted them in 1652 added this one to the beginning: "Old men go to Death, Death comes to Young men." [22] Milton at the time he wrote the sonnet was appreciably older than he or Edward King was when *Lycidas* was written, but he was still creatively young, his great poem probably not yet started. Very soon he would copy Hercules and go down to hell to help restore the dead to life. Doing this would involve the same effort of will as is sketched out in this sonnet, awakening from a dream possession by a female muse to a cold winter morning, encompassed by darkness and danger. The effort of *Paradise Lost* is to turn memory into prophecy. This sonnet is the first stage in this process, escaping the embrace of the dead and delivering the experience intact, with all of its pain. With "I waked" the act of resistance is sudden and complete, his refusal to be claimed by the past.

In this context the sonnet's concern with childbirth is paramount. The analogy between parturition and literary creation was a cliché when Sir Philip Sidney used it to open *Astrophel and Stella,* and frequently it was man's compensation for what a female Freud might call womb envy. In neither case, however, is the creation *ex nihilo.* The artist, too, is penetrated and possessed and, if not strong enough, will be left in silence. So many and fertile are the conceptions with which memory holds him, that the effort to render them with anything like the clarity of their original impression will leave him, at best, pale and faint. The gap between the absolute certainty of the experience and its inevitably inadequate reproduction in words is figured repeatedly in Milton's poetry—as in the paralysis of Shakespeare's reader, the lady's paralysis in *Comus,* and, eventually triumphantly, in the son's stasis in *Paradise Regained.* In this sonnet Milton is in a position very close to Jonson's: not paralyzed and bedridden, but blind and in bed, dependent upon his will to resist the siren's song.

One further element which makes the resistance so difficult is the sexual power of the dream. Appreciating it gives the clue to how Milton turned the subliminal into the sublime. The purification ceremony which monopolizes the sonnet's octave is, as he takes care to remind us, derived from the Old Testament. In Leviticus 12 the woman who has given birth to a female child, as Milton's wives had, "shall be unclean two weeks . . . and shall continue in the blood of her purifying threescore and six days." During this time "she shall touch no hallowed thing, nor come into the sanctuary." When the days of her purifying are completed, then she shall bring an offering "unto the door of the tabernacle of the congregation, unto the priest." This ceremony had its second biblical reference in the New Testament, in the passage I have already mentioned in Luke 2, where the Virgin Mary accomplishes the days of her purification. The ceremony continued into the Catholic and then Protestant churches, where it came to be known as the churching of women, the title given to it in the 1552 Book of Common Prayer.

In several curious ways Milton's sonnet is tightly bound to this ceremony, so that the veiled vision is not merely a representation of his blindness or dream state, but a literal enough description of the woman at the purification ceremony, in which a veil was traditionally worn. Then there is the psalm which, until 1662, was the centerpiece of the ceremony, number 121, *Levavi oculos*. In the Great Bible version, used in the prayer book, its closeness to Milton's sonnet comes not only in its opening image—"I have lifted up mine eyes"—but also in its description of the creator of heaven and earth as one who "shall neither slumber nor slepe"; and, more pointedly, "he that kepeth thee wil not slepe." [23] And the psalm closes with a promise that the Lord will "preserve thy going out, and thy coming in," a link between the ceremony's traditional location at the church door and the sonnet's closing with a going away and a coming back.

It is tempting now to see the ceremony of churching as yet one more example of man's contempt for woman, so that even her part in the creation of life is interpreted as something unclean from which she needs to be purified. There is probably much in this, but it needs to be added that the ceremony had a function which was of some importance to the woman. It gave her a period when, because of her "uncleanness," she could recover from childbirth without having to resume sexual relations. Therefore, the ceremony had an erotic force, a sign of the resumption of lovemaking after a long period of abstinence. In Milton's sonnet the eroticism may be signaled in his trust to have "full sight of her in heaven without restraint." "Restraint" is a word which crops up with potentially strong sexual connotations in *Paradise Lost*.[24] Here the poem touches on an idea which has never been far beneath the surface of this chapter, that of the nature of the resurrected body. In his epic Milton gives fuller consideration to the lost opportunities for continued sexuality as man is gradually refined to a state of angelic bliss. Here, in the sonnet, the real alternative is starkly described—that a lost lover is lost forever, never to be restored. As the gospel has it, "when they shall rise from the dead, they neither marry, nor are given in marriage; but are as the angels of God in heaven" (Matthew 22:30). One implication of these words is that "my late espoused saint" will forever be just that, to be seen but not to be touched. Indeed, it could hardly be otherwise for Milton, assuming that Mary Powell was saved too, for a polygamous heaven is not a Christian ideal. The eternal loss is conveyed by the syntax, as all the promise of "as yet once more I trust to have" is diluted to make "have" not a marker of possession, franking the "mine" which begins the sentence, but only part of a phrasal verb "have . . . sight of." The sight is full, which is a double compensation for a blind man; but poetry is the creation of the fancied sight which lays the living upon the dead and the dead upon the living.

PART FOUR

The Commonwealth

10 "New Things Succeed": Proverbs

Milton's use of the ceremony of the purification of women after child-birth in his sonnet "Methought I saw" seems slightly odd when we take into account his apparently increasing Puritan militancy during the 1650s, for Puritan objections to the ceremony were long-standing, bound up with hostility to the Book of Common Prayer. Alternative Puritan editions of the prayer book did not dare to leave the service out, but by retaining the designation "priest" for such services as public and private baptism and the churching of women, rather than "minister," which replaced it in the other services, the compilers seem to have been suggesting "as a silent but intelligible sign, that these services were added for apparent conformity, but that the use of them was to be discouraged."[1] In James I's reign several Puritan women were prosecuted, ecclesiastically and civilly, for not wearing a veil during the ceremony, and Milton himself has at least one slighting reference to the service as prescribed in the prayer book.[2] And yet the sonnet seems to accept churching as legitimate and even desirable.

Perhaps the oddness fades a little if we realize that the churching of women, while suspected as a relic of papist superstition by some Puritans, was tolerated and practiced by the majority, and Nonconformist objections to the new prayer book at the Savoy Conference in 1661 did not include rejection of the ceremony. Changes in some of its details were asked for, namely its location in the church, the choice of the psalm, and the omission of the offering.[3] Churching, it would seem, was a ceremony which straddled superstition and custom. As the first it should clearly be unacceptable to all Protestants, but as the second it might be acceptable to most, depending, of course, on its source. Superstitions cannot normally be traced to a source, beyond the conspiracy theory that the church of Rome invented them to keep the people in ignorance. Custom, however, is rooted in popular practice, and militant Puritanism often based its arguments upon the recovery of traditions which had become obscured by the Norman conquerors. In similar fashion, religious matters were traced back to the practices of the primitive church, a fountain muddied by Roman superstition—hence Milton's careful stipulation in his sonnet that the purification ceremony was franked by "the old Law." Their emphasis upon the old law brought mockery upon Puritans as would-be restorers of Judaism, but it was really a source of their strength, keeping them close to their Reformation origins. From early in the sixteenth century English culture, unlike the rest of Europe, gave the Old Testament a privileged place; two of Milton's three long poems are on Old Testament subjects.

In the first Book of Common Prayer, in 1549, the title of the service had been, simply, "The Order of the Purification of Women," recalling the words of Leviticus concerning "the blood of her purifying" and "the days of her purifying."[4] The second prayer book, in 1552, changed the title to "The Thanksgiving of Women after Childbirth, Commonly Called the Churching of Women," apparently because of objections to and misunderstandings over the earlier title.[5] Significantly, the 1552 revision added, after the preface, an explanation "Of Ceremonies, Why Some be Abolished, And Some Retained." This essay acknowledged the divisions which already existed in the kingdom as the first stirrings of Puritanism were felt. On the one hand were men who "thynke it a great matter of conscience to departe from a pece of the least of their Ceremonies (thei be so addicted to their old customs:) and again on the other side, some be so new fangled, that thei would innovate all thyng, and so do despise the old, that nothyng can like them, but that is new."[6] As the established church tried to do, right up to the time of Laud, the prayer book compilers trod carefully a path between the two extremes. Although many ceremonies were abolished, the most valued were retained: and those of the new party, who "would rather have al devised anewe," they admonished with the charge that "thei cannot reasonably reprove the old only for their age without bewraying of their owne foly." The reason was obvious: "they ought rather to have reverence unto them for their antiquitie, if they wyl declare themselves to be more studious of unitie and concord, then of innovacions and newe fanglenes, which (asmuche as may be with the true setting furth of Christes Religion) is always to be eschewed."[7] The question begged here is what is really meant by new and old.

Puritan was a term adopted initially by the precisians' enemies, but its use was an accurate enough reflection of their call for a continued reformation so that the church could be returned to "pure" biblical principles.

What seemed to their opponents to be an unrestrained desire for novelty was in their eyes a continuing restoration of the true, old Christianity. William Tyndale summarized his use of "purification" in Leviticus 12 as the "purging" of women, that is, the removal of impurities.[8] Purging the church and then the state was defended in the same terms by whichever side attempted it. *Reformation* could be interpreted as the altering of things for the better—in other words, replacing the old with the new—or it could be presented as the return of things to their correct, old form. The *OED* quotes this from John Trapp's commentary on the Psalms (1657): "that grave and simple Psalmodie . . . so much used of old, and by this blessed Reformation restored to the Church." Richard Lovelace, in prison and surveying the state and the clamors for further reformation, sees them as calls not for restoration, as the Puritans claim, but for the destruction of old values:[9]

> A *Reformation* I would have,
>   As for our griefs a *Sov'reign* salve;
> That is, a cleansing of each wheel
>   Of State, that yet some rust doth feel:
>
> But not a Reformation so,
>   As to reform were to o'erthrow;
> Like watches by unskilful men
>   Disjointed, and set ill again.

No wonder that *restoration* was a word used keenly by both sides. To those who claimed that Charles II's return was a restoration of the proper order, Milton replied at the beginning of *Paradise Lost* with praise for that greater man who will "restore us, and regain the blissful seat."

In all of this *common* is an important word, for in a country split into factions the chief sense is of a common belief or purpose which has been lost, something once shared by all but now shattered by novelty. All factions, of course, believe that theirs is the way back to restoration of that golden age. In their revision of its title from "Purification of Women" to "Thanksgiving," the prayer book editors took care to remind their readers that the ceremony was *commonly* called "the Churching of Women." This is consistent with the book's designation as the Book of Common Prayer. The defense of ceremonies which were retained was based on a need for "unity and concord," without which "it is not possible to kepe any ordre or quiet discipline in the churche."[10] Now, order and discipline are at least as much Puritan ideals as they are Anglican ones; think of the organized community of rowers in Marvell's "Bermudas." But the desirability of all working together in a commonwealth came under some pressure on both sides. For the Puritans there were Calvinist doctrines which taught that at least half the people alive were reprobate, and for the higher-ranking supporters of the king there was the already well-established sense that common people should not have the same rights as they; "the common sort" was a frequent term of contempt. It is clear that both of these pressures could be found across any line of division. There were plenty of Puritan gentry who had contempt for the common sort, and plenty of supporters of the royal cause whose theology, when it came to matters of salvation and damnation, was virtually indistinguishable from Calvinism. Henry Vaughan, for example, in "The Relapse," thanks God for having saved him from a fate which has already swallowed up thousands of his fellow citizens:

> My God, how gracious art thou! I had slipped
>   Almost to hell,
> And on the verge of that dark, dreadful pit
>   Did hear them yell,
> But O thy love! thy rich, almighty love
>   That saved my soul,
> And checked their fury, when I saw them move,
>   And heard them howl.

You can call this "love" only when your sense of a common lot has been severely attenuated, if not extinguished altogether.

Puritan opposition to the Book of Common Prayer was based explicitly upon hostility to its retention of practices and ceremonies "not agreeable to the Scriptures." [11] But behind this was a deep hostility to the whole notion of uniformity of belief and worship. By 1645 any use of the Book of Common Prayer in any public or private place was punishable first by fine and then by imprisonment. "The Directory for the Public Worship of God" with which Parliament replaced it kept to the minimum the observation of common ceremonies; for example, it left to each congregation to decide how and how often Communion should be celebrated, and replaced the burial service with the direction that "the dead body, upon the day of burial, be decently attended from the house to the place appointed for public burial, and there immediately interred, without any ceremony." [12] It may be that Milton, writing in the late 1650s, when in his own opinion, extreme factionalism had threatened, if not doomed, the Commonwealth, was including in this very personal sonnet an essentially political point: that just as ceremony binds the living to the dead, so it keeps the living united to each other—so long as the ceremony is grounded upon good ancient custom, not vain superstition.

The most ancient custom was, by definition, to be found in Genesis. There supporters of a true commonwealth of shared interests could find their original precedent, when Adam delved and Eve spun; as in "Upon Appleton House" (441–456):

> This scene again withdrawing brings
> A new and empty face of things,
> A levelled space, as smooth and plain
> As cloths for Lely stretched to stain.
> The world when first created sure
> Was such a table rase and pure.
> Or rather such is the *toril*
> Ere the bulls enter at Madril.
>
> For to this naked equal flat,
> Which Levellers take pattern at,
> The villagers in common chase
> Their cattle, which it closer rase;
> And what below the scythe increased
> Is pinched yet nearer by the beast.
> Such, in the painted world, appeared
> D'Avenant with the universal herd.

Marvell's perspective, shifting from the garden of Appleton House to the common grazing land of the village, presents him with an image of the complex changes being undergone by English society, the gentry's park being threatened with encroachment by the Levellers' insistence that all should be in common. The hint comes in the way the cattle crop the grass, so close that, as often happened to common land, the pasture becomes increasingly unproductive. A universal herd needs more and better land.

Yet opposition to the enclosure of land was by no means a principle of the Puritan Commonwealth. Resistance to enclosure had been an important part of crown policy from the beginning of the sixteenth century, and Royalist poets exhibited a more or less sentimental attachment to the rights of common land. Here is Richard Corbett praising his father:[13]

> His conscience, like his diet, such
> As neither took, nor left too much:

> So that made Laws were useless grown
> To him, he needed but his own.
> Did he his Neighbours bid, like those
> That feast them only to enclose?
> Or with their roast meat rack their rents,
> And cozen them with their consents?
> No; the free meetings at his board
> Did but one literal sense afford;
> No *Close* or *Acre* understood,
> But only *love* and *neighbourhood.*

This is all part of Corbett's world view, which looks back to an ideal time when all the country danced to the same tune. Much of the anti-Puritanism of his poems is aimed at the Puritans' supposed avariciousness, as they enclose and take to themselves what was once common to all. His best poem is "A Proper New Ballad, Intitled the FAERIES' FAREWELL: or GOD-A-MERCY WILL: to be Sung or Whistled to the Tune of Meadow Brow by the Learned; by the Unlearned, to the Tune of FORTUNE." The details of this title are important. The country is not divided into classes or estates, only into the learned and unlearned, bound together by their love of ballads. This is Corbett's ballad:

> Farewell, Rewards and *Faeries,*
>   Good Housewives now may say;
> For now foul Sluts in Dairies
>   Do fare as well as they;
> And though they sweep their Hearths no less
>   Than Maids were wont to do,
> Yet who of late for Cleanliness
>   Finds *six-pence* in her Shoe?
>
> Lament, lament, old Abbies,
>   The Fairies lost Command:
> They did but change Priests' *Babies,*
>   But some have changed your *Land;*
> And all your Children sprung from thence
>   Are now grown *Puritans:*
> Who live as *Changelings* ever since
>   For love of your Demains.
>
> At Morning and at Evening both
>   You merry were and glad,

So little Care of Sleep or Sloth
   These Pretty ladies had.
When *Tom* came home from labour,
   Or *Cis* to Milking rose,
Then merrily, merrily went their Tabor,
   And nimbly went their Toes.

Witness those Rings and Roundelays
   Of theirs, which yet remain,
Were footed in Queen *Mary's* days
   On many a Grassy Plains;
But, since of late *Elizabeth,*
   And later *James,* came in,
They never danced on any heath
   As *when the Time hath been.*

By which we note the *Fairies*
   Were of the old Profession;
Their Songs were *Ave Maries,*
   Their Dances were *Procession.*
But now, alas, they all are dead,
   Or gone beyond the Seas,
Or Farther for Religion fled,
   Or else they take their Ease.

A Tell-tale in their Company
   They never could endure,
And who so kept not secretly
   Their Mirth, was punished sure.
It was a just and Christian Deed
   To pinch such black and blue.
O, how the Common wealth doth need
   Such Justices as you!

Now they have left our Quarters
   A *Register* they have,
Who looketh to their Charters,
   A Man both *Wise and Grave;*
An hundred of their merry Pranks
   By one that I could name
Are kept in Store, con twenty Thanks
   To *William* for the same.

I marvel who his Cloak would turn
   When *Puck* had led him round,
Or where those Walking Fires would burn,
   Where *Cureton* would be found;
How *Broker* would appear to be,
   For whom this Age doth mourn;
But that their Spirits live in Thee,
   In Thee, old *William Chourne*.

To *William Chourne* of Stafford Shire
   Give Laud and Praises due,
Who every Meal can mend your Cheer
   With Tales both old and true.
To *William* all give Audience,
   And pray ye for his Noddle,
For all the *Fairies'* Evidence
   Were lost, if that were Addle.

The secret mirth of the fairies in the sixth stanza is a good way of describing the success of a community with common interests. They have no need for explicit communication, for the delight in being a member of the community is as much a matter for private enjoyment as for public celebration. But the poem's sadness derives from the sense that all is slipping away. People are still decent: good housewives still sweep their hearths properly, but there is no secret ceremony to reward them for this, as with the old custom of leaving sixpence in her shoe. How fragile it all is, depending finally upon one good, old man who, when he slips into senility, will take with him the most valuable part of English communal history.

Several times in the poem Corbett glances at enclosure, in the takeover of what used to be the monastery demesnes, and in the now neglected rings and roundelays which were footed in Mary's days "on many a grassy plain." Many grassy plains were now enclosed in the name of a more efficient agriculture. Corbett would pin the blame for this on Puritan cupidity. Certainly, the necessity of enclosure was printed deep in the Puritan mentality. To take one example, Lucy Hutchinson's fragment of autobiography opens with a short history of her country whose ruling metaphor is of walls and fences:

Britain hath been as a garden enclosed, wherein all things that man can wish, to make a pleasant life, are planted and grown in her own soil . . .

Better laws and a happier constitution of government no nation

ever enjoyed, it being a mixture of monarchy, aristocracy, and de-
mocracy, with sufficient fences against the pest of every one of those
forms—tyranny, faction, and confusion; yet it is not possible for
man to devise such just and excellent bounds, as will keep in wild
ambition, when prince's flatterers encourage that beast to break his
fence . . . And in the just bounds, wherein our kings were so well
hedged in, the surrounding princes have with terror seen the reproof
of their usurpations over their free brethren.[14]

Her crowning judgment is that here God had "enclosed a people . . . out
of the waste common of the world, to serve him with a pure and undefiled
worship." [15] Set her instinctive attraction toward enclosure against Shak-
erly Marmion's opening of a poem in praise of Robert Dover's "Annual
Sports at Cotswold":[16]

> Hear! You bad owners of enclosed grounds,
> That have your souls as narrow as your bounds!
> When you have robbed the earth of her increase,
> Stored up that fading treasure, and spoke peace
> Unto your wretched thoughts, the barren field
> Of Cotswold, and those emulous hills shall yield
> A crop of honour unto Dover's name,
> Richer than all your stacks or barns contain!

The sports which Dover established provide a good illustration of how
custom and common tradition could be differently interpreted. His purpose was to restore the practices of a once vigorous peasantry, rather in
the spirit of James I's *Book of Sports*. John Cole, contrasting such a
healthy country pursuit with the city's decadence, plays on the word *common:*[17]

> Who's this reneweth the old world, and brings
> Tempe to Cotswold? Draws the sports of kings
> From far Olympus hither? Makes the games
> Of Hyde Park common as their City dames,
> Drawn in their hackney-coaches? Here none pay
> As there, to see the follies of the day,
> Nay, of the night, committed, and that sport
> Bought dearer by a second. Our resort
> Upon these plains is better; like the spring,
> Each in his native habit, where the ring
> Of country gentles, and the neighbourhood,

Practise their sports (their emblems), free and good;
Sports harmless where the hound and nimble horse,
O'erruns the quickest eye (no master's purse);
Sports lawful as their author (not within
The Statute); war-like sports, where the loud din
Of cannons drown the common peoples' cries,
And with their breath and smoke thicken the skies.
    Ask you the author's name? Dover is he
To whom Fame sounds in Epiphonemy.

Cole prefers to the commonness of the city dames' ostentation the common people's cries of shared delight. His opening claim that Dover renews the old world is important, for it challenges the inevitable Puritan opposition to the games as merely another form of the kind of superstitious cultivation of libidinous excess which marked such ceremonies as dancing round the Maypole. Indeed, the collection of poems which celebrated Dover's enterprise was largely an anti-Puritan project. Davenant's offering to it is typical in its contrast of Puritan envy with Dover's openness:[18]

Money at Cotswold Games shall yearly fly,
Whilst the Precise and Envious shall stand by,
And see his Mineral Fountain never dry;

His girls shall dowerless wed with heirs of birth;
His boys plough London widows up like earth,
Whilst Cotswold bards carol their Nuptial Mirth!

Again, the image revealingly proposes an extension of common ownership of land. Lovelace, writing in the 1650s, looks back to a golden age when there were no fences and no inhibitions, all sharing all:[19]

Love then unstinted, Love did sip,
And cherries plucked fresh from the lip,
    On cheeks and roses free he fed;
Lasses like autumn plums did drop,
And lads, indifferently did crop
    A flower, and a maidenhead.

Then unconfined each did tipple
Wine from the bunch, milk from the nipple,
    Paps tractable as udders were;
Then equally the wholesome jellies,

Were squeezed from olive-trees, and bellies,
    Nor suits of trespass did they fear.

"Suits of trespass" plays on their nakedness and their freedom from law-suits for trespassing on private land. But Lovelace's poem is merely a mas-turbatory fantasy. By this time, with the Levellers destroyed and the par-liamentary gentry well in control, it had been firmly established that the maintenance of common land was not in the best interests of the Com-monwealth.

If we go back into the sixteenth century we can find support for the enclosure of common land in one of the most popular books of poetry in English literary history, Thomas Tusser's *Five Hundred Points of Good Husbandry,* first issued in 1557 as *A Hundred Good Points of Hus-bandry,* but expanded through many editions, and still a popular work well into the seventeenth century. Among his many pieces of advice, Tus-ser included a sustained defense of enclosure. It offers (chapter 52, 37–48):[20]

More plenty of mutton and beef,
    corn, butter, and cheese of the best,
More wealth anywhere (to be brief),
    more people, more handsome and prest,
Where find ye? (go search any coast)
    than there where enclosure is most.

More work for the labouring man,
    as well in the town as the field:
Or thereof (devise if ye can)
    more profit what countries do yield?
More seldom where see ye the poor,
    go begging from door unto door?

In contrast, common land encourages promiscuous grazing, theft, and general thriftlessness ("champions" means common land) (chapter 52, 97–132):

For commons these commoners cry,
    enclosing they may not abide:
Yet some be not able to buy
    a cow with her calf by her side.
Nor lay not to live by their work,
    but thievishly loiter and lurk.

The Lord of the town is to blame,
   for these and for many faults mo.
For he that doth know of the same,
   yet lets it unpunished go.
Such Lords ill example doth give,
   where varlets and drabs so may live.

What footpaths are made, and how broad!
   annoyance too much to be borne:
With horse and with cattle what road
   is made through every man's corn!
Where champions ruleth the roost,
   there daily disorder is most.

Their sheep when they drive for to wash,
   how careless such sheep they do guide!
The farmer they leave in the lash,
   with losses on every side.
Though any man's corn they do bite,
   they will not allow him a mite.

What hunting and hawking is there!
   corn looking for sickle at hand:
Acts lawless to do without fear,
   how yearly together they band.
More harm to another to do,
   than they would be done so unto.

More profit is quieter found
   (where pasture in several be:)
Of one silly acre of ground,
   than champion maketh of three.
Again what a joy is it known,
   when men may be bold of their own!

Tusser may have been old-fashioned in many ways, and was certainly inefficient himself—he frequently failed at making a living from the land—but this support for enclosure had, nearly a century later, become the established common sense, shared by all but the two extremes, sentimental Royalists and the lowest peasant class.

True common sense, one assumes, should be shared by all, just as the common wealth is everyone's—but there is a problem which consideration of anything *common* involves. Often common sense is what we assume we possess while all around us are people obviously lacking it; but if we are the only ones with it, then it ceases to be common. Another word which became more common with use was *commonplace*. Originally it translated the Latin *locus communis*, "explained by Cicero . . . as a general theme or argument applicable to many particular cases" (*OED*). Through the sixteenth and seventeenth centuries its positive meaning gradually deteriorated, from "a striking or notable passage, noted for reference or use in a book of commonplaces," to "a common or ordinary topic . . . an everyday saying . . . a platitude or truism." By the nineteenth century it had come to mean "anything common or trite."

In *In Memoriam* Tennyson heaps scorn upon the commonplaces which are offered for Arthur Hallam's loss:[21]

> One writes, that "other friends remain,"
>   That "loss is common to the race"—
>   And common is the commonplace,
> And vacant chaff well meant for grain.
>
> That loss is common would not make
>   My own less bitter, rather more:
>   Too common! Never morning wore
> To evening, but some heart did break.

Tennyson was probably the last poet whose commonplaces became part of the common stock. He ended a tradition which began in the Renaissance, for no matter how elevated or low the sixteenth- or seventeenth-century poet, he knew that a major purpose behind his poetry was to tap the resources of common wisdom. Tusser, as low and functional a poet as one can find, takes care to harness the advice he offers to the stock of commonplaces which all in the country share. The stanzas quoted above show how he constantly veers towards proverbial forms of expression, as in "Where champions ruleth the roost / there daily disorder is most" or "Again what a joy is it known, / when men may be bold of their own!" Often the proverbs are clearly recognizable, and still current, as in this piece of advice regarding the folly of constantly moving to new houses and land, whether one is rich or poor:[22]

> The stone that is rolling can gather no moss,
>   who often removeth is sure of loss.
> The rich it compelleth to pay for his pride;
>   the poor it undoeth on every side.

More often the effect is proverbial, an impression that a commonly recognized truth is being pithily expressed, as in this instruction:[23]

> Friend, harrow in time, by some manner of means,
>   not only thy peason, but also thy beans.
> Unharrowed die, being buried in clay,
>   where harrowed flourish, as flowers in May.

Move right up the ranks of poets and the effect is similar. Milton ends
a sonnet on his blindness "They also serve who only stand and wait." Is
this an existing saying, proverb, or commonplace, or did Milton invent
it? If the first, then its received truth confirms his individual resolve and
helps him pluck a purpose out of enforced passivity. If the second, then
the blindness has already begun to help him move from passivity to the
active creation of proverbial lessons from which all may learn. His individual pain becomes a commonplace, just as a poet such as Lovelace
works to transform his own confinement into a maxim which asserts that
"stone walls do not a prison make, nor iron bars a cage." But the process
is two-way, for, like all good proverbs, this epigram has a double nature.
The more it asserts mental freedom from physical confinement, the more
it presents a mind forced to stare at stone walls and iron bars. Marvell's
"An Horatian Ode" is a lesson in the ambiguity of proverbs: critics have
queued up to explain how it is possible to read maxims such as "'Tis
madness to resist or blame / The force of angry heaven's flame" or "the
same arts that did gain / A power, must it maintain" as for or against
Cromwell. But his commonness ensures that he will remain a puzzle.
Charles, in contrast, "nothing common did or mean."

In addition to *commonplace, proverb,* and *maxim,* there are a dozen or
more terms which describe compressed, memorable statements of general
truth, such as *saw, adage, sentence,* even *epigram.* But *proverb* keeps closest to the ideas which lie behind such words as *common, old,* and *custom.*
Like William Chourne in Corbett's poem, the proverb is one of our last
links with a past which in so many respects seems to be another country.
Indeed, it helps teach us the customs of that country, for few of us cook
broths or change horses today. Because they expressed commonly accepted notions of the truth, proverbs could be held to be the simplest
forms of expression—hence their easy use by a poetaster such as Tusser
(the water poet was fond of them too). But because they were so often
compressed, even elliptical, they could, equally, take on a parabolic obscurity. The Geneva Bible's explanation of the word *proverb,* in its introduction to the book which collects large numbers of them, emphasizes

the gravity and depth of these apparently simple verses: "this word, Prov-
erbe, or parable, signifieth a grave and notable sentence, worthy to be
kept in memory"; and the Authorized Version translators replaced "parable" with "proverb" in their rendering of Proverbs 1:6, making it parallel to a *dark saying:*

> A wise man will hear, and will increase learning: and a man of
> understanding shall attain unto wise counsels:
> To understand a proverb, and the interpretation; the words of the
> wise, and their dark sayings.[24]

St. John reports Christ's words regarding his parables like this, in the
Authorized Version's translation (16:25): "These things have I spoken
unto you in proverbs: but the time cometh when I shall no more speak
unto you in proverbs, but I shall show you plainly of the Father." And the
disciples reply with relief (16:29): "Lo, now speakest thou plainly, and
speakest no proverb."

And yet *proverb* has remained a term for the most easily assimilable
expression of common sense, the kind of thing which Sir Walter Scott
recognized as most valuable in Tusser's verses when he praised his attain-
ment of "a sort of homely, pointed, and quaint expression, like that of the
old English proverb, which the rhyme and the alliteration tended to fix in
the memory of the reader." [25] In a highly functional work, made to be read
by busy men, the proverbial expression of directions ensured that they
would be clear and easily fixed in the mind.

Elizabethan poetry never moved far away from the proverbial, as
Shakespeare's sonnets amply testify.[26] Sometimes whole poems could be
constructed out of proverbs, as in this example by Robert Southwell,
where virtually every line may be traced back to a common saying:[27]

Times Go By Turns

The lopped tree in time may grown again,
Most naked plants renew both fruit and flower;
The sorriest wight may find release of pain,
The driest soil suck in some moistening shower;
Times go by turns, and chances change by course,
From foul to fair, from better hap to worse.

The sea of fortune doth not ever flow,
She draws her favours to the lowest ebb;
Her tides hath equal times to come and go,

Her loom doth weave the fine and coarsest web;
No joy so great but runneth to an end,
No hap so hard but may in fine amend.

Not always fall of leaf, nor ever spring,
No endless night, yet not eternal day;
The saddest birds a season find to sing,
The roughest storm a calm may soon allay:
Thus, with succeeding turns, God tempereth all,
That man may hope to rise, yet fear to fall.

A chance may win that by mischance was lost;
The net that holds no great, takes little fish;
In some things all, in all things none are crossed;
Few all they need, but none have all they wish.
Unmeddled joys here to no man befall;
Who least, hath some; who most, hath never all.

Written in the early 1590s by an imprisoned Jesuit, the poem shows the potential political uses of the proverb, as it teaches how to be content with a little, be patient, learn to wait for times to change. Move forward sixty years and see how Roland Watkyns consoles himself for the loss of his living under the Commonwealth, and teaches his readers how to wait for better times:[28]

The Changes

The painful Bee, which to her hive doth bring
Sweet honey, in her tail retains a sting.
Our sweetest joys are interlined with cares,
No field of corn but hath some choking tares.
The stream, which doth with silent motion slide
Is oftentimes disturbed with wind and tide.
Who sits today in Honour's lap and sings,
God soon can change his tune and clip his wings.
Sometimes the Sea doth ebb, and sometimes flow,
Now with, anon against the tide we row;
No haven's so secure but some ill blast
May toss the ship, and break the stately Mast:
Who now in Court doth dance and lift his head,
Tomorrow droops, and sickly keeps his bed.
The King may beg and beggars may command.

Higher Cedars fall when little shrubs do stand.
The sweetest comfort I do feel, or find,
Though fortune change, is not to change my mind.

In either case the proverb not only makes its political point but also relates it closely to the experience of life at the most basic level—as in the
images of cultivation, lopped trees, dry soil, and cornfields choked with
tares. The process works both ways. Tusser's stanza about harrowing in
due time is literally advice for "February's husbandry," but it takes little
imagination to see how it could act figuratively as a religious lesson to
repent in time, or political advice to prepare our defenses before we are
attacked.

Proverbs serve as a common link between the highest and lowest forms
of poetry. John Crouch's balled "Two Antagonists in Love" uses a proverb to satirize the excesses of love—the same proverb might just as well
epitomize *Lycidas*:[29]

Those that do die for Love, deserve no slander;
    but with *Love's* holy Martyrdom be Crowned,
Perhaps you cannot imitate *Leander*,
    for every man is not born to be drowned.

Here is another balladeer, Richard Burton, telling the old story of the
substitute bride in "The Glory of the West." As she removes her veil the
clown finds that he has married the maid, not the mistress:[30]

but plucking off their veils, they soon perceived the jest;
This youngster when he did behold,
    he had lost his Mistress and his Gold;
Faith I might a look quoth he,
    before that I had leapt so free;
But now the proverb you may plainly see,
    marriage and hanging goes by destiny.

It may be only a light thing, but its development is revealing. As the veil
is plucked off, so the proverb becomes clear. As in the case of biblical
parables, the sense of proverbs is realized only when related to experience: to the inexperienced they remain dark sayings.

Thomas Shipman wrote "The Royal Martyr," a poem on the death of
Charles I, on the third anniversary of the execution, when he was still

only twenty years old. In it he tried to relate his youthful innocence to the national guilt which spread through the whole state (7–12):[31]

> In Proverbs he his wisdom often shrouds:
> As *Phoebus* sometimes wears a Cloak of Clouds.
> Their knowledge wisest Nations thus conveyed,
> And in such Cabinets their Jewels laid.
> And these are some of Ours—, *viz.* Night follows Day
> And purest Gold is lessened by Allay.

This is not very sophisticated poetry, but it fits its subject well, as Shipman's naïveté frustrates his efforts to apply such commonplaces to the state of the nation. Instead the proverbs drive him back to a realization that the best he could do was merely to stand and wait, which was not enough (39–44):

> The first part of the *Proverb's* so far right.
> But now, alas, I am o'erwhelmed with night!
> Thus in a harmless state of youth I stood;
> I did no harm, but, ah! I did no good.
> My influence, like to Winter Suns, did show;
> They scorch not, but yet nothing make to grow.

Again, we can imagine Tusser making good literal use of the sterility of winter suns.

That proverbs should be so plain and so dark, and should frequently relate to cultivation and husbandry, gives them a common identity with herbs, the most easily found but mysteriously useful of plants. In their magic use lay the oldest wisdom of the common people. This is the attendant spirit talking to the elder brother in *Comus* (616–636):

> Care and utmost shifts
> How to secure the Lady from surprisal,
> Brought to my mind a certain shepherd lad
> Of small regard to see to, yet well skilled
> In every virtuous plant and healing herb
> That spreads her verdant leaf to the morning ray,
> He loved me well, and oft would beg me sing,
> Which when I did, he on the tender grass
> Would sit, and hearken even to ecstasy,
> And in requital ope his leathern scrip,

And show me simples of a thousand names
Telling their strange and vigorous faculties;
Amongst the rest a small unsightly root,
But of divine effect, he culled me out;
The leaf was darkish, and had prickles on it,
But in another country, as he said,
Bore a bright golden flower, but not in this soil:
Unknown, and like esteemed, and the dull swain
Treads on it daily with his clouted shoon,
And yet more med'cinal is it than moly
That Hermes once to wise Ulysses gave.

The herb, called "haemony," has engendered much critical debate over its identity and over Milton's purposes in employing it here. For our concerns, however, the interesting point is the contrast between the shepherd lad and the dull swain. Both are from the common sort. The lad is "of small regard to see to," and the swain is "dull," but the latter is as much an intellectual description as a visual one, whereas the lad is a skilled interpreter of nature. The divide between them is almost an allegory of the state of the nation as perceived by poets of all sides; it fits Corbett's "Faeries' Farewell" quite nicely, for instance. The mass of the people have lost contact with the land they live on, and what was once their common wisdom survives only in the brains of isolated individuals.

Herbs are humble things, small, unsightly, unknown, unesteemed to the point that they are often trodden on, but they have great political purposes. George Herbert's *A Priest to the Temple* is a statement of Anglican idealism, setting forth the priest's duty to ensure that his flock is obedient to God. This involves, naturally, a view of an ordered society in which relative degrees of knowledge and ignorance are as necessary as relative degrees of power and wealth. Chapter 23, "The Parson's Completeness," begins with an account of the priest's role as a judge: "In judging, he followes that, which is altogether right; so that if the poorest man of the Parish detain but a pin unjustly from the richest, he absolutely restores it as a Judge; but when he hath so done, then he assumes the Parson, and exhorts to Charity." [32] This is soon followed by directions to the priest to be his flock's physician, something which "is done by seeing one Anatomy, reading one Book of Phisick, having one Herball by him." Knowledge of herbs is doubly useful, for it not only helps heal the people, but provides material for instructive parables too, "even as our Saviour made plants and seeds to teach the people." [33] That the one person in the parish with the power such knowledge gives should be the parson is self-

evident, for books of physic and herbals were written in Latin and therefore out of the ken of even those parishioners who could read English.
For the purposes of a well-governed hierarchy it was necessary that
knowledge be so confined, and the model extended from the parish to the
state. Herrick's poem "To the King, to Cure the Evil" praises the monarch's "Blest Hand, which has the powers / Of all those supple-healing
herbs and flowers."

In reality it was not the king who knew the use of herbs but the College
of Physicians, and its monopoly came under vigorous attack in 1649
when Nicholas Culpeper translated its *Pharmacopoeia* into English, following it in 1653 with *The English Physician Enlarged, with 369 Medicines Made of English Herbs* . . . He was bitterly attacked by the vested
interests and accused of all forms of sectarian excess, including atheism,
but the books were increasingly popular, their huge sales and frequent
reprints bearing out the great interest the people had in restoring what
had once, supposedly, been common knowledge. Culpeper's emphasis on
astrology got his herbal a bad name later but made it doubly attractive to
Englishmen of the seventeenth century, for, as Milton's "haemony"
shows, the curative and restorative powers of herbs struck those who experienced them as a form of magic.

The very names of herbs testified to their properties, as evinced in an
anonymous poem which appeared in the *Westminster Drollery* of 1672:[34]

On His Mistress' Garden of Herbs

Heart's-ease, an herb that sometimes hath been seen
In my love's garden plot to flourish green,
Is dead and withered with a wind of woe;
And bitter rue in place thereof doth grow.
The cause I find to be, because I did
Neglect the herb called time, which now doth bid
Me never hope, nor look once more again
To gain heart's-ease, to ease my heart of pain.
One hope is this, in this my woeful case,
My rue, though bitter, may prove herb of grace.

Heart's-ease, the wild pansy, has a host of alternative names, including
love-lies-bleeding, herb constancy, herb trinitatis, and, made famous by
Shakespeare, love-in-idleness; it may also be the "pansy freaked with jet"
of *Lycidas*. But heart's-ease is the most expressive name because of its
double medicinal function: it acted as an aid to sufferers from heart disease and was popularly thought to be the source of an effective love po-

tion.[35] But "No herb can cure love," and the poem's edge comes from its relation to this proverb. And another well-known one says that "Rue and thyme both grow in one garden," playing on the obvious double senses of those two herb names. Rue's alternative name, however, is herb of grace, as Ophelia tells Gertrude; and Milton uses the herb to introduce Adam's prophetic vision which takes up most of the last two books of *Paradise Lost* (11:412–415):

> Michael from Adam's eyes the film removed
> Which that false fruit that promised clearer sight
> Had bred; then purged with euphrasy and rue
> The visual nerve, for he had much to see . . .

Behind this there are probably memories of failed efforts to treat Milton's blindness with herbs, but this treatment works. This is the grace which, as in his sonnet on his "late espoused saint," purges away obstacles to full sight, giving Adam something more complete and enlightening than mere human vision in the fallen world. So, in the anonymous herb poem rue is proved to be a herb of grace. It purges the lover's delusions, persuading him never to hope nor look again. The pun at the close on *prove herb* and *proverb* is likely to be more accessible to American readers, who still have an unaspirated pronunciation of *herb*.

The kinds of proverb which prove herbs true are essentially things of the countryside. Shakespeare's Warwickshire childhood and youth gave him an access to them which was already lost to the citizens of London; Milton's herbs seem to come more from reading than from experience. Robert Herrick is a splendid example of a Londoner whose poetry gained hugely from his having to live for long periods in the country, in spite of his often-recorded loathing for Devonshire. Like George Herbert, another poetical parson, Herrick obviously found proverbs a source of wisdom which could be appreciated by all levels of the society to which he ministered. Sometimes he constructs whole poems out of a string of proverbs, as in "Love me Little, Love me Long":

> You say, to me-wards your affection's strong;
> Pray love me little, so you love me long.
> Slowly goes far: The mean is best: Desire
> Grown violent, does either die, or tire.

Favorite lessons are recast in a more compressed form as he, like Herbert, apparently invents proverbs himself. In "The Country Life . . . ," a poem dedicated to Emdymion Porter, Herrick advises this groom of the king's bedchamber to get out of court and city and enjoy an existence where (21–24)

> to thy corn-fields thou dost go,
> Which though well soiled, yet thou dost know,
> That the best compost for the Lands
> Is the wise Master's Feet, and Hands.

In "A Good Husband" this lesson is recast to the more succinct, and therefore more proverbial, closing couplet:

> A master of a house (as I have read)
> Must be the first man up, and last in bed:
> With the Sun rising he must walk his grounds;
> See this, View that, and all the other bounds:
> Shut every gate; mend every hedge that's torn,
> Either with old, or plant therein new thorn:
> Tread o'er his glebe, but with such care, that where
> He sets his foot, he leaves rich *compost* there.

Herbert included this in his *Outlandish Proverbs,* linking it to the other proverb about the master's eye fattening the horse: "The masters eye fattens the horse, and his foot the ground."

Herbert and Herrick were men of relatively high rank—Herbert of very high estate—who both held fast to an ideal of state founded on common interest in decades during which England was slipping into factionalism. The lesson they taught was one of the necessity for condescension, not in the more modern sense of patronizing, but in its pure meaning of yielding consent to and acquiescing in the practices of others. The key text for this sense of an ideal community in which high and low work together is in St. Paul's Epistle to the Romans (12:3–8, 16):

> For I say, through the grace given unto me, to every man that is among you, not to think of himself more highly than he ought to think; but to think soberly, according as God hath dealt to every man the measure of faith.
> For as we have many members in one body, and all members have not the same office:
> So we, being many, are one body in Christ, and every one members one of another.
> Having then gifts differing according to the grace that is given to

us, whether prophecy, let us prophesy according to the proportion of faith;

Or ministry, let us wait on our ministering: or he that teacheth, on teaching;

Or he that exhorteth, on exhortation: he that giveth, let him do it with simplicity; he that ruleth, with diligence; he that sheweth mercy, with cheerfulness . . .

Be of the same mind one toward another. Mind not high things, but condescend to men of low estate. Be not wise in your own conceits.

This is Herbert's opening to chapter 35 of *A Priest to the Temple,* a chapter titled "The Parson's Condescending":

The Country Parson is a Lover of old Customes, if they be good, and harmlesse; and the rather, because Countrey people are much addicted to them, so that to favour them therein is to win their hearts, and to oppose them therin is to deject them. If there be any ill in the custome, that may be severed from the good, he pares the apple, and gives them the clean to feed on.[36]

Herrick was a lover of old customs too, and often when one goes to check popular practice in something like *Brand's Popular Antiquities* the only source is a poem by Herrick. Customs once common through the country, which were vigorously suppressed during the Commonwealth period and then wiped out completely by the move to the cities, have their sole memorial because this poet took such delight in them. But it was not a simple delight, for even the most apparently innocent of his poems has its political purposes too. Thus, "Corinna's Going a Maying" poses a challenge to Puritan prohibitions of the May ceremony. A more subtle example is the poem in which country customs, herbs, and proverbs all fuse into a defense of common interests against the factionalism brought upon the country by militant Puritanism:

    Ceremonies for Candlemas Eve

Down with the Rosemary and Bays,
    Down with the Mistletoe;
Instead of Holly, now upraise
    The greener Box (for show).

The Holly hitherto did sway;
    Let Box now domineer;

Until the dancing Easter-day,
   Or Easter's Eve appear.

Then youthful Box which now hath grace,
   Your houses to renew;
Grown old, surrender must his place,
   Unto the crisped Yew.

When Yew is out, then Birch comes in,
   And many Flowers beside;
Both of a fresh, and fragrant kin
   To honour Whitsuntide.

Green Rushes then, the sweetest Bents,
   With cooler Oaken boughs;
Come in for comely ornaments,
   To readorn the house.
Thus times do shift; each thing his turn does hold;
New things succeed, as former things grow old.

As with most of Herrick's poems, it is not possible to date this even approximately. It could have been written at any time between, say, 1620 and 1648, when it was published in *Hesperides,* but the 1648 publication date suits our purposes well enough. Militant Puritanism was triumphant. For a man with Herrick's Anglican and Royalist sympathies the times had become completely untunable. Puritan opposition to the celebrations of the old religious calendar had long been a topic of grim humor. In Jonson's *Alchemist,* a generation earlier, one of the extreme brethren cannot stop himself from correcting Christmas to Christ-tide. But by the 1640s these caricatures were in power, with Parliament legislating against such pagan and papist practices as Christmas celebrations and dancing around the Maypole. Candlemas Eve would be a spectacularly offensive title for any Puritan to consider, combining as it does candles and masses, and being concerned with the Virgin Mary. Herrick compounds the offense by showing how the celebrations for Candlemas Eve fit into a pattern of essentially pagan markings of the year's cycle.

So far so good, and we might judge the poem to be a gentle, almost innocent celebration of a tradition under threat. But it is much stronger than such a sentimental reading allows, largely because of the proverbial ending which Herrick gives it. To end with an epigrammatic proverb is a well-established form of poetic closure, as in many sonnets. Here its purpose is to break into, and complete, the cycle with which the poem could potentially go on and on. As the year's ceremonies go round, so do the stanzas, with Herrick stepping in to change the form and to remind us of the common truths which such a cycle embodies. In part he is recalling the experience of writing his own celebratory poems—"Thus times do shift" remembers the "Argument" which begins *Hesperides:* "I sing of *Times trans-shifting:* and I write / How *Roses* first came *Red,* and *Lilies White.*" But trans-shifting times need further definition. This is, after all, a poem about revolution. The seventeenth century saw the first applications of that word to great political movements, but it contains within itself an ambiguity which Herrick's poem addresses. A principal idea behind revolution is of a total break with the past, a new order replacing the old. But revolution also contains a cyclic view of history, of time going round with things repeating themselves. Choose between two proverbs: "Times change and we with them" or "There is nothing new under the sun."

Herrick's poem begins "Down with." In the rural society which he celebrates this is the call of happy families saying farewell to Christmas and looking forward to Easter. But superimposed upon it are echoes of the New Model Army's use of the same phrase to pull down the idolatrous trappings encouraged by Laud and the Stuarts. By 1648 the Puritans had succeeded, but is success succession? To succeed is more cyclical than revolutionary. Only kings can succeed one another; any other form of succeeding is illusory. So *"New things succeed, as former things grow old"* turns out not to be a proverbial support for upheaval and change, but is instead a redefinition of *new* and *old*. Rosemary, bays, and mistletoe were once new, become old, and are taken down, but will, as times shift round again, be hailed as new once more. The vital thing is the proverb, for it expresses the will of the people, their common sense. Apparently hijacked by Cromwell and his army, it is redefined as a support for stability and continuity.

In its way, too, Herrick's poem presents a counterview to Milton's sonnet. Candlemas Day was the feast of the purification of the Virgin Mary after the birth of Christ. Whereas Milton's sonnet is private and austere, using the purification image to demonstrate the great divide between us and the past, Herrick's purification is a celebration of continuity, community, and restoration.

11 "Enjoy the Time": Going Round and Standing Still

The 1640s and 1650s are known as the period when the world was turned upside down, in accord with the Puritan extremists' favorite image taken from the Bible's description of the disciples' purpose: "These that have turned the world upside down are come hither also" (Acts 17:6). It was used by the Puritans' enemies ironically. "The World is Turned Upside Down," a ballad written in 1646, has as its theme the new order's prohibition of Christmas, as in these stanzas, the third and final one:[1]

> Command is given, we must obey,
> And quite forget old Christmas day:
> Kill a thousand men, or a Town regain,
> We will give thanks and praise amain.
> The wine pot shall clink,
> We will feast and drink.
> And then strange motions will abound
> *Yet let's be content, and the times lament,*
> *You see the world turned upside down.*
> . . . . . .
>
> To conclude, I'll tell you news that's right,
> Christmas was killed at *Naseby* fight:
> Charity was slain at that same time,
> Jack Tell truth too, a friend of mine,
> Likewise then did die,
> Roast beef and shred pie,
> Pig, Goose and Capon no quarter found.
> *Yet let's be content, and the times lament,*
> *You see the world is quite turned round.*

246

As Hyder Rollins explains in his introduction to this ballad, it is only one of many complaints in the 1640s against the Puritans' prohibition of Christmas celebrations. But he also points out that the complaint against the neglect of these festivities went back to much earlier in the century. There is a ballad written long before the Puritans were in power, titled "A Song Bewailing the Time of Christmas, So Much Decayed in England."[2] In effect, Herrick's trans-shifting times were shifting themselves from the beginning of the century, and whereas one image to describe this was turning things upside down, an equally if not more common one was of things turning round and round. There are words for this sensation which imply that the whole thing is under control: *revolution* is one, *cycle* another. Other words, however, describe the experience not from a still point of observation, as Herrick does when he celebrates the yearly cycle, but from within the experience, conveying the alarming lack of control felt by those living in an age of swift and sudden change. *Vertigo* is one such. It, and its cognate *vertiginous,* are essentially seventeenth-century words. Volpone's ambition to drink until his roof whirls round with the vertigo introduces a host of literal and figurative uses.

The association of drink and dizziness is one explanation for the popularity of vertiginous images. Drunkenness was an attractive way of shrugging off defeat; it also helped explain it. "The Round-head's Race" takes its cue from Isaiah's image of Egypt as a country whose perverse spirit has caused it to err "as a drunken man staggereth in his vomit" (19:14), and presents England as a state caught up in a fit of giddiness:[3]

> I will not say for the World's store,
>   The World's now drunk, (for did I)
> The Faction which now reigns would roar,
>   But I will swear 'tis giddy.
>
> And all are prone to this same Fit,
>   That it their Object make,
> For every thing runs Round in it,
>   And no form else will take.

The rest of the poem plays on the various circles which the giddy Round-heads pursue. Consolation might be found in this movement too. The old idea of the wheel of fortune could make such a revolution seem only a way of raising up what will eventually fall crashing to earth, as in this poem also collected in *The Rump:*[4]

The Advice

Ne'er trouble thyself at the Times nor their turnings,
  Afflictions run circular, and wheel about,
Away with these Murmurings, and these Heartburnings,
  With the Juice of the Grape we'll quench the Fire out,
Ne'er chain, nor imprison thy Soul up in sorrow,
What fails us today, may befriend us tomorrow,
We'll scorn our Content from others to borrow.

Though Fortune hath left us we'll strive to regain her,
  And court her with Cups till her Favourite come,
Then with a Courage untamed we'll maintain her,
  And silence the noise of the Enemy's Drum,
We'll link her unto the Man most deserving,
Shall keep her at work, as well as from starving,
She shall not hereafter be at her own Carving.

I hold him a Novice in Human affairs,
  Thinks whirlings in State a wondrous thing,
To daub up old Ruins with dirty repairs,
  And instead of a Sceptre to set up a Sling.
Such Atoms of Greatness are but Fortune's laughter,
She fattens them up till they're fitted for slaughter,
Then leaves them at *Tyburn* to Tittar and Tauter.

Another revolutionary theme often played on by the poets, following Donne, was the new astronomy, which put in doubt the regularity of planetary orbitings. Things do not simply go round and round, but they go round in a spiral. As in the case of vertigo, the movement is eccentric, a kind of falling sickness. In Donne's *Anniveraries* even the sun is held to suffer from it:[5]

> nor can the sun
> Perfect a circle, or maintain his way
> One inch direct; but where he rose today
> He comes no more, but with a cozening line,
> Steals by that point, and so is serpentine.

Proverbs offer a solace for vertiginous feelings, as for most things: as the widow tells Petruchio, "He that is giddy thinks the world turns round," (*Taming of the Shrew* V.ii.20). But by the 1650s it was hard for all but the most revolutionary not to feel that the world itself was out of control. Lovelace's lines are typical enough:[6]

> See all the world how't staggers,
>   More ugly drunk than we,
> As if far gone in daggers,
>   And blood it seemed to be.

Donne's conclusion, some forty years earlier, was that a world which was governed by the inconstant notions of men was one which had no place for "solidness and roundness."[7] Jonson, true to his classical beliefs, found solidness and roundness within himself, as in the great blob which he told William Burlase to paint. The Cary-Morison ode opens with a circular movement as the brave infant of Saguntum reenters his mother's womb to die as soon as he is born; but the poem's structure shows another way of dealing with the giddy world in its movement from "turn" and "counter-turn" to "stand." Finding how to stand still is one of the great concerns of seventeenth-century poetry, reaching its most decisive point in Milton's Jesus at the end of *Paradise Regained,* who finally repels Satan by the purest form of standing still.[8]

In speculating upon the motives for the infant's action, Jonson recalls its context: a town besieged and now taken by Hannibal, whose troops set about razing it to the ground, doing "the deeds of death, and night, / Urged, hurried forth, and hurled / Upon the affrighted world." There, already, sits in place the most common rhyme of the century. It comes easily to Milton in *Lycidas,* as he imagines King's bones hurled to the bottom of the monstrous world, and to Marvell at the end of "Upon Appleton House" (761–764):

> 'Tis not, what once it was, the world,
> But a rude heap together hurled,
> All negligently overthrown,
> Gulfs, deserts, precipices, stone.

Seventeenth-century poetry offers many more examples. Whether the worldview creates the rhyme or the rhyme the view is a moot point, but the easy collocation of a spinning world which hurls everyone and everything around, together with the natural play on *world* and *whirled,* led to much vertiginous poetry. Joseph Fisher sent the world spinning round in a morris dance poem in 1633. Until the end, all seems to be going well in the best of all possible whirls:[9]

A Morisco

The sky is glad that stars above
　Do give a brighter splendour:
The stars unfold their flaming gold,
　To make the ground more tender:
The ground doth send a fragrant smell,
　That air may be the sweeter:
The air doth charm the swelling seas
　With pretty chirping metre:
The sea with rivers' water doth
　The plants and flowers dainty:
The plants do yield their fruitful seed,
　That beasts may live in plenty:
The beasts do give both food and cloth,
　That man high Jove may honour:
And so the world runs merrily round,
　When peace doth smile upon her.
Oh then, then oh: oh then, then oh:
　This jubilee last for ever,
That foreign spite or civil fight,
　Our quiet trouble never!

This is where poetry and movement part company. The dance may lead to a dervishlike loss of full consciousness, but the poet, striving for a similar effect—the third line from the end must be the lamest in the whole century—only betrays his anxieties. Twenty years later, when "civil fight" had become commonplace, Lovelace wrote this:

Cupid Far Gone

What so beyond all madness is the elf,
　Now he hath got out of himself!
　His fatal enemy the bee,
　Nor his deceived artillery;
　His shackles, nor the rose's bough
Ne'er half so nettled him as he is now.

See! at's own mother he is offering,
　His finger now fits any ring;
　Old Cybele he would enjoy,
　And now the girl, and now the boy.
　He proffers Jove a back caress,
And all his love in the antipodes.

Jealous of his chaste Psyche, raging he,
    Quarrels the student Mercury;
    And with a proud submissive breath
    Offers to change his darts with Death.
    He strikes at the bright Eye of Day,
And Juno tumbles in her milky way.

The dear sweet secrets of the gods he tells,
    And with loathed hate loved heaven he swells;
    Now like a fury he belies
    Myriads of pure virginities;
    And swears, with this false frenzy hurled,
There's not a virtuous she in all the world.

Olympus he renounces, then descends,
    And makes a friendship with the fiends;
    Bids Charon be no more a slave,
    He Argus rigged with stars shall have;
    And triple Cerberus from below
Must leashed t'himself with him a hunting go.

This looks forward to the frenzy of much Restoration poetry, and it is born out of a similar sense of futility. Behind the flimsy Cupid fiction is a self-portrait of a drunken, sodomizing, brawling, self-loathing individual. The keynote is the abandonment of Olympus, for Lovelace in his last decade was keenly interested in his standing as a poet. But it is difficult to turn giddiness into poetry unless you yourself can stand still and observe it. Lovelace tries this in "The Ant," where he sees the whole world as a round of eaters being eaten (31–36):

Thus we unthrifty thrive within Earth's tomb,
    For some more rav'nous and ambitious jaw:
The grain in th'ant's, the ant's in the pie's womb,
    The pie in th'hawk's, the hawk's i' th'eagle's maw:
So scattering to hoard 'gainst a long day,
Thinking to save all, we cast all away.

In "Advice to my Best Brother" he presents the world as a whirligig (25–28):

But this eternal strange Ixion's wheel
Of giddy earth, ne'er whirling leaves to reel

> Till all things are inverted, till they are
> Turned to that antic confused state they were.

The poem as a whole is counsel to keep one's balance: build low, have a "breast of proof," and realize that the extremes between which one is hurled are, in essence, indistinguishable from each other:

> For tell me how they differ, tell me pray,
> A cloudy tempest, and a too fair day.

This is Lovelace's version of the many proverbs which teach that *fair* and *foul* are not contrasts but, ultimately, the same thing.

In one poem, "A Fly About a Glass of Burnt Claret," he sets up contrasts of wet and dry, hot and cold, heaven and hell, life and death, and projects himself into the middle of these extremes as a noble, heroic fly who is hurled around his small universe. At its center is the glass of burnt claret, a "liquid fire . . . more fatal than the dry." The contemporary method of cooling wine was to drop a ball of snow in it, but in this case "A snowball-heart in it let fall, / And take it out a fire-ball." In spite of the danger, the fly crawls to the brim as the poet looks wonderingly on (37–56):

> What airy country hast to save,
> Whose plagues thou'lt bury in thy grave?
> For even now thou seem'st to us
> On this gulf's brink a Curtius.
>
> And now th'art fall'n (magnanimous fly)
> In, where thine ocean doth fry,
> Like the sun's son who blushed the flood,
> To a complexion of blood.
>
> Yet see! my glad auricular
> Redeems thee (though dissolved) a star,
> Flaggy thy wings, and scorched thy thighs,
> Thou li'st a double sacrifice.
>
> And now my warming, cooling breath
> Shall a new life afford in death;
> See! in the hospital of my hand
> Already cured, thou fierce dost stand.

Burnt insect! dost thou reaspire
The moist-hot-glass, and liquid fire?
I see! 'tis such a pleasing pain,
Thou wouldst be scorched, and drowned again.

Noble and heroic perhaps, but insignificant and suicidal when seen from the lofty perspective of the wielder of the little finger of Fate. The story of Curtius, who plunged into an abyss which opened up in the forum at Rome, thereby sacrificing himself to the gods to save the city, crops up several times in the poetry of the interregnum. Thomas Shipman, after chastising himself for having been too young to help Charles, resolves:[10]

If I to *Brutus's* glory may not come;
I dare, with *Curtius,* tempt a noble doom;
And plunge into the Gulf to rescue *Rome*.

In other words, he is resolved upon some desperate action to avenge the dead king, even if it results in his own death. But these are naive heroics. Lovelace's vision is much cooler. He looks down upon himself as a man with no illusions left, who, for some obscure reason, is required to behave as if he were an idealist with a cause to fight for. The vision comes at the very place which, in most Royalist poetry, is the center of forgetfulness, the rim of the wineglass. In this sense "The Grasshopper," from his earlier volume of poetry, written in the 1640s, is revealingly inconsistent: it mocks the insect at the beginning for its nightly drunkenness, which caused it to forget to lay up against winter, and it ends with a resolve to live in visions created by an "o'erflowing glass." A decade later, his eye fixes on the fly and its crazed heroics, as it wittingly goes through a cycle of loss, restoration, loss.

Lucasta, the presiding genius of Lovelace's poetry, looks down on the world as Lovelace himself looks at the fly, in another poem in the later volume, "Lucasta Laughing":

Hark how she laughs aloud,
Although the world put on its shroud;
Wept at by the fantastic crowd,
   Who cry, One drop let fall
From her, might save the Universal Ball.
      She laughs again
      At our ridiculous pain;
And at our merry misery

> She laughs until she cry;
>   Sages, forbear
>   That ill-contrived tear,
>   Although your fear,
> Doth barricado Hope from your soft ear.
>   That which still makes her mirth to flow,
>   Is our sinister-handed woe,
>   Which downwards on its head doth go;
>   And ere that it is sown doth grow.
>   This makes her spleen contract,
>   And her just pleasure feast;
>   For the unjustest act
>   Is still the pleasant'st jest.

In his first volume, *Lucasta,* the lady acts benevolently. Deserted by the poet in the opening poems—"To Lucasta, Going Beyond the Seas" and "To Lucasta, Going to the Wars"—he returns to her in the final poems as a redemptress, healing the poet and the nation of their wounds. In "Calling Lucasta from her Retirement" she wakes from her "dead vault" to bring about a state in which (29–30)

> No storms, heats, colds, no souls contentious,
> Nor civil war is found—I mean, to us.

And in "Aramantha," the pastoral which ends the volume, she transforms and harmonizes a landscape ravaged by civil war; Marvell took the hint from this for his Maria in "Upon Appleton House." Now, however, merriment and misery hang so close together that tears of laughter and tears of anguish are indistinguishable. "Lucasta Laughing" stands on the edge of the cynicism which took over the lyric in the second half of the century. It is saved from toppling over by Lovelace's inclusion of himself among the fantastic crowd—the pronouns are *our,* not *their*—but the final two lines, with their contrasted superlatives, are as bitter as anything written in the century. Again, the conditioning image is a giddy one— "sinister-handed woe" is a seed which spirals down instead of up, like some kind of crazed bean.

Lovelace's "merry" is only one more example of an adjective whose connotations grew increasingly cynical through the century. *Merry England* meant, originally, a land which was "pleasant, delightful in aspect or conditions" (*OED*), but this meaning gave way to the image of a country of mindless revelers. Charles II came to be known as the "merry monarch," but the epithet had, incongruously, and therefore to some extent ironically, been applied by Lovelace to his father under the guise of the grasshopper in the 1640s:

> Up with the day, the sun thou welcom'st then,
>   Sport'st in the gilt-plaits of his beams,
> And all these merry days mak'st merry men,
>   Thyself, and melancholy streams.

This, the third stanza of "The Grasshopper," is followed by the sickle, frost, and the grasshopper's winter fate, to become green ice—a cynical turn to the old proverb about being "as merry as a cricket." His son's merriness was not so much innocent as frenzied, at least if we take the view of it intended by the phrase's apparent originater, the Earl of Rochester, in his "Satire on Charles II" (10–15):[11]

> Nor are his high Desires above his Strength,
> His Sceptre and his Prick are of a Length,
> And she may sway the one, who plays with th'other
> And makes him little wiser than his Brother.
> Restless he rolls about from Whore to Whore
> A merry Monarch, scandalous and poor.

We can see the word turning at the beginning of the century, when Viola calls Feste "a merry fellow [who] car'st for nothing." She means, inoffensively, that he has no worries; but he picks up the potential insult and insists that he does "care for something; but in my conscience, sir, I do not care for you" (*Twelfth Night* III.i.26–29).

The whirligig of time is an image which needs explanation now: we would more readily understand *merry-go-round,* one of the final resting places of *merry,* whose other senses, apart from the connections with Christmas and widows, seem to be confined to mild drunkenness and, in the phrase *merry hell,* to describe mindless disturbance and upheaval. This phrase has strong associations with drink too, as in the *OED*'s example from *The Transport Workers' Song Book* (1926): "We don't get drunk to fight the boss / Or kick up merry hell." Carelessness is the origin of the word's fate, as in Herrick's "To Live Merrily, and to Trust to Good Verses," where the intention is to ride a merry-go-round of poetry and drink into oblivion:

> Now is the time for mirth,
>   Nor cheek, or tongue be dumb:

For with the flowery earth,
    The golden pomp is come.

The golden Pomp is come;
    For now each tree does wear
(Made of her Pap and Gum)
    Rich beads of *Amber* here.

Now reigns the *Rose,* and now
    Th'*Arabian* Dew besmears
My uncontrolled brow,
    And my retorted hairs.

Homer, this Health to thee,
    In Sack of such a kind,
That it would make thee see,
    Though thou wert ne'er so blind.

Next, *Virgil,* I'll call forth,
    To pledge this second Health
In Wine, whose each cup's worth
    An Indian Common-wealth.

A Goblet next I'll drink
    To *Ovid;* and suppose,
Made he the pledge, he'd think
    The world had all *one Nose.*

Then this immensive cup
    Of *Aromatic* wine,
Catullus, I quaff up
    To that Terse Muse of thine.

Wild I am now with heat;
    O *Bacchus!* cool thy Rays!
Or frantic I shall eat
    Thy *Thyrse,* and bite the *Bays.*

Round, round, the roof does run;
    And being ravished thus,
Come, I will drink a Tun
    To my *Propertius.*

Now, to *Tibullus,* next,
    This flood I drink to thee:

But stay; I see a Text,
    That this presents to me.

Behold, *Tibullus* lies
    Here burnt, whose small return
Of ashes, scarce suffice
    To fill a little Urn.

Trust to good Verses then;
    They only will aspire,
When Pyramids, as men,
    Are lost, i' th' funeral fire.

And when all Bodies meet
    In *Lethe* to be drowned;
Then only Numbers sweet,
    With endless life are crowned.

Like everything else in Herrick's verse, his oblivion is a self-conscious one. The poem, celebrating the time of Ovid's golden pomp, is meant to demonstrate a spiral into complete intoxication. There is an alchemical metaphor running through "flowery," "golden," "rose," and "retorted" in the opening stanzas, which gives the idea of superfluities being burned away until the truly sublime state of forgetfulness is achieved. But this being Herrick, the opposite happens. The more he strives for Volpone's vertigo, the more the poem spirals down into his self. Tibullus is the sticking point—"But stay." The least ambitious and least known of the great Roman poets, his example provides the text upon which the last three verses comment. One comment is that only poetry survives. But this is self-perplexing, for Tibullus is the one classical poet who had no wish for immortality. His is a sobering name, for his contented acceptance of oblivion guaranteed the survival of his poems as unique examples of self-effacement, making Herrick's striving after absorption into the great tradition seem all the more forced because of the survival he so much yearns for. And then there is the question of what it is that survives. Tibullus is a name and a text, nothing more: the merest remnant, a handful of ashes, while the man and his body have been virtually annihilated. Herrick's final image is of a double absorption, of bodies merging into each other and of bodies being drowned in Lethe. The same image makes the end of "Corinna's Going a Maying" so sad: "All love, all liking, all delight / Lies drowned with us in endless night." It all makes the effort to live merrily— that is, to lose oneself in drink—seem at best futile. At worst, which is where the poem ends, it is a worse than futile experience, leading to an intensification of the sadness which underlies all human endeavor. As the biblical proverb puts it, "Even in laughter the heart is sorrowful" (Proverbs 14:13).

In the popular poetry the drinking catches were, in form, circular things, going round the three voices. In content one might assume that they would be buttresses for carefree enjoyment. This is one of the best, perhaps by John Crouch, which appeared in *Mercurius Democritus* in 1652:[12]

> Bring your Lads and your Lasses along Boys,
> We'll traverse the ground with a Song Boys;
> We'll sup with delight, and we'll shorten the night,
> And our mirth shall do nobody wrong Boys.
>
> We will sing, we will sport, and we'll play boys,
> All the night long till 't be day boys;
> Then home with our Lasses, and drink wine in glasses,
> And honestly for it we'll pay boys.
>
> Then to the green Woods we'll repair boys,
> With our Lasses that looketh so fair boys;
> We'll dance it and trip it, and merrily clip it;
> And shorten the hours and days boys.

It is not difficult to see how hollow the merriment is, hedged in by protestations of innocence and the realization that everything has to be paid for. The aim to shorten time is not too far removed from Marvell's determination, caught between time's chariot and deserts of oblivion, to make the sun run even faster. Two years later Crouch printed another catch whose merriment is even more circumscribed. He introduced it like this: "There were a Company of good fellows the last week as they were sadly merry, in their Cups, they to pass away a *Winters* morning, in a dumb voice made this mournfull Melody following."[13]

The century was marked by many particularly severe winters, so that the cycle of the seasons became even more noticeable than usual. This catch offers a charm to shorten those most tedious nights of midwinter:

> A Charm against Cold, Frost, Ice and Snow,
>   hail, rain, and stormy weather,
> Shall make the cold wind his own Nails go blow,
>   till we are merry together.

Bring forth good cheer, Tap your Christmas beer,
    and make a Rousing fire,
With friendship and joy conclude the old year,
    for then the New one is nigher.

Music strike up, unto this Crowned Cup,
    true hearts we will remember,
And he that denies to turn his Liquor up,
    we'll end him with *December*.

'Tis Sack, rich Sack, that can no Treason smother,
    Wine opens the breast,
    And gives our cares rest,
And makes us to love one another.

Hostile elements are chased away by beer, but the drink gradually releases the otherwise repressed hostilities which divide men from each other, and those who do not join in reveal the treasons which their breasts contain. The chorus is, like all drunken states, an illusion of openness, carelessness, and mutual concord. There is nothing sentimental here, for not even a drink can drown the sadness which the merriment intensifies.

The proverb says "As long lives a merry man as a sad." Herrick's "Best to be Merry" seems, by its title, to be an exercise on this theme:

Fools are they, who never know
How the times away do go:
But for us, who wisely see
Where the bounds of black Death be:
Let's live merrily, and thus
Gratify the *Genius*.

The preacher of Ecclesiastes is behind this and other of Herrick's mirthful poems, for he recommended men to eat, drink, and be merry, the actions which "shall abide with him of his labour the days of his life" (8:15). He, too, was haunted by the realization that the wise man and the fool both die the same, with no more remembrance of the one than of the other (2:14–16). Herrick's poem is equally tormented. It presents a merriment which is not natural, but forced. The wise man's merry life is lived against the odds, tinged always with the knowledge of death. It would be better to be a fool, with no such knowledge, for then merriment is natural; and it may be that we should not read the opening couplet as contemptuous dismissal of a whole section of humanity, but, rather, as a definition.

There are two kinds of people: fools, who live and die ignorant of their condition; and the wise, who are constantly aware of it. The title tells you which it is better to be. "Children and fools have merry lives," as another proverb has it.

Robert Gomersal wrote a fine poem built around the same proverb with which Herrick closed "Ceremonies on Candlemas Eve," as its title floridly demonstrates: "Upon Our Vain Flattery of Ourselves That the Succeeding Times Will be Better Than the Former." Man, unable to believe in the cycle which Herrick celebrates, hurtles from one experience to another, in Gomersal's jaundiced view, always beginning in hope and ending in disillusion. The closing sequence of the poem brilliantly mimics the spiral of disappointment as man reels toward age and death—partly by its *till*-governed syntax and partly by the recollection of the thousands and millions of kisses which Martial's *carpe diem* lover offers his mistress (33–60):[14]

> Be it joy or be it sorrow,
> We refer all to the morrow,
> That we think will ease our pain,
> That we do suppose again
> Will increase our joy, and so
> Events, the which we cannot know,
> We magnify, and are (in sum)
> Enamoured of the time to come.
>   Well, the next day comes, and then
> Another next, and so to ten,
> To twenty we arrive, and find
> No more before us than behind
> Of solid joy, and yet haste on
> To our consummation:
>   Till the baldness of the crown,
> Till that all the face do frown,
> Till the forehead often have
> The remembrance of a grave;
> Till the eyes look in, to find
> If that they can see the mind;
> Till the sharpness of the nose,
> Till that we have lived to pose
> Sharper eyes, who cannot know
> Whether we are men or no;
> Till the tallow of the cheek,

Till we know not what we seek,
And at last of life bereaved,
Die unhappy, and deceived.

In "To Enjoy the Time" Herrick finds, typically, another association of death to rhyme with "merry":

While Fate permits us, let's be merry;
Pass all we must the fatal Ferry:
And this our life too whirls away,
With the Rotation of the Day.

Rotation began as a term to describe "the action of moving round a centre, or of turning round . . . an axis" (*OED*) and was applied to planetary movements. "Rotation of the Day" carries much of this sense of the planet wheeling round and round, but its principal sense is the one which developed early in the century, of things "coming round again in succession." The *OED*'s first citation of this sense is an influential one, from Henley's translation of the *City of God*: "That rotation and circumvolution of misery and blisse, which he [Origen] held, that all mankind should run in." The poem's slight discordancy comes from its opposition of merriment and whirling round rather than, as is usual, their being seen as elements of each other. It is as if, finally and unexpectedly, Herrick has come up with a definition of merriment as stasis rather than movement.

In this context we can see how puzzling in his best-known poem:

To the Virgins, to make much of Time

Gather ye Rose-buds while ye may,
  Old Time is still a flying:
And this same flower that smiles today,
  Tomorrow will be dying.

The glorious Lamp of Heaven, the Sun,
  The higher he's a getting;
The sooner will his Race be run,
  And nearer he's to Setting.

That Age is best, which is the first,
  When Youth and Blood are warmer;
But being spent, the worse, and worst
  Times, still succeed the former.

> Then be not coy, but use your time;
>   And while ye may, go marry:
> For having lost but once your prime,
>   You may for ever tarry.

Christian *carpe diem* describes it neatly, and once one has swallowed this oxymoron, then all falls into place. The pious answer to those who counsel experience at all costs, because of the oblivion which awaits us all, is to follow St. Paul's advice, and marry rather than burn (1 Corinthians 7:9)—and marry betimes. Coyness, constantly associated with virginity in *carpe diem* poetry, is here opposed not to irresponsible behavior but to wedlock. This is the normal way to read the poem, but I find it difficult to sustain. Gathering rosebuds is, after all, a plural act, easily relatable to men, who can crop maidenheads as long as they live, but more difficult to relate to the (presumably) female virgins of this poem. Either the phrase means "Have sexual experience while you can," or it means "Become more and more beautiful." This ambiguity is carried over from the title, where "make much of" means either that the virgins should treasure each moment or that they should fill each moment with action. To the assertion that these are much the same thing, I would demur when virginity is in question. For virgins to act means that they will sustain an unrestorable loss. Virgins who make much of time by treasuring their virginity stay virgins. Those who act do not. The second stanza emphasizes the uniqueness of the action by pinning the whole time span to the rotation of one day. This is the more striking because the sun's (supposed) orbiting is traditionally opposed to man's limited timespan—"suns that set may rise again." Here, however, everything is rotating and has just the one orbit, so that the poem's great sense of movement, carried by the weak-rhyming participles, is set within strict limitations. As the third stanza implies, the movement is not so much rotation as a spiraling down.

Once the first age is spent then good gives way to bad, which gives way to worse and worst. How does a virgin *spend* her time? One answer may be that she stays a virgin, although I think that the sense is more likely to be active than passive, spending not hoarding nature's coin. This, too, is the more probable sense of the "prime" of the last stanza. Virgins can lose their prime by not acting, but "but once" indicates one act rather than a gradual fading away. In either sense, however, the poem reduces itself to a denial that anyone, virgin or not, can do anything to alter her condition. Losing her prime will happen whether she does or does not act: and while "go marry" may well be good Christian advice on how to make best use of her fate, I am tempted to read it as I suspect many a

seventeenth-century reader would have done, with "marry" not an imperative but an interjection. The *OED* defines it as "an exclamation of
asseveration, surprise, indignation, etc.," originating in the use of the Virgin Mary's name as an oath. It quotes from 1601: "He thinketh all lost in
tumbling of books / Of marry go looks." Perhaps we are close here to a
source of the word *merry-go-round.*

There is a Christian view of marriage which allows a form of perpetual
virginity, a pious version of the merry-go-round. Herrick advances it in
several of his epithalamia, and also in this poem, addressed to his favorite
lady, Julia:

> *Julia's Churching, or Purification*
> Put on thy *Holy Filletings,* and so
> To th' Temple with the sober *Midwife* go.
> Attended thus (in a most solemn wise)
> By those who serve the Child-bed mysteries.
> Burn first thine incense; next, when as thou see'st
> The candid Stole thrown o'er the *Pious Priest;*
> With reverend Curtsies come, and to him bring
> Thy free (and not decurted) offering.
> All Rites well ended, with fair Auspice come
> (As to the breaking of a Bride-Cake) home:
> Where ceremonious *Hymen* shall for thee
> Provide a second *Epithalamie.*
> *She who keeps chastely to her husband's side*
> *Is not for one, but every night his Bride:*
> *And stealing still with love, and fear to Bed,*
> *Brings him not one, but many a Maidenhead.*

When the ceremony is performed as diligently as Herrick describes it
here, then, as in his Candlemas Eve poem, the result is a cycle of restoration, not a spiraling into oblivion—the return of *merry* to *Mary* perhaps.
Childbirth is a fitting event on which to focus this mystery, for we tend to
gloss over too easily the great dangers which it held for a woman in an
age of primitive gynecological practices. In truth, poets have almost always glossed over them, but they lie just under the surface of many love
poems—hence the natural yoking of the death images of *carpe diem* poetry to the purposes of seduction. Donne, whose wife endured eleven
pregnancies in fifteen years, and eventually died soon after labor, put
some of her fears into a poem as light as "The Flea," which weaves into
its games of seduction images of pregnancy, blood, and death. For most

virgins, making much of time was a matter of enjoying the little that was granted to them.

To come through childbirth, then, was a reason for thanksgiving. Herrick's poem presents it as a return to the beginning of the circle, a restoration to full virginity after the hazardous postnatal period has been survived. Mysteriously the purification ceremony, when properly observed, returns the woman to the condition she had been in as a bride. The language is carefully chosen to lead toward the closing epigrams. "Auspice" goes back to the *auspex,* the interpreter of omens who supervised marriage ceremonies; and *hymen* was already in use in the sense of the virginal membrane. Everything in this ideal state is magically given back to her, with the church the symbolic location where even the most vulnerable of human beings can be restored.

The idea of a continuous restoration attracted George Herbert too.[15] Often in *The Temple* the sinful condition of man is characterized as a mindless rotation; "Sin's Round" is the most obvious example, where his offenses "course it in a ring." Another is "Giddiness," where man whirls between mood and mood in as frenzied a fashion as any drunken Cavalier. Herbert's final judgment of this rotation is (21–28):

> Surely if each one saw another's heart,
> There would be no commerce,
> No sale or bargain pass: all would disperse,
> And live apart.
>
> Lord, mend or rather make us: one creation
> Will not suffice our turn:
> Except thou make us daily, we shall spurn
> Our own salvation.

The clinching pun is "suffice our turn," which makes creation a process of continuous adaptation to man's giddiness, and restoration of him to the condition in which he started out. Identity depends upon constancy. Giddiness, man's natural state, would deny him such a settled center, and would deny the community any such center also, with men unable to trust one another, all dispersing and living apart. Only God's fiction holds it all together—a massive act of creative will which freezes movement into stasis.

Man resists, but resistance is absorbed into the creation. All of this is most powerfully symbolized in the one still place in the turning world, the church. In "Church Monuments" Herbert, kneeling in prayer, sees all around him dissolving elegantly into, a true community at last, "the good fellowship of dust." Identity means man's acceptance that he does not have the individuality which his naturally giddy state persuades him he is so much in need of. This is a matter for all creation, and everything in and about the church acts as a model to teach the lesson: as in Herrick's poem on Julia's churching, where all the items of the ceremony—vestments, incense, ritual, and offerings—make the individuals—woman, midwife, priest—part of an event with a mysterious power greater than could be conceived by the mere totaling of the units which make it up. So, in Herbert's church, mere pieces of wood, stone, and glass make up a building of immense strength.

As all architects and builders know, strength is derived from the resistance of materials. This is one of the points made in the poem which takes the reader from the first section of *The Temple*, "The Church-Porch," into "The Church" itself:

> *Superliminare*
>
> Thou, whom the former precepts have
> Sprinkled and taught, how to behave
> Thy self in church; approach, and taste
> The church's mystical repast.
>
> Avoid profaneness; come not here:
> Nothing but holy, pure, and clear,
> Or that which groaneth to be so,
> May at his peril further go.

Groaning is the elemental sound of Herbert's volume, the marker of man's condition as an afflicted, repentant creature. But other things groan too. Here it is the piece of timber which makes up the lintel over the entrance to the church, the *superliminare* of the title. Like another piece of wood in Christian history the lintel is in a tragic position, being the vital element which ensures man a way into salvation but which has no entry itself. This is to suppose that wood has feelings. Herbert's disciple, Henry Vaughan, wrote a poem on this very premise, for even a piece of wood is part of the creation which "groaneth and travaileth" to be with God (Romans 8:22–23). In "The Timber" Vaughan reflects on the past life of a piece of seasoned wood (1–12):

> Sure thou didst flourish once! and many springs,
> Many bright mornings, much dew, many showers

Passed o'er thy head: many light *hearts* and *wings*
Which now are dead, lodged in thy living bowers.

And still a new succession sings and flies;
Fresh groves grow up, and their green branches shoot
Towards the old and still enduring skies,
While the low *violet* thrives at their root.

But thou beneath the sad and heavy *line*
Of death, dost waste all senseless, cold and dark;
Where not so much as dreams of light may shine,
Nor any thought of greenness, leaf or bark.

To be out of time and life, the succession of seasons and generations, is the timber's apparent fate. But its identity is not lost, for at times of great storms it can be felt to murmur and groan (13–20):

And yet (as if some deep hate and dissent,
Bred in thy growth betwixt high winds and thee,
Were still alive) thou dost great storms resent
Before they come, and know'st how near they be.

Else all at rest thou liest, and the fierce breath
Of tempests can no more disturb thy ease;
But this strange resentment after death
Means only those, who broke (in life) thy peace.

Resentment, in the sense of a feeling of trouble or loss, is a good word to describe Herbert's lintel too, as it holds up and absorbs the great weight of the building while straining to be allowed to enter. In the English church this doorway was the location for the churching ceremony, so perhaps Herrick, with his fondness for the origins of ritual, set his poem to Julia on the same threshold. Milton's "Methought I saw" sonnet describes a threshold experience as well—the kind of dream state which we may now call subliminal.

The "Church" section of *The Temple* is a building held together by the subliminal tensions of the protagonist, who appears in nearly all of its poems. These often take the form of a frustrated narrative, the promised journey from *A* to *Z* either getting stuck halfway or turning back on itself and going back to *A*. "Sin's Round" obviously does this, building its tower of Babel and smashing it down again. More subtly, the poems on either side of it show immobility rather than promised movement. The one before it is "Hope":

> I gave to Hope a watch of mine: but he
>   An anchor gave to me.
> Then an old prayer-book I did present:
>   And he an optic sent.
> With that I gave a vial full of tears:
>   But he a few green ears:
> Ah Loiterer! I'll no more, no more I'll bring:
>   I did expect a ring.

Hope and Herbert are playing some kind of transactional game, with Herbert, as usual, the loser. What he loses is hope, leaving him in the condition where there is no point in further movement—as the proverb has it, "Hope deferred maketh the heart sick." The irony lies in calling Hope a loiterer, for, had he been able to read the signs correctly, Herbert would have perceived a promising narrative, taking him from the time-piece to the green ears. The important words are *but* and *and,* for they reveal the protagonist's subliminal desires. "But" in response to the anchor signals lack of understanding, even disappointment; "and" shows that the telescope holds out hope for him; then "but" to the green ears turns the whole transaction sour. He is back where he started. But this is what he really wants, the ring which he expected. Hope offers a narrative, leading to salvation. He prefers to go round and round in the same place.

After "Sin's Round" comes "Time," the most entertaining poem in *The Temple:*

> Meeting with Time, "slack thing," said I,
> "Thy scythe is dull; whet it for shame."
> "No marvel Sir," he did reply,
> "If it at length deserve some blame:
>   But where one man would have me grind it,
>   Twenty for one too sharp do find it."
>
> "Perhaps some such of old did pass,
> Who above all things loved this life;
> To whom thy scythe a hatchet was,
> Which now is but a pruning-knife,
>   Christ's coming hath made man thy debter,
>   Since by thy cutting he grows better.

And in his blessing thou art blest:
For where thou only wert before
An executioner at best;
Thou art a gard'ner now, and more,
    An usher to convey our souls
    Beyond the utmost stars and poles.

And this is that makes life so long,
While it detains us from our God,
Ev'n pleasures here increase the wrong,
And length of days lengthen the rod.
    Who wants the place, where God doth dwell,
    Partakes already half of hell.

Of what strange length must that needs be,
Which ev'n eternity excludes!"
Thus far Time heard me patiently:
Then chafing said, "This man deludes:
    What do I here before his door?
    He doth not crave less time, but more."

The setting is a doorway, the threshold of death, over which many a man stumbles. Others pass through with little trouble, for whereas every other door may be shut this one is always open. Donne's two dying poems offer both possibilities, the door at which he tunes his instrument in readiness to join the choir of saints and the door through which his sins have led many to hell.[16] But the best gloss on Herbert's poem comes from a poem earlier in *The Temple*, "My soul doth love thee, yet it loves delay" ("Justice I"). Time's comment that "this man deludes" is exactly right, for Herbert is playing with time. Meeting death at the door is a disconcerting experience, and only an experienced player of games could cope as well as he does, seizing the initiative instead of panicking. The delight of the poem is to see how the most correct and orthodox expressions of piety can be used for wholly impious purposes, preferring a love of delay over a love of God. Everything Herbert says to Time, from the second stanza to the beginning of the fifth, is a good Christian acceptance of death in a world redeemed by Christ's love. And yet Time understands it for what it is, a mere playing for time. The proper response at death's door is to walk through, not stop at the threshold and utter pieties. In the fleshly sense Herbert wins the game, Time's withdrawal taking him back to the place he began.

"The Church" opens on the threshold and closes in "Love III" at the same place, still reluctant to move forward—"Love bade me welcome: yet my soul drew back." There has been a faltering "entrance in," but it needs all Love's persuasion, even a taking of Herbert's hand, to lead him further forward. This is a positive breaking of the circle with which the main body of *The Temple* closes, but the volume as a whole still has its reservations. Rather in the manner of Bunuel's *Exterminating Angel*, the third section, the long seminarrative poem "The Church Militant," moves back from the man in the church to the Church itself. This poem initially promises the movement of progression, the Church's advance from its origins in the east being traced by way of Egypt, Greece, Rome, Spain, and Germany, to its arrival in a properly Protestant Britain. But this is a poem of the 1630s, and Herbert knows that the idea that Christianity has found its true place is an illusion. The poem moves on to trace Sin's pursuit of the Church, and a narrative of progress becomes a narrative of rotation, the rhymes emphasizing the circle which all things trace (259–271):

> Yet as the Church shall thither westward fly,
> So Sin shall trace and dog her instantly:
> They have their period also and set times
> Both for their virtuous actions and their crimes.
> And where of old the Empire and the Arts
> Ushered the Gospel ever in man's hearts,
> *Spain* hath done one; when Arts perform the other,
> The Church shall come, and Sin the Church shall smother:
> That when they have accomplished the round,
> And met in th' east their first and ancient sound,
> Judgment may meet them both and search them round.
> Thus do both lights, as well in Church as Sun,
> Light one another, and together run.

Despite the impression of advance, even running on to America, the movement is illusory, for the same distance is kept between the Church and Sin, who sits on the next horse on the merry-go-round.

"The Church Militant" is not quite the final poem of the volume. Herbert closes it with a brief envoy, asking God to give the lie to a Sin which teaches that the cross is "common wood," a memory perhaps of the piece of wood which stands above the church door.

12 "Sir, You Have Not Missed": Civilized Behavior

The great pleasure given by Herbert's "Time" comes from the unexpected courtesy which the deathly visitor displays. Meeting with Herbert, and being rebuked like some tardy tradesman, Time responds to the poet's slightly offensive "slack thing" with a civilized "Sir" and, having given his brief explanation for his delay, listens patiently while he is lectured about his place in the scheme of things. Even when his patience runs out, his chafing expresses itself not in a quick flash of the scythe, but in a wry acceptance that he is an unwelcome visitor in spite of his host's protestations to the contrary. To appreciate the poet's vulgarity we need only move forward twenty years and think of a more civilized character also on the threshold of death, who did nothing common, made no protests, but simply "bowed his comely head, / Down, as upon a bed."

It has always been tempting to see the Cavalier-Roundhead contrast as one of the polished and urbane against the violent and uncouth—the comely head surrounded by a bloody-handed mob applauding the execution. This cliché, though taken to the point of caricature, has much truth in it. Although it is possible to point to many Colonel Hutchinsons in Parliament's ranks, there were many more who took a simple, crude delight in breaking anything beautiful or elegant which they could lay their hands on. Indeed, Hutchinson is a case in point. In her memoir of him, his wife, shortly after lamenting this opponents' caricaturing of Puritans as "an illiterate, morose, melancholy, discontented, crazed sort of men," tells this story:

> The parliament had made orders to deface the images in all churches. Within two miles of his house there was a church, where Christ upon the cross, the virgin, and John, had been fairly set up in a window over the altar, and sundry other superstitious paintings, of

270

the priest's own ordering, were drawn upon the walls. When the order for rasing out those relics of superstition came, the priest only
took down the heads of the images, and laid them carefully up in his
closet, and would have had the church officers to have certified that
the thing was done according to order; whereupon they came to Mr
Hutchinson, and desired him that he would take the pains to come
and view their church, which he did, and upon discourse with the
parson, persuaded him to blot out all the superstitious paintings, and
break the images in the glass; which he consented to, but being ill-
affected, was one of those who began to brand Mr Hutchinson with
the name of Puritan.[1]

Despite the civilized tones of the narrative and the courteous behavior of
Hutchinson, the fanatic gleam is obvious. The very certainty of his zealous possession enables him to behave as if he were perfectly justified in
smashing up the stained glass, and allows her to write about it with the
slightly pained air of someone who senses that her husband's altruism
had not been appreciated by all. But this is the same man who, when he
faced a painful death imprisoned in Sandown Castle, said simply, "'Tis
as I would have it: 'Tis where I would have it."[2]
    One way of understanding such iconoclasm as Hutchinson's is to see it
in terms of the ear against the eye, Puritan emphasis upon the spoken
word confronting Anglican values of ceremony and ritual designed to
work principally in images. True, this yields some odd results if taken
back to earlier in the century. Jonson's bias, for instance, is almost always
for the ear over the eye, a preference which came to a devastating head in
the argument with Inigo Jones over the primacy of image or language in
the masques. In the 1630s, however, zeal was seen as essentially a matter
of verbal expression while Laudianism moved increasingly toward visual
demonstrations of faith. The chief lesson of Herbert's "Time" is to know
when to be silent, for even the best words in the wrong mouth are merely
wind. Images were less likely to be so abused or to be treated ambigu-
ously, as William Strode explains in his account of the fine stained-glass
windows of Fairford church:[3]

> Each pane instructs the Laity
> With silent eloquence: for here
> Devotion leads the eye, not ear,
> To note the catechising paint,
> Whose easy phrase doth so acquaint
> Our sense with Gospel that the Creed

In such a hand the weak may read:
Such types even yet of virtue be,
And Christ, as in a glass we see.

"Catechising paint" makes the point succinctly. Words being slippery, dangerous things, their ideal use was in a set form of questions and answers which allowed neither ambiguity nor the possibility of individual inspiration. Images were likely to be more reliable in controlling the wandering imagination.

Strode's poem is not, like Corbett's on the same subject, a sustained piece of anti-Puritanism. It comes to the phenomenon of iconoclasm only after a sustained meditation upon the way the images work upon the pious viewer. Stuck in the middle of the meditation is one passage of discordant wit: how do you throw a church out of a window (39–42)?

But would you walk a turn in Paul's?
Look up; one little pane enrolls
A fairer temple: fling a stone
The Church is out o' the windows thrown.

The oddness comes from the capriciousness of the idea. All the reverence and wonder which Strode feels at the sight of these marvelous windows does not prevent from popping into his head the idea that he could very easily pick up a stone and score a direct hit. The poem closes, as Corbett's does, by wondering why the Puritans have left the windows alone; so, in a sense, this wayward thought of vandalism helps prepare the way for a reminder of the real vandals of the state. But really the Puritans are only incidental, one further threat to the windows which have long been under siege (59–70):

The wondrous art hath equal fate
Unfenced and yet inviolate:
The Puritans were sure deceived,
And thought those shadows moved and heaved,
So held from stoning Christ: the wind
And boisterous tempests were so kind
As on his Image not to prey,
Whom both the winds and seas obey.
At Momus' wish be not amazed;
For if each Christian heart were glazed

Detail from one of the windows of the Church of St. Mary, Fairford, surprisingly spared by Puritan iconoclasts. This may be the window to which Strode's poem refers: the smaller building in the background looks very like the church itself.

> With such a window, then each breast
> Might be his own Evangelist.

Not only Puritans, winds, and tempests but anyone and anything threaten them, for even a civilized observer such as Strode could see in them an opportunity to test his marksmanship or display his wit. Momus was dissatisfied with man because of the opacity of his breast. Place a window there, he said, so that his breast could be seen. Strode has, wittingly or not, allowed a peep into his own.

Civilized behavior means commerce and transaction, a condition unlikely to be reached if Momus' wish were granted, as Herbert realized in "Giddiness." But Momus, of course, was a classical figure, so his notion of a window was likely to be different from Strode's. While there were glass windows in ancient times, they were a rarity. A seventeenth-century window, stained glass or not, offered only a very limited kind of transparency, a feature which Herbert plays on in "The Elixir" (9–12):

> A man that looks on glass,
>   On it my stay his eye;
> Or if he pleaseth, through it pass,
>   And then the heav'n espy.

The difficulty is to do both things at once, look at the glass and look through it and beyond. In "The Windows" Herbert uses the cracked and flawed glass which normally filled seventeenth-century window space to describe the priest's role. Both are supposed to be transparencies through which the light can shine but are obviously inadequate for the task (1–5):

> Lord, how can man preach thy eternal word?
>   He is brittle crazy glass:
> Yet in thy temple thou dost him afford
>   This glorious and transcendent place,
>   To be a window, through thy grace.

The answer to Herbert's opening question is to fill the space with stained glass, thereby giving the crazy patternings a purpose and sense of design (6–15):

> But when thou dost anneal in glass thy story,
>   Making thy life to shine within
> The holy Preachers; then the light and glory

More rev'rend grows, and more doth win:
Which else shows wat'rish, bleak, and thin.

Doctrine and life, colours and light, in one
When they combine and mingle, bring
A strong regard and awe: but speech alone
Doth vanish like a flaring thing,
And in the ear, not conscience ring.

Again there emerges the preference for the eye over the ear. Given the arguments which raged over preaching in the 1620s and 1630s, it would not be wrong to see one of Herbert's purposes in this poem to be offering a proper definition of the word. Preaching should not be an expression of the inspired self—this would be crazed at worst, at best empty of content—but should be a controlled expression of received doctrine. As he put it in *A Priest to the Temple,* "the character of his Sermon is Holiness; he is not witty, or learned, or eloquent, but Holy."[4] The lesson is that transparency is not a synonym for honesty, nor is it necessarily desirable. Artifice, whether in the creation of the artist or in the manners of civilized behavior, is the way to win a strong regard and awe—so long, of course, as the victory is God's, not one's own.

One of Herbert's most civilized encounters occurs in front of a stained-glass window, in the poem "Lovejoy":

As on a window late I cast mine eye,
I saw a vine drop grapes with *J* and *C*
Annealed on every bunch. One standing by
Asked what it meant. I (who am never loth
To spend my judgment) said, It seemed to me
To be the body and the letters both
Of *Joy* and *Charity.* Sir, you have not missed,
The man replied; It figures JESUS CHRIST.

I don't know what Herbert means by his title, at least insofar as it relates to the poem. Perhaps it recalls St. Paul's advice to the Galatians to live in a civilized way, eschewing "envyings, murders, drunkenness, revellings, and such like," preferring instead the "fruit of the Spirit," which is "love, joy, peace, longsuffering, gentleness, goodness, faith, meekness, temperance" (5:21–23). The link may be between fruit and the vine dropping grapes on the window, whose lesson is not drunkenness, but the letters *J* and *C.*[5] Other items in St. Paul's list seem to fit the encounter too, notably gentleness, faith, and meekness. Herbert's questioner can be seen to possess these qualities, first asking his opinion and then agreeing wholeheartedly that Herbert's answer is right on target. The poem seems to be a celebration of the way a church's stained-glass window will inspire its viewers to a realization that Christ's message is bound up with the two great Christian values, joy and charity.[6] The eye has led the way toward the true interpretative words which bind a community of worshipers, here symbolized by the agreement between Herbert and his questioner.

And yet such a reading is surely wide of the mark, for it leaves out all of the poem's discordant elements, most obviously the piece of self-characterization which sits at the poem's center: "I (who am never loth / To spend my judgment) said." The self-denigration signals a disturbance, something in the memory of the incident which has perplexed Herbert and shaken his opinion of himself. The other discordant element in the poem is the original question, for a moment's thought shows it to have been quite unexpected. It is hard to think how any literate person in seventeenth-century England—or even in godless twentieth-century England, for that matter—could look at the letters *J* and *C* on a church window and not know what they signified. The questioner is not a child, as we discover in the final line, so perhaps he is illiterate; but his courteous response at the poem's end implies that he is Herbert's equal and would, therefore, be recognized as such through his bearing, dress, and tone of voice. If so, why does he ask a question whose answer is so obvious?

I can answer this best by rewriting Herbert's poem. My apologies for the lame rhyme and wretched meter:

> As on a window late I cast mine eye,
> I saw a vine drop grapes with *J* and *C*
> Annealed on every bunch. One standing by
> Asked what it meant. I (who am never loth
> To spend my judgment) said, it seemed to me
> To be the body and the letters both
> Of *Jesus Christ*. Yes, sir, was his reply,
> You have not missed; It figures JOY and CHARITY.

Looking back at the encounter Herbert realizes that some kind of test was involved, which he did not pass. Asked to interpret *J* and *C*, he had assumed that the questioner wanted more than the obvious answer which he would, for example, offer to a child. So he moved forward one interpretative step and offered *joy* and *charity*. The man's response, despite its apparent agreement, was a rebuke, restoring the primary values of the letters. The lesson is that it is dangerous to allow one's wit to lose hold of the essential Christian truth, that Christ is the source of everything good. But this is a questioner who sits so sly, for had Herbert answered instinctively, not allowing his "judgment" any play, he would have been open to the rebuke that his interpretation was dull and unthinking. Answer each man according to his capacity, and such a questioner should be given more than would be offered to an illiterate. This is what Herbert did, offering the man an insight into the hieroglyphic mysteries whereby letters can signify multiple levels of meaning. One lesson of the poem is that for people of Herbert's—and the questioner's—learning, there can be no such thing as a simple response. Everything is stained by interpretation and its attendant sense of loss. Rather than emphasizing and supporting an idea of community, the poem does the opposite, turning the most apparently civilized encounter into a contest of wit and faith, dividing men from each other, and leaving the poet with an impaired sense of his own value as the interpreter of God's word.

This appreciation that the words one uses, even the most apparently simple ones, are out of control and potentially dangerous, is a theme of Herbert's work which Henry Vaughan seized upon. In the preface to the second edition of his *Silex Scintillans* (1655) and in several of his poems in that volume, he describes how a writer's words can lead other men— whole generations perhaps—into ruin. A "soul-killing issue" is how he describes the phenomenon in his preface, a theme treated explicitly in poems such as "Idle Verse" and implicitly in "The Daughter of Herodias," one of the earliest treatments of Salome in the English tradition:

> Vain, sinful art! who first did fit
> Thy lewd loathed *motions* unto *sounds,*
> And made grave *music* like wild *wit*
> Err in loose airs beyond her bounds?
>
> What fires hath he heaped on his head?
> Since to his sins (as needs it must,)
> His *art* adds still (though he be dead,)
> New fresh accounts of blood and lust.
>
> Leave then young sorceress; the *ice*
> Will those coy spirits cast asleep,
> Which teach thee now to please his eyes
> Who doth thy loathsome mother keep.

> But thou hast pleased so well, he swears,
> And gratifies thy sin with vows:
> His shameless lust in public wears,
> And to thy soft arts strongly bows.
>
> *Skilful enchantress* and true bred!
> Who out of evil can bring forth good?
> Thy mother's nets in thee were spread,
> She tempts to *incest,* thou to *blood.*

Here is a web of artifice spun by Salome and her mother, but not only by them, for the poem's initial contempt is aimed at the artist, the original choreographer, whose dance patterns Salome employed. He may be long dead, but his damnable art continues to seduce and tempt succeeding generations to sin; as Vaughan put it in his preface: "These *vipers* survive their *parents,* and for many ages after (like *epidemic* diseases) infect whole generations, corrupting always and unhallowing the best-gifted *souls,* and the most capable *vessels.*" The lesson is a sobering one, that "the more acute the *author is,* there is so much the more danger and death in the *work.*" The implications are political as well as moral. The beheaded John the Baptist is an obvious analogue for the dead Charles, whose execution occurred shortly before *Silex Scintillans* was published. Vaughan's question is how far the writers of idle verse created the mindset which brought about such an appalling event.

As in so much else, he was taking his lead from George Herbert, who reportedly hovered between a hope that his poems might "turn to the advantage of any poor soul," in which case they should be printed, and a fear that they might be harmful, and should therefore be burned. "The Church-porch" opens with a defense of poetry:

> Thou, whose sweet youth and early hopes enhance
> Thy rate and price, and mark thee for a treasure;
> Hearken unto a Verser, who may chance
> Rhyme thee to good, and make a bait of pleasure.
>   A verse may find him, who a sermon flies,
>   And turn delight into a sacrifice.

The brief account of Herbert's life which the printers prefixed to *The Temple* stated that "by his example, exhortations, and encouragements" he "drew the greater part of his parishioners to accompanie him dayly in the publick celebration of Divine Service." [8] The greater part, not all, one might cynically say—and perhaps it was the younger generation who held back; hence the poem's address to those blessed with early hopes, who might otherwise evade a preacher's example and exhortation. But Herbert was well aware of the dangers of the enterprise, for poetry's pleasurable bait depends much more than a sermon does upon the operations of chance. Outside the church, as part of the world, the book is out of control. While it might work for good, it might just as easily do the devil's work, the bait being taken but the fish lost. And, after all, Herbert's fears were justified, his poems having become in this century favorite texts for atheist critics to demonstrate that providential patterns are merely fictional constructs.

Herrick was another poet who hovered between eternity and the fire, so far as his poems were concerned. *Hesperides* ends with "The Pillar of Fame," a proud proclamation that no matter what else happens to the state, this volume is fixed to stand the judgment of time:

> Firm and well fixed foundation.
> Out-during *Marble, Brass,* or *Jet,*
>   Charmed and enchanted so,
>   As to withstand the blow
>   Of   overthrow,
>   Nor   shall   the   seas,
>   Or   OUTRAGES
>   Of   storms   o'erbear
>   What   we   up-rear,
>   Though   Kingdoms   fall,
> This   pillar   never   shall
> Decline   or   waste   at   all;
> But stand for ever by his own
> Firm and well fixed foundation.

As has often been rightly noted, *Hesperides* needs to be read as a total collection for full pleasure to be gained from the individual poems. A great part of the enjoyment comes from sharing Herrick's occasional weariness at the task he is engaged on and his trepidation that he might not be able to finish it. Tongue in cheek, he includes people as subjects for his poems because they expect it, because it will make his book shine the brighter to get a particularly noble name in it, or to fulfill a family debt. Some four-fifths of the way through he includes a poem "To his kinsman M. Tho. Herrick, who desired to be in his Book":

> Welcome to this my College, and though late
> Th'ast got a place here (standing candidate)

It matters not, since thou art chosen one
Here of my great and good foundation.

The jokes come in "candidate" and "foundation," both of which continue the college metaphor. But the foundation, as in "The Pillar of
Fame," is all the poems which have gone before, on top of which Thomas
Herrick can sit and be elevated higher than he really deserves, just as any
future recipient of the funds of a college foundation owes his position—
and his future fame—to the charitable person who gave the gift. "Candidate" is even more mischievous, pointing to his kinsman's usefulness in
filling up one more piece of the white pages which remain until the book
is completed. The final poem in *Hesperides* is accordingly a celebration
of a job well done, and Herrick fills it with many of the typographical
details which have been scattered through the volume: the shaped poem,
italics marking the inferior materials in line 2, and the capitalized "OUT-
RAGES" in the central section—the capitals signaling the huge importance
of what has been done to king and country in the 1640s, the context for
so many of the poems in the collection. "Set" in the opening line—
"Fame's pillar here, at last, we set"—has at least two technical senses
which fit Herrick's use of it here. One is "to place in a certain sequence in
a literary work, in writing or in print"; the other, "to place (type) in the
order in which it is to be printed from" (*OED,* 15c and 72). The poem is
a miniature compendium of the varieties of print into which the triumphant author has seen his written sheets transferred.

Yet only a few poems earlier Herrick included this last dip back into
doubt and depression:

To his Book

Go thou forth my book, though late;
Yet be timely fortunate.
It may chance good-luck may send
Thee a kinsman, or a friend,
That may harbour thee, when I,
With my fates neglected lie.
If thou know'st not where to dwell,
See, the fire's by: *Farewell.*

This is a very circumscribed survival, nothing like immortality. Probably
the flames await, unless a lucky chance supplies one person who will keep
it from the fire—or an even worse fate, for in one poem Herrick specu-

lates on its use to wipe backsides. Who knows, perhaps even the kinsman Thomas Herrick might be the one proud enough of his name's presence in it to keep it alive a little longer. A better savior, however, would be the lady to whom many of the individual poems in *Hesperides* are addressed. This poem occurs a few pages earlier:

> *His last request to Julia*
> I have been wanton, and too bold I fear,
> To chafe o'er much the Virgin's cheek or ear:
> Beg for my Pardon *Julia; He doth win*
> *Grace with the Gods, who's sorry for his sin.*
> That done, my *Julia*, dearest *Julia*, come,
> And go with me to choose my Burial room:
> My Fates are ended; when thy *Herrick* dies,
> Clasp thou his Book, then close thou up his Eyes.

Like "To his Book," this is marked by a reluctance to detach himself from the book which has been so long a part of him that the thought of its separate existence is perplexing to the point of anxiety. His death would mean his book's death too if the book were really his. It is not, of course—that is one of the points of the volume's closing couplet, added at the end of "The Pillar of Fame":

> To his Book's end this last line he'd have placed,
> *Jocund his Muse was; but his Life was chaste.*

The jocund muse is not to be held as the measure of the man's life, which was chaste. On such distinctions lie the hopes of salvation and the fear of damnation. Yet, as Herbert and Vaughan argued, even a chaste life may not save one from the soul-killing effects of a jocund muse. So there is as much ambiguity in Herrick's instructions to Julia as in Herbert's commission to Ferrar either to print the poems or to burn them. Julia should, as part of the proper observance of his death, close up his eyes and clasp his book. But "clasp" goes in different directions. One is the hope that she will embrace it, at least ensuring its survival, at best taking his words to her and making them part of her life. However, *clasp* has an older sense of shutting up a book and leaving its contents buried, as in Hooker's use of the word (cited by the *OED*): "sermons are the keys . . . and do open the scriptures; which being but read, remain, in comparison, still clasped." So intimate is the connection between Herrick's death and the book's clasping that the image of a coffin comes through in the final line.

Alongside his hopes for immortality there is a form of resentment that the book should have a survival and life of its own after his death, particularly when its reading could lead to misinterpretation of the life and character of its writer.

An earlier poem in *Hesperides,* also titled "To his Book," literally consigns the poems to a coffin, as a preferred alternative to their misuse or neglect:

> If hap it must, that I must see thee lie
> *Absyrtus*-like all torn confusedly:
> With solemn tears, and with much grief of heart,
> I'll recollect thee (weeping) part by part;
> And having washed thee, close thee in a chest
> With spice; that done, I'll leave thee to thy rest.

The tears, washing, and use of spice parallel the frequent directions to Julia, in various poems scattered through the volume, directing her on how to prepare Herrick's body for its funeral—making the identity of Herrick and his poems even stronger. *Recollect* is one of those favourite *re*–words of the seventeenth century, like *restore* and *renew.* We distinguish its two senses now by difference in pronunciation, but in Herrick's poem it means both "remember" and "collect together again." "Absyrtus," more familiarly Apsyrtus, was Medea's half brother. She hacked him to pieces and threw them into the sea so that his pursuing father Aeetes would be delayed by having to retrieve them for proper burial. Humorously the analogy is of Herrick picking up sheets which have been scattered by negligent readers, but the double sense of "recollect" gives the image its more serious tinge. Apsyrtus's name means "swept away," making him an obvious Orpheus figure. The poet tearfully remembering his poems and the occasions which inspired them is reclaiming them as his own when they have been misappropriated by others. Any poet who sees how perversely his poems are read and interpreted might well wish to recollect them and bury them away. Henry Vaughan's preface to *Silex Scintillans* earnestly entreats readers to ignore his earlier verse; but he had no need to worry, since there was little sign that anyone had bothered to read them. Herrick's poems had not yet gone into print (with a few exceptions), but his poems were being circulated in manuscript, were being widely read, and were taking on a life of their own.[9]

Eleven poems in *Hesperides* are addressed to his book. One of them comes immediately after "Julia's Churching, or Purification" (see above, page 263) and should be read as a continuation of it:

Before the Press scarce one could see
A little-peeping-part of thee:
But since th'art Printed, thou dost call
To show thy nakedness to all.
My care for thee is now the less;
(Having resigned thy shamefacedness:)
Go with thy Faults and Fates; yet stay
And take this sentence, then away;
Whom one beloved will not suffice,
She'll run to all adulteries.

"Julia's Churching" closes with the ideal wife coming reverently to her husband's bed, bringing him, mysteriously, a maidenhead each night. "To his Book" presents the counterimage, as if thoughts of his poems turned Herrick's mind to adultery and divorce. Coincidentally, they seem to have acted in a similar way in Milton's mind, the disespousal of his awakening after his dead wife's nocturnal visitation paralleling the muse's nightly visits from which he wakes each morning ready to write something more heroic than the "rage / Of Turnus for Lavinia disespoused" (*Paradise Lost* 9:16–17). Herrick's promiscuous book has caused him to divorce it—the meaning, I assume, behind the imperatives "Go" and "away." In part he is doing what every good author does, apologizing for the various kinds of error which can slip into its printing: this is the meaning of "Faults" in line 7. More particularly, he is lamenting the loss of control over what should be his, an inevitable consequence of publication. In manuscript, shown now and then to selected readers, all that was given to the world was an occasional peep. Now the poems are common property, and with them has gone Herrick's name too. *Publish* seems to be the unspoken pun behind the poem. One of its common senses was to proclaim the guilt of an offender—here Herrick is publishing his poems' adulteries; the other common sense, ironically enough, was to proclaim the banns of marriage (as in the 1662 Book of Common Prayer).

The odd thing in all of this is that, so far, the poem had not been published. Our reading of *Hesperides* as, in part, a continuing account of Herrick's preparation of the volume for the press is suddenly blocked here as he projects himself into a future time. In terms of the metaphor, he is a husband whose wife is still faithful, but who finds himself anticipating an inevitable cuckolding—a piece of wit which informs the words "Press" and "Printed," emphasizing their sexual undertones. The images are of pressure, indentation, black ink on virginal white sheets of paper, the taking of the one maidenhead which, without the mysterious cere-

monial of the preceding poem, is all the woman has to offer. It is a view
of women's sexuality which seems completely opposite to the image presented in "Julia's Churching," the one sexual experience opening up adul-
terous floodgates. Really, though, the opposition is only superficial, for
the idea that a woman is either a perpetual virgin or a perpetual whore
comes down to the same caricatured view held by most seventeenth-
century poets. Rochester's veering between visions of women who will
not give anything and who give all to anyone repeatedly is only an extreme example of what most of the love poetry of the century had been
leading toward. In "The Platonic Lady," for example, he makes double
use of *press:*

> I could Love thee till I die,
>   Wouldst Thou Love me Modestly;
> And ne'er press, whilst I love,
>   For more than willingly I would give;
>   Which should sufficient be to prove
>   I'd understand the Art of Love.
>
> I hate the Thing is called Enjoyment,
>   Beside it is a dull employment,
> It cuts off all that's Life and fire,
>   From that which may be termed Desire.
>   Just like the Bee whose sting is gone,
>   Converts the owner to a Drone.
>
> I love a youth, will give me leave
>   His Body in my arms to wreathe;
> To press him Gently and to kiss,
>   To sigh and look with Eyes that wish.
>   For what if I could once Obtain,
>   I would neglect with flat disdain.
>
> I'd give him Liberty to toy,
>   And play with me and count it Joy.
> Our freedom should be full complete,
>   And nothing wanting but the feat:
>   Let's practice then, and we shall prove,
>   These are the only sweets of Love.

The same lady might well be the "Mistress Willis" whom he described as

> Bawdy in thoughts, precise in Words,
>   Ill natured though a Whore,
> Her belly is a Bag of Turds,
>   And her Cunt a Common shore.

Herrick wrote many poems praising the virginal purity of his mistresses. He also wrote this:

> *Upon Some Women*
>
> Thou who wilt not love, do this;
> Learn of me what Woman is.
> Something made of thread and thrum;
> A mere Botch of all and some.
> Pieces, patches, ropes of hair;
> In-laid Garbage everywhere.
> Out-side silk, and out-side Lawn;
> Scenes to cheat us neatly drawn.
> False in legs, and false in thighs;
> False in breast, teeth, hair, and eyes:
> False in head, and false enough;
> Only true in shreds and stuff.

Of course, there is a long tradition of misogynist verse into which such caricatures fit; and Herrick gives himself a let-out clause by confining the portrait to "some women." Still, the general term "Woman" in line 2 puts the poem at odds with its title. The apparent contradiction clears up a little, however, if we realize that Herrick is describing not only women but also something even more important to him, his poems; for the ordering of the volume makes "Upon Some Women" follow immediately upon another "To his Book" poem:

> Like to a Bride, come forth my Book, at last,
> With all thy richest jewels over-cast:
> Say, if there be 'mongst many gems here; one
> Deserveless of the name of *Paragon:*
> Blush not at all for that; since we have set
> Some *Pearls* on *Queens,* that have been counterfeit.

Again, here are virgin blushes to contrast with the catalogue of falsities in the next poem. The connection is the more obvious because of the closing image, although whether it is the pearls which are counterfeit or the queens is not easy to decide.

I would choose the pearls, if only because they complete the poem's bookmaking conceit. Any connection with jewels is likely to attract Herrick's attention—the son of a goldsmith, and apprenticed to one himself—so he imagines his book appearing not as any run-of-the-mill volume of poems, but in a fine binding decorated with precious stones. This image occurs several times in *Hesperides,* notably in "To his Closet-Gods," where the jewel-book-woman yoking is even more curiously presented:

> When I go Hence ye *Closet-Gods,* I fear
> Never again to have ingression here:
> Where I have had, what ever thing could be
> Pleasant, and precious to my Muse and me.
> Besides rare sweets, I had a Book which none
> Could read the Intext but my self alone.
> About the Cover of this Book there went
> A curious-comely clean *Compartlement:*
> And, in the midst, to grace it more, was set
> A blushing-pretty-peeping Rubelet:
> But now 'tis closed; and being shut, and sealed,
> Be it, O be it, never more revealed!
> Keep here still, *Closet-Gods,* 'fore whom I've set
> Oblations oft, of sweetest Marmelet.

I have kept to the 1648 text here. The Oxford edition emends "compartlement" to "compartiment," taking up the *OED*'s suggestion that the word means "the fine binding of a book"—although there are precious few other examples of its use. "Intext," too, is a rarity. It is a word which ought to gain currency today, although Herrick's is the only recorded use: the *OED*'s suggested meaning is "the text or matter of a book." Both words are part of the poem's depiction of closets within closets, with, at the heart of the mystery, the "rubelet," another Herrick nonce word. This is defined as "a little ruby" by the dictionary, but the poem's prefixture "blushing-pretty-peeping," gives it a clitoral sense. That most private place, once seen and known, has lost its unique value for ever.

So, the counterfeit pearls of "To his Book" are to be contrasted with the real, genuine pearls which Herrick's bride-book wears, a sign that only his has the genuine intext, while the majority are false throughout, superficially attractive, but really "in-laid Garbage." The poem plays one other game, a typographical one, for its jewels are sizes of type, "set" in the order in which they are to be printed. "Pearl" is the name of the smallest size of type (in the seventeenth century, at least), "Paragon" is one of the largest.[10] This little poem has its political implications too when we remember Herrick's instinctive setting of Charles and his queen in the largest sizes of type, as in

T O   T H E   K I N G,
To Cure the Evill

or the two poems which follow each other, T O   T H E   K I N G and T O   T H E   Q U E E N E.

Putting the king and queen in paragon is instinctive good manners on Herrick's part. Without such courtesies states fall apart, marriages collapse into adultery, counterfeit jewels are passed off as genuine, and badly printed books issue from the press. Herbert's *Temple* made its own revolutionary statement in its preliminaries. Instead of the expected dedication to someone of influence or importance, it appeared naked of all such gestures. As Nicholas Ferrar explained in "The Printers to the Reader":

> The dedication of this work having been made by the Authour to the *Divine Majestie* onely, how should we now presume to interest any mortall man in the patronage of it? Much lesse think we it meet to seek the recommendation of the Muses, for that which himself was confident to have been inspired by a diviner breath then flows from *Helicon*. The world therefore shall receive it in that naked simplicitie, with which he left it, without any addition either of support or ornament, more then is included in it self.

Herrick would have understood Herbert's sending his book naked into the world as an example of the proper respect this saintly figure—as Herbert was already coming to be known—thought fitting for poems dedicated to the praise of God. But Herrick would have known, too, that with the explosion of printed material in the 1640s, many books were pouring from the press presented in the crudest possible form, with many Puritan writers taking pride in their refusal to give apologies or dedications. As is so often the case with Herbert, his practice came curiously close to the sectarians' ways of doing things in the next decade. In this case Herrick would agree with St. Paul's warning that "evil communications corrupt good manners" (1 Corinthians 15:33). So *Hesperides* offers elaborate preliminaries, including a portrait, title page with large crown ornament, and a poem dedicating the book to the Prince of Wales. The poem's title is an example of paragon and pearl, with intermediate sizes of type also, as if to show how carefully rank and order have been considered:

TO THE MOST
I L L V S T R I O V S,
A N D
Moſt Hopefull P R I N C E,
C H A R L E S,
Prince of *Wales.*

Then follows an errata page, apologizing for the faults which have cropped up in the printing. The best of these is the restored line "Ah! woe is me, woe, woe is me" in "The Fair Maid's Song," which the printer had set as "Ah! woe woe woe woe woe woe is me." To be fair, though, the printer had not done badly, with only sixteen errors listed by Herrick— fewer than one every twenty pages. Still, the poet seems rather grumpy about even these few, and he adds this little poem to explain that the faults were not his:

> For these Transgressions which thou here dost see,
> Condemn the Printer, Reader, and not me;
> Who gave him forth good Grain, though he mistook
> The Seed; so sowed these Tares throughout my Book.

"Transgressions" and "condemn" seem a hard judgment on the printer, but they fit the biblical image which follows of sowing tares among wheat, the evil action of the "enemy" in one of the parables of the sower in Matthew 13.

It may seem a nit-picking point, but Herrick's use of "grain" rather than "wheat" recalls another piece of biblical sowing, that connected with the resurrection in Paul's First Epistle to the Corinthians, in verses which follow soon after the one quoted above, that "evil communications corrupt good manners." Paul says (15:35–38, 42–44):

> But some men will say, How are the dead raised up? and with what body do they come?
> Thou fool, that which thou sowest is not quickened, except it die:
> And that which thou sowest, thou sowest not that body that shall be, but bare grain, it may chance of wheat, or of some other grain:
> But God giveth it a body as it hath pleased him, and to every seed his own body . . .
> So also is the resurrection of the dead. It is sown in corruption; it is raised in incorruption:
> It is sown in dishonour; it is raised in glory; it is sown in weakness; it is raised in power:
> It is sown a natural body; it is raised a spiritual body. There is a natural body, and there is a spiritual body.

Herrick is purifying his book on the threshold, ridding it of all blemishes so that he can guarantee its immortality, for, as poems such as "Julia's Churching" show, only a proper regard for every detail makes the ceremony deliver its mysterious restoration. Sown in corruption—the printer devil doing his best to add imperfections—*Hesperides* will emerge cleansed and immortal.

Toward the end of the volume there is a small group of poems which depend upon the image and value structures traced so far. The first is the short "His Grange," whose curious title his editor, L. C. Martin, describes as "not yet convincingly explained."

> How well contented in this private *Grange*
> Spend I my life that's subject unto change:)
> Under whose Roof with *Moss-work* wrought, there I
> Kiss my *Brown wife,* and *black Posterity.*

"*Grange*" might be understood in its primary sense, still current in the seventeenth century, of a "repository for grain," that is, a granary. Even so gentle a poem, being Herrick's, has thoughts of death built into it, in the parenthetical reminder to himself that his life is not as unmoving as his moss-covered house might suggest. The house lodges a life subject to change, but it lodges, too, the seeds of Herrick's immortality. Behind the literal wife and children we ought to imagine a brown study and black printer's ink, Herrick's meditations leading to poems which will not be subject to change.

Brown and black are colors not normally preferable to white. This is even true of grain. Thomas Tusser, in "A digression . . . concerning Tillage," explains that[11]

> White wheat or else red, red rivet or white,
> far passeth all other, for land that is light.
> White pollard or red, that so richly is set,
> for land that is heavy is best ye can get.

In contrast,

> Grey wheat is the grossest, yet good for the clay,
> though worst for the market, as farmers may say.

But white has one very negative connotation which stretches back to the Old Testament and which was still not entirely figurative in seventeenth-century England. This is the metaphor of the next poem in the volume:

> *Leprosy in Houses*
> When to a House I come, and see
> The *Genius* wasteful, more than free:
> The servants *thumbless,* yet to eat,
> With lawless tooth the flower of wheat:
> The Sons to suck the milk of Kine,
> More than the teats of Discipline:
> The Daughters wild and loose in dress;
> Their cheeks unstained with shamefacedness:
> The Husband drunk, the Wife to be
> A Bawd to incivility:
> I must confess, I there descry,
> A House spread through with *Leprosy.*

White runs through the leprous household, in the "flower of wheat" (the pure white flower of the grain) eaten by servants rather than by the young children for whom it should be saved, the milk sucked by the sons, and the blushless cheeks of the daughters. Leprosy is normally used as a figurative equivalent to uncleanness. Here Herrick matches this quality to its whiteness, for, as any writer knows, there is nothing more obscene than a white page with not a mark of ink, brown or black, upon it.

The poem which follows returns to Herrick's grange and, in contrast to the household he has just described, explains how anyone who crosses his threshold should behave:

Good Manners at Meat

This rule of manners I will teach my guests,
To come with their own bellies unto feasts:
Not to eat equal portions; but to rise
Farced with the food, that may themselves suffice.

The modern literary senses of *farce* do not become current until toward the end of the seventeenth century. They originated in short dramatic works whose sole object was to inspire laughter: in this sense farce occurred in English from early in the sixteenth century. Its connection with the verb *farce,* meaning "to stuff or cram in," came from the use of such short pieces as interpolations in the intervals of medieval religious drama. We can compare the later history of the word *gag*, which developed from "something thrust into the mouth to keep it open" (sixteenth century, *OED*) to "expressions, remarks . . . interpolated or substituted by the actor" (nineteenth century). *Gag* has a further relevant sense, to retch. Herrick's poem is an admonition to his guests—or readers, for books are made to be digested—to eat according to their capacities. They should not try to match each other's capacities, but be content with what fills them, not farce themselves to the point of gagging. The wordplay is on *farced* and *fast,* possibly recalling the old proverb that "He whose belly is full believes not him who is fasting," which has implications not only with regard to social justice but also for readers of Herrick's book, who should not try to cram too much speculation into poems which will not bear it.

The "rule of manners" is a phrase which epitomizes much seventeenth-century verse, particularly Herrick's. It takes us back to the beginning of this chapter and to Herbert's courteous encounters with figures who appreciate the value of civilized transactions. It might also have a meaning distinctively Hesperidean, in that *rule* has a special typographical sense too, of "a thin slip of metal . . . used for separating headings, columns of type, articles, etc." (*OED,* first example 1683). So perhaps, following the ink of "His Grange" and the paper of "Leprosy in Houses," this poem helps set everything up for the press. As if to underline the point, the next poem has *rule* again:

Anthea's Retractation

Anthea laughed, and fearing lest excess
Might stretch the cords of civil comeliness:
She with a dainty blush rebuked her face;
And called each line back to his *rule* and *space*.

Nothing is more civilized than a volume of poems. The typographical layout of line and space makes each poem appear regular in construction, attractive to the eye, and self-controlled in keeping well away from the margins of the page. On the same level of civilization is Anthea, whose laughter is quite the opposite of Lovelace's Lucasta's. Far from being aimed at others' misery or overflowing into hysteria, the merest hint of its excessiveness leads to a blush and the restoration of her normal countenance. Herrick's word for it is "retractation," humorously incongruous in its echoes of the great Augustine's correction of his former writings when related to these simple acts of generous courtesy—Anthea's, in not wishing to disturb the civilized atmosphere around her, and Herrick's, in noticing her behavior and praising her for it. But the incongruity is only an apparent one, for Anthea's behavior is a measure by which all should be judged. "Retractation" is the admission and correction of error, as important in a drawing room as it is in the preliminary matter to a book or in theological debate. Without a general capacity for believing that one can make errors, the whole state is as fragile as a stained-glass window.

PART FIVE

Men and Women

13 Playing with Snakes: Embarrassing Positions

Anthea blushes several times in *Hesperides*. The first is probably the best known, in "The Shoe Tying":

> *Anthea* bade me tie her shoe;
> I did; and kissed the Instep too:
> And would have kissed unto her knee,
> Had not her Blush rebuked me.

This is quintessential Herrick, taking all the delight possible in flirtation with no fear that things will go too far. A blush is confined to the face, so he must be squinting upward as he kisses, expecting the rebuke—hoping for it, probably, if the rest of the poems are any guide. In any case his ambition is still a limited one, going no further than the knee. The poem's deeper interest lies in conjecturing what Anthea's ambitions are. To answer would probably require more knowledge of seventeenth-century etiquette than we actually possess. How common was it for ladies to ask gentlemen to tie their shoelaces? Perhaps the cumbersomeness of dresses, tightness of bodices, or temporary absence of maids made it more common than it would be today. Even so, its erotic potential must have been more pronounced, for women's legs were a more hidden, and therefore more exciting, prospect than their breasts.

A few poems earlier in *Hesperides* comes "Julia's Fall," where the mere glimpse of a leg is a heightening experience:

> *Julia* was careless, and withal,
> She rather took, than got a fall:
> The wanton *Ambler* chanced to see
> Part of her leg's sincerity:

And ravished thus, It came to pass,
The Nag (like to the *Prophet's Ass*)
Began to speak, and would have been
A telling what rare sights h'ad seen:
And had told all; but did refrain,
Because his Tongue was tied again.

The plot of the poem is that Julia has fallen from her horse, the *"Ambler"* and "Nag" of lines 3 and 6. Perhaps she fell while Herrick tried to help her mount it. He, of course, would not see, or would pretend not to, and is thus denied the sight—or pretends to be denied—which the horse has been granted. But unlike the story of Balaam's ass, this incident offers no prophetic vision. As usual with Herrick, full sight is denied, and he is left with the pleasure of imagining what he might have seen. Worth imaginative interpretation, too, is the nature of Julia's fall. Herrick makes a nice distinction here between taking a fall and getting one. Carelessness is the cause, and the effect is of a gentle tumble rather than anything sudden or hurtful. How far carelessness is brought about by design is open to conjecture. In either case, the shoe-tying or the fall, Herrick's focus is on the natural intimacies of civilized life, which offer glimpses and suggestions all the while. They must remain only tentative and unrealized for civilization to survive, and thus depend upon a continuous and repeated collusion between the sexes. He knows the accident is designed. She knows that the courteous gesture is a form of flirtation. Blushing is partly a measure of apprehension at what might happen, partly a revelation that something has already happened.

An appearance of carelessness is the vital thing in all of this, as one of Herrick's best-known poems explains:

Delight in Disorder

A sweet disorder in the dress
Kindles in clothes a wantonness:
A Lawn about the shoulders thrown
Into a fine distraction:
An erring Lace, which here and there
Enthralls the Crimson Stomacher:
A Cuff neglectful, and thereby
Ribbands to flow confusedly:
A winning wave (deserving Note)
In the tempestuous petticoat:
A careless shoe-string, in whose tie

I see a wild civility:
Do more bewitch me, than when Art
Is too precise in every part.

There is a designed carelessness in the structure of this poem. Apparently
a string of epigrams continuing the opening couplet, all hanging on "kindles," it turns out at the end to be all the subject of "bewitch." First the
impression is of the clothes themselves being inflamed into wantonness,
each item expressing its excitement in its fall from order. But the sentence
which makes up the whole poem finally comes clean by admitting that
this is all the poet's bewitchment, a retrospective reinterpretation of the
kindling, enthralling distractions which the poem has listed. Two games
are being played here: the woman's, in carefully neglecting to be precise
in her dress; the poet's, in displacing his and her emotions onto the
clothes which stand between them.

Another syntactic game teases the reader in "The Maiden-Blush":

So look the mornings when the Sun
Paints them with fresh Vermilion:
So Cherries blush, and Catherine pears,
And Apricots, in youthful years:
So Corals look more lovely Red,
And Rubies lately polished:
So purest Diaper doth shine,
Stained by the Beams of Claret wine:
As *Julia* looks when she doth dress
Her either cheek with bashfulness.

From the title we expect, and seem to get, a poem about a flower, the
maiden-rose, known as maiden's-blush. Only in the final couplet do we
find that we have to revise our expectations—and we have to do this
twice. "When she doth dress" is so cunningly placed that what had
seemed to be a poem about things which have the most delicate of pink
colors now seems to be about Julia's body as she dresses herself. But the
only thing being dressed is her cheeks. The shift is from the most brazen
of sights, a woman dressing in front of a man, to one of the most civilized,
the blush of a bashful virgin. In most of the examples which Herrick offers blushing is an intensification of beauty which occurs in youthful
things—new days or young apricots—or, as in the corals and rubies, it
represents their true color. Only the claret-stained white linen allows a
peep into other forms of reddening, and Herrick takes care to make this

298 MEN AND WOMEN

one the image which leads into the final couplet; but even this is only a peep, the staining being really the effect of light playing through the wine onto the linen.

Stain introduces the prospect of other causes for blushing than mere bashfulness. Virginal responses have built into them all of the sensuality which the most experienced courtesan could display; all that is lacking is knowledge. In its place are suspicion and apprehension, for which the blush is the marker. Herrick could be quite crude about driving this point home, as in these two poems, which stand fourth and fifth in *Hesperides*. They follow the first of his "To his Book" poems, and both are on the same theme; hence their titles.

Another
To read my book the Virgin shy
May blush, (while *Brutus* standeth by:)
But when He's gone, read through what's writ,
And never stain a cheek for it.

Another
Who with thy leaves shall wipe (at need)
The place, where swelling *Piles* do breed:
May ever Ill, that bites, or smarts,
Perplex him in his hinder-parts.

Herrick regularly pleads that his poems are, at worst, merely jocund and will give no offense to well-intentioned readers. The first of these poems claims that in spite of their reputation there is nothing that could really shock even a virgin. The second, as if to test this claim, uses its scatological image to describe the most uncharitable of readers, those who would happily rip out pages to wipe their backsides clean. The first reader blushes not because of what the poems contain, but because Brutus stands by. Only her apprehension of what he may think of her provokes this response. She does not want him to know that she knows so much, but she knows as much as Herrick can offer. Her blush is not a response to content, but a preserver of reputation, and to be seen to be embarrassed by Herrick is a guarantee of her privileged virginal status. In her way she uses Herrick's book as selfishly as the next reader. The link between them is that they both have stained cheeks.

In "The Broken Crystal" Herrick give his tiny version of *The Golden Bowl*. Here the blush seems to be the common response which any one of us makes to our own clumsiness, but again the poet digs a little deeper:

To Fetch me Wine my *Lucia* went,
Bearing a Crystal *continent:*
But making haste, it came to pass,
She brake in two the purer Glass,
Then smiled, and sweetly chid her speed;
So with a blush, beshrewed the deed.

"*Continent*" is Herrick's warning that the gentle surface covers disturbing emotions. Its position seems deliberately ambiguous. As a substantive, qualified by the adjective "Crystal," it would mean simply a container, although the use in such a small context of a word normally devoted to large spaces gives a mock-heroic tinge to the incident. But "*continent*" may equally be an adverb meaning self-restraining, a word which had a specialized meaning of behaving with sexual self-restraint. Lucia's chasteness, leading to the maiden-blush which she offers at the poem's end, is belied by her hasty carelessness. The clumsy breaking of the glass is akin to the cracking of continents in the greater world, a sign of turbulence beneath the surface. Her blush is her realization of this and, more to the point, an apprehension that he realizes it too.

Herrick's blushing ladies are ideal virgins, so packed with emotional intensity that the slightest breach of everyday decorum opens up possibilities of erotic pleasure. Not surprisingly, the ballad poetry presents a much plainer view of relations between the sexes. The odd trembling virgin appears in it, but we are much more likely to encounter women as capable of frank expression of their feelings as any man. In "A New Merry Dialogue Between John and Bess the Two Lusty Brave Lovers of the Country" (1656) Laurence Price presents, in Bess, a woman who knows exactly what she wants. John, "a bachelor bold and brave," promises her a good life if she will marry him. She replies (stanzas 7–11):[1]

Kind *John* I protest thou art welcome to me,
    since thou art come for to woo me;
Ten thousand to one but we two shall agree,
    now thou com'st lovingly to me,
Thy love and thy labour is not lost in vain,
For thus in few words I will tell thee here plain,
If thou com'st at midnight I'll thee entertain,
    I know no harm thou'lt do me.

I have kept my maiden-head twenty long year,
    before you come to woo me,

And many a brave gallant that loved me dear,
    made suit often unto me:
But I for my own part could love never a man,
Let them use the chiefest of skill that they can,
Until the time came that I met with my *John,*
    I know no harm thou'lt do me.

You promised me gold and you promised me fee,
    when you came first for to woo me,
Because that I your true Lover should be,
    these knacks you proffered unto me:
You promised me scarfs and you promised me rings,
Silk gown and silk apron and many brave things,
The which to my presence much comfort it brings,
    I know much good you will do me.

Gay garments are good sir of which I accept,
    now you so lovingly woo me,
Your Silver is better I do it respect,
    both those are welcome unto me,
But your proper person exceeds all the rest,
For you are the creature that I do love best
I had rather have you than have gold in my chest,
    for I know no harm you'll do me.

To bind up the bargain and finish the strife,
    seeing you come hither to woo me,
I prithee come quickly and make me thy wife,
    I know no harm you'll do me.
And when we are married thou shalt have thy will
To clip and to kiss and to use thine own will,
I am thine own true love and so will be still,
    now I come merrily to thee.

Money and fine clothes are useful extras so far as Bess is concerned, but
the balladeer makes it clear that her choice of John is based principally
on his virility, the "proper person" which exceeds all the rest. Her refrain,
that he will do her no harm but much good, is an appreciation of the
sexual promise which he offers. Still, she is continent enough not to give
her appetite control over her appreciation of the need for self-protection.
She has reached the ripe old age of twenty with her virginity intact, in
spite of many temptations, and her offer that John may clip and kiss and
have his will with her is contingent upon their getting married. Although

she has none of the bashfulness of Herrick's virgins, she still has their self-control.

In "The Two Jeering Lovers" Price presents "A pleasant new dialogue between Dick Downright of the Country, and pretty, witty Nancy of the citie." Really, in spite of the title, only one of the lovers jeers. While Dick keeps telling Nancy how much he loves her, and has done "these seven long winters," she continually replies with contempt, as here (stanzas 9–11):[2]

> Thy eyes stand asquint,
>   thy nose stands awry,
> Thy mouth stands aside,
>   and thy beard's never dry:
> Thy Chaps all beslabbered
>   and thy lips are amiss,
> 'Twould make a maid loath
>   for to give thee a kiss.
>
> Thy Shoes are untied,
>   and down at the heels,
> Thy Stockings ungartered,
>   which thou dost not feel,
> Thy Codpiece unbuttoned,
>   thy breeches bepissed,
> These are nasty actions,
>   say what you list.
>
> Take this for an answer
>   I will thee not have,
> There's the door and the way,
>   now go walk like a Knave,
> Go home to thy Country
>   and kiss Country *Joan,*
> For sweet-heart in *London*
>   thou art like to have none.

Finally even Dick has had enough and makes to leave, telling her that she behaves so badly she ought "either to be hanged / or be tied to a Cart," at which Nancy reverts to complete gentleness (stanza 13):

> Nay stay my sweet *Richard,*
>   let's kiss and be friends,
> For what I said to thee

> I'll make thee amends.
> If thou'lt be my Husband
>   I will be thy Wife,
> And I'll be constant to thee
>   all the days of my life.

The poet's moral is that women can play any role they wish:

> Their wits are so nimble,
>   they can in an hour
> Turn sour into sweetness
>   and sweetness to sour.

Price puts it all down to nimble wits, but even his own ballad, simple as it is, implies more; for Nancy's changed approach to Dick is as much emotional as intellectual, an instinctive response to his sudden disdain for her. Price's ballads are the crudest forms of seventeenth-century verse, but he shares with his most sophisticated contemporaries some of the bafflement at the feelings and behavior of women. Of all the fleeting things, they presented the greatest pleasure in judging between design and accident.

Sometimes this pleasure was denied. When all pretense at virginal behavior was dropped, the poets' responses were scathingly resentful. Henry Bold, writing around the same time as Price's ballads, addresses a lady who has shown too little forbearance:[3]

> Chloris, forbear a while, do not o'erjoy me;
> Urge not another smile, lest it destroy me.
> That beauty pleases most, and is best taking,
> Which soon is won, soon lost, kind yet forsaking.
>   I love a coming lady, faith! I do;
>   But now and then I'd have her scornful too.
>
> O'er cloud those eyes of thine, bo-peep thy features;
> Warm with an April shine, scorch not thy creatures:
> Still to display thy ware, still to be fooling,
> Argues how rude you are in Cupid's schooling.
>   Disdain begets a suit, scorn draws us nigh:
>   'Tis cause I would and cannot, makes me try.
>
> Fairest, I'd have thee wise: when gallants view thee
> And court, do thou despise; fly, they'll pursue thee.

Fasts move an appetite, make hunger greater;
Who's stinted of delight falls to 't the better.
   Be kind and coy by turns, be calm and rough,
   And buckle now and then, and that's enough.

After this lyric's appearance (in a slightly different form) in *Sportive Wit* in 1656, it occurs in at least seven other collections. Clearly, it appealed to Restoration tastes, which took pleasure in the satirical portraits of man-eating women in Rochester's poems or Wycherley's plays. But at its heart is the same impulse which motivates Herrick, that women should play the virgin, no matter how well-developed their appetites or how thorough their knowledge. "Dissemble well" is how Edmund Waller puts it in "To Flavia":

   'Tis not your beauty can engage
   My wary heart;
   The sun, in all his pride and rage,
   Has not that art;
   And yet he shines as bright as you,
   If brightness could our souls subdue.

   'Tis not the pretty things you say,
   Nor those you write,
   Which can make Thyrsis' heart your prey;
   For that delight,
   The graces of a well-taught mind,
   In some of our own sex we find.

   No, Flavia! 'tis your love I fear;
   Love's surest darts,
   Those which so seldom fail him, are
   Headed with hearts;
   Their very shadows make us yield;
   Dissemble well, and win the field.

If Flavia hopes to make headway she must learn to pretend that her feelings are genuine, for without the impression of true love upon them her practiced wiles will get her nowhere. They have to seem to emerge from natural feelings, like the blushes which are employed by Herrick's virgins.

Most of Waller's ladies knew exactly what was required, and behind his lightest poems we can feel the pressure which made civilized wooing such an exciting game. While Dick and Nancy were prepared to express themselves as openly as possible, the gentry loved in code, and of all the poets Waller was cryptographer in chief. Here he is replying to a lady who, as the title explains, had given him a silver pen:

To a Lady, From Whom he Received a Silver Pen

Madam! intending to have tried
The silver favour which you gave,
In ink the shining point I dyed,
And drenched it in the sable wave;
When, grieved to be so foully stained,
On you it thus to me complained:

"Suppose you had deserved to take
From her fair hand so fair a boon,
Yet how deserved I to make
So ill a change, who ever won
Immortal praise for what I wrote,
Instructed by her noble thought?

I, that expressed her commands
To mighty lords, and princely dames,
Always most welcome to their hands,
Proud that I would record their names,
Must now be taught an humble style,
Some meaner beauty to beguile!"

So I, the wronged pen to please,
Make it my humble thanks express,
Unto your ladyship, in these:
And now 'tis forced to confess
That your great self did ne'er indite,
Nor that, to one more noble, write.

This is only a trifle, but, because it is so self-reflexive, it takes us far into appreciation of a society which was powered by suggestion and innuendo. It links the wit of early seventeenth-century poetry with the concern for nuances of behavior which the Restoration carried into the eighteenth century. She has given him the pen ostensibly as a sign of her favor, but really so that he might write the poem to and about her. In fact the pen writes two poems: the whole four stanzas, which are Waller's, and the second and third, which are the pen's. This automatic writing is a protest against Waller's intention, which had been to try the pen out by writing on and to some meaner beauty. Instead he finds his thoughts diverted upward toward the noble lady whose favor indicates her interest in him. She gets her poem and the promise that she will get sole use of Waller's pen. The sexual suggestion is obvious enough in the language of the first stanza, but the poem also makes it clear that sexual favors are not given for nothing, but have to be bought.

Lovelace plays a similar game with Ellinda's glove in the poem of that title:

> Thou snowy farm with thy five tenements!
>   Tell thy white mistress here was one
>   That called to pay his daily rents:
> But she a gathering flowers and hearts is gone,
> And thou left void to rude possession.
>
> But grieve not pretty ermine cabinet,
>   Thy alablaster lady will come home;
>   If not, what tenant there can fit
> The slender turnings of thy narrow room,
> But must ejected be by his own doom?
>
> Then give me leave to leave my rent with thee;
>   Five kisses, one unto a place:
>   For though the lute's too high for me;
> Yet servants knowing minikin nor base,
> Are still allowed to fiddle with the case.

Raymond Williams thought this "strange poem" worth a mention in *The Country and the City*, as one through which "we see momentarily more of the actual seventeenth-century life than in the poems of retirement."[4] He does not say exactly what we do see, but he is probably thinking of how, in the 1640s, management of property and estates devolved heavily upon widows—actual ones, when their husbands died in battle; grass widows, if they were away fighting or had fled. Lovelace gets enough innuendo into "rents," by way of the word "daily," to make his role as tenant farmer sexual and mercenary. Behind the coded kisses upon the sockets of the glove lies the message that he knows what his function is. She will not allow him to penetrate her, but may let him masturbate her, playing with the case rather than plucking the lute.

In "Of Her Passing Through a Crowd of People" Waller takes his favorite lady into the most embarrassing of situations, a crowd in which she is pressed and squeezed:

As in old chaos (heaven with earth confused,
And stars with rocks together crushed and bruised)
The sun his light no further could extend
Than the next hill, which on his shoulders leaned;
So in this throng bright Sacharissa fared,
Oppressed by those who strove to be her guard;
As ships, though never so obsequious, fall
Foul in a tempest on their admiral.
A greater favour this disorder brought
Unto her servants than their awful thought
Durst entertain, when thus compelled they pressed
The yielding marble of her snowy breast.
While love insults, disguised in the cloud,
And welcome force, of that unruly crowd.
So the amorous tree, while yet the air is calm,
Just distance keeps from his desired palm;
But when the wind her ravished branches throws
Into his arms, and mingles all their boughs,
Though loath he seems her tender leaves to press,
More loath he is that friendly storm should cease,
From whose rude bounty he the double use
At once receives, of pleasure and excuse.

Waller shares with Herrick a delight in recording quirks of behavior and fragments of experience, but he has little of the older poet's voyeuristic guilt. His pleasure comes from registering the mock-heroic quality of such encounters—hence the apparently ridiculous comparisons of the experience to the sun in chaos, ships and flagships, and trees in a storm. Really, though, they are not so ridiculous; not from Sacharissa's point of view, anyway. Crowds are terrifying, and only images of chaos and storm do justice to their ability to annihilate identity. Waller's focus is on the way her "servants" seem to do their best to preserve role and identity even while pressed right up against her: in lines 13–14 the poem allows a glimpse of the greater crowd around them and her, any member of which would gladly take the opportunity which intimate proximity would offer. Their pressure allows any of the servants to change his role too and take an advantage which years of service could not guarantee. Again, the poem may be only a trifle, but it understands and conveys, in a way in which more apparently serious poems fail to, how thin a shell of civilization covers turbulent passions. Not quite articulated, but heavily implied, is Sacharissa's response to the situation. Crowds and their pressure breed panic. Its absence in Waller's careful recording of the scene indicates some degree of willing abandonment to the experience on her part. He cannot be sure, of course, but his use of "insults" gives both possibilities, for as well as its common modern sense, "to assail with offensively dishonouring or contemptuous speech or action" (*OED*, well established by the seventeenth century), it still had its earlier, primary sense, "to exult . . . boast, brag, vaunt, glory, triumph." To be the central point of attraction for a mass of worshipers, no matter how sordid the individual action, is a triumphant release of civilized repressions. This, at least, is how Waller imagines the situation. We might call his vision unhealthy, but that will not invalidate it once we accept that even the purest noble breasts hide impure impulses—rather like Strode's civilized gentleman who suddenly imagines the possibility of flinging a stone through Fairford windows.

A fair number of mid-seventeenth-century poems enjoy digging into the mud which lies at the bottom of silver fountains. Marvell's "Young Love" is a famous piece on child molestation. Not so well known is Waller's variation on this theme:

From a Child

Madam, as in some climes the warmer sun
Makes it full summer ere the spring's begun,
And with ripe fruit the bending boughs can load,
Before our violets dare look abroad;
So measure not by any common use
The early love your brighter eyes produce.
When lately your fair hand in woman's weed
Wrapped my glad head, I wished me so indeed,
That hasty time might never make me grow
Out of those favours you afford me now;
That I might ever such indulgence find,
And you not blush, or think yourself too kind;
Who now, I fear, while I these joys express,
Begin to think how you may make them less.
The sound of love makes your soft heart afraid,
And guard itself, though but a child invade,
And innocently at your white breast throw
A dart as white, a ball of new fall'n snow.

Swift, whose jaundiced eye took great pleasure in noting the peccadillos of servants, has a pertinent comment in his account of how one of his ideal societies took care to see that its children were not exploited:

"Males of Noble or Eminent Birth . . . are dressed by Men until four Years of Age, and then are obliged to dress themselves."[5] The child who speaks Waller's poem is certainly older than four. Indeed, he speaks exactly like a man, but this may not be so much a consequence of Waller's gaucherie, not having a novelist's or dramatist's ability to imitate a child's speech patterns, as it is a recognition of the precociousness which children in this century often displayed.[6] Still, whatever the reason, the child's precious mode of speech is central to the poem's embarrassing context, the very onset of puberty, when what had previously been innocent becomes suddenly fraught with innuendo. Madam's blush may be a recognition that the object of her careful attention has ceased to respond like a child. The polite fog of the language he uses is not easy to pierce, but her recoiling from giving him the caresses with which she had previously been so free, signaled by the blush and the fact that she thinks herself too kind, is described as a reaction to his articulation. "While I these joys express" is his way of describing the new experience—partly a reference to the words which make up the poem, but principally his surprisingly self-assured recognition that she has noticed his first erection and has begun to think how she may soften it. This would be the blush apprehensive, as Touchstone might have called it; but if we take Swift's observation of female behavior into account, there is equally the possibility that here is the blush of guilt, having been found out in her harmless pleasures.

As Donne's flea poem implies, there were good self-preservative reasons for women to explore other ways of finding sexual satisfaction than the one which so often led to childbirth and death. Waller's *jeu d'esprit* "The Marriage of the Dwarfs" is based on the witty idea that the two tiny people were born for each other: would that all lovers were in their happy position of having only the one ideal partner. But in expressing this he raises the ghost which haunted all seventeenth-century heterosexual experience. While the male dwarf would be handicapped by the simple physical difficulties of trying to couple with a woman of normal size, the female faces something more extreme (13–18):

> To him the fairest nymphs do show
> Like moving mountains, topped with snow;
> And every man a Polypheme
> Does to his Galatea seem;
> None may presume her faith to prove;
> He proffers death that proffers love.

That last line reverberates beyond its witty context here, as a simple fact of the century's sexual relations.

Suckling's poem on the candle and the various uses to which it could
be put is only the most blunt expression of a general male suspicion that
women could live without them. In "Ellinda's Glove" Lovelace ends the
poem by presenting himself as a kind of glorified candle for Ellinda's use.
In "Her Muff" he makes a more resolute attack on the female mystery:

> 'Twas not for some calm blessing to deceive,
> Thou didst thy polished hands in shagged furs weave;
>> It were no blessing thus obtained,
>> Thou rather wouldst a curse have gained,
> Than let thy warm driven snow be ever stained.
>
> Not that you feared the discol'ring cold,
> Might alchemise their silver into gold;
>> Nor could your ten white nuns so sin,
>> That you should thus penance them in
> Each in her coarse hair smock of discipline.
>
> Nor Hero-like, who on their crest still wore
> A lion, panther, leopard or a boar,
>> To look their enemies in their hearse;
>> Thou wouldst thy hand should deeper pierce,
> And, in its softness rough, appear more fierce.
>
> No, no, Lucasta, destiny decreed
> That beasts to thee a sacrifice should bleed,
>> And strip themselves to make you gay;
>> For ne'er yet herald did display,
> A coat, where sables upon ermine lay.
>
> This for lay-lovers, that must stand at door,
> Salute the threshold, and admire no more:
>> But I, in my invention tough,
>> Rate not this outward bliss enough,
> But still contemplate must the hidden muff.

From the evidence of Hollar's engravings the large fur muff was only one
element in an elaborate, all-enveloping costume which, if topped by a
mask, presented a forbiddingly enclosed image to the world. Lovelace's
language is almost as precious as Waller's child's, with its references to
her flesh as "warm driven snow," her fingers as "ten white nuns," and the
alchemical and heraldic imagery which runs throughout. The point is
close to Waller's too, for the rarefied tone is a deliberate dressing up of
some very basic urges, as tender skin encases itself within the fur and hair

"Destiny decreed / That beasts to thee a sacrifice should bleed": a lady in muff and mask. Wenceslaus Hollar, 1643.

of gloves and muff. Sadomasochistic impulses are hinted at in the nunlike penance and the slaughtering of animals. Lovelace's effort is to look through these and dent the self-sufficiency at the heart of the image. Lucasta, with her fingers in her muff, is protecting them from the world as carefully as she preserves her other muff from contact with anything else than her own fingers. His pose is aggressive, but the final determination to undress and penetrate her, with its clichéd recall of Donne's lay-lovers image, seems mere bluster.

In "Lucasta's Fan, With a Looking-Glass in It" Lovelace focuses on

Struthocamelus Straus

Tab. **XXI**

"Ostrich, thou feathered fool and easy prey": John Johnstone's *Natural History of Birds* was published ca. 1650, around the same time as Lovelace's poem on Lucasta's fan.

another item in the catalogue of female impedimenta as an image of woman's protection of her body from male assault:

> Ostrich! Thou feathered fool, and easy prey
>   That larger sails to thy broad vessel need'st;
> Snakes through thy gutter-neck hiss all the day,
>   Then on thy iron mess at supper feed'st.
>
> Oh what a glorious transmigration
>   From this to so divine an edifice
> Hast thou straight made! near from a winged stone
>   Transformed into a bird of paradise!

Now do thy plumes for hue and lustre vie
    With th'arch of heaven that triumphs o'er past wet,
And in a rich enamelled pinion lie
    With sapphires, amethysts, and opals set.

Sometime they wing her side, then strive to drown
    The day's eye's-piercing beams, whose am'rous heat
Solicits still, till with this shield of down
    From her brave face, his glowing fires are beat.

But whilst a plumy curtain she doth draw,
    A crystal mirror sparkles in thy breast,
In which her fresh aspect whenas she saw,
    And then her foe retired to the west,

Dear engine that o' th' sun got'st me the day,
    Spite of his hot assaults mad'st him retreat!
No wind (said she) dare with thee henceforth play
    But mine own breath to cool the tyrant's heat.

My lively shade thou ever shalt retain
    In thy enclosed feather-framed glass,
And but unto our selves to all remain
    Invisible thou feature of this face!

So said, her sad swain overheard, and cried
    Ye gods! for faith unstained this a reward!
Feathers and glass t' outweigh my virtue tried?
    Ah show their empty strength! The gods accord.

Now fall'n the brittle favourite lies, and burst!
    Amazed Lucasta weeps, repents, and flies
To her Alexis, vows herself accursed
    If hence she dress herself, but in his eyes.

This is a better poem than "Her Muff," partly because it is funnier and partly because it reaches out to wider issues. This would be a good poem to use for speculation about political subtexts. From the ostrich at the beginning to the fallen favorite at the end, it describes a society which increasingly evades contact with the world outside the court. Only a great smash can bring it to its senses. The poem's humor comes from the ostrich who fronts the poem. His transmigration works in two ways: his own feathers, dyed, have turned from the drab to the glory of the rainbow, but they metamorphose the elegant Lucasta, as she fans her way across the room, into the ungainly figure of an ostrich, as ill equipped as that creature traditionally is to cope with her environment. Such fans with inlaid mirrors were common enough items, superficially doubly useful but, as the gems indicate, really only excuses to lay vanity upon vanity. Lovelace's scorn is drawn to the opportunities they offer to keep out the world and encourage self-absorption. The target is not so much the feathers and glass, which can be broken easily enough, but the hidden fan which needs to be stripped of its affectations and restored to the mindless, snake-devouring "gutter-neck" of the opening stanza.

Playing with snakes rather than devouring them is the topic of one of Waller's stranger poems:

To a Fair Lady, Playing With a Snake

Strange! that such horror and such grace
Should dwell together in one place;
A fury's arm, an angel's face!

'Tis innocence, and youth, which makes
In Chloris' fancy such mistakes,
To start at love, and play with snakes.

By this and by her coldness barred,
Her servants have a task too hard;
The tyrant has a double guard!

Thrice happy snake! that in her sleeve
May boldly creep; we dare not give
Our thoughts so unconfined a leave.

Contented in that nest of snow
He lies, as he his bliss did know,
And to the wood no more would go.

Take heed, fair Eve! you do not make
Another tempter of this snake;
A marble one so warmed would speak.

At least, the situation seems odd to us now, but we ought to bear in mind Thorn-Drury's laconic note on the poem, quoting an earlier editor of Waller: "Keck says, 'Twas formerly not unusual among our English ladies for coolness in the hot weather to carry a snake in their sleeve.' "[7] Discovering whether or not the carrying of snakes was a common practice is not entirely whimsical where this poem is concerned. If Chloris is doing something which many a well-bred English lady would have done, then Waller is aiming at the whole sex, not one aberrant member of it who carries her teasing of men to uncomfortable lengths. The snake becomes one more impediment to add to the muff and fan, more obstructive to the man's approach because it cannot easily be removed or broken. After all, the idea that snakes could help keep a body cool is an unconvincing one, their cold-bloodedness merely leaving their body temperature at the same level as their environment. It would be a useful fiction, however, for the sex to gain some innocent enjoyment under the guise of necessity.

Chloris' playing with the snake is a consequence of her "starting" at love. By this Waller means that she recoils from it. The proverb about carrying a snake in one's bosom is redefined when the snake is, as this one certainly is, only a grass snake, not a viper. Unlike the real thing, this will not bite no matter how it is used, although Waller playfully hints in the final stanza that even a harmless snake might be pushed too far and be moved to respond, as the child did in his "From a Child." The poem belongs to a long-established tradition of voyeuristic poetry which fantasizes the pleasure which women derive from having creatures crawling over their bodies—going back in English to Skelton's *Philip Sparrow* and, ultimately, to Ovid's Corinna. Characteristically, Waller's example is the more salacious in that Chloris' innocence and youth is a more ironically conceived state than Jane Scrope's naïveté—or Marvell's nymph's, for that matter. Chloris is well aware of what she is doing, allowing the snake all the scope which her rejected lover is denied. Hers is a flaunted self-sufficiency aimed at humiliating the man with a living symbol of his impotence—"playing with," in the title, epitomizes the sexual relations of a society which, at one extreme, employed snakes, muffs, fans, and candles and at the other tried to sustain fanciful ideas of Platonic love.

Poets such as Suckling and, later, Rochester claimed to see through the whole illusion and wrote plainly about the dildoes which underlay it. Waller's poetry is more interesting than theirs because of his willingness to dwell on the illusions rather than just sweep them away. At times his tone is celebratory rather than critical, as in the poem which in 1645 he titled "On the Friendship Betwixt Sacharissa and Amoret" and, later, more generally, "On the Friendship Betwixt Two Ladies":

> Tell me, lovely, loving pair!
> Why so kind, and so severe?
> Who so careless of our care,
> Only to yourselves so dear?

By this cunning change of hearts,
You the power of love control;
While the boy's deluded darts
Can arrive at neither soul.

For in vain to either breast
Still beguiled love does come,
Where he finds a foreign guest,
Neither of your hearts at home.

Debtors thus with like design,
When they never mean to pay,
That they may the law decline,
To some friend make all away.

Not the silver doves that fly,
Yoked in Cytherea's car;
Not the wings that lift so high,
And convey her son so far;

Are so lovely, sweet, and fair,
Or do more ennoble love;
Are so choicely matched a pair,
Or with more consent do move.

The comparison of the ladies to debtors who never intend to pay is revealing enough. Not only are men shut out of their relationship, but they are never going to be allowed entry. Waller seems perfectly happy at such an arrangement, and although the poem gestures at protest, it ends with the admission that the pair are so happily self-contained that their beauty is doubly enhanced. If the poem has anything negative in its tone, it is envy rather than resentment.

Such a poem marks, in the society Waller inhabited at least, the ascendancy of female values. Suckling, who constantly took the aggressively masculine role, mocked this movement repeatedly. His favorite technique for reducing women to their sensual common denominator is to collapse the lyric with an anticlimactic deflation, as he does in his best-known poem:

Why so pale and wan fond Lover?
Prithee why so pale?
Will, when looking well can't move her,

> Looking ill prevail?
> Prithee why so pale?
>
> Why so dull and mute young Sinner?
> Prithee why so mute?
> Will, when speaking well can't win her,
> Saying nothing do 't?
> Prithee why so mute?
>
> Quit, quit, for shame, this will not move,
> This cannot take her;
> If of her self she will not Love,
> Nothing can make her,
> The Devil take her.

One answer to the opening question might be that the paler and wanner one is, the more ladylike, and therefore the more attractive to a sex which prefers its own kind. Suckling's opinion of this is caustic enough. What really attracts women is virility—looking well—and if they are not attracted by this then there is no point in unmanning oneself.

As in Lovelace's lyrics, there are political undertones to such pieces, although in Suckling's case they are a good deal further beneath the surface. But if the major philosophical emphasis of the court-centred culture in the 1630s was upon a harmonious, love-centered society, epitomized by the ideally married king and queen and buttressed by the increased importance of ceremony in church and state, then passionate, violent emotions were dangerously marginalized. Suckling's poems frequently focus their resentment upon the women who apparently run the whole show; undressing the powerbroking Lady Carlisle is only one example. His scorn for the fond lover who tries to play their game is an only slightly displaced contempt for the more general emasculation which acts on him too. His "To a Lady that Forbid to Love Before Company" tells its story in its title. It opens with ribbons, fan, and muff and closes in acknowledgment of impotence:

> What no more favours, not a Ribbon more,
> No fan, nor muff to hold as heretofore?
> Must all those little blisses then be left,
> And every kiss we have become a theft?
> May we not look ourselves into a Trance,

Let our souls parley at our eyes, not glance,
Nor touch the hand, nor by soft wringing there
Whisper a love that none but eyes can hear?
Not free a sigh, A sigh that's there for you,
Dear must I love you, yet not love you too?
Be not so nice Fair, sooner shall they Trace
The feathered Travellers from place to place,
By prints they leave i'th'Air, and sooner say
By what right line the last star made his way
That fled from heaven to us, than guess or know
How our loves first did spring, or how they grow;
Love is all spirit, fairies sooner may
Be taken Tardy when they night-tricks play
Than we; we are too safe I fear, that rather
Would they could find us both in bed together!

At its fullest this lovemaking is all hint and gesture, with nothing of substance, and this, too, is becoming attenuated by her embarrassment. Herrick loves this kind of game, and the fairies image which Suckling brings
in at the end might well have carried for him a positive valuation of such
unconsummated wooings. Suckling's values are different, so that his
poem moves in contrary directions. The elegant syntax of the second half,
culminating in the assertion that love is all spirit and in the fairies image,
carries the lady's ideal view—something so soft and insubstantial that it
can scarcely be felt or traced—while the final lines restore the plain
speaking of the opening half of the poem, showing up the trick for what
it is, the dishonest preference by stupid people for embarrassment over
frankness.

In Suckling's verse such constraints lead to real hatred. There are few
more contemptuous poems than his "Proffered Love Rejected":

It is not four years ago,
    I offered Forty crowns
To lie with her a night or so:
    She answered me in frowns.

Not two years since, she meeting me
    Did whisper in my ear,
That she would at my service be
    If I contented were.

I told her I was cold as snow
    And had no great desire;
But should be well content to go
    To Twenty, but no higher.

Some three months since or thereabout,
    She that so coy had been,
Bethought herself and found me out,
    And was content to sin.

I smiled at that, and told her I
    Did think it somewhat late,
And that I'd not repentance buy
    At above half the rate.

This present morning early she
    Forsooth came to my bed,
And *gratis* there she offered me
    Her high-prized maidenhead.

I told her that I thought it then
    Far dearer than I did,
When I at first the Forty crowns
    For one night's lodging bid.

This is pure wish-fulfillment revenge, the man totally in control, the woman reduced to begging for his favors and being utterly humiliated. At their initial contact, when he frankly offered to buy her, she acted as if she were anything but a marketable object. A mere four years of history has proved him right with a vengeance—even to the location of her offering herself at his bed. This empty, vicious poem reveals only Suckling's impotence as he gets his pleasure from speaking rather than acting. Similar scenes are played out frequently in the court poets' lyrics. Lovelace, in "Love Made in the First Age: To Chloris" sets the delights of an imagined Eden of free and frank relationships against the games Chloris wants him to play. He ends the poem by preferring masturbation:

Now, Chloris! miserably crave
The offered bliss you would not have;
    Which evermore I must deny,
Whilst ravished with these noble dreams,
And crowned with mine own soft beams,
    Enjoying of myself I lie.

Again, the scene is obviously fictional, the disdainful Chloris being willed to the poet's bed to be subjected to a humiliating rejection.

Of all the poets who versified their impotence by projecting it into either female embarrassment or female self-absorption, the most interesting is Andrew Marvell. In "Clorinda and Damon" he attempts a reverse "Coy Mistress," the shepherd in the dialogue persuading the shepherdess to give up her sensual pleasures and turn to joint Christian worship instead:

Clor	Damon, come drive thy flocks this way.
Dam	No, 'tis too late; they went astray.
C	I have a grassy scutcheon spied,
	Where Flora blazons all her pride.
	The grass I aim to feast thy sheep:
	The flowers I for thy temples keep.
D	Grass withers; and the flowers too fade.
C	Seize the short joys then, ere they vade,
	Seest thou that unfrequented cave?
D	That den?
C	Love's Shrine.
D	But virtue's grave.
C	In whose cool bosom we may lie
	Safe from the sun.
D	Not heaven's eye.
C	Near this, a fountain's liquid bell
	Tinkles within the concave shell.
D	Might a soul bathe there and be clean,
	Or slake its drought?
C	What is't you mean?
D	These once had been enticing things,
	Clorinda, pastures, caves, and springs.
C	And what late change?
D	The other day
	Pan met me.
C	What did great Pan say?
D	Words that transcend poor shepherd's skill,
	But he e'er since my songs does fill:
	And his name swells my slender oat.
C	Sweet must Pan sound in Damon's note.
D	Clorinda's voice might make it sweet.
C	Who would not in Pan's praises meet?
Chorus	Of Pan the flowery pastures sing,

> Caves echo, and the fountains ring.
> Sing then while he doth us inspire;
> For all the world is our Pan's choir.

This kind of pastoral dialogue was one of the most popular forms in the century, normally set to music to be sung by a man and a woman to the appropriate audience of nobility or gentry. Here the woman's part is the forward one, with her evocations of her own body in the landscape she offers of grassy scutcheons, flower-beds, and the unfrequented cave set to be love's shrine. The man's part is all coyness, in the worst sense of the word, as he transfers his tumescent powers to his songs and oat-pipe.

William Empson is right to fix on Marvell's homosexuality. It is probably a bias which conditions much of the love poetry of the 1630s and 1640s. Lovelace fleeing from Lucasta's arms claims to be chasing a new mistress, but the embrace he pursues is a masculine one:

> Tell me not (Sweet) I am unkind,
>   That from the nunnery
> Of thy chaste breast, and quiet mind,
>   To war and arms I fly.

The wordplay is on "arms," Lucasta's having been abandoned in preference for the arms of war, but the flight is real enough, and resolved only at the end of the volume when, in "Aramantha," he goes to kill her but is disarmed by her instead. The images are of the passive male being overcome by the stronger female (365–370):

> His arms hung up and his sword broke,
> His ensigns folded, he betook
> Himself unto the humble Crook:
> And for a full reward of all,
> She now doth him her shepherd call,
> And in a SEE of flow'rs install.

Marvell acts out similar scenes in his garden poems as he lies down under the onslaughts of aggressive vegetation. He frequently portrays himself as recoiling from erotic experience. In "The Definition of Love" this seems to be the principal condition for any kind of human achievement: as long as love is not consummated the world keeps its roundness and spins around its axis. In "The Gallery" heterosexual love is defined

in cerebral terms, with a final stanza which transforms all that goes before:

> Clora, come view my soul, and tell
> Whether I have contrived it well.
> Now all its several lodgings lie
> Composed into one gallery;
> And the great arras-hangings, made
> Of various faces by are laid;
> That, for all furniture, you'll find
> Only your picture in my mind.
>
> Here thou art painted in the dress
> Of an inhuman murderess;
> Examining upon our hearts
> Thy fertile shop of cruel arts:
> Engines more keen than ever yet
> Adorned a tyrant's cabinet;
> Of which the most tormenting are
> Black eyes, red lips, and curled hair.
>
> But, on th'other side, th'art drawn
> Like to Aurora in the dawn;
> When in the East she slumbering lies,
> And stretches out her milky thighs;
> While all the morning choir does sing,
> And manna falls, and roses spring;
> And, at thy feet, the wooing doves
> Sit perfecting their harmless loves.
>
> Like an enchantress here thou show'st,
> Vexing thy restless lover's ghost;
> And, by a light obscure, dost rave
> Over his entrails, in the cave;
> Divining thence, with horrid care,
> How long thou shalt continue fair;
> And (when informed) them throw'st away,
> To be the greedy vulture's prey.
>
> But, against that, thou sit'st afloat
> Like Venus in her pearly boat.
> The halcyons, calming all that's nigh,

Betwixt the air and water fly;
Or, if some rolling wave appears,
A mass of ambergris it bears.
Nor blows more wind than what may well
Convoy the perfume to the smell.

These pictures and a thousand more
Of thee my gallery do store
In all the forms thou canst invent
Either to please me, or torment:
For thou alone to people me,
Art grown a numerous colony;
And a collection choicer far
Than or Whitehall's or Mantua's were.

But, of these pictures and the rest,
That at the entrance likes me best:
Where the same posture, and the look
Remains, with which I first was took:
A tender shepherdess, whose hair
Hangs loosely playing in the air,
Transplanting flowers from the green hill,
To crown her head, and bosom fill.

The first six stanzas form a gentle love poem celebrating the varieties of experience which love offers, from the erotic and aesthetic to the amused and alarmed. But the final stanza returns to the threshold of the affair to convey the disappointment inherent in all human contact between the opposed sexes. In it "posture" and "took" are slightly loaded words. Posture girls had not yet come into being, but the careful placing of the word in Marvell's gallery ensures that we pick up all its connotations of artifice and carry them into "took," which has much the same sense that it has in Herrick's "Upon Julia's Clothes," where Julia's silks are the glittering fly which takes the poet as an angler takes a fish. There has been, through the poem, an increasing innuendo that the artist is not, as it first seems, Marvell, but Clora—from "I have contrived," "thou art painted," and "th'art drawn," through "thou show'st" and "thou sit'st," to "thou canst invent." What had seemed undesigned might, after all, have been carefully planned. Marvell's bewilderment could only be settled by a return to the moment when he first saw her. There is the carefully posed virginal image which outshines all the rest and which, while it still remains there, can no more be restored to the center of his consciousness than he can wind back time. The more intimate one's relationship, the more fragmented the personality becomes with whom one is dealing. Their integrity lies far back, getting further away all the time, at the first blush— although whether the blush was one of apprehension or of guilt will always be a matter of doubt.

14 "Such Delights I Meant to Say": Roses and Hair

"... the first Chorus beginning may relate the course of the city each eve[n]ing every one with mistresse, or Ganymed, gitterning along the streets, or solacing on the banks of Jordan, or down the stream."[1] Milton's draft outline to the opening of his planned tragedy on the burning of Sodom had obvious contemporary relevance—for "Jordan" read "Thames." He recalled it early in *Paradise Lost*, describing Belial's reign (1:500–505):

> and when night
> Darkens the streets, then wander forth the sons
> Of Belial, flown with insolence and wine.
> Witness the streets of Sodom, and that night
> In Gibeah, when the hospitable door
> Exposed a matron to avoid worse rape.

That allusion is not just to the attempted rape of Lot in Genesis 19, but also to its analogue in Judges 19, where the Levite's concubine is pushed over the threshold to be raped by the drunken citizenry of Gibeah. The first edition of *Paradise Lost* reads, at lines 504–505, "when hospitable doors / Yielded their matrons to prevent worse rape." The alteration to the single matron in the second edition points more directly toward the narrative in Judges, probably because the consequence of this event was a vicious civil war between the tribes of Israel and Benjamin, leading to the deaths of tens of thousands of men.

Milton's moral point is clear enough, that a society ruled by the values of Belial will eventually tear itself to bits, as England had done. He has sexual points to make too. One is that heterosexual rape is, in the scale of things, preferable to homosexual rape; at least, this is the only mean-

ing that seems possible for "avoid worse rape." The matron in the Judges
narrative is not likely to have agreed with this. Her fate was to be raped
to death. But Milton obviously believes that the rape of the Levite would
have been an even greater abomination. Another point is that by drawing
a parallel between Cavalier society and the sons of Belial of both biblical
narratives, Milton is more than hinting at the homosexual bias of this
society, or at the least of its bisexuality, as if a mistress or a Ganymede
were things indifferent.

Much of *Paradise Lost* offers an embedded commentary on the sexual
concerns of seventeenth-century England. The continuously emphasized
nakedness of Adam and Eve mocks the elaborate costumes of city and
court—"naked majesty" is a phrase which could never have been applied
to the king and queen. Clothes, muff, fan, and shoe fetishisms are given
no place, except in the satirical fringes of the poem. The most telling passage comes in book 4, where clothes are related directly to impotence and
frigidity (739–743):

> Handed they went; and eased the putting off
> These troublesome disguises which we wear,
> Straight side by side were laid, nor turned I ween
> Adam from his fair spouse, nor Eve the rites
> Mysterious of connubial love refused . . .

The passage goes on explicitly to criticize primitive Puritan hostilities to
sexual relationships, but ingrained in these lines is a pertinent reading of
more civilized behavior too, as if Milton knew well how empty the new
Restoration society was. It continued Cavalier attitudes which, soaked in
drink, ensured that direct, intimate sexual contact remained an exception. It is the man here who turns away first, an impotence which crops
up repeatedly in the many drinking songs of the interregnum, as in this
one by the Earl of Orrery:[2]

> 'Tis wine that inspires,
> And quencheth love's fires;
> Teaches fools how to rule a state:
> Maids ne'er did approve it,
> Because those that love it,
> Despise and laugh at their hate.
>
> The drinkers of beer
> Did ne'er yet appear

In matters of any weight:
 'Tis he whose design
 Is quickened by wine,
That raises things to their height.

 We then should it prize,
 For never black eyes
Made wounds which this could not heal:
 Who then doth refuse
 To drink of this juice,
Is a foe to the Common-weal.

That wine raises things to their height is rather an empty boast, surrounded as it is by the further claims that wine quenches love's fires and heals wounds made by black eyes. It is not merely that being flown with wine offers an attractive defense of impotence, but that it channels this impotence into a contempt for women, as in the scorn for the maids who refuse to get sodden themselves.[3] In part Orrery is being ironic, offering a thinly disguised counsel of despair for those who hold on to the old values in hard times, but his reading of the situation is relevant enough, matching political and sexual impotence.

Milton's digression in praise of married love which follows the lines quoted above from book 4 closes with a return to the sleeping postcoital couple by way of a contemptuous gibe at the contemporary aristocratic society, the games it plays and the poems it reads (763–774):

Here Love his golden shafts employs, here lights
His constant lamp, and waves his purple wings,
Reigns here and revels; not in the bought smile
Of harlots, loveless, joyless, unendeared,
Casual fruition, nor in court amours
Mixed dance, or wanton mask, or midnight ball,
Or serenade, which the starved lover sings
To his proud fair, best quitted with disdain.
These lulled by nightingales embracing slept,
And on their naked limbs the flowery roof
Showered roses, which the morn repaired. Sleep on
Blest pair . . .

"Gitterning along the streets," from the Sodom draft, means the playing of serenades on the guitar, as here. In this passage "quitted" means "re-

paid" as well as "left alone," so that not only is the lady not worth the
serenade she is offered, but the real purpose of the serenade itself is not
persuasion or compliance, but increased disdain. Like fine clothes and
jewels, fine love poems are barriers to intimacy, not the seductive things
they pretend to be. The roses which shower down on the naked, embracing pair are central to Milton's restoration of a poetic imagery which the
love lyrics had debased.

Already when Shakespeare used the rose as the presiding image of his
sonnets he was recalling a tradition of rose-centered love poetry half as
old as time. His twists were to use the image for the purposes of homosexual love and to remind his lover that, unlike their use by other poets,
his roses have thorns. The rose was such a conventional image in love
poetry that when the seventeenth-century lyric poets came to use it they,
too, gave it an ironic or bitter edge. Waller's "Go, Lovely Rose" is probably the best-known example, with its sudden, sadistic impulse in the
final stanza, telling the rose directly, and the lady implicitly, to die. Herrick's "Upon Roses" has a similar purpose, achieved in a slightly more
subtle way:

> Under a Lawn, than skies more clear,
> Some ruffled Roses nestling were:
> And snugging there, they seemed to lie
> As in a flowery Nunnery:
> They blushed, and looked more fresh than flowers
> Quickened of late by Pearly showers;
> And all, because they were possessed
> But of the heat of *Julia's* breast:
> Which as a warm, and moistened spring,
> Gave them their ever flourishing.

"Ruffled" is a cleverly chosen epithet for the roses, bringing with it all
kinds of connotations, none of which can be ruled out of the poem. It has
various senses of disordering or discomposing; it relates to various treatments of dress or its accessories; it describes agitated states of mind; and
it describes physical agitation too, including one meaning specifically related to the rough-handling of women. "Nestling" and "snugging"
would seem to exclude the negative elements of these connotations of
ruffle, except that, as so often in Herrick's poems, we soon have to revise
our views of the poem's scene, and with them to reinterpret the roses'
comfort. Originally we are presented with a landscape, the roses standing
out in a clump—another sense of *ruffle*—from the stretch of level ground

which they lie beneath. But the lawn, it turns out, is the fine linen veil with which Julia covers the exposed part of her breasts in which the cut roses nestle. This kind of blush is almost a technical, aesthetic term. Herrick explains it most elaborately in "The Lily in a Crystal," describing the subtle contrast of colors when red flowers set against white skin are perceived through a gauzelike veil. But behind the aesthetics lies an apprehension of the stifling, life-destroying impulses of this culture: the contrast between the now dying flowers in Julia's breast and still living flowers under the other kind of lawn is pressed home in the final lines. Ideally the goddess gives them their color, warmth, and life. Really, her picking and wearing them has accelerated their opening out and imminent decay. They will no more be ever flourishing than will their wearer, except, of course, in Herrick's poem, where the golden moment is fixed for all time.

Whether picked or still growing, roses stand as the essential symbol of woman and, more pointedly, of man's wish to ruffle her, or at the least to open her out and force her into a position of vulnerability. An anonymous poem written probably sometime in the 1640s is worth mention here because it professes to be written by a woman:[4]

On a Rosebud Sent to her Lover

The tender bud within herself doth close
With secret sweetness till it prove a rose;
And then as fit for profit as for pleasure
Yields sweet content to him that gains the treasure:
    So she that sent this, yet a bud unblown,
    In time may prove a rose, and be your own.

This rings true as a woman's self-description because it lacks the subdued hostility of many rose poems. The blowing to which the rosebud aspires is entirely positive, a full blossoming out to display and share its sweet content to the lover. Now look at a rose poem by a very unaggressive male poet. William Hammond addresses his sister, who is mourning her husband's death immoderately:

The Rose

After the honey drops of pearly showers,
    Urania walked to gather flowers:
"Sweet Rose," I heard her say, "why are these fears?
    Are these drops on thy cheek thy tears?

By those thy beauty fresher is, thy smell
   Arabian spices doth excel."
"This rain," the Rose replied, "feeds and betrays
   My odours; adds and cuts off days:
Had I not spread my leaves to catch this dew,
   My scent had not invited you."
Urania sighed, and softly said, " 'Tis so,
   Showers blow the Rose, and ripen woe;
For mine, alas! when washed in floods sweet clean,
   Heaven put his hand forth, and did glean."

George Saintsbury calls this "a characteristic and charming thing"—a fair description, for Hammond is as gentle a poet as one can find in the century. The rose is an emblem of his dead brother-in-law whom his sister, under the guise of Urania, mourns in the final lines. Practically, however, the poem is a counsel to her to open herself out to life's vulnerabilities. The raindrops on the rose are at first figuratively perceived as tears but become increasingly literal, opening the flower and making it fully blown. Beauty and death are subtly blended, for the rain-induced odor has attracted Urania to the rose and she will, quite probably, put forth her hand and glean it. For such a desirable flower the process of growth into bloom hastens its sudden death—"adds and cuts off days."

In Hammond's poem "blow" has a more negative sense than in the anonymous poem quoted just before it, as if it were being moved closer to meanings which derive from the other verb *blow*, with senses such as "inflated" or "stale." It is not difficult to see why such connotations were added to the word. Shakespeare's Sonnet 15 gives the clue, with its image of men increasing as plants, holding in perfection but a single moment. That moment is the full-blown one, followed immediately by decay, so that a blown rose may be either a flower in full bloom or one that has experienced its full bloom and is now decaying (the word *overblown* remained rare).

The senses of *blow* become further confused when the word's most basic meaning is recalled. Richard Fanshawe introduced this English confusion into his translation of a poem by Gongora:

A Rose
Blown in the Morning, thou shalt fade ere Noon:
   What boots a Life which in such haste forsakes thee?
Th' art wondrous frolic being to die so soon:
   And passing proud a little colour makes thee.

If thee thy brittle beauty so deceives,
  Know then the thing that swells thee is thy bane;
  For the same beauty doth in bloody leaves
  The sentence of thy early death contain.

Some Clown's coarse Lungs will poison thy sweet flower
  If by the careless Plough thou shalt be torn:
  And many *Herods* lie in wait each hour
  To murder thee as soon as thou art born.

Nay, force thy Bud to blow; Their Tyrant breath
Anticipating Life, to hasten death.

Never at any point does this poem move its focus away from the rose, so that to describe its subject as a woman is to misrepresent it. And yet it is very difficult to resist the parallel. So common and so instinctive is the association of woman and rose, through phrases such as "passing proud" and "brittle beauty," that it would take someone entirely unfamiliar with Renaissance poetry to read the poem as a piece of casually cruel contempt for a flower rather than a studied rejection of female beauty. Embedded in the sonnet's third quatrain, in the sour breath of the peasant and the "careless Plough," are implications of violence and rape, although the tyrants of the couplet whose breath will force the buds to open out are as likely to be wandering, flower-gathering virgins as country clowns.

When it comes down to it, breathing was probably the only positive action which female beauty could be allowed to take. Once we move above the class which did the menial work, then, apart from a little embroidery and, later on, bearing children, women could be described quite fairly as "things without use." The words are Waller's, from his poem "To Chloris":

Chloris! what's eminent, we know
Must for some cause be valued so;
Things without use, though they be good,
Are not by us so understood.
The early rose, made to display
Her blushes to the youthful May,
Doth yield her sweets, since he is fair,
And courts her with a gentle air.
Our stars do show their excellence
Not by their light, but influence;

When brighter comets, since still known
Fatal to all, are liked by none.
So your admired beauty still
Is, by effects, made good or ill.

Even by the poem's end it is still difficult to see what their use is: sexual submission certainly—that is the yielding of "her sweets"—but it leads only to the vague terms "influence" and "effects." The first of these, at least, is only slightly more substantial than breathing. Indeed, a verse in the Apocrypha parallels the two terms when describing the effects of the personified Wisdom: "For she is the breath of the power of God, and a pure influence that floweth from the glory of the Almighty" (Wisdom 7:25, Geneva). All Chloris is being told to do is to open herself out for smelling and plucking, the one way she can be of influence in the world.

Herrick has a short poem in which the most distinctive grammatical element of the seventeenth-century love lyric, the imperative, makes one of its most curious appearances:

> On Julia's Breath
> Breathe, *Julia*, breathe, and I'll protest,
>   Nay more, I'll deeply swear,
> That all the spices of the East
>   Are circumfused there.

Circumfuse is a nice Jonsonian word to describe the sweet effects of Julia's breathing, but it scarcely disguises the inanity of a life which the poem reduces to the lowest common denominator of existence. Telling her to breathe is to fix her precisely at the level of a rose, whose purpose is merely to blow: no other action is necessary or called for. Action is the prerogative of the male, while the woman's duty is simply to exist—so that even in this very short poem Herrick takes most care to define and redefine what he must do: protest, and more than protest. In a more famous poem, a little later in *Hesperides*, for a change, the lady delivers the imperatives:

> To Anthea, Who May Command Him Any Thing
> Bid me to live, and I will live
>   Thy Protestant to be:
> Or bid me love, and I will give
>   A loving heart to thee

A heart as soft, a heart as kind,
    A heart as sound and free,
As in the whole world thou canst find,
    That heart I'll give to thee.

Bid that heart stay, and it will stay,
    To honour thy Decree:
Or bid it languish quite away,
    And 't shall do so for thee.

Bid me to weep, and I will weep,
    While I have eyes to see:
And having none, yet I will keep
    A heart to weep for thee.

Bid me despair, and I'll despair,
    Under that *Cypress* tree:
Or bid me die, and I will dare
    E'en Death, to die for thee.

Thou art my life, my love, my heart,
    The very eyes of me:
And hast command of every part,
    To live and die for thee.

"Protestant" was an inspired change. It seems that earlier versions had words such as "supplicant" or "votary," but they lack the humor of "Protestant," with its connotations of religious radicalism and orthodoxy. As antipapists Protestants were simultaneously revolutionaries and followers of the true Christian tradition, so that Herrick can use the word to present himself as an obedient yet passionate worshiper of Anthea. But the commitment is all his and is, ultimately, commitment to nothing, for Anthea's imperatives are illusory. Whatever she orders he will do, whether it be to love or to leave; and since all his actions come to the same thing, proof of his true heart, the content of her command is immaterial. All she really needs to do is breathe.

In another brief poem in *Hesperides*, "Upon a Virgin Kissing a Rose," the action of the title is revised down to merely breathing upon it:

'Twas but a single *Rose,*
    Till you on it did breathe;
But since (me thinks) it shows
    Not so much *Rose,* as Wreath.

Wreath means a cluster, so Herrick is describing the opening out of the flower as it is breathed upon, the obviously single bud spreading its petals and now looking as if it has multiplied. This is a fairly fragile lyric, but it can take some interpretative pressure. For the virgin to breathe upon the rose is something of an experiment, forcing into full bloom a bud which in its closed state images herself; or at least this is how Herrick perceives her action, for his "me thinks" is a slightly distancing parenthesis. It is as if, in the gentlest possible way, the girl is experimenting upon the rose: simultaneously testing the power of her breath and observing what the process of opening involves.

Repeatedly, roses have this kind of effect upon the women who handle them in seventeenth-century poems. Marvell's child, little T. C., plays her first games of dominance with them, and the most grown-up lady of all, Milton's Eve, has her first intimations of clothing as she stands among some: "Veiled in a cloud of fragrance, where she stood, / Half spied, so thick the roses bushing round / About her glowed . . ." But probably the most influential blending of woman and rose came earlier in the century, in Ben Jonson's best-known poem:[6]

Song. To Celia

Drink to me only with thine eyes,
  And I will pledge with mine;
Or leave a kiss but in the cup,
  And I'll not look for wine.
The thirst that from the soul doth rise
  Doth ask a drink divine;
But might I of Jove's nectar sup,
  I would not change for thine.
I sent thee late a rosy wreath,
  Not so much honouring thee
As giving it a hope that there
  It could not withered be.
But thou thereon didst only breathe,
  And sent'st it back to me;
Since when it grows, and smells, I swear,
  Not of itself, but thee.

As Jonson's editors religiously remind us, this lyric is a stitching together of various passages from the *Epistles* of Philostratus: but Jonson's emphasis is quite his own—not love happily accepted, but love proffered and rejected.

Like most of Jonson's love poems, the rejection is implicit from the start. "Only" qualifies both the drinking of the first half and the breathing of the second. Initially the idea that they should drink to each other only in glances could promise different contexts for their relationship— possibly collusion, so that although she may actually drink to someone else she will, with her eyes, signal her feelings for him; or satiety, so that the only drinking which can now be done is symbolic rather than actual; or rejection, so that Jonson's response to her refusal to mix pledges with him is to remove the contact to a less tangible level where he has more room for interpretation. It transpires that the first "only" does signal rejection: we appreciate this when the second "only" reveals the disappointment implicit in the "but" which begins the line. Rather than accept his roses she did with them the least distinctive thing she could, only breathing on them before sending them back. The closing lines may not be quite the compliment they seem. They certainly relate to the long-hallowed tradition that the truly beautiful woman outscents the roses. Philostratus has: "Send what is left of them back, since their scent is not now just of roses but also of you."[7] Jonson goes further, not even mingling the scents of the roses and Celia, but claiming that her scent has submerged theirs. This excess may be just the point at which the poem springs its trap, for we are still waiting to see how and why the immortality which Jonson had promised to his wreath has been denied; that is the force of "but" when it follows "a hope that there / It could not withered be." Logically, if Celia is the principle of abiding beauty, her overpowering of the roses should ensure their survival, for now they share her identity, having lost their own. But the wreath still grows—her breath having encouraged the roses to be full-blown—and can only be growing toward an eventual withering. Smelling of Celia, they now smell of mortality. This is as Jonson would have it. As in Herrick's poem in which the virgin's kiss turns the rose into a wreath, so behind Jonson's rose wreath is an image of his own poems and their claim to immortality. An easier and more certain route to that goal is to sup Jove's nectar, but Jonson would still prefer to write to Celia, whose beauty, so determined by her own coldness and the depredations of time, is already a dying thing.

George Herbert chose rather to take the drink divine than to write to any Celias of his acquaintance. Roses, then, had to be rejected—for example, one in "Virtue" is included in the catalogue of fleeting things which, in spite of their beauty, cannot rival the attractions of a lump of seasoned timber. At best, as in "Life," roses are a *memento mori*, their only real use in the world being, after their death, the material for medicines which cure the flesh—not a necessarily positive recommendation, in Herbert's view, if by doing so they prolong life or lessen affliction. At worst, which is their common state in this world, they offer the material for temptation and have to be dealt with accordingly. Only one rose deserves to be accepted and nourished. "Church-rents and Schisms" opens with this address:

> Brave rose, (alas!) where art thou? in the chair
> Where thou didst lately so triumph and shine,
> A worm doth sit, whose many feet and hair
> Are the more foul, the more thou wert divine.

Herbert's being a Protestant utilization of the rose imagery of the Song of Songs, none of that book's erotic content is allowed entry. However, the church as rose does realize some of the Song's sexual potential in *The Temple* through the unlikely route of Herbert's mother. When Henry Vaughan praised Herbert as one of the truest sons a mother ever ever had, he must have been thinking of mother church, not of Magdalen Herbert.[8] But Herbert's Latin poetry is full of extravagant flourishes in praise of his recently dead mother, making the second stanza of "Church-rents and Schisms" emotionally, if not intellectually, ambiguous:

> Why doth my Mother blush? is she the rose,
> And shows it so? Indeed Christ's precious blood
> Gave you a colour once; which when your foes
> Thought to let out, the bleeding did you good,
> And made you look much fresher than before.
> But when debates and fretting jealousies
> Did worm and work within you more and more,
> Your colour faded, and calamities
>   Turned your ruddy into pale and bleak:
>   Your health and beauty both began to break.

It is hard, after reading the hyperboles of the Latin poetry, not to imagine that there is some residual sense of his mother's last years in this image of the withering rose. Those hyperboles belong to the Petrarchan tradition, as Herbert repeatedly addresses his mother in terms conventionally associated with the address of a lover to his mistress.[9] In *The Temple* such poetry occurs only in forms of ironic parody, as in "The Rose," Herbert's most vicious rejection of the world and its pleasures. Unlike in "Church-rents and Schisms" the rose in this poem is destroyed not by a canker from within, but by the poet's own hand:

Press me not to take more pleasure
    In this world of sugared lies,
And to use a larger measure
    Than my strict, yet welcome size.

First, there is no pleasure here:
    Coloured griefs indeed there are,
Blushing woes, that look as clear
    As if they could beauty spare.

Or if such deceits there be,
    Such delights I meant to say;
There are no such things to me,
    Who have passed my right away.

But I will not much oppose
    Unto what you now advise:
Only take this gentle rose,
    And therein my answer lies.

What is fairer than a rose?
    What is sweeter? yet it purgeth.
Purgings enmity disclose,
    Enmity forbearance urgeth.

If then all that wordlings prize
    Be contracted to a rose;
Sweetly there indeed it lies,
    But it biteth in the close.

So this flower doth judge and sentence
    Worldly joys to be a scourge:
For they all produce repentance.
    And repentance is a purge.

But I health, not physic choose:
    Only though I you oppose,
Say that fairly I refuse,
    For my answer is a rose.

There is a sense in which Herbert himself is the rose. "Press me not"
floats the idea that it is the flower speaking, preferring natural life and
death to a pressing which will preserve it artificially in a flattened outline
which is only a caricature of its identity. But it soon emerges that the rose

is the poem's object, not subject—the counter in a game which Herbert and his antagonist are playing. I assume the antagonist is a woman, for the passing on of a rose is a familiar romantic gesture. The normal pious response is simply to refuse the temptation, as in another poem in *The Temple*, "The Quip," where part of the jeering world's disdain for Herbert is based upon his rejection of its concept of beauty (5–8):

> First, Beauty crept into a rose,
> Which when I plucked not, "Sir, said she,
> Tell me, I pray, Whose hands are those?"
> But thou shalt answer, Lord, for me.

In "The Rose," however, Herbert seems to accept the proffered flower, thereby entering a game which is as complicated in its way as the one which Jesus and Satan play out in *Paradise Regained,* for, as in that contest of wits, any movement which Herbert makes is calculated to trap him. The Freudian slip in the third stanza is part of the strategy. This kind of revision is a favorite trick of Herbert's—as in "Love Unknown," where the depressed narrator says that "some had stuffed the bed with thoughts, / I would say thorns." Here the revision signals a refusal to accept the register of love poetry. "Delights" would have offered the illusion that he was prepared to play. "Take," in the next stanza, seems to do so, but we cannot be sure how literal the offer is. Perhaps it simply means "take as an example," or perhaps he is holding out the rose to be taken back. Probably both are right, for the antagonist's gesture to take the rose from Herbert is forestalled in the sixth stanza by his closing of his hand around it. When he opens his fist in the next stanza, he reveals a bloody palm and a mess of crushed petals and thorns (and perhaps thoughts too) leading to the resurrection pun on the rose's name at the end of the poem.

As at the beginning of "The Collar," Herbert uses a violent gesture to announce his refusal to play—apt enough for this member of a proud and aggressive family. It is the more disturbing here because it is a violence on the side of righteousness, and therefore not one which is corrected or for which he is rebuked. If we could separate the rose from the woman this would not matter, but there is too much accumulated tradition behind the blushing flower to keep us from glimpsing the misogynist fantasy in the final stanzas.

The rose offered other ways of expressing hostility than Herbert's puritanical iconoclasm. For the love poets it provided an opportunity to displace their resentments and focus their violence upon it rather than upon the woman. Thomas Duffett's poem plays out the familiar scene of the rejected lover left only with the dying flower as the emblem of his defeated expectations:[10]

On a Rose Taken From Francelia's Breast

Poor hapless emblem of Amyntor's heart,
　Thy blooming beauty's overcast;
Deep shades of grief seem to o'erspread each part,
　Yet still thy fragrant sweets do last.

Thou wert not, when my dearest nymph is kind,
　In all thy pride so blessed as I,
She gone, my wounded heart thy fate does find,
　So does it droop, and so will die.

What joyful blushes did thy leaves adorn,
　How gay, how proudly didst thou swell,
When in Francelia's charming bosom worn,
　That Paradise where Gods would dwell.

Oh had my heart thy happy place possessed,
　It never had from thence been torn,
But like a Phoenix in her spicy nest,
　It still should live and ever burn.

No wonder thy perfume so near thy death
　Still lasts, though thy vermilion's gone:
Thy sweets were borrowed from her sweeter breath,
　Thy fading colour was thy own.

See how my burning sighs thy leaves have dried,
　Where I have sucked the stolen sweets:
So does the amorous youth caress his bride,
　And print hot kisses in her lips.

Hadst thou ungathered fall'n among the rest
　Lost and forgotten thou hadst been,
Thou hadst not flourished in Francelia's breast
　Nor been the subject of my pen.

Amber dissolved and beaten spices smell,
　That gold is valued most that's proved;
Coy beauty's lost, but lasting fame will tell
　Their praise that love and are beloved.

Behind all the complimentary gestures which claim that Francelia is more beautiful than the rose and could, if she wished, give it enduring life, lies a barely suppressed hostility which emerges in the image of the amorous youth with his bride at his mercy. In the poem's logic he sucks life out of her just as Amyntas has killed the rose by breathing his burning sighs upon it. Francelia refuses to be dissolved or beaten—staying coy is shorthand for her independence—and the man can only waste the flower instead, under the pretense that immortality can be achieved only through affliction.

Most sinister of all is Waller's lesser-known rose poem "The Bud." In it the object of his attentions has less opportunity to be coy, her youth rendering her more liable to give way to his advances:

> Lately on yonder swelling bush,
> Big with many a coming rose,
> This early bud began to blush,
> And did but half itself disclose;
> I plucked it, though no better grown,
> And now you see how full 'tis blown.
>
> Still as I did the leaves inspire,
> With such a purple light they shone,
> As if they had been made of fire,
> And spreading so, would flame anon.
> All that was meant by air or sun,
> To the young flower, my breath has done.
>
> If our loose breath so much can do,
> What may the same in forms of love,
> Of purest love, and music too,
> When Flavia it inspires to move?
> When that, which lifeless buds persuades
> To wax more soft, her youth invades?

The rose is usually an emblem of blushing cheeks, but Waller's bud harks back to an older tradition. Like the rubelet at the heart of Herrick's book, this flower is the clitoris. Waller's breath encourages it to open out, the sweet pleasures of cunnilingus preparing the way for a rougher invasion. Detached and forensic is his scrutiny of the bud; he carefully observes how it opens, its coloring as it does so, and the passion which such movement and color promise. This contrast between the flower's excitement and Waller's control is emphasized by the first stanza's seeming to encourage some third party to observe the scene. We might guess—or hope—that the "you" who sees how full-blown the bud is will be the woman herself, toward whom most rose poems are directed. But Flavia remains talked about rather than talked to, so that the reader is involved in what has turned out to be a coolly voyeuristic enterprise. It is cruel too. The violence begins casually with "I plucked it," and ends with the final image of an irresistible deflowering.

The nastiest element in the poem is its suggestion that the girl is complicit in the action, her initial gesture being aimed at catching the adult man's attention, promising in time a full disclosure which his persuasion simply accelerates. The word which carries the implication is, as usual, "blush," offering just the tinge of color to catch the passer's eye, and just the promise of virginal innocence to inspire his salacious interest. Between rape and seduction lies only a flimsy barrier, constructed out of the interpretation of signals, gestures, and symbols such as the rose. Often the mere fact that women dress and prepare themselves to allure is excuse enough for the male to justify his actions; and, more than this, it stimulates the illusion that the man is the real victim, of forces more powerful than any he can muster. Much of the imagery of seventeenth-century love poetry is of traps and snares, as in the title of one of Herrick's rose-gathering poems:

> How His Soul Came Ensnared
> My soul would one day go and seek
> For Roses, and in *Julia's* cheek,
> A richess of those sweets she found,
> (As in an other *Rosamond*.)
> But gathering Roses as she was;
> (Not knowing what would come to pass)
> It chanced a ringlet of her hair,
> Caught my poor soul, as in a snare:
> Which ever since has been in thrall,
> Yet freedom, she enjoys withal.

Personifying his soul as "she" sows deliberate confusion into the poem, mixing up the traditional images of a rose-gathering female's vulnerability to assault with the equally traditional subtlety of the snares which women spread for unwary men. It makes the last line ambiguous. Either Herrick's soul finds freedom in its thralldom to Julia, or, while Herrick is enslaved Julia stays free. Some of this ambiguity informs the second "she" in the poem, the one gathering roses. She may be his soul, who had gone out on such an errand, or the Julia which she encounters, who is doing the same thing. If the second, then the parenthesis of the next line creates powerful parallels between this tiny poem and the heroine of a much longer one who, in a state of mindlessness, with roses bushing round about her, falls victim to assault.

As Satan approaches Eve, Milton's comparison of her to a country girl emphasizes her simple innocence. The effect on the devil is, ironically, that (9:459–462)

> Her graceful innocence, her every air
> Of gesture or least action overawed
> His malice, and with rapine sweet bereaved
> His fierceness of the fierce intent it brought.

"Rapine sweet" is a suggestive oxymoron, supported by the dozens of lyric poems which argue that some force or deception is not only necessary but desired too—only in this case the irony is that it describes the woman's action, not the man's. But perhaps this scene does not break down simply into male versus female, for Milton makes much, earlier in the poem, of the angels', and particularly Satan's, ambiguous sexuality; and, indeed, as he seduces Eve he uses at least as many female snares as male assaults. Not the least formidable of his weapons is his serpentine beauty, described in terms which echo earlier descriptions of Eve's hair: both curl many a wanton wreath to lure the eye.

Robert Graves made much of Milton's obsession with women's hair, apparently not realizing that the repeated focusing on Eve's loose, flowing locks is part of the poem's strategy to conquer and sequester the most treasured territory of the lyric poem. In *Lycidas* the lyric is associated directly with flowing hair as Milton contrasts his own prophetic endeavors with the immediate rewards which can be gained from writing love poems (64–69):

> Alas! What boots it with uncessant care
> To tend the homely slighted shepherd's trade,
> And strictly meditate the thankless muse,
> Were it not better done as others use,
> To sport with Amaryllis in the shade,
> Or with the tangles of Neaera's hair?

In the Trinity College manuscript "Or with" originally read "Hid in," bringing the image even closer to the many lyrics which treat the snares and traps of women's hair. Its relating of the hair to the "shade" of the previous line glances at the greatest erotic promise of all, to be entirely covered by the woman's hair, as in Lovelace's poem:

To Amarantha, That She Would Dishevel Her Hair

> Amarantha sweet and fair
> Ah braid no more that shining hair!
>   As my curious hand or eye,
> Hovering round thee let it fly.
>
> Let it fly as unconfined
> As its calm ravisher, the wind;
>   Who hath left his darling th' East,
> To wanton o'er that spicy nest.
>
> Every tress must be confessed
> But neatly tangled at the best;
>   Like a clue of golden thread,
> Most excellently ravelled.
>
> Do not then wind up that light
> In ribbons, and o'er-cloud in night;
>   Like the sun in's early ray,
> But shake your head and scatter day.
>
> See 'tis broke! Within this grove
> The bower, and the walks of love,
>   Weary lie we down and rest,
> And fan each other's panting breast.
>
> Here we'll strip and cool our fire
> In cream below, in milk-baths higher:
>   And when all wells are drawn dry,
> I'll drink a tear out of thine eye.
>
> Which our very joys shall leave
> That sorrows thus we can deceive;
>   Or our very sorrows weep,
> *That joys so ripe, so little keep.*

Here the situation is the classic one of urging the woman no more to attempt to control her hair, but to let it loose. Male locks flowed profusely in the seventeenth century—Lovelace's portrait shows him in a typically Cavalier pose with hair down to his shoulders—so the incentive for women to pin up or braid their hair was very strong. There are few gestures so self-absorbed as the braiding of one's hair, or few transformations so dramatic as releasing it from its confinement with one shake of the head, as in Lovelace's poem. From the point at which she lets it loose Aramantha becomes a whole landscape in which Lovelace can lose himself. The many parallels between Eden and Eve work to similar effect in *Paradise Lost*.

This is Herrick again, on the next page of *Hesperides* from the soul-ensnared poem:

Upon Julia's Hair, Bundled Up in a Golden Net
    Tell me, what needs those rich deceits,
    These golden Toils, and Trammel-nets,
    To take thine hairs when they are known
    Already tame, and all thine own?
    'Tis I am wild, and more than hairs
    Deserve these Mashes and those snares.
    Set free thy Tresses, let them flow
    As airs do breathe, or winds do blow:
    And let such curious Net-works be
    Less set for them, than spread for me.

The plea is the same as Lovelace's, but more craftily done in its realization of the sexual control which tightly bound hair bespeaks. If anything is bundled up in the gold net it is the man who longs for the hair to flow free. His claim to be wild is mocked by the acknowledgment that he is already caught in the trap—the short poem is packed with synonyms for *snare*—and his call for Julia to let herself go is merely naive; he does not realize that the parallel between loose hair and passion is only illusory, for the woman is always in control of her responses. Braided, beribboned hair is erotic precisely because it circumscribes passion with civilized control. Lovelace imagines one sudden movement of the head letting all go free, but this comes only after a careful unpicking of pins and unweaving of plaits, a movement longer and more designed than the removal of jewelry.

A similar blend of looseness and control comes in Herrick's definition of his ideal woman:

What Kind of Mistress He Would Have
    Be the Mistress of my choice,
    Clean in manners, clear in voice:

Be she witty, more than wise;
Pure enough, though not Precise:
Be she showing in her dress,
Like a civil Wilderness;
That the curious may detect
Order in a sweet neglect:
Be she rolling in her eye,
Tempting all the passers by:
And each Ringlet of her hair,
An Enchantment, or a Snare,
For to catch the Lookers on;
But her self held fast by none.
Let her *Lucrece* all day be,
Thais in the night, to me.
Be she such, as neither will
Famish me, nor over-fill.

Virgin by day, whore by night is every man's ideal, but note that Herrick's Lucrece has only her chastity in common with her Roman original. Otherwise, her behavior is all calculated flirtation. Nor is his Thais the original insatiable harlot, her demands being not so inordinate that Herrick is taxed beyond his powers. In effect, the day-night contrast is only apparent, not real—possibly an index of Herrick's own moderation, or possibly a suggestion that all women are the same compound of passion and restraint.

If the second, then Herrick is only repeating what had become a familiar thought. Here is Davenant facing the perplexity of so much passion bound up in so much control:

To Mistress E. S. Married to an Old Usurer

In your black Hair Night may securely lie,
Whilst yet you sleep; but when you wake, the sky,
Your Face, will be enlightened with your Eye.

Your Hair does serve to ease and rescue sight,
As Shades resist the piercing force of light:
Your Eyes and Hair atone the day and Night.

Why should a Soldier thus his praises spend,
On what he loves and cannot comprehend?
Our work is to attain, not to commend.

But Wealth has married Wealth; with Youth Age joins
His feeble heat, and melts his withered Loins,
Not to engender Men but sev'ral Coins.

Bright eyes, fair complexion, under raven tresses are imagined as day and night setting each other off, the great pleasure being the moment when day breaks as Mistress E. S. emerges from sleep. But she wakes to see the old miser she has married, not the lusty soldier who cannot comprehend the waste. She has no trouble in reconciling her youth to his age: that wealth should marry wealth is as natural to her as that night should follow day. And she remains unattainable. Davenant claims that his duty is not merely to commend, but the first two stanzas are pure commendation, giving her the praise which the finest love lyrics offer. Here is a woman who can dishevel her hair but who has to face none of the consequences of the act—in particular the pregnancies which coupling with a younger man would lead to.

In short, women must always calculate. Men like to imagine them as rosebuds, passive, vulnerable, waiting to be plucked and breathed into life; but the register of their control over their passions and destinies is their hair. In "Io," a song written for *The Imposture* and published in his 1646 volume of poems, James Shirley used the binding up and letting free of hair as an index of the state of the nation:[11]

You Virgins that did late despair
    To keep your wealth from cruel men,
Tie up in silk your careless hair,
    Soft peace is come again.

Now Lovers' eyes may gently shoot
    A flame that wo'not kill:
The Drum was angry, but the Lute
    Shall whisper what you will.

Sing *Io, Io,* for his sake,
    Who hath restored your drooping heads,
With choice of sweetest flowers make
    A garden where he treads.

Whilst we whole groves of Laurel bring,
    A petty triumph to his brow,
Who is the Master of our Spring,
    And all the bloom we owe.

In the second half of the poem the virgins are roses whose drooping heads have been raised by the bringer of peace, as the garden of England is restored. This is a figurative parallel to the literal action of the opening stanza, in which their hair is carefully braided with silk ribbons. It had been let down in readiness for the rape which commonly follows an invading army. There are several calculations involved here. One is merely practical, that it is better to prepare for trouble; another, that braided hair is more provocative; a third, that acquiescence is better than resistance when the odds are so uneven. War is man's ideal state of affairs, one in which Davenant's uncomprehending soldier need never "commend," but easily attains what he considers rightfully his. But peace is, *pace* Hobbes, the normal condition of mankind, and woman is the better equipped to survive and triumph in that state: "The Drum was angry, but the Lute / Shall whisper what you will."

15 Poetry and Push-Pin: Loyalties

The game of passion which men and women play with each other was the most enduring of the fleeting things which the seventeenth-century poets celebrated, achieving its triumphant apotheosis in the marvelous mob of elegant gentlemen and ladies who play their parts in *The Rape of the Lock*. It may have been hedged in by thoughts of violence and death, as the *Rape* frequently is, but it was powered all the time by wit and humor. Even that most saturnine of Miltonic heroes, the blinded, suffering Samson, finds room for a joke in the middle of his contest with Dalila. To her complaint that "In argument with men a woman ever / Goes by the worse, whatever be her cause," he replies sardonically, "For want of words no doubt, or lack of breath" (903–905). A little earlier Dalila protests that she has betrayed her husband not for material gain, but out of loyalty to her nation and her religion. Samson responds by asserting the laws of love and nature which ought to have bound her to him, and, moreover, he protests that her argument from patriotism is false because the two states are really one. Note the slide in these lines from "thy country" to "our country" (885–895):

> Being once a wife, for me thou wast to leave
> Parents and country; nor was I their subject,
> Nor under their protection but my own,
> Thou mine, not theirs: if aught against my life
> Thy country sought of thee, it sought unjustly,
> Against the law of nature, law of nations,
> No more thy country, but an impious crew
> Of men conspiring to uphold their state
> By worse than hostile deeds, violating the ends
> For which our country is a name so dear;
> Not therefore to be obeyed . . .

347

In part, this affirms that a wife's nationality is her husband's, not the one she was brought up in; but it also revises the Israel-Philistia conflict into a civil war. The parallels with Milton's own first marriage are obvious enough. Whatever the other reasons for Mary Powell's desertion, it would have been impossible not to make some connection between it and the formal outbreak of the war which occurred at virtually the same time. In a society under such extreme pressures sexual relations became merely one more of the high stakes being played for. The betrayals involved were sometimes ridiculous enough to be merely funny; sometimes they were tragic; most often they occupied the large middle ground between.

Mary Powell came back three years later, probably at the prompting of her hard-beset family, who saw no other way of salvaging money and property with the imminent defeat of the Royalist cause. Similar scenes must have been played out at all levels of society, and not only during the 1640s but also in the decades leading up to war when the country began to split into factions. The echoes continued well into the next decade too, as demonstrated in the ballad printed by John Hammond in March 1656. Hammond was one of the few Puritan balladeers, but he printed enough material of general, apolitical interest to make his attitude in this piece a matter of conjecture. Hyder Rollins, apparently going by the title, suggests that the Cavalier values are successful. They are upheld by the girl in resistance to her Roundhead suitor. This is the first half of the ballad:[1]

No Ring, No Wedding
Young-man
Sweet-Heart I come unto thee,
   hoping thy Love to win,
I mean to try, thy courtesy,
   and thus I do begin:
If thou wilt be my Sweeting,
   then I will be thy Dear,
What think'st of me, shall I have thee,
   thou pretty Cavalier?

Maid
Good Sir you do but mock me,
   your mind is nothing so,
You'll speak of Love, my thoughts to prove,
   and then away you'll go:
For if you be a Round-head,
   (as to me it doth appear,)

You cannot (yet,) your fancy set,
   upon a Cavalier.

Young-man

Sweet-Heart I speak in earnest,
   thy beauty hath me ta'en,
And my true-love, to thee (my Dove,)
   for ever shall remain:
My true affections to thee,
   such zealous thoughts doth bear,
If thou consent, I am content,
   my pretty Cavalier.

Maid

Your Sect is bent to false-hood,
   and I indeed am jealous,
That this is but, the shell o' th' Nut,
   though your pretence be zealous:
You have no cause to blame me,
   but I have cause to fear,
'Twould be your sport, to win the Fort,
   and spoil the Cavalier.

Young-man

My dearest do not doubt me,
   my Heart and Tongue agree,
Now *Cupid's* Dart, hath pricked my Heart,
   I love no Lass but thee:
Tomorrow we'll be married,
   then take it for no jeer,
In word and deed, I am agreed,
   to wed my Cavalier.

Maid

Sweet Sir you are too hasty,
   to speak of such a thing,
If I should yield, to you the Field,
   where is your Wedding-Ring:
Your Bride-Gloves and your Ribbons
   with other things that were,
Fit for a Bride, all things provide,
   I'll be your Cavalier.

Young-man

These are but Ceremonies,
   belong to Popery,
Therefore we will, not use them still
   but all such toys defy:
We'll hand in hand together,
   conjoin (with joyful cheer,)
Few words we'll need, I'll do the deed,
   with thee sweet Cavalier.

It is possible, just for once, that Rollins has misinterpreted the text. The title is something of a come-on for the audience, promising the traditional woman's victory, but allowing it finally neither to her nor to the lusty young Puritan. There is a second part to the ballad, entirely different in form, which purports to be "the maiden's answer":

Sweet-Heart for thy sake,
   I will never make,
Choice of any other,
   Then by *Cupid's* Mother,
     freely speak,
It's at thy choice my dearest Love,
   Either to leave or take.

I, thy Mary gold,
   Wrapped in may fold,
Like the golden client,
   To the Sun's suppliant,
     show it's gold:
Display thy beams by glorious Sun,
   And I'll to thee unfold.

Those bright locks of hair,
   Spreading o'er each ear,
Every crisp and curl,
   Far more rich than Pearl,
     doth appear:
Then be thou constant in thy love,
   And I will be thy Dear.

Till I have possessed,
   Thee whom I love best,

I have vowed for ever,
In thy absence never,
   to take rest:
Deny me not thou pretty little one,
    in whom my hopes are blessed.

If a kiss or two,
Can thee a favour do,
Were it more than twenty,
Love indued with plenty
   Lovers know:
For thy sweet sake, a thousand take,
    For that's the way to woo.

It doth grieve my heart,
From thee for to part,
It is to me more pleasant,
Ever to be present,
   where thou art:
Yet in the absence of a Friend,
    My love shall never start.

As to me thou'rt kind,
Duty shall me bind,
Ever to obey thee,
Reasons so doth sway me,
   to thy mind,
Thou hast my heart, where e'er thou art,
    Although I stay behind.

In the Bed or Bark,
I will be thy mark,
Couples yet more loving,
Never had their moving,
   from the Ark:
Welcome to me my only joy
    All times be it light or dark.

As Rollins points out, it is unlikely that this is all the woman's last word: the stanzas describing the lover's hair and the "pretty little one" sound more like the young man's continued entreaty. Really, it all seems like a different piece, and well may be—Hammond not trying hard enough to bind together two oddments. The "no ring, no wedding" argument disappears without the necessary concession's having been won, and this second half is more concerned with the matters which exercised much seventeenth-century love poetry: how to promise loyalty during absence, and how to trust such promises. Developing from the valedictions of late sixteenth-century poetry, the theme became more pronounced as circumstances dictated continued and prolonged absences. Whereas the first half of the ballad has an almost bantering tone, the second, with its hints of dark times and separations, remembers the more harrowing experiences of the 1640s. Part of Dalila's submission in her defense is that Samson's liberty (804–810)

> Would draw thee forth to perilous enterprises,
> While I at home sat full of cares and fears,
> Wailing thy absence in my widowed bed;
> Here I should still enjoy thee day and night
> Mine and love's prisoner, not the Philistines',
> Whole to myself, unhazarded abroad,
> Fearless at home of partners in my love.

Behind such lines lies the old mistrust of women's voracious sexual appetite. Left to their own devices, weak and frail vessels that they are, temptation will surely meet and conquer them. Herrick's long, semididactic poem "The Parting Verse, or Charge to his Supposed Wife When he Travelled" is packed with doubts and warnings:

> Go hence, and with this parting kiss,
> Which joins two souls, remember this;
> Though thou beest young, kind, soft, and fair,
> And may'st draw thousands with a hair:
> Yet let these glib temptations be
> Furies to others, Friends to me.
> Look upon all; and though on fire
> Thou set'st their hearts, let chaste desire
> Steer thee to me; and think (me gone)
> In having all, that thou hast none.

These are the first ten lines, enough for a normal Herrick poem on such a theme, but it continues for another seventy-four lines. The poem becomes increasingly ridiculous as Herrick's fantasies grow, to the point where he imagines her being taken against her will, and continues to instruct her on how to bear herself in such circumstances (53–64):

But if boundless Lust must scale
Thy Fortress, and will needs prevail;
And wildly force a passage in,
Banish consent, and 'tis no sin
Of Thine; so *Lucrece* fell, and the
Chaste *Syracusian Cyane*.
So *Medullina* fell, yet none
Of these had imputation
For the least trespass: 'cause the mind
Here was not with the act combined.
The body sins not, 'tis the Will
That makes the Action, good, or ill.

It will doubtless be a comfort to her to know that if she is raped the action can still be a good one.

That Herrick should lose his footing in such a context is revealing. This poem has none of the self-mockery which makes most of his poems work so well. Perhaps the relationship was too close for him to jest about it. He does better when saying goodby to a lady who, presumably, meant a little less to him:

His Parting From Mrs Dorothy Keneday

When I did go from thee, I felt that smart,
Which Bodies do, when Souls from them depart.
Thou did'st not mind it; though thou then might'st see
Me turned to tears; yet did'st not weep for me.
'Tis true, I kissed thee; but I could not hear
Thee spend a sigh, t'accompany my tear.
Me thought 'twas strange, that thou so hard shouldst prove,
Whose heart, whose hand, whose every part spake love.
Prithee (lest Maids should censure thee) but say
Thou shed'st one tear, when as I went away;
And that will please me somewhat: though I know,
And Love will swear't, my Dearest did not so.

I can praise this best by observing how Hardy-like it is—the moment of parting frozen into a memory of puzzled disappointment, like "Love the Monopolist," where the woman turns away just a second too soon for the departing lover's peace of mind. The echo from Donne at the beginning of Herrick's poem does little except to show that he had Donne's valediction in mind. But this is a more moving poem than Donne's, rooted in a real, not idealized, experience; and from line 3 it explores in gentle subtlety the games which he and Dorothy play. That she did not "weep for me" is an ambiguous protest: "for" might mean either in sympathy with him or because he wanted her to. His own distraction is qualified by his capacity, among all his tears, to notice every movement she makes and fails to make. There is a marvelous sense, too, of the way her body tenses in resistance to his tearful embrace, in the image of what had always promised to be so loving proving, at the crisis of the relationship, to be so hard. The poem ends not in any great sense of betrayal or disillusion, but in the appreciation that although the rules of the game have had to be slightly revised, it is still worth playing, so long as she is prepared to offer the merest gesture toward the fiction that they could ever be lovers.

The implication is that in guessing at this—or any—woman's intentions, no man can distinguish between the artful and the artless. Whether Dorothy Kennedy showed so little emotion out of self-control or because she felt nothing is impossible for Herrick to know. He may suspect, but he cannot be sure, for the real vulnerability at such moments of parting is the woman's, not his. He has freedom to range and feed on new pastures, as many Cavalier farewell lyrics testify. When the Cavalier girl tells her Roundhead lover "Thou hast my heart, where e'er thou art, / Although I stay behind," she admits to a surrender which a lady such a Mistress Kennedy was wise not to acknowledge, even if she had lost her heart. And if she did weep after his departure and told him so, he could not believe it, for she might cry the same simply to keep the flirtation going.

Fanshawe opposes the artful and the artless in an absence poem which closes on an echo of Herrick's "Delight in Disorder":

On a Lady that Vowed not to Curl her Hair till her Brother Returned from Beyond Sea

Celia hath for a brother's absence sworn
(Rash oath) that since her tresses cannot mourn
In black, because unshorn Apollo's hair
Darts not a greater splendour through the Air;
She'll make them droop in her neglect: forget
Those rings which her white hand in order set,
And curiously did every morning curl
Into a thousand snares the wanton purl.
But they, are disobedient to command;
And swear they own no homage to her hand;
That Nature is their Mistress, in her name

The privilege, which they were born to, claim;
Scorning to have it said the hair gave place
To the perfections which all parts do grace:
So wind themselves in wreaths, and curl now more
By carelessness, than by her care before.
Like a crisped Comet which the stars pursue
In throngs, and mortals with pale horror view
Threat'ning some great man's death, such light displays
Her brow: Or like a Saint crowned with Rays.
Lady, what boots neglect of face or hair?
You must use art if you will grow less fair.

Behind the compliment that Celia's natural beauty is greater than anything which cosmetic aids could add lies the insinuation that she is well
aware of this. The neglect of herself which should keep her from pleasure
is really a carefully contrived encouragement to male advances—particularly so because her design is located in the snares of curling hair. The
poem is cruder than Herrick's, but it has its psychological interest too, in
the speculation that she may or may not be conscious of the effect her
tangled hair now has. Neglect signals a dropping of defenses and inhibitions. Had the poem referred to an absent husband the insinuation would
go too far; but an absent brother encourages us to think of virginal innocence which, in aiming to be chaste, reveals its real desires.

A virginal game is played out in one of Waller's most voyeuristic
poems, "The Fall." This quintessential seventeenth-century lyric seems to
be built upon the flimsiest of afterechoes of an event: a slight indentation
in the ground and some dirt on a dress. And yet Waller gives it a title
directly related to the greatest moment in human history:

See! how the willing earth gave way,
To take the impression where she lay.
See! how the mold, as loth to leave
So sweet a burden, still doth cleave
Close to the nymph's stained garment. Here
The coming spring would first appear,
And all this place with roses strow,
If busy feet would let them grow.
Here Venus smiled to see blind chance
Itself before her son advance,
And a fair image to present,
Of what the boy so long had meant.

A very low-cut bodice for summer, but veil, fan, and gloves promise
to hide more than is discovered. Wenceslaus Hollar, 1641.

'Twas such a chance as this, made all
The world into this order fall;
Thus the first lovers on the clay,
Of which they were composed, lay;
So in their prime, with equal grace,
Met the first patterns of our race.
Then blush not, fair! or on him frown,
Or wonder how you both came down;
But touch him, and he'll tremble straight,
How could he then support your weight?

> How could the youth, alas! but bend,
> When his whole heaven upon him leaned?
> If aught by him amiss were done,
> 'Twas that he let you rise so soon.

Again Waller's tone is that of the amused observer, mocking the naïveté of the young couple but also envious of their situation. By one accidental slip the flirtation has been transformed. She leaned on him and he fell, bringing her down with him. All this happened in a place frequented by many people, so that one of the sources of Waller's amusement is his perception of how the passions break through the crust of civilized behavior. By chance the refined young couple—he having courted her politely for so long—find themselves acting out their sexual performance in public, and Waller's scrutiny picks out the messy detail of her stained dress, careful not to miss anything which can add to their embarrassment. Her blush and frown are recorded as apparent signals of her disapproval, although they also register her realization that a step has been taken away from the stasis of flirtation toward the now more probable act of lovemaking. Any fault is attached to her for leaning on him too heavily, so that although chance is blamed twice for having brought the fall about, the real villain of the piece is the woman who will tease the man to the point where she will press her body against him but not allow any response.

In poems in which he is a protagonist Waller replays the situation, picturing himself as a paralyzed victim of flirtation. His "Song" does this most amusingly:

> Peace, babbling Muse!
> I dare not sing what you indite;
> Her eyes refuse
> To read the passion which they write.
> She strikes my lute, but, if it sound,
> Threatens to hurl it on the ground;
> And I no less her anger dread,
> Than the poor wretch who feigns him dead,
> While some fierce lion does embrace
> His breathless corpse, and licks his face;
> Wrapped up in silent fear he lies,
> Torn all in pieces if he cries.

In manuscript this poem's title is "Banished if he made Love," which gets the situation just right. This is poetry for a society wholeheartedly devoted to flirtation and resistant to any show of real passion. What strong feeling there is here is aimed only at blocking positive movement toward fruition. Waller seems to pin all the blame on her anger, but his own timorousness is the real target of the poem, brought out fully in the final image of frozen suspense as the lion licks the poor wretch's face. She permits no response or reaction, no matter how provocatively he is teased. He claims to resent such tyranny but is a willing victim, taking his pleasure in the game which holds them back from any expression of real feeling. The game is explored further in "The Self-Banished":

> It is not that I love you less,
> Than when before your feet I lay;
> But to prevent the sad increase
> Of hopeless love, I keep away.
>
> In vain, alas! for everything
> Which I have known belong to you,
> Your form does to my fancy bring,
> And makes my old wounds bleed anew.
>
> Who in the spring, from the new sun,
> Already has a fever got,
> Too late begins those shafts to shun,
> Which Phoebus through his veins has shot;
>
> Too late he would the pain assuage,
> And to thick shadows does retire;
> About with him he bears the rage,
> And in his tainted blood the fire.
>
> But vowed I have, and never must
> Your banished servant trouble you;
> For if I break, you may mistrust
> The vow I made—to love you too.

This really goes a step back from the "Song," for now the rules require that the lovers not meet at all. Like the lion in that poem, the bleeding wounds, rage, and fire in the blood of this one are merely shadows of passion, words instead of deeds. The wit of the final stanza is, in its way, Waller's equivalent to Marvell's "Definition of Love": "proof" that the truest expression of feeling can be only an intense solipsism. For all his protestations that he is a victim, Waller's wit discloses his complicity in the arrangement. Cynically, he can profess love while never having to do anything to support the profession; more idealistically, he can retreat into a truth which is entirely self-defined, mirroring a society in which each member exists only for and within the self.

In the wider world it is not difficult to see why this game of flirtation should have been so attractive, particularly in the 1630s. By maintaining stasis and self-absorption, it reinforced the belief that all change was an illusion. Love poetry usually presents two viewpoints, even if one is only implicit. And if equivalent wit is allowed to each side, then the consequence is a stalemate to which all ideal games aspire. A minor example of the phenomenon is Sir Francis Kynaston. In the public world his efforts in the 1630s were toward establishing what, at best, would have been a cultural irrelevance: an academy which, in *Love's Labours Lost* fashion, would have allowed its members secluded study of literature and science. His love poems, *Cynthiades*, are records of largely fruitless flirtation, with titles such as "On Her Looking Glass," "On Expressions of Love," "On Her Coyness," "On a Parting Kiss." These are all very Petrarchan, but often in the worst sense, for they replace passion with self-regarding gesture. In "To Cynthia, On a Short Visit" the repeated images of fire and flame are words only, not in any real way related to the situation which has generated the poem:[2]

> Giving thee once a visit of respect,
> Because I some affairs could not neglect,
> Which much concerned me, brooking no delay,
> I only kissed thine hand, and went away:
> How aptly, Cynthia, didst thou then enquire,
> Whether I came to thee but to fetch fire:
> It was too true, for yet I never came
> To visit thee, but I did fetch a flame,
> Religious fire, which kindled by thine eyes,
> Still made my heart thy beauty's sacrifice;
> But though I, like Prometheus, never stole
> Celestial fire to give a living soul
> To any earthen statue, stone, yet he
> More mercy finds from Jove, than I from thee;
> Though he to Caucasus be bound for ever,
> A ravenous vulture tiring on his liver,
> His pain is not augmented, but the same.
> But mine, like Vesta's never-dying flame,
> Although to burn my heart it never cease,
> Like oil of gold yet it doth still increase,

An everlasting lamp, for fires that come
From heaven still do burn, but not consume.

Flames which burn and do not consume epitomize the passionlessness of
the whole thing. Kynaston's one point of contact with the real world is
the memory of the moment when he kissed her hand. Out of this, with
her complicity, he spins the fiction of pain and suffering which spans
heaven and hell. Here we may be culturally miles away from the ballad
of the Roundhead boy and Cavalier girl, but the experiences of both
poems are not so far removed: the purpose of both is to avoid resolution,
leaving each of the characters the impression that they have made contact
and influenced the other, while they actually remain locked within their
competing fictions—here, that he is a man too busy to make the real
movement toward her, she that she really influences him.

A better poet than Kynaston, Lovelace, presents the situation with
more self-awareness:

> *To Lucasta, Going to the Wars*
> Tell me not (Sweet) I am unkind,
>   That from the nunnery
> Of thy chaste breast, and quiet mind,
>   To war and arms I fly.
>
> True; a new mistress now I chase,
>   The first foe in the field;
> And with a stronger faith embrace
>   A sword, a horse, a shield.
>
> Yet this inconstancy is such,
>   As you too shall adore;
> I could not love thee (Dear) so much,
>   Loved I not honour more.

The illusion that she cares, and can be provoked into showing that she
does, is carried by the teasing reference to a new mistress, designed to
stimulate her jealousy. This will immediately be assuaged by the tacit
promise that he will be chaste—the only embrace he pursues being a martial one. But this is an illusion too, betrayed by the summarizing of the
war he flees to as "a sword, a horse, a shield." In that anachronistic shield
is a signal that the sought-after battlefield is a landscape of the mind, a
relic of the ideal days of chivalry when honor was a real, sustainable concept, relevant to all forms of human behavior.

To profess a love of honor in the 1640s was as devious a claim as the profession of love for another person. An apparently trivial poem, very popular in the 1640s and 1650s, captures beautifully the forms of treachery which professions of honor and loyalty only thinly disguise. Its apparent triviality is a consequence of its genre, the pastoral dialogue, which produced some of the most vapid verse of the period. Yet the poem has claims to our attention. It was popular enough to exist in a variety of versions—making a definitive text impossible to determine—and for a long time it has been included among Andrew Marvell's poems. It was probably written a little too early to be his, but the ascription to him, fairly happily accepted by a number of Marvell's editors, hints at something of substance under the trite surface:[3]

<blockquote>

A Dialogue Between Thrysis and Dorinda

Dorinda When death shall part us from these kids,
           And shut up our divided lids,
           Tell me, Thyrsis, prithee do,
           Whither thou and I must go.
Thyrsis   To the Elysium.
Dorinda   Oh, where is't?
Thyrsis   A chaste soul can never miss't.
Dorinda I know no way but to our home,
           Is our cell Elysium?
Thyrsis   Turn thine eye to yonder sky,
           There the milky way doth lie;
           'Tis a sure but rugged way,
           That leads to everlasting day.
Dorinda There birds may nest, but how can I
           That have no wings and cannot fly?
Thyrsis   Do not sigh, fair nymph, for fire
           Hath no wings yet doth aspire
           Till it hit against the Pole:
           Heaven's the centre of the soul.
Dorinda But in Elysium how do they
           Pass eternity away?
Thyrsis   Oh, there's neither hope nor fear,
           There's no wolf, no fox, no bear.
           No need of dog to fetch our stray,
           Our Lightfoot we may give away;
           No oat-pipe's needful; there thy ears
           May sleep with music of the spheres.

</blockquote>

Dorinda Oh sweet! Oh sweet! How I my future state
              By silent thinking antedate:
              I prithee let us spend our time to come
              In talking of Elysium.
Thyrsis   Then I'll go on. There sheep are full
              Of sweetest grass and softest wool;
              There birds sing consorts, garlands grow,
              Cool winds do whisper, springs do flow.
              There always is a rising sun,
              And day is ever but begun.
              Shepherds there bear equal sway,
              And every nymph's a Queen of May.
Dorinda Ah me, ah me!
Thyrsis   Dorinda, why dost cry?
Dorinda I'm sick, I'm sick, and fain would die.
              Convince me now that this is true
              By bidding with me all adieu.
Thyrsis   I cannot live without thee, I
              I'll for thee, much more with thee, die.
Chorus   Then let us give Corillo charge o' the sheep,
              And thou and I'll pick poppies, and them steep
              In wine, and drink on't even till we weep,
              So shall we smoothly pass away in sleep.

It is easy to see why this should have been thought of as Marvell's. It has his favorite collision between the naive and the experienced, a scene repeated on many levels in later poems, whether it be Marvell himself looking at little T. C. or the mowers in "Upon Appleton House," or the wily Cromwell trapping the royal actor in "An Horatian Ode." The tongue is in the cheek too, as Thyrsis meets the nymph's complaints with the austere admonition that she should direct her thoughts toward the rugged way. That is a characteristic of Marvell, as is the concern with timelessness: passing eternity away is, after all, the issue at the heart of "To his Coy Mistress," whose first section postulates an eternal lovemaking—what only Adam and Eve could have done to avoid anticlimax—and whose final section aims at accelerating time to the same effect, so that one lifetime equals one complete act.

Thyrsis promises Dorinda an eternity which is one act of pleasure, never completed but always on the rise, like the eternal spring toward which the refugees sail in "Bermudas." As there, this vision is corrupting, so that a poem which begins with an innocent question ends in a suicide pact. By projecting such an attractive alternative life, Thyrsis makes their present existence unbearable. He imposes on her naïveté his own inability to live in a world compounded entirely of fleeting things, sudden hopes or fears, work and rest, seasons, days and nights, and, most tellingly, different roles and stations in life. That every shepherd should be equal and every shepherdess the queen of May is a prescription for an entirely solipsistic existence, calculated to arouse her most passionate responses. Looking at the poem coolly, we are asked to enjoy the little drama of a world-weary man tainting a simple girl's image of the world to the point that she can bear to live no longer. More significantly, perhaps, is that seventeenth-century audiences enjoyed the poem so much that it was set to music by three different composers. We should imagine the dialogue being performed by such characters as Herrick and his Julia. Their pleasure in it came from the opportunity it presented to act out their real-life roles, he the sophisticated, worldly-wise man instructing her in the realities of life, she the innocent, willing to be instructed, putty in his hands.

And yet, as everyone knows, these are really only temporary, strategic positions. *Paradise Lost* recognizes this when it authoritatively proclaims through its first eight books that Adam lived for God alone, Eve for God in him, and then in its ninth shows the opposite happening, Eve going for godhead by herself, he following only to stay with her. In its much smaller way "Thyrsis and Dorinda" also subverts the accepted roles of man and woman, for while Thyrsis appears to be in control of the dialogue, he is actually the one who responds, and, as Herbert repeatedly demonstrates, power lies with the questioner, not with the giver of answers. Dorinda's questions are naive but devastating because they strike at the root of his anxiety that she may lose her innocence and share his tainted view of the world. As she presses him to explain, he constructs an image of eternal life and eternal love designed only to save her from realizing that all that awaits them is annihilation. His ideal state is for him to know and for her to be ignorant, protector and protected; but she finally challenges him to convince her of the truth of the illusion, so that any act other than suicide would now be treachery. Innocence has its designs and is crafty in pursuit of them.

For this reason the prevailing image of much of the best seventeenth-century love poetry is of a game. "Thyrsis and Dorinda" may play it to the ultimate stalemate, but most lyric poems focus on single moves, always with a sense of the passions which, if not controlled by the rules of the game, would promise apocalypse. Herrick writes of the breaking of a bracelet of pearl and the glimpses which this tiny act gives of discontent and revenge:

The Bracelet of Pearl: to Silvia

I brake the bracelet 'gainst my will;
    And, wretched, I did see
Thee discomposed then, and still
    Art discontent with me.

One gem was lost; and I will get
    A richer pearl for thee,
Than ever, dearest *Silvia,* yet
    Was drunk to *Antony.*

Or, for revenge, I'll tell thee what
    Thou for the breach shalt do;
First, crack the strings, and after that,
    Cleave thou my heart in two.

The pregnant phrase is "'gainst my will." Of course it was done against his will; an accident, not a deliberate act of provocation. Yet *Hesperides* is full of such revealing accidents, performative equivalents of Freudian slips, and the unnecessary assertion that he did it accidentally is almost a form of protesting too much. Silvia's discomposure is apparently a reflection of her anger at his negligence, but it also signals some appreciation of the vengeful passions which underlie the act. "Discomposed" bears just the right sense of disturbing something carefully arranged—a disturbance which the rest of the poem tries to recompense by moving the situation back into the register of wooing poetry. But the broken heart at the poem's end, though a traditional enough image, has a greater than figurative force because of its parallel to the bracelet. Her countermove to his may be the one which finishes the game cruelly. His mistake was to have shown his feelings, a move which has left him vulnerable to whatever expression of discontent she wishes to make.

This is the pleasure of the game, that while the players are held in stasis by the rules which govern behavior, there is always the promise of excitement, the one moment which might transform everything. Thomas Stanley was probably attracted to a poem by Marino because it described such a sudden move. He translated it like this:[4]

The Snow-ball

Doris, I that could repel
All those darts about thee dwell,
And had wisely learned to fear,
'Cause I saw a Foe so near;

I that my deaf ear did arm,
'Gainst thy voice's powerful charm,
And the lightning of thine eye
Durst (by closing mine) defy,
Cannot this cold snow withstand
From the whiter of thy hand;
Thy deceit hath thus done more
Than thy open force before:
For who could suspect or fear
Treason in a face so clear,
Or the hidden fires descry
Wrapped in this cold outside lie?
Flames might thus involved in ice
The deceived world sacrifice;
Nature, ignorant of this
Strange Antiperistasis,
Would her falling frame admire,
That by snow were set on fire.

One unexpected act has transformed the whole game of wooing in which, up to this point, she sent signals and he affected cool disdain. Then she threw a snowball at him, so apparently artless a revelation of her feelings that, while it artfully preserves her position as a mere player in a game, it hurls him into an entirely new state of burning commitment. By such fleeting moments are whole lives changed.

On the other hand, some games appear to be heading toward resolution or transformation, but the necessary move is never made. Henry Reynolds' "Song" teases the reader by promising revelation but never delivering it:[5]

Was it a form, a gait, a grace,
    Was it their sweetness merely?
Was it the heaven of a bright face,
    That made me love so dearly?

Was it a skin of silk and snow,
    That soul and senses wounded?
Was't any of these, or all of these,
    Whereon my faith was founded?

Ah, no! 'twas a far deeper part
    Than all the rest that won me:

> 'Twas a fair-clothed but feigning heart
> I loved, and has undone me.

The lyric idealism of the first two stanzas seems suddenly compromised by the "far deeper part" of the third. If she had really let him enter her, then the game would be over; but rather than the part we expect we get "heart" and are returned to the game of fruitless wooing. "Deeper" is not the salacious literalism we might have anticipated, but a figurative epithet meaning "hypocritical," "cunning," "impossible to fathom." Instead of undoing her, he has been undone.

As might be expected, Herrick is the player par excellence, often setting his affairs within actual games. One such is "Laugh and Lie Down," named after a card game popular with English poets; Skelton includes it in "Why Come Ye Not to Court?" Snap is probably the closest we have to it now, a child's game in which the noise overrides any necessary skill. This is the poem, *in toto:*

> Y'ave laughed enough (sweet) vary now your Text;
> And laugh no more; or laugh, and lie down next.

Obey the rules is the warning here, or change the game from one in which you merely tease to one in which you have to make a move too. But the rules may, in some cases, pave the way toward betrayal, as in "Chop-Cherry." This game was designed to humiliate mildly the child who tried to get a bite out of a suspended cherry:

> Thou gav'st me leave to kiss;
> Thou gav'st me leave to woo;
> Thou mad'st me think by this,
> And that, thou lov'dst me too.
>
> But I shall ne'er forget,
> How for to make thee merry;
> Thou mad'st me chop, but yet,
> Another snapped the Cherry.

Another good rhyme for "merry." Snapping the cherry, as opposed to merely chopping at it, is just the move which Herrick dare not make, for it breaks the suspense which is the prevailing condition of the game. He thought that playing it as if it were to go on forever would hold them in their constant relationship, but such frozen states are childish illusions, as her betrayal demonstrates.

Still, the illusion of constancy is what matters, rather than the betrayals of real experience, for only in the illusion can the lover pretend that he has found something to stand against the flux of time. Childhood games as trivial as cherry-pit, draw-gloves, or stool-ball were building-blocks of the eternal pillar. Most childish of all was push-pin, a game which became in the seventeenth century, according to the *OED*, "the type of trivial or insignificant occupation." But Herrick knew well enough that any way of passing the time was as good as any other, given a partner prepared to play the same game, to fend off the knowledge that with all our loyalties and betrayals, we are still only and always temporary:

> *To Anthea*
> Come *Anthea*, know thou this,
> *Love at no time idle is:*
> Let's be doing, though we play
> But at push pin (half the day:)
> Chains of sweet bents let us make,
> Captive one, or both, to take:
> In which bondage we will lie,
> Souls transfusing thus, and die.

Notes

Introduction

1. Jeremy Bentham, *The Rationale of Reward* (1825), bk. 3, in vol. 2 of *The Works of Jeremy Bentham*, ed. John Bowring (Edinburgh, 1843), p. 253.
2. A. J. Smith, ed., *John Donne: The Complete English Poems* (Harmondsworth, 1971), p. 378.
3. Waller's poems are from G. Thorn-Drury, ed., *The Poems of Edmund Waller* (London, 1893).
4. Herrick's poems are from L. C. Martin, ed., *The Poetical Works of Robert Herrick* (Oxford, 1956).
5. Joseph Strutt, *Sports and Pastimes of the People of England,* 2d ed. (London, 1810), p. 349.
6. Lauro Martines, *Society and History in English Renaissance Verse* (Oxford, 1985), pp. 1–17.
7. Lovelace's poems are from Gerald Hammond, ed., *Richard Lovelace: Selected Poems* (Manchester, 1987).
8. Herbert's poems are from C. A. Patrides, ed., *The English Poems of George Herbert* (London, 1974).
9. Lines 65–66, 157–159, 199–202, 293–294, 297–298, 400–402. "Rest" means the stake held in reserve in the card game primero; "six and seven" is a dicing term.
10. Amy Charles, *A Life of George Herbert* (Ithaca, 1972), p. 43.
11. Patrides, *English Poems of Herbert*, p. 94.
12. Jonson's poems are from George Parfitt, ed., *Ben Jonson: The Complete Poems* (Harmondsworth, 1975).
13. S[amuel] Schoenbaum, *William Shakespeare: A Compact Documentary Life* (Oxford, 1977), p. 315.
14. Parfitt, *Ben Jonson,* pp. 393–394 (ll. 787–806).
15. Bentham, *Works,* 2:254.
16. Wallace Stevens, William Carlos Williams, and Thomas Hardy, respectively.

1. Obduracy

1. Corbett's poems are from J. A. W. Bennett and H. R. Trevor Roper, eds., *The Poems of Richard Corbett* (Oxford, 1955).
2. Ibid., p. xxv.
3. "Rous subscribes the poem 'Rich. Oxon.,' yet goes on to suggest that it may not be by Corbett but by a Puritan"; ibid., p. 155.
4. Carew's poems are from Rhodes Dunlap, ed., *The Poems of Thomas Carew* (Oxford, 1970).
5. The printed title, "Upon the King's Sickness," is vague enough to refer to James or Charles. One ms. describes it as having been written "when K:Iames was sicke," i.e., his fatal illness in 1625. But even with allowance made for conventional hyperbole, description of James as "sober, strong and young" is singularly inappropriate. Charles had smallpox in 1633.
6. For the text of Townshend's poem, see *Modern Language Review,* 12 (1917), 422.
7. Fanshawe's poems are from N. W. Bawcutt, ed., *Sir Richard Fanshawe: Shorter Poems and Translations* (Liverpool, 1964).
8. Hyder Rollins, ed., *A Pepysian Garland: Black-Letter Broadside Ballads of the Years 1595–1639* (Cambridge, Mass., 1922), pp. 415–419.
9. Davenant's poems are from A. M. Gibbs, ed., *Sir William Davenant: The Shorter Poems and Songs from the Plays and Masques* (Oxford, 1972).
10. Ibid., p. 359.
11. Ibid., p. 412.

2. "All Time's Story"

1. *The Rump: or an Exact Collection of the Choycest Poems and Songs Relating to the Late Times . . .* (1662), pt. 1, p. 41.
2. This is the text of Gongora's poem:

Sella el tronco sangriento, ne lo oprime
De aquel dichosomente desdichado,
Que de las inconstancias de su hado
Esta picarra apenas le redime;

Piedad comun, en vez de la sublime
Vrna, que el escarmiento le ha negado,
Padron le erige en bronce imaginado,
Que en vano el tiempo las memorias lime.

Risueño con el tanto como falso
El tiempo quatro lustros en la visa
El cuchillo quiça embainava agudo.

De'l sitîal despues al cadahalso
Precipitado, ó quanto nos avisa!
O quanta trompa es su exemplo mudo!

3. ". . . no tomb was erected in the Minster. The body of the great Earl of Strafford was left where it had been quietly interred after his death . . . in the family vault of the little church at Wentworth Woodhouse. On the wall above, he kneels in stone, a figure not without force and dignity though sculpted by a clumsy hand. The inscription is respectful but restrained, as though at the time those who composed it were loth to say too much. 'His soul through the mercy of God lives in eternal bliss, and his memory will never die in these kingdoms'"; C. V. Wedgwood, *Thomas Wentworth, First Earl of Strafford 1593–1641: A Revaluation* (London, 1961), p. 395.

4. See Brian Morris and Eleanor Withington, eds., *The Poems of John Cleveland* (Oxford, 1967), pp. xxxiii–xxxiv. Cleveland's poems are taken from this edition.

5. Ibid., p. xxxiv. Rose Macaulay seems to have written her novel *They Were Defeated* in order to argue that this poem must have been written by a woman.

6. *ΕΙΚΩΝ ΒΑΣΙΛΙΚΗ. The Portraiture of His Majesty King Charles I*, ed. Catherine M. Phillimore (Oxford, 1878), p. 6.

7. Wedgwood, *Thomas Wentworth*, p. 396.

8. For the whole poem see George Parfitt, ed., *Silver Poets of the Seventeenth Century* (London, 1974), p. 132.

9. The precursor of this poem is Jonson's "An Epistle to a Friend, to Persuade Him to the Wars" (*The Underwood* 15).

10. *History of the Rebellion and Civil Wars in England* (Oxford, 1888), bk. I, sec. 63, p. 37. Clarendon goes on to say (I.64): "And upon this Observation persons of all conditions took great licence in speaking of the person of the duke, and dissecting all his infirmities, believing they should not thereby incur any displeasure of the king. In which they took very ill measures; for from that time almost to the time of his own death the king admitted very few into any degree of trust who had ever discovered themselves to be enemies of the duke, or against whom he had ever manifested a notable prejudice. And sure never any prince manifested more a most lively regret for the loss of a servant than his majesty did for this great man, in his constant favour to his wife and children."

11. In Frederick Fairholt, ed., *Poems and Songs Relating to George Villiers, Duke of Buckingham*, Percy Society, Early English Ballads, vol. 29 (London, 1850), p. 9.

12. John Milton, *A Defence of the People of England*, vol. 4 of *Complete Prose Works*, trans. Donald Mackenzie (New Haven, 1962), p. 408.

13. Fairholt, *Poems Relating to Buckingham*, p. 77.

14. Ibid., p. 35.

15. The ballad's full title is "The Tragedy of Doctor Lamb, The great supposed Conjurer, who was wounded to death by Sailors and other lads, on Friday the 14 of June, 1628. And died in the Poultry Counter, near Cheapside, on the Saturday morning following." The full text is in Rollins, *A Pepysian Garland*, pp. 278–282.

16. Fairholt, *Poems Relating to Buckingham*, p. 77.

17. Ibid., p. 75. For Townley and Ben Jonson, see Chapter 5.

18. Ibid., p. 52.

19. In another anti-Buckingham poem, "Charon and the Duke," Felton is presented as the duke's rival in love for Charles; ibid., p. 56.

20. Ibid., p. 54.

21. Ibid., p. 51.
22. James Shirley, *Poems. 1646* (facsimile, Menston, 1970).
23. Fairholt, *Poems Relating to Buckingham,* p. 78. One manuscript claims this poem was "made by D. Donn."

3. Doing Nothing Common

1. Hyder Rollins, *Cavalier and Puritan: Ballads and Broadsides Illustrating the Period of the Great Rebellion 1640–1660* (New York, 1923), p. 120.
2. It ends:

> So his retreat hath rectified that wrong;
> Backward is forward in the Hebrew tongue.
> Now the Church Militant in plenty rests,
> Nor fears, like th'Amazon, to lose her breasts.
> Her means are safe; not squeezed until the blood
> Mix with the milk and choke the tender brood.
> She, that hath been the floating ark, is that
> She that's now seated on Mount Ararat.
> Quits Charles; our souls did guard him northward thus
> Now he the counterpart comes south to us.

3. Norman Ault, ed., *Seventeenth Century Lyrics from the Original Texts,* 2d ed. (New York 1950), p. 33.
4. King's poems are from Margaret Crum, ed., *The Poems of Bishop Henry King* (Oxford, 1965).
5. Godolphin's poems are from George Saintsbury, ed., *Minor Poets of the Caroline Period,* vol. 2 (Oxford, 1906), pp. 227–261.
6. Ault, *Seventeenth Century Lyrics,* pp. 146–47.
7. Ibid., p. 147.
8. For a discussion of the dating of this poem, see H. A. Margoliouth's review of Wilkinson's edition of Lovelace's poems, *Review of English Studies,* 3 (1927), 93–94.
9. "TO THE KING, Upon his Coming With his Army Into the West." "*Best of Kings*" recalls Jonson's epigram to James I.
10. Lucy Hutchinson, *Memoirs of the Life of Colonel Hutchinson* (London, 1908), p. 266.
11. Herrick offers a pastoral treatment of the same theme in a longer poem, "A Pastoral Sung to the King: Montano, Silvio, and Mirtillo, Shepherds."
12. For representations of Charles as a Roman emperor, see Graham Parry, *The Golden Age Restored* (Manchester, 1981), p. 221.
13. Fanshawe was made the prince's secretary of war in 1644. According to the *Dictionary of National Biography* (Oxford, 1909) (hereafter cited as *DNB*), he "exercised much influence in the prince's councils, and it was largely owing to him that the party left the mainland."
14. Adolphus William Ward, *DNB,* s.v. Charles II.
15. Vaughan's poems are from Alan Rudrum, ed., *Henry Vaughan: The Complete Poems* (Harmondsworth, 1976).
16. Morris and Withington, *Poems of John Cleveland,* p. 87.

17. Phillimore, ΕΙΚΩΝ ΒΑΣΙΛΚΗ, p. 190.
18. Rollins, *Cavalier and Puritan*, pp. 151–152.
19. Crum, *Poems of Henry King*, p. 209.
20. Herrick's editor (p. xxxviii) lists five poems definitely datable to 1647 and two other possibles.

4. "Light and Airy Man"

1. Text of *Conversations* from Parfitt, *Ben Jonson: The Complete Poems*. This sentence is lines 376–377 in Parfitt's edition.
2. *Timber: or Discoveries*, in ibid., lines 756–770.
3. *Conversations*, 629.
4. *Timber*, 794–801.
5. George Parfitt, ed., *The Poetaster* (Nottingham, 1979), p. 6.
6. See, for example, Ovid Junior's speech in I.ii (*Poetaster*, p. 14) beginning "and give me stomach," concerning those who "would dread more / To be thought ignorant than be known poor."
7. The next few epigrams continue the theme: IX tells readers not to look "for strict degrees of rank"; X is addressed to "My Lord Ignorant"; XI attacks a noxious lord; and XV is "On a Court-Worm."
8. For Eliot's poem see Ian Donaldson, ed., *Ben Jonson: Poems* (Oxford, 1975), p. 327.
9. See C. H. Herford and Percy Simpson, eds., *Ben Jonson*, vol. 1 (Oxford, 1925), p. 94.
10. The poem was Zouch Townley's. Details of the incident are given in ibid.
11. Ibid., p. 242.
12. Ibid.
13. Parfitt, *Poetaster*, p. 101. Perhaps Milton remembered these lines for his tormented hero at the opening of *Samson Agonistes*.
14. Wesley Trimpi, *Ben Jonson's Poems: A Study of the Plain Style* (Stanford, Calif., 1962), pp. 193–194.
15. Parfitt, *Poetaster*, p. 99.
16. Ibid., p. 98.
17. Ibid.
18. *Conversations*, 330–333.
19. The visit to Drummond occurred in 1618–19. Jonson had been writing court masques since 1605.
20. The text of the poem is in Parfitt, *Ben Jonson: The Complete Poems*, p. 312.
21. Text in Herford and Simpson, *Ben Jonson*, vol. 6 (Oxford, 1941), p. 368.
22. Edward Partridge, ed., *Bartholomew Fair* (London, 1964): Induction, lines 17–20 of Partridge.
23. See the Arden edition of *Measure for Measure*, ed. J. W. Lever (London, 1965), pp. xlviii–l.
24. Overdo's (or mad Arthur's) tirades against tobacco parallel the king's in *A Counterblast to Tobacco*. Another parallel with the *Counterblast* is James's harping on the concept of a warrant—e.g., "how a custom springing from so vile a ground . . .

should be welcomed upon so slender a warrant"—with Trouble-All's obsession with Overdo's warrant.

25. *OED*, s. vv. *break* v. 2f, *broken* 7.

26. In manuscript "The cassock, cloak and gown" reads "cloak, cassock, robe and gown." The change was probably made to avoid a potentially humiliating reference to Charles, the obvious bankrupt wearer of the robe.

27. The *OED* dates the first recorded use of the word in this sense to 1611.

28. The couplet is omitted in Benson's two editions of the poems (1640) as well as in some manuscripts. The Folio text of *The Underwood* includes it.

29. See Donaldson's note, *Ben Jonson: Poems*, p. 240.

30. Herford and Simpson, *Ben Jonson*, 1:91.

31. Ibid., p. 92.

35. Michael Hattaway, ed., *The New Inn* (Manchester, 1984), pp. 203–204.

36. Quoted by George B. Tennant in his edition of *The New Inn*, Yale Studies in English, 34 (New York, 1908), p. 291.

5. "The Utmost Bound of a Fable"

1. V.xii. He is accused of "feigning lame, gout, palsy, and such diseases."

2. *Discoveries*, 1–15.

3. Ibid., 1349–57.

4. Letter to the Earl of Newcastle, Herford and Simpson, *Ben Jonson*, 1:213.

5. *Discoveries*, 1159–71.

6. Ibid., 2565–69.

7. Ibid., 1305–10.

8. Here my interpretation of the Saguntum infant image differs from that of Richard Peterson, who sees it as an ironic example, not to be copied; *Imitation and Praise in the Poems of Ben Jonson* (New Haven, 1981), pp. 203–206.

9. Ibid., p. 221.

10. *Discoveries*, 1358–69. This paragraph immediately follows the one which considers that "our life is like a play."

11. Herford and Simpson, *Ben Jonson*, 1:113.

12. *Discoveries*, 3383–95.

13. Ibid., 3742–47.

14. Herford and Simpson, *Ben Jonson*, 1:103.

15. I have preferred Ian Donaldson's text in *Ben Jonson: Poems*. Parfitt has "wants" for "want" in line 5.

16. Jonson described it as "the vulgar censure of his play by some malicious spectators;" Hattaway, *The New Inn*, p. 204.

17. Ibid.

18. Jones is actually described as "asinigo"; for the play on "faussebraies" see the *OED*; for Gill see Chapter 6.

19. *Ben Jonson: Poems*, p. 250.

20. Quoted in Herford and Simpson, *Ben Jonson*, 1:181.

21. Ibid., p. 183.

6. A Justly Suspected Easiness

1. *Conversations*, 4–7: "Said he had written a discourse of poesy both against Campion and Daniel, especially this last, where he proves couplets to be the bravest sort of verses . . ."
2. For the complete text of Gill's poem, see Herford and Simpson, *Ben Jonson*, 11:346–348. Zouch Townley wrote an attack on Gill's poem, in defense of Jonson; see ibid., pp. 348–349.
3. For the text see Donaldson, *Ben Jonson: Poems*, pp. 328–329.
4. Milton's poems are from John Carey, ed., *John Milton: Complete Shorter Poems* (London, 1971); and Alastair Fowler, ed., *John Milton: Paradise Lost* (London, 1971).
5. Herford and Simpson, *Ben Jonson*, 2:377.
6. *Discoveries*, 2128–33.
7. Herford and Simpson, *Ben Jonson*, 8:528–529.
8. Ibid., p. 533.
9. Ibid., p. 537. The quotation is from Sir John Cheke.
10. Ibid., p. 543.
11. "An Expostulation with Inigo Jones," 69–70.
12. "Malui . . . longo & acri studio ad illam laudem veram contendere, quam properato & praecoci stylo falsam praeripere"; *The Works of John Milton*, vol. 12 (New York, 1936), p. 248.
13. *Discoveries*, 2104.
14. See the seventeenth-century examples given for *enthusiast* and *enthusaism* in the *OED*.
15. Carey, *Milton: Shorter Poems*, pp. 341–343.
16. From *Eikonoclastes*, in *Complete Prose Works*, vol. 3 (New Haven, 1962), p. 361.

7. "You Never Saw Thing Made of Wood So Fine"

1. See the article on the navy in *Encyclopaedia Britannica*, 11th ed. For much of the information on the navy in the Civil War I have relied on J. R. Powell, *The Navy in the English Civil War* (Hamden, Conn., 1962).
2. The poem's full title is "On His Majesty's Great Ship Lying Almost Finished in Woolwich Dock. Anno. Dom. 1637. and afterwards called The Sovereign of the Seas."
3. In his edition of Waller's poems G. Thorn-Drury suggests 1627, while allowing that the poem's references to piracy might suggest a date in the next decade.
4. In *Otia Sacra* (1648), in L. Birkett Marshall, ed., *Rare Poems of the Seventeenth Century* (Cambridge, 1936), p. 69.
5. In *Parthenia Sacra* (1633), in Marshall, *Rare Poems*, p. 106.
6. There are many versions of this poem. This text is from Ault, *Seventeenth Century Lyrics*, pp. 113–114.
7. The poem was not published until 1673. Ault dates it "before 1639."
8. "His Age, Dedicated to his Peculiar Friend, Mr *John Wickes*, Under the Name of *Posthumus*," 57–64.

376 NOTES TO PAGES 167–185

9. "Advice to my Best Brother, Colonel Francis Lovelace," 1–16.
10. *Cavalier and Puritan*, p. 16.
11. Text in C. H. Firth, ed., *Naval Songs and Ballads* Navy Records Society, vol. 33 (London, 1908), 45–46.
12. Powell, *The Navy in the Civil War*, p. 3; see also p. 10.
13. Firth, *Naval Songs*, p. 38.
14. Marvell's poems are from Elizabeth S. Donno, ed., *Andrew Marvell: The Complete Poems* (Harmondsworth, 1972).
15. Ibid., p. 266.
16. Firth, *Naval Songs*, p. xxviii.
17. E.g., Paul J. Korshin: "among his lyric poems only one, 'Bermudas,' visualises the harmonious coexistence of Nature and her despiser, Man"; *From Concord to Dissent: Major Themes in English Poetic Theory 1640–1700* (London, 1973), p. 69.
18. In his Arden edition of *The Tempest* (London, 1964) Frank Kermode reprints William Strachey's *True Reportery of the Wracke* (published in *Purchas His Pilgrimes*, 1625), including this anecdote: "the Birds would come flocking to that place, and settle upon the very armes and head of him that so cryed, and still creepe neerer and neerer . . . by which our men would weigh them with their hand, and which weighed heaviest they tooke for the best and let the others alone, and so our men would take twentie dozen in two houres of the chiefest of them" (p. 138).
19. "Advice to my Best Brother . . . ," 17–28.
20. Cotton Mather, quoted in *DNB*.

8. A Just Recompense

1. The one other was W. Hall; see George Williamson, *Seventeenth-Century Contexts* (London, 1960), p. 138.
2. M. Lloyd, *Modern Language Notes*, 75 (1960), 103–108. See Carey's note to line 100, *Milton: Complete Shorter Poems*, p. 246.
3. Saintsbury, *Minor Poets*, 2:513.
4. Ibid., p. 517.
5. Ashmore's volume of translations from Horace and other poems appeared in 1621. See Marshall, *Rare Poems*, pp. 1–2.
6. From *A Collection of Miscellanies* . . . (1687), ibid., pp. 160–161.
7. David Masson, *Life of John Milton* (London, 1859), p. 606. For the Latin text see Ernest C. Mossner, ed., *Justa Edovardo King*, Facsimile Text Society no. 45 (New York, 1939).
8. M. Lloyd, *Notes and Queries*, n.s., 5 (1958), 432–434.
9. "In quo nihil immaturum praeter aetatem."
10. "Qua via lata patet, qua pronior area lucri"; "Ad Patrem," 69.
11. "Paterne rure . . . evolvendis Graecis Latinisque scriptoribus summum per otium totus vacavi"; *The Works of John Milton*, vol. 3 (New York, 1933), pp. 120–121.
12. Arthur C. Sprague, ed., *Samuel Daniel: Poems and A Defense of Rhyme* (Chicago, 1930), pp. 161–163.
13. ". . . dum alii vectores vitae mortalis frustra satagerent."
14. ". . . immortalem anhelans."
15. Neil Rhodes, ed., *John Donne: Selected Prose* (Harmondsworth, 1987), p. 67.

16. Ibid., p. 71.
17. "Formerly Milton's Paradise Lost had been my chief favourite, and in my excursions during the Voyage of the Beagle, when I could take only a single small volume, I always chose Milton"; Darwin, *Autobiography,* ed. Gavin de Beer (Oxford, 1983), p. 49.
18. From *The Tenure of Kings and Magistrates:* "the mercy which they pretend, is the mercy of wicked men; and their mercies, we read, are cruelties . . . Lastly, a dissembl'd and seditious pity, fain'd of industry to begett new discord"; in C. A. Patrides, ed., *John Milton: Selected Prose* (Harmondsworth, 1974), p. 251.
19. From poems by Henry King, William More, John Cleveland, and Joseph Beaumont.

9. Caught in the Web of Dreams

1. "To Althea From Prison," 25–32.
2. Most American editions of *Paradise Lost* carry the misprint "blushing" for "bushing," anticipating one of my later themes.
3. *OED,* s.v. "incarnation," 5: "Flesh-colour, carnation; a pigment or dye of this colour" (quotation from the *Art of Limning,* 1575).
4. *OED,* s.v. "sciagraphy."
5. Suckling's poems are from Thomas Clayton, ed., *The Works of Sir John Suckling,* vol. 1 (Oxford, 1971). In line 37 "heart" is often emended to "hair."
6. Saintsbury, *Minor Poets,* 2:195.
7. The chief exceptions are O. B. Hardison, *The Enduring Monument* (Chapel Hill, N.C., 1962); and Arnold Stein, *The House of Death* (Baltimore, 1986).
8. "Slack" may have this sexual meaning, but see Herbert's "Love III."
9. "The Question and Answer," 7–12, from *Poems Divine and Humane* (1641); in Marshall, *Rare Poems,* p. 11.
10. The poem occurs in a scene (III.v) in which a dead innkeeper's ghost waits on his customers; Ault, *Seventeenth Century Lyrics,* p. 13.
11. Strode's poems are from Bertram Dobell, ed., *The Poetical Works of William Strode* (London, 1907).
12. Saintsbury, *Minor Poets,* vol. 2, p. 314.
13. "On the Death of my Dear Brother, Mr Richard Flatman," ibid., p. 374.
14. A comparable case with Flatman's is Henry Vaughan's. The untitled poems in *Silex Scintillans* are about his dead brother William and they too convey how difficult it is to comprehend how bodily corruption can be reconciled with biblical promises of resurrection.
15. This is the final epitaph section to his second poem on the death of Mary Prideaux ("On the Same M. M. P.").
16. Randolph's poems are from John Jay Parry, ed., *The Poems and Amyntas of Thomas Randolph* (New Haven, 1917).
17. It is common in modernizing seventeenth-century texts to change the *my self* to *myself,* but because this poem plays on a distinction between Herrick and his self, I have kept the original form.
18. An interesting parallel comes in Herrick's "The Vision," which begins "Me thought I saw (as I did dream in bed) . . ."

19. *Edolon* (XI.476) is translated by Richard Lattimore as "mere imitations of perished mortals," by Robert Fitzgerald as "the after-images of used-up men."
20. *OED,* s.v. "idolum."
21. Text in G. Blakemoor Evans, ed., *The Plays and Poems of William Cartwright* (Madison, Wis., 1951), pp. 484–485.
22. F. E. Hutchinson, ed., *The Works of George Herbert* (Oxford, 1941), p. 356.
23. See *The First and Second Prayer Books of Edward VI,* Everyman edition (London, 1949), pp. 428–429.
24. In discussing angelic intercourse, 8:678.

10. "New Things Succeed"

1. Francis Procter, *A New History of the Book of Common Prayer,* rev. Walter M. Frere (London, 1910), p. 134. George Herbert, in *Musae Responsariae,* has a poem defending the ceremony against the attacks of the Puritan Andrew Melville; see Chapter 11, note 15, below.
2. Procter, *A New History,* p. 639. For Milton's comment, see E. S. LeComte, *Notes and Queries,* 199 (1954), 245–246.
3. Procter, *A New History,* p. 187.
4. The English renderings go back to William Tyndale's Pentateuch (1530).
5. So much can be understood from Hooker's defense of the ceremony: "Howbeit God forbid wee should cease performing this dutie when publique order doth draw us unto it, when it maie be so easilie don, when it hath ben so longe executed by devout and vertuous people, god forbid that being so many waies provoked in this case unto so good a dutie, wee should omitt it, onlie because there are other cases of like nature wherein we cannot so convenientlie or at the least wise doe not performe the same vertuous office of pietie. Wherein wee trust that as the action it selfe pleaseth God so the order and manner thereof is not such as maie justlie offend anie. It is but an overflowing of gall which causeth the womans absence from the Church during the time of her lying in to be traduced and interpreted as though she were so long judged *unholie* and were thereby shut out or sequestred from the house of God according to the ancient leviticall law. Whereas the verie common law it selfe doth not so hold, but directlie professeth the contrarie, she is not barred from thence in such sort as they interpret it, nor in respect of anie unholines forbidden entrance into the Church, although her abstaininge from publique assemblies, and hir aboad in seperation for the time be most convenient. To scoffe at the manner of attire then which could be nothing devised for such a time more grave and decent, to make it a token of some follie committed for which they are loath to showe their faces, argueth that great devines are sometime more merrie then wise"; W. Speed Hill, ed., *Folger Library Edition of the Works of Richard Hooker,* vol. 2 (Cambridge, Mass., 1977), p. 408.
6. *First and Second Prayer Books,* p. 324.
7. Ibid., pp. 325–326.
8. "Purging" is taken from the marginal note in the anonymous Matthew's Bible (1534), a version which used Tyndale's translation of the Pentateuch. It reads: "a lawe howe wemen shoulde be purged after their delyverence."
9. "To Lucasta From Prison," 29–36.

10. *First and Second Prayer Books*, p. 325. The defense ends on a patriotic note. Ceremonies are a way of binding together the nation, not the world: "And in these our doinges, we condemne no other nacions, nor prescribe any thing, but to our owne people only. For we think it convenient that every country should use such ceremonies, as they shal think best to the settyng furth of Goddes honour or glory, and to the reducyng of the people to a most perfect and godly lyvyng without errour or Superstcion. And that they shoulde put awaye other thynges, whiche from tyme to tyme they perceyve to be moste abused, as in mennes ordinances it often chaunceth diversely in diverse countreyes" (p. 326).

11. From the Millenary Petition, in Procter, *A New History*, p. 137.

12. Ibid., p. 161.

13. "Upon the Death of his Own Father," 33–44.

14. "The Life of Mrs Hutchinson Written by Herself," in *Memoirs of Colonel Hutchinson*, p. 3.

15. Ibid.

16. From *Annalia Dubriensa* (1636), in Christopher Whitfield, *Robert Dover and the Cotswold Games* (Evesham, 1962), p. 210. Like Carew, Marmion died soon after going north with the king's army in 1639.

17. Whitfield, *Robert Dover,* p. 190.

18. However, Davenant's poem was not included in the *Annalia.* Thomas Randolph's contribution to the volume, "An Eclogue on the Noble Assemblies Revived on the Cotswold Hills," describes the Puritan opposition to Dover's enterprise in some detail (49–60):

    Some melancholy swains about have gone
    To teach all Zeal, their own complexion:
    Choler they will admit sometimes I see
    But Phlegm, and Sanguine no Religions be.
    These teach that Dancing is a Jezebel;
    And Barley-break, the ready way to Hell.
    The Morris, *Idols;* Whitsun-ales can be
    But profane Relics of a Jubilee!
    These in a Zeal, t'express how much they do
    The Organs hate, have silenced Bag-pipes too;
    And harmles May-poles, all are railed upon
    As if they were the towers of *Babylon.*

19. "Love Made in the First Age: To Chloris," 13–24.

20. Thomas Tusser, *Five Hundred Points of Good Husbandry,* ed. Geoffrey Grigson (Oxford, 1984), pp. 137–138.

21. The opening stanzas of poem XXXVI.

22. Tusser, *Five Hundred Points,* p. 20.

23. Ibid., p. 83.

24. The Geneva Bible's rendering is: "To understand a parable, and the interpretation."

25. In Tusser, *Five Hundred Points,* pp. 315–320.

26. "Sweets grown common," "lilies that fester," etc.

27. Text from Norman Ault, ed., *Elizabethan Lyrics* (London, 1986), p. 195. Another good example is Dyer's "The Lowest Trees Have Tops."

28. From *Flamma sine Fumo: or Poems Without Fictions* (1662), in Marshall, *Rare Poems*, p. 201.
29. The ballad appeared in Crouch's *Mercurius Fumigosus*, August 1654. He may not have been its writer. Text in Rollins, *Cavalier and Puritan*, pp. 348–351.
30. From a sheet printed ca. 1649. Burton was the printer. Text in Rollins, *Cavalier and Puritan*, pp. 256–264.
31. In Shipman's *Carolina: or Loyal Poems* (1683; facsimile ed., Farnsborough, 1971). In his preamble to the poem he claims that it was written January 30, 1652.
32. Hutchinson, *Works of George Herbert*, p. 260.
33. Ibid., p. 261.
34. Ault, *Seventeenth Century Lyrics*, p. 384.
35. Herrick's "To Pansies" plays similarly on the herb's two uses:

> Ah, cruel Love! must I endure
> Thy many scorns, and find no cure?
> Say, are thy medicines made to be
> Help to all others, but to me?
> I'll leave thee, and to *Pansies* come;
> Comforts you'll afford me some:
> You can ease my heart, and do
> What Love could ne'er be brought unto.

See also his "How *Pansies* or *Hearts-ease* Came First."
36. Hutchinson, *Works of George Herbert*, p. 283.

11. "Enjoy the Time"

1. George Thomason dates the ballad April 8, 1646. Text in Rollins, *Cavalier and Puritan*, pp. 161–162.
2. Ibid., p. 160.
3. *The Rump*, pt. 1, p. 66.
4. Ibid., p. 322.
5. "An Anatomy of the World: the First Anniversary," 268–272.
6. "A Loose Saraband," 25–28.
7. "An Anatomy of the World: the First Anniversary," 299.
8. Cf. Thomas May's poem above, p. 71.
9. Ault, *Seventeenth Century Lyrics*, p. 83.
10. "The Royal Martyr," 47–49.
11. Rochester's poems are from Keith Walker, ed., *The Poems of John Wilmot, Earl of Rochester* (Oxford, 1984).
12. Rollins, *Cavalier and Puritan*, p. 325.
13. In *Mercurius Fumigosus*, December 1654; text in Rollins, *Cavalier and Puritan*, p. 352.
14. From *Poems* (1633); in Ault, *Seventeenth Century Lyrics*, pp. 84–86.
15. In his Latin poem on the churching ceremony, George Herbert stressed the concept of renewal:

> And so the wife, feeling guilty
> For plucking the apple, groans for bearing children

As if she had been cursed; but now, as if blessed,
She rightly comes back to the ripe and mild God
From whom once, when he raged, she ran away
The Latin Poetry of George Herbert, trans. Mark McCloskey and Paul R. Murphy
(Athens, Ohio, 1965), pp. 20–21.

16. "Hymn to God my God, in my Sickness" and "A Hymn to God the Father." In the latter the play on his name, *Donne* and *done*, means that there is probably a pun on *door* and *doer* too.

12. "Sir, You Have Not Missed"

1. Hutchinson, *Memoirs*, pp. 65, 79.
2. Ibid., p. 380.
3. "On Fayrford Windows," 20–28.
4. Hutchinson, *Works of Herbert*, p. 233.
5. In "The Bunch of Grapes," later in *The Temple*, joy is the immediate association which the grapes stimulate: "Joy, I did lock thee up . . ."
6. In early English Bible versions *agape* was rendered *love* rather than *charity*.
7. Izaak Walton recounts how Herbert asked Arthur Woodnoth to deliver the poems to Nicholas Ferrar, with this instruction. See Patrides, *English Poems of Herbert*, p. 29.
8. Hutchinson, *Works of Herbert*, p. 4.
9. However, L. C. Martin's statement that Herrick's reputation stood high in the 1620s (*Poetical Works of Herrick*, p. xvii) is not generally believed now.
10. *Gem* has a typographical sense too, but the *OED* examples date only from the nineteenth century.
11. In "October's Husbandry," in Tusser, *Five Hundred Points*, p. 43.

13. Playing with Snakes

1. Rollins, *Cavalier and Puritan*, pp. 409–413.
2. The ballad was registered in May 1656; text in ibid., pp. 414–419.
3. From *Poems, Lyric, Macaronic, Heroic* (1664); text in Ault, *Seventeenth Century Lyric*, pp. 308–309.
4. Raymond Williams, *The Country and the City* (London, 1973), p. 25.
5. Ricardo Quintana, ed., *Gulliver's Travels and Other Writings* (New York, 1958), p. 39.
6. E.g., John Evelyn's prodigy who died very young, or Cowley's verse romances written at the age of ten.
7. Thorn-Drury, *The Poems of Edmund Waller*, p. 334. I have not found any independent support for this idea, apart from this nineteenth-century ancedote reported by Augustus Hare: "Madam du Quaire had met Lady Colin Campbell at dinner and sat opposite to her, but she did not know her. She could not help being attracted by the necklace she wore, it was so very extraordinary. After a time it seemed to be moving by itself. She fancied at first that this must be a delusion, but, putting up her glasses, she certainly saw the necklace writhing round Lady Colin's

throat. Seeing her astonished look, Lady Colin said, 'Oh, I see you are looking at my snake: I always wear a live snake round my throat in hot weather: it keeps one's neck so cool'; and it really was a live snake"; *In My Solitary Life,* ed. Malcolm Barnes (London, 1953), p. 199.

14. "Such Delights I Meant to Say"

1. *John Milton, Poems: Reproduced in Facsimile from the Manuscript in Trinity College, Cambridge* (Menston, 1972), p. 40.
2. In Henry Lawes's *Airs and Dialogues I* (1653); text in Ault, *Seventeenth Century Lyrics,* pp. 288–289.
3. "Maids" could refer to male virgins: the *OED*'s last example of its use in this sense is in 1641.
4. The poem is in manuscript only, in the British Museum (B.M. Add. Ms. 22118; before 1649); text in Ault, *Seventeenth Century Lyrics,* p. 232.
5. Saintsbury, *Minor Poets,* vol. 2, p. 515.
6. I have preferred the punctuation of Ian Donaldson's edition here. Parfitt has "Drink to me, only, with thine eyes."
7. Parfitt's translation, in *Ben Jonson: Complete Poems,* p. 512.
8. "We have had many blessed Patterns of a holy life in the *Brittish Church* . . . I shall propose but one to you, the most obedient *Son* that ever his *Mother* had"; from *The Mount of Olives,* in L. C. Martin, ed., *The Works of Henry Vaughan* (Oxford, 1957), p. 186.
9. E.g., from the seventh poem in "Memoriae Matris Sacrum":
   > Here you shall be, and I,
   > Every day on perfumes banqueted—
   > The smells of many herbs. Just
   > Wear your real face, one like
   > The way I feel; do not listless
   > Mix with memory your face.
   > If with polar looks we come
   > To disagreement, we will break
   > The fragile flower odours, and among the other
   > Blossoms budding, our joys linked in fate
   > Will dissolve in grief away.

   McCloskey and Murphy, *The Latin Poetry of George Herbert,* p. 139.
10. From *New Poems, Songs, Prologues and Epilogues* (1676); text in Marshall, *Rare Poems,* pp. 54–55.
11. Text in Shirley, *Poems. 1646,* p. 44, and in Ault, *Seventeenth Century Lyrics,* p. 148.

15. Poetry and Push-Pin

1. Rollins, *Cavalier and Puritan,* pp. 396–401.
2. Saintsbury, *Minor Poets,* vol. 2, pp. 168–169.

3. Text in Donno, *Andrew Marvell: Complete Poems,* pp. 21–22. In one ms. it is attributed to "H. Ramsay." It was first printed in 1659.
4. G. Miller Crump, ed., *The Poems and Translations of Thomas Stanley* (Oxford, 1962), p. 30.
5. Printed in Henry Lawes's *Airs and Dialogues II* (1655); text in Ault, *Seventeenth Century Lyrics,* p. 148.

Index

Italicized page numbers indicate that a poem is both quoted and discussed.